The Philosophy of Human Nature

IMPRIMI POTEST:

Daniel H. Conway, S.J.

Praep. Prov. Missourianae

NIHIL OBSTAT:

Frederic C. Eckhoff

Censor Deputatus

IMPRIMATUR:

✝ Joseph E. Ritter

Archiepiscopus Sancti Ludovici

Die 27 Januarii 1953

The Philosophy of
Human Nature

GEORGE P. KLUBERTANZ, S.J.

Assistant Professor of Philosophy
Saint Louis University

New York

APPLETON-CENTURY-CROFTS, INC.

Test editions copyright 1949, 1951,
by George P. Klubertanz

PRINTED IN THE UNITED STATES OF AMERICA

Preface

No realistic philosophy can be considered complete unless it includes a philosophy of nature. The philosophy of human nature is an area where most of the problems of the philosophy of nature occur, some of them in a crucial form. Moreover, the philosophy of human nature is an absolute prerequisite for a philosophically grounded ethics. Clearly, then, a knowledge of the philosophy of St. Thomas Aquinas requires a study of the philosophy of human nature.

Nor is it an easy task to discover and present St. Thomas's thought on man. For this philosophic thought is contained on the one hand in summary form and often under a deductive guise in the two *Summae;* on the other hand, the *Disputed Questions* are fragmentary and polemical by their nature, and the *Commentaries* follow an order and an emphasis that is no longer directly useful. Moreover, where St. Thomas presumed basic philosophical understanding and a knowledge of the pertinent evidence, present-day students, unfamiliar with both, are unable to gain much more than a superficial verbal mastery.

Finally, the philosophy of nature is in close material contact with the natural sciences. The problems and questions that arise out of this contact are dated by their very nature; the problems of this third quarter of the twentieth century are not those of the first and second quarters, let alone those of the thirteenth century.

Consequently, a textbook that aims to present a Thomistic philosophy of human nature must meet many difficult requirements. It simply cannot be put together out of snippets of texts, culled at random from St. Thomas's closely integrated works. St. Thomas's thought must be re-thought in the modern setting. Great effort must be made to present the basic evidences unmistakably

and in such an order that the student is able, most likely for the
first time, to gain a truly intellectual and philosophic insight into
human nature. Finally, as many of the major contemporary problems must be met as is consistent with the abilities of the author
and the student and the limitations of class time available.

The present text is an attempt to meet these exacting standards.
It was first used in a preliminary form in 1949. Out of classroom
experience and the suggestions of many generous friends there
grew a thoroughly revised text, which was published in a temporary edition in 1951. Further classroom testing and discussions
with other teachers have produced a number of minor changes and
a few additions. Basically, however, this edition is the same as that
of 1951.

Only a very unusual class could complete the entire text as it
stands. Paragraphs which can easily be omitted are marked with
an asterisk. It is suggested that these paragraphs be assigned for
private reading and study by the students, though in particular
cases they may well be brought into the actual classroom discussion. Where these suggested omissions do not gain enough time,
each individual teacher will have to make his own selection, considering the needs of his present class and the possibility of sup-
plying in other courses what is omitted from this (for example,
where the habits are thoroughly taught in the ethics courses,
Chapter XII could be postponed).

It is my prayerful hope that this text will serve as an effective
medium by which the student can make his own some of the insights of St. Thomas Aquinas, to attain thereby a philosophic understanding of human nature in himself and others, and thus be
enabled better to reach God, the author and goal of that nature.

G.P.K.

Saint Louis University

Table of Contents

The Philosophy of Human Nature

CHAPTER I

Introduction

1. What is the philosophy of human nature?

You can look on every university course as either the answer to a question or the solution of a problem.

There is no advantage in knowing the answer to a question if you do not know what question you are trying to answer. So, in the beginning of every course, you must try to find out—at least in a general way—the location and the nature of the problem you are studying.

The question that is asked in the philosophical study of man is obviously, What is man? Put in this simple way, the question seems excessively easy to answer; and if there is anything difficult about it, those difficulties already seem to be adequately studied by biology and experimental psychology, with perhaps some help from sociology and history. Is there, then, any point in attempting to give a philosophical answer to the question, What is man?

2. A question can have many meanings

Do all these various sciences mean the same thing when they ask, What is man? The question is so simple that it seems it can have only one meaning. A few examples, though, may help us to understand that even simple questions sometimes are complicated.

Suppose a housewife wants to bake a spice cake, but does not know what it contains. She asks a chemist friend and receives an answer that begins, "It contains five kinds of carbohydrates, namely $C_{12}H_{22}O_{11}$. . . ." This is a perfectly correct answer, but it is of no help to the housewife. So she goes to another friend who is a dietician and is told, "Fifty grams of spice cake contain about one hundred and sixty calories. . . ." Then she meets a neighbor who says, "You will need flour, sugar, shortening. . . ." It is easy to see that, though all the answers were correct and were replies to the housewife's question, only the last *answered* that question.

Suppose an art critic, a historian, a chemist, and a geometrician each spend an hour studying Raphael's *Madonna and Child* and then write up their observations. The four accounts will be quite different; if they are properly done, they will all be true; even if one of them is an exhaustive study in its special field, it will not make the other accounts useless. Or suppose that a literary critic, a theologian, and a printer each study Lloyd Douglas's *The Big Fisherman* and compare their results.[1]

In these examples, it is quite clear that each of the investigators studied the same thing, the same reality. We might reflect, then, and ask ourselves: Are there facts, independent of each other, that one investigator will stress and the others simply omit—for example, the date of birth of the artist and the chemical nature of the materials with which he worked? Are there various insights, various truths seen? Are there differences in method?

3. Knowledge or knowledges?

The fact that a question can have several correct answers suggests that there is more than one way of knowing a thing. Perhaps we might hold that there are only different degrees of knowing— for example, completely and incompletely, perfectly and imperfectly. Or is there perhaps more than one kind of knowledge? Many people have said that there is only one real knowledge and that other so-called forms of knowledge are merely incomplete ways of looking at things or else only dreams, phantasy, fiction— even nonsense.[2]

Those who say that there is only one real knowledge do not

---

[1] It is an interesting—and often surprising—experience for a group of people to try an experiment like this.

[2] For readings and examples of some of these attitudes, see below, Appendices B, D, E, F, pp. 361-63, 368-77.

agree about what that one real knowledge is. For example, rationalists deny experimental science and faith on the ground that there must be a rational proof for everything that is held; some, like Averroes, have denied value to faith, history, and experience, saying that only the deductive syllogism gives knowledge. Fideists and traditionalists assert that only faith is true knowledge because the human mind is incapable of getting truth by itself. Mathematically minded philosophers admit the value of mathematics and mathematically influenced knowledge and so imply that reality is quantified matter. Positivists restrict knowledge to the purely experimental sciences, saying that the use of reason beyond experience is a meaningless exercise of that power. Some scientists restrict knowledge to the natural sciences (physics, chemistry, biology and the related dependent sciences) and mathematics.

Now, it is completely legitimate, and sometimes even necessary, to prescind from other knowledge and other forms of reality when one is engaged in the pursuit of a particular scientific knowledge of a limited object: [3] a man cannot simultaneously be acting as a physicist, a historian, and an artist. But when he goes so far as to say that there is only one kind of knowledge, he is making a double mistake. He is denying the experience that there are other forms of knowledge, and he is denying (at least by implication) a smaller or greater part of reality. He is implicitly saying, "I refuse to admit as real what I cannot know in this way or that way."

It is characteristic of the "Sunday-supplement mind" to consider the pronouncements of a motion picture star on international politics significant and important, or those of a gossip columnist on social relations. It is a sign of equal ignorance and credulity to take the ill-considered conclusions of a great physicist on the nature of God or of man for more than they are intrinsically worth. The only intelligent, realistic, and unbiased position is that in fact

[3] The advantage gained from such precision seems to have been the occasion for the one-sided views we have been considering. The resplendent success of some one method (logic, mathematical analysis, controlled experiment) can tempt a man to apply it everywhere.

there are many distinct kinds of knowledge. How and why this must be so should be clearer at the end of this course.

4. Experimental psychology and the philosophical study of man

Since the philosophical study of man seems to be most closely related to experimental psychology, some parallels and contrasts may help to make the relation of the two clearer.[4]

EXPERIMENTAL PSYCHOLOGY   PHILOSOPHY OF HUMAN NATURE

A. Starting Point

Specific facts [5] that are precise and detailed. They are demonstrated to be universal in fact [6] by techniques that more or less closely involve laboratory testing of many individuals.

Facts that need not be specific, but must be very accurately determined. They are ideally demonstrated to be universal by a proof that gives the reason for their being universal.[7]

For example, this science investigates the various conditions that can have an influence on memory; it considers how much different persons forget after a week, a month, a year; it tests the advantages and disadvantages of various techniques of remembering.

For example, the philosopher tries to see as clearly as possible what "to remember" means; he investigates this action to see what he can learn about the nature of man from it; he relates this action to other actions of man in terms of the nature thus revealed.

Or the scientist, studying sensation, tries to find out by careful measurement in many instances the relation between the intensity of a stimulus and the intensity of a resulting sensation.

Or the philosopher, studying sensation, investigates its nature, as this is revealed in the fact that it needs a material stimulus, and is measurable.

[4] For a fuller development of this point, see below, Appendix K, especially section 8, pp. 393–96.

[5] By "specific facts" are meant the very specialized results characteristic of the sciences. For example, it is found that the speed of a nerve impulse is so many centimeters per second at a given temperature.

[6] The demonstration of fact (*quia est: that* something is so) needs complicated procedures of choice of cases, elimination of disturbing causes, and so forth, when the scientist intends to find out whether something always occurs.

[7] Called the *propter quid* demonstration. By discovering the cause of an effect, it can show the universality of an effect without the roundabout process of studying many individual cases.

B. Methods

The scientist almost always uses elaborate techniques of observation, usually involving instruments and some form of measurement. The scientist tends to base the value of his conclusions on the completeness of his coverage of cases. From these cases, he develops an explanatory hypothesis which must then be checked by further "verifying" experiments. When this second stage is completed, he states his conclusions in terms of laws of behavior.

The philosopher's techniques are usually not elaborate, though they must by all means be careful and accurate. Measurement in itself is usually irrelevant. When knowledge through instruments is used, the instruments themselves are rather a condition. The technique of the philosopher is usually a rigorous use of reflection and/or analysis. From an experience, he passes by means of reflection-analysis to consideration of what it is that he has observed and of its mode of being.

C. Type of Conclusion

As far as possible, the scientist states his conclusions quantitatively. In general, what he is looking for is the connections between various facts, the conditions that modify the fact, and the consequences this fact may have in relation to other facts.

The philosopher states his conclusions in terms of nature and mode of being. What he is looking for is the answer to these questions: What kind of activities are these? What kind of being is man?

For example, the scientist concludes that retention is better when learning-practice is spaced than when it is continuous; that for any given individual there is a constant factor in learning efficiency.

For example, the philosopher concludes that memory has a relation to the body, since it is governed at least partly by conditions of matter and motion; that it is a distinct power because it has a distinct formal object.[8]

In the light of these considerations we can see that both the experimental psychologist and the philosopher of human nature have true forms of organized knowledge about man. Both investigators strive to see what man is; both try to find the causes of human activities. But the experimental psychologist wants to know

[8] It is to be expected that a person who has not studied these subjects will have only a vague notion of what the conclusions thus expressed mean, and that he will not as yet know why they are asserted.

how the various human activities can be classified, measured (if possible), and predicted and seeks to express them as accurately as possible. When the psychologist looks for the causes of human actions, he looks principally [9] for formal conditions and formal relationships (for example, what actions always, or at least ordinarily, precede other actions). The philosophy of human nature also wants to know what man does—and as accurately as possible, though it is not directly interested in measuring these actions; rather its interest lies in them as action and being and as a revelation of man's nature. When the philosophy of human nature asks for the causes of human action, it looks for proximate and remote principles (efficient, formal, material) and for efficient and final causes as well.

5. The philosophy of human nature and metaphysics [10]

Metaphysics (or the philosophy of being) follows a method of procedure that is very much like the method used by the philosophy of human nature. Thus, it proceeds by induction, insight, and analysis (and/or deduction) to arrive at principles that apply analogously [11] to all beings or to all things that have their act of existing in a certain way (some principles, for example, apply only to created being). Thus metaphysics is concerned with the structure of being in terms of act and potency, and less directly

[9] Principally, though not exclusively. To some extent, he looks for material causes and efficient causes of motion or change. On the other hand, final causes and the efficient causes of being are usually not dealt with by any science—though there is no reason why any scientist should deny what he himself does not use.

[10] For a more detailed discussion of this relationship and of the evidence that needs to be considered, see below, Appendix K, pp. 397–99.

[11] Analogy is midway between univocation (application or use in identically the same way) and equivocation (application or use in two or more completely different ways). It is in a way a relational predication, either through causality or through a similitude of proportions; cf. below, section 93, D, E, F.

Do not confuse this with the so-called "argument from analogy" in the sense in which this is understood in rhetoric and in biology. In the latter case, a similitude of proportions is used *to infer a fact*. But the philosopher does *not* use his similitude of proportions to infer at all; he uses it to understand something he experiences or infers.

with matter and form, which metaphysics considers rather as instances of act and potency.

Since man is a being, the principles and conclusions of metaphysics apply to him and to his nature, his activities, and so forth. In this sense, metaphysics is implicit throughout the philosophy of human nature.

But man is not just a being (in general); he is a particular kind of being, with his own proper nature and his own significantly unique activities. Therefore, it would be totally incorrect to think of the philosophy of human nature as "applied metaphysics," and it would be almost as great an error to think of it as a branch of metaphysics.[12] On the other hand, an excessive separation of the philosophy of human nature from metaphysics would also have unfortunate consequences.[13]

Briefly, the task of the philosophy of human nature in relation to metaphysics is this: In the course of considering man philosophically, one must make new inductions, which are based on the evidence proper to living things and to man as such. In making these inductions, one rediscovers metaphysical principles in a more particularized field of experience and being. Sometimes, the principles of metaphysics thus discovered will need to be expressed in a new formulation suited to the special nature of the subject, man. Furthermore, whereas metaphysics deals directly with being and only indirectly with essence or nature, the philosophy of human nature studies man as a being having a special, proper nature.

[12] By "applied metaphysics" is meant the univocal use of metaphysical principles in the explanation of a particular being. Such a procedure would result in overlooking all that is special to man. Almost the same consequences would result from considering the philosophy of human nature as a branch of metaphysics.

[13] To cut off the philosophy of human nature from metaphysics (as if it were simply a diverse kind of knowledge) would be to prevent the student from understanding man as a being.

Some persons might be inclined to think that the "philosophy of human nature" is just a collection of points, some of which pertain to metaphysics, some to experimental psychology, some to the "philosophy of nature." In Appendix K, an effort is made to investigate the proper nature of the philosophy of human nature.

6. Organization and method

The general topic which the philosophy of human nature considers is the question, What is man? This question must be broken down into a number of more particular questions. And before they can be intelligently approached and correctly answered, a preliminary question about the unity of man must be placed. For, unless a man is *one* being, there is no point in asking *what kind* of being he is. The question is a hard one to answer; but it is absolutely necessary that the unity of man should be known before we can answer many of the questions that arise later on.

Once we have solved the problem of the unity of man, we have to ask ourselves, What does man do? For it is only through the activities of things that we can discover their nature.[14] And since we find many kinds of activities in man, each one of these kinds needs to be studied in itself. When this has been done, we can take up the question of the nature of man with a solid hope of answering it.

In this procedure the method of proof becomes clear. The *point of departure* cannot be the nature, essence, or being of man. We can only begin with man's sensible qualities and with his activities —in other words, with the data of external observation and introspection. In making this beginning, it is of the utmost importance that the data really be given; if facts are overlooked or falsified, or if pseudofacts are invented, we cannot hope to arrive at the true nature of man. The examples of human activities which furnish our data have been drawn both from common experience and from the investigations of experimental psychology.[15] Examples

---

[14] The reason for this statement will be clear after the chapters dealing with knowledge have been completed.

[15] This course does not presuppose a course in experimental psychology. That is why terms used in that science are always defined when they are referred to and examples are also drawn from other fields that can be expressed in non-technical terminology.

Some readings in experimental psychology are suggested at the end of each chapter. If anyone wishes more detailed suggestions, or wishes to explore other areas where scientific psychology may furnish valuable data for the phi-

from experimental psychology are used freely because they are often more concise and directly relevant to the particular phase of the question under discussion.

Because of this starting point, the method of proof can be called inductive. By "induction" is meant the discovery or finding (*inventio*) of the data on which an organized or systematic knowledge of real things is based. However, we cannot be content simply with establishing and recounting these data—for example, that man has sense perception or emotion, or that he uses language. We must try to see what these data can tell us about the nature of man. So at this point we use philosophical analysis and reflection (for example, the method of analysis by formal object, or the principle that a thing and its way of acting are proportioned to each other). Our effort is to discover and follow the intelligible relations that are present in our data. Conclusions reached in this way can frequently be used as premises in further argumentation to reach further conclusions. At times, these further arguments may be deductive (for example, the argument by which we prove the spirituality of the soul), proceeding from a nature discovered by induction and analysis to other properties not manifested in experience.

After all this has been done, it is possible to reconsider the whole course of the argument, but this time in reverse. Such a return movement of thought [16] has two functions. First, it enables us to check on the accuracy with which the inductive-analytic movement was conducted. Secondly, it gives us complete certitude, in that it changes the argumentation from a demonstration of fact to a demonstration by cause. In other words, at the conclusion of the second movement, we can not only say, "Man acts thus and so," but also, "Having such a nature, man must act thus."

---

losopher, he can find selected starting-points for his investigations in G. P. Klubertanz, S.J. "The Psychologists and the Nature of Man," *Proceedings of the American Catholic Philosophical Association,* XXV (1951), 66–88.

[16] In the terminology of Aristotle and St. Thomas Aquinas, the entire first movement is called the "way of discovery" (*via inventionis*); the second, the return movement is called the "way of judgment" (*via iudicii*).

Hence, we can describe the philosophy of human nature as an organized, unified, and certain knowledge about the nature of man, derived from experience through an analysis of his activities, characteristics, and powers.

In the entire course of this argument, practically no notice is taken of other systems. In the first place, it does not seem possible to learn—all at once and in the same moment of thought—facts, the conclusions implied in those facts, other conclusions drawn from them by thinkers, and the critique that must be directed against them. "Divide and conquer" is as true in the mastery of a field of learning as it is in power politics and battle strategy.

In the second place, no philosophical system can be grasped piecemeal, conclusion by conclusion; neither can it be judged and evaluated in that way. To understand those who differ in their explanations of reality, it is necessary to see their doctrines as wholes; then their stand can be properly evaluated. Selected readings for various systems are indicated in the appendix, together with hints that will help the reader to find their key points.

This book is in two parts. The first part, or text, presents the philosophy of human nature in a straightforward, organized progression of thought. Each chapter takes a particular phase or part of the general question, discusses its meaning, and works through the data to an answer. After this has been done at length, the essential results of the discussion are summed up in definitions and proofs in syllogistic form.[17] Finally, each chapter is concluded with a group of suggested readings, which will serve to bear out experimental data, offer examples, present certain points in a more extensive fashion or in a different way, or, occasionally, exemplify opposing positions. In almost every chapter, some scientific readings have been suggested in addition to the philosophical treat-

[17] These proofs and definitions may well seem obscure and without content if they are read apart from the chapter whose results they embody. Therefore, teacher and student should refer to the appropriate preceding discussion in considering and learning these proofs and definitions.

In the groups of definitions attached to each chapter, some terms are italicized; these are the more important terms, and their definitions should be memorized.

ments; both Catholic and non-Catholic authors are mentioned, in order that the student may more clearly see that the positions arrived at are purely rational, and do not presuppose the acceptance of the Catholic faith.

The second part of the book contains two groups of appendices. The first group is a guide to opposing philosophical systems, offering not only selected readings in English, but offering in each case suggestions that will help toward an understanding of the philosophy of man that is contained or implied in each given system. Moreover, the basic points of criticism are indicated, together with references for further reading and study.

The second group of appendices is a series of brief discussions of points that are important but are not directly part of the course. They would interrupt the straightforward march of the argument. Unfortunately, there are no adequate English treatments of these accessory points available. Since the needs of the students must be considered as well as the logical requirements of the course, this second group of appendices is offered in the hope that some very urgent modern questions will thereby be answered.

7. Readings

Jacques Maritain, *Introduction to Philosophy*, trans. by E. I. Watkin (New York, Sheed and Ward), pp. 111–23.

Henry V. Veatch, "Some Suggestions on the Respective Spheres of Science and Philosophy," *Thomist*, III (1941), 177–216.

Robert J. Henle, S.J., "A Note on Professor Joad's *How Our Minds Work*," *The Modern Schoolman*, XXV (1948), 193–96.

Alfred North Whitehead, *Science and the Modern World* (New York, Macmillan, 1925), pp. 80–81, 214. This contains some strong statements on the unwarranted extension of scientific method.

James Collins, "Philosophical Discussion in the United States: 1945," *The Modern Schoolman*, XXIV (1947), 65–81. This is a brief presentation of the views of certain writers who in general hold that experimental science is the only valid form of knowledge.

CHAPTER II

The Unity of Man

8. Preliminary: the notion of unity

We cannot hope to successfully answer the question, What is man? unless we know whether man is one being or not. Consequently, the first problem that faces us is the problem of the unity of man. And before we can attack even the problem of the unity of man, we must have a very accurate understanding of the meaning of unity, and must be ready to recognize its signs and conditions. But we cannot completely solve the problem of the unity of man at this point; it will be taken up again in Chapter XIII.

What do we mean when we say X is one? The word "one" here does not mean the first of the series of numbers we use when we count. It means that the thing we are talking about is not divided into many [other things].[1] Hence "one" means an attribute of the subject itself. This is the kind of meaning we attach to the word when we ask, before buying a car or a dishwasher, whether it is "all in one piece." The abstract term, "unity," will similarly mean "actual indivision" ("undividedness").

Unity may be of many kinds. A thing may be actually undivided, and it may also not be capable of being divided. For example, a geometrical point is that which has position but no size: it is thus not only actually one, but indivisible. An indivisible unity is known as "simplicity." On the other hand, a thing may be actually undivided, but at the same time divisible. Though actually not divided, it *can* be divided: it is divisible in potency. For example, a line that is not divided is actually one, but it can be divided

[1] This type of unity is technically called *transcendental,* because it transcends (goes beyond) the particular category of number and is found in all the categories of being.

indefinitely. Such a unity that includes a potential multiplicity of parts is called "a unity of composition."

The unity of composition is again divided into several types, depending upon the relation of the parts to each other and to the whole. For parts may be parts of a whole by their very nature (intrinsic unity), as the parts of an animal belong together, or they may have been formed into a whole by something superadded to their nature (accidental unity), as the bricks of a house are one by their place and arrangement.

The loosest kind of accidental unity is unity in activity only. For example, a group of boys form a team (therefore a unit) to play a game; a car and its driver are united in the series of activities involved in driving the car; a carpenter and his hammer form a unit in hammering a nail. In all these cases, the things united are clearly distinct (multiplied), except so far as they are engaged in the same activity, which is the "something superadded" making for unity. This kind of unity may be called "dynamic."

A more closely knit kind of accidental unity is found in distinct beings that are also united to some extent in being. For example, the parts of a watch make up one watch as long as they are together according to their proper arrangement in the watch (even though the watch is not running); the parts of a table need have no specific action together, yet they make up one table so far as they are together according to a spatial arrangement; single stones piled together make up one heap—in a unity that is perhaps the weakest of its kind, for though the stones really make up one heap, the unity of the heap is only the being-together-in-space. This kind of unity may be called "static."

All these forms of the unity of composition are in one sense or another extrinsic unities, in the sense that the unity, or wholeness, of them is in one way or another outside the nature of the parts as beings or things—the unity is "something superadded" (accidental). The intrinsic unity, on the contrary, is characterized by this, that according to the whole nature of the parts they are ordered to each other and to the whole.

The first example of a natural or intrinsic unity is to be found in a being that is a composite of substance and accidents (for example, a piece of wood and its shape, color, hardness).[2] Created substance has existence *in itself;* still, it is in need of further determinations distinct from itself in order to exist. It is thus by its nature ordered to the accidents which complete it. On the other hand, accidents by their very nature are modifications and determinations of a subject that is substance; hence by their very nature, not by something superadded, they are such as to exist *in substance* and to be united to it, in a per accidens unity.

The second type of natural or intrinsic unity, called "per se unity," is found within substance, wherever a substance is composite even as substance (that is, is composed of the substantial principles: matter and form), and consequently is capable of division even as substance. Such a composite substance would have substantial parts that themselves are not substances. This kind of unity is called "substantial unity"; and the term "per se unity," when used without qualification, ordinarily means substantial unity.

Unity is:
- simple, if it is without parts.
- composite, if it is a whole composed of parts; the parts are potentially or virtually present.

Composite unity can be
- accidental (extrinsic)
  - in operation or activity (dynamic), for example, driver and car, horse and rider
  - in being (static), for example, a table, a heap of stones.
- intrinsic
  - per accidens
    - accident and substance
    - accidents of a substance among themselves
  - per se, within substance, of substantial principles.[3]

[2] The examples of accident-substance composition and of substantial composition given here are presumed as established in metaphysics. We will see later that they are also established in the philosophy of human nature.

[3] This scheme is not complete, nor is the terminology entirely fixed. Some authors used the term "per accidens" for accidental; some have a three-fold

9. Criteria and conditions of unity

Some types of unity are directly perceptible; for example, many instances of unity in space (the table or watch mentioned above) can be immediately seen or experienced in some sensible fashion. Other kinds of unity cannot be so experienced; and in order to discover whether or not unity is to be found in such instances some criteria must be used.

The most difficult, and, for our present purposes, the most important kind of unity is the substantial unity of composition. Being substantial, it is not precisely as such perceptible by sensory experience. But this does not mean that it is either mysterious or hidden. To discover it, we have only to engage in some reflection and a careful analysis of the evidence.

A thing can be known to us so far as it manifests itself to us. These manifestations either are, or at least take place through, some activity.[4] For example, we know that an electric iron is hot when it heats something else (our hand, a thermometer); something is known to be heavy when it presses down; we know that an automobile has a motor when we see it moving independently down the street. By an induction of this kind we can come to see how it is that we learn to know a thing from its activities. Reflection will show us that this must be so. A thing can act according to its mode of being, and only in that way. For an action implies that the agent is in act. This principle is summed up in the phrase "action follows being" (*agere sequitur esse*).

Now, if action follows being, then the unity of being can be known through the unity of activity. If a thing had only one activity, then its nature, and the unity of that nature, would be

___

classification. The unity of substance and accident could be called "per se" because it is natural, or "per accidens," in the sense that the accident becomes one with the subject by inherence. (Moreover, per se unity usually involves both a unity within substance [whether simple or composite] and a single act of existing.)

[4] As we shall see in Chapter VI, even such static qualities as shape are known to us through other directly sensible qualities, and these in turn through their action upon us.

very readily discoverable. But it is to be expected that composite things have many activities (at least more than one). We must therefore say that a composite thing that is really one can be known to be such through the unity of its several activities. In other words, though at some times or from one point of view a thing may have many activities, yet the activities of one thing must, at least, at other times or from a different point of view, be joined into one, composite activity.

All activity is for an end; every agent acts for a goal (*omne agens agit propter finem*). Again, to be understood, this principle must be considered inductively. Thus, local motion is identified and specified by its direction or term: an *upward* movement, a trip *north*, a ride to *Chicago*. In a similar fashion, a process is identified and specified by its product: a change that leads to a new size is augmentation; a change that leads to a new quality is an alteration; a process that leads to the suspension of a substance in a solvent is a dissolving. When we ask a person, "What are you doing?" we ask the question because we see an activity going on and wish to know the product or term of that activity in order to know what the activity is. Therefore, our question about the unity of activities is immediately translated into a question about the unity of the goal of those activities.

We can argue from the unity of the end of activity to substantial unity, because of the close relationship between the thing that acts (the agent) and its activity. A careful reflection will bring this relationship clearly before our mind. Whatever acts in itself, or is the real subject of action, can only be something that exists in itself, that is, an existing substantial unit, or *supposit*. Not only must we say, "What does not exist cannot act," but, "Whatever exists only in another, can act only as in a subject." Since action flows from nature [5] to end, it would be a contradiction to imagine

---

[5] By "nature" we mean the intrinsic substantial principle of activity. It is the same as the essence considered in relation to activity. We are not presuming that man has a nature; we are trying to understand what nature is, so

that the end—the good—of any particular supposit could simultaneously not be its good, but immediately and in itself the good of another. If the parts of a whole are so many supposits, they cannot act primarily and directly for the good of the whole without contradicting the independence of their being. Or, put conversely, whatever has various parts that act primarily and directly for the good of the whole is a supposit or substantial unit.

Note that it is not enough that the parts of a given whole should act for *one* end in order that we may immediately conclude that that whole is a single supposit. The parts of a camera, for instance, work for the one end of taking pictures; the parts of an automobile work for the one end of transportation. Yet the parts of the camera do not act for the good of the camera—they work for the good of the photographer; and the parts of the automobile do not work for the good of the automobile—they work for the good of the driver. The one end that each machine works for is extrinsic to the machine itself. Hence neither camera nor automobile is a supposit, for the one end of a supposit must be an intrinsic end, the good of the whole. Every supposit, then, acts directly and primarily for its own good, and only secondarily or remotely for the good of another.

In order that one substantial whole may be actually one substantial being, its components must be principles of being; they cannot be complete beings in themselves. Two substantial acts make two beings; consequently, there can be only one substantial act in a being that is substantially one. On the other hand, there must be at least one substantial act in a being that is actually one substance; for if all its parts were to be potencies in the order of substance, there would be no being in act at all. Consequently, if a being is substantially composite, it must be a composite of act and potency.[6]

---

that we can discover whether man has a nature, and what that nature is. These two steps will be worked out in Chapters III and XIII.

[6] This discussion of substantial composition is but preliminary; it will be taken up in great detail in Chapter III.

10. The question: Is a living thing one or many beings?

A man, a dog, a tree is in some sense each one being. If they were not, we could not experience them, could not point to them, could not talk about them. Their unity in space and—in some sense—in activity is so obvious that we need not ask, Are they one? The only question to be asked is, In what sense is a living thing one? or, What kind of unity does a living thing have? Is the unity of a living thing substantial or merely accidental? The evidence here is complex and manifold, and needs very careful consideration.

First of all, can anything that is extended in space really be called *one* thing? To be extended in space means to have parts that are not identical. If my hand and my foot are really distinct and different, how am I really one being? To be extended in space is not merely to have parts which are outside of other parts; it is to be a composite of such parts; and therefore, in a way, it is to be those many parts.

The evidence from activity causes much more of a problem. Every one of us experiences conflicts within himself—how can one being be in conflict with itself? And if we look at scientific evidence, there seems to be even more reason for doubting unity. Biochemists say that a man's body is composed of oxygen, hydrogen, carbon, and many other elements. Psychiatrists find sick individuals who are "multiple personalities," and frequently these personalities are strangers one to another. Doctors can take skin and bones and flesh, and even whole organs (like a gland), out of one body, keep them alive outside of the body, and transplant them into another person. And so a person's body seems to be many living things: cells and tissues and organs.

Now that we have seen that there is a problem about the unity of man, we will proceed to a detailed examination of the evidence. This evidence can conveniently be divided into two kinds: that drawn from external observation of man and other living things, and that drawn from our own experience of ourselves. Under the first heading, we shall consider the evidence for and against human unity; then we shall take up the evidence for unity drawn from our own experience (in section 16).

11. The evidence for unity. A. From the outside: the finality of human activities

a. From anatomy and neurology we learn that the various tissues and organs are not simply attached to one another externally. In addition to the distinct organs (eyes, glands, and so forth), there are other parts of the body whose function is to unify and coördinate the other distinct parts. The circulatory system brings food and oxygen to all parts of the body and carries away their waste products. Then there are the endocrine [7] and nervous control-systems, whose function is to keep all the particular functions balanced, in harmony with each other, and adjusted to the requirements of the whole. Therefore, even at this level, we can see that the good of the whole is the controlling end of the parts.

b. Human activities are interrelated. Vegetative (biological) life in a man not only nourishes and produces man as a vegetable; it brings the body to full perfection and keeps it in good working order as a sentient organism. By their very nature as vegetative processes of a particular kind, the activities of digestion, nourishment, growth, repair, and so forth—all these vegetative processes in a man or an animal are ordered to the body inasmuch as that body is sentient.[8] For example, the processes of growth in a dog embryo not only make nourishment and growth possible for the future, but precisely as vegetative processes in this dog produce and nourish the organs of sensation (eyes, ears, and so forth). The same thing is true in a man. What is nourished by vegetative activity, what has been developed by that activity, is the sentient body. And again in man the activities of the senses serve to arouse

[7] The "endocrine control system" comprises a group of glands which secrete their products (called "hormones") directly into the blood stream. Most of these secretions stimulate or excite other organs and tissues; some of them inhibit or retard the activity of organs and tissues. In this way, the endocrine glands act as controls upon the activity of the living thing.

[8] If the natural ordering of these activities were not for the good of the whole, we would have no way of distinguishing between health and disease.

and develop intellectual understanding. Man's senses, his desires, his motor activities, are such that by them he can adjust himself as a whole to his environment and can improve and better himself. The interlocking of all these levels of activity in man will become clearer as this study progresses; even at this stage, enough evidence is present for us to say that the natural ordering of the different levels of activity in a man (and proportionately in an animal) is for the good of the whole.

c. Psychological personality depends on the body. When a person is in good health he usually feels well and can sense and think clearly. When he has a high fever, his sensory and intellectual processes are sometimes disturbed, and then we speak of a delirium. The continuance of consciousness depends on the integrity of the brain; a severe blow on the head deprives a person of consciousness. Drugs which in one way or another chemically injure the nervous system or interfere with its functioning have corresponding effects upon knowledge and emotion. Injuries to particular parts of the brain have special effects upon particular parts or aspects of imagination, memory, recognition, and emotion. Endocrine imbalance (as in cretinism, involutional melancholia) [9] brings about mental deficiency and emotional imbalance corresponding to the kind of deficiency. Electrical stimulation of the brain (for example, in the course of an operation) can cause a person to become aware of various images.

d. The body is influenced by conscious states. The feeling of shame results in blushing; anger causes a flow of adrenalin and so brings about a fast pulse and heavy breathing; fear produces paleness and trembling. This dependence is even more clear in

[9] *Endocrine imbalance* is the state in which one or several endocrine glands secrete notably more or less of their special hormone than is suited to functioning of the rest of the system of glands and tissues. *Cretinism* is a dwarf condition caused by deficiency of thyroid secretion in infancy or early childhood; among typical features we find: retarded growth, mental deficiency, coarsening of the features. *Involutional melancholia* is a marked psychic depression and vasomotor disturbance; it is frequently connected with a subnormal concentration of oestrin in the blood; at least some of the symptoms are relieved by injections of theelin (one of the forms of the hormone oestrin).

abnormal cases. A violent emotional shock can bring about hysterical paralysis [10] or the inability to feel pain in some part of the body. Worry can cause gastric ulcers. Finally, in some dramatic cases of sensitivity, the mental image of a swelling in the shape of a rose-petal will produce a swelling of just that shape in the spot where it is imagined to be.

We have taken a brief look at the evidences which lead us to conclude that a man is one being, a substantial unit. But we cannot have a full understanding of this unity until we have considered and correctly located the evidence for multiplicity in man. We will consider the evidence for multiplicity in four stages (which are somewhat parallel to the four divisions of the argument for unity).

12. The counter-evidence for plurality: I. The multiplicity of parts necessarily involved in every extended body

The first difficulty against the unity of man is that he is made up of many parts. Now the multiplicity of parts is based on the very nature of continuous extension. A more careful consideration of extension will show that the plurality of spatial parts is not an actual but a potential plurality. For example, a line contains any number of parts (smaller lines) and points *potentially*, not actually. The potential presence of parts in a line means that any given line can be cut into smaller lines; yet, before it is cut either really or mentally, the smaller part-lines have no distinct real existence nor are they distinctly understood. In the same way, there are no actual points in the make-up of a continuous, undivided line, though they can very easily be designated. So, too, a hand or any

[10] A psychoneurotic condition involving loss of movement in arms, legs, speech organs. Hysterical anesthesia is the loss of function of some sense, for example, deafness, blindness, loss of sense of touch or of pain. These hysterical conditions usually involve no organic nervous disturbance; frequently do not correspond to the anatomical distribution of the affected part; reflexes remain normal. Explanations of hysteria mention these factors: heightened suggestibility, retracted field of consciousness, maladjustment or emotional shock, dissociation; all of these are psychic factors, though they may well be connected with organic conditions at some points. Cf. D. B. Klein, *Abnormal Psychology* (New York, Holt, 1951), pp. 268–72, 274–80.

other organ in the living body is not an actually distinct quantity. Because of the special characteristics of organs, they are easily thought of as distinct. In such cases, the distinction is actualized by the mind. Hence, a being extended in space has as such only a potential multiplicity, which does not contradict or interfere with an actual unity.

13. The counter-evidence for plurality: II. The presence of chemical elements and substances in the living body

Physical, chemical, and biological theory usually holds these as true: (*a*) elemental particles (protons, electrons) are found as such in all complex units; (*b*) chemical elements are found as such, distinctly, in chemical compounds; (*c*) elements and compounds are found as such in physical compounds like living things; (*d*) cells—according to some persons—are distinct beings in a multicellular living thing. If those who propound such theories were to use the terminology of the present chapter, they would say that all composite material units are accidental units. Because these theories are backed by weighty evidence, it is necessary for us to review it briefly and evaluate it in order that we may see how it is related to the evidence for the unity of living things.

(1) All complex material units are composed of particular kinds of simpler matter, in definite proportions. Thus, if a chemist wishes to produce water, he combines two parts of hydrogen to one of oxygen. If a living thing could be produced in a laboratory, a very definite set of proteins, carbohydrates, and so on would be necessary.

(2) In the destruction of a complex material unit, certain simpler matter is recovered, and that in the same proportions which went to make it up.

(3) Any complex material being has some of the "qualities" of its constituents; for example, its total weight is the sum of the weights of these parts; some of its activities can be predicted from a knowledge of the activities of these parts.

(4) In the larger physical compounds, some parts have special

activities related to their own structure; for example, the eye is partly composed of transparent matter, and it is the only part of a large animal that is directly sensitive to actual color.

(5) The microscope shows that large living things are composed of cells; that growth takes place by division of these cells; that nourishment takes place within the cell; that muscular contractions are the sum total of the contractions of the muscle cells, and so forth.

(6) In certain types of illnesses, certain cells or certain types of cells seem to escape from the unity of the body and continue living a vegetative life of their own to the detriment of the organism (tumors, leukemia, perhaps cancer).

(7) Chemical elements are present in compounds. The spectrograph [11] of a living thing, for example, shows the characteristic spectrum lines of water, carbon, and so forth; by the use of "tagged atoms" (radiocarbon, and so forth), particular particles of matter can be traced in a living thing, and their location in it definitely established; in crystalline structures, the constituent elements are arranged in regular patterns; the whole theory of stereochemistry presupposes that atoms and molecules in other substances are also arranged in very definite spatial patterns.

(8) Light, heat, and electricity all deal with the movements of definite particles in a material thing and imply that electrons and even atoms are able to move about in the substance.

These evidences [12] lead, first of all, to a general view of the mate-

[11] A spectrograph is an image or picture (or diagram) of a spectrum. There are two kinds of spectra: continuous and line (band) spectra. For example, when ordinary sunlight is passed through a prism or grating, the familiar band of colors is produced; there are no gaps or dark lines. But when light has been passed through a layer of gas, liquid, or solid, some rays are selectively absorbed, and the place of these rays is marked by dark lines or bands in the spectrum. (Line spectra can also be produced in other ways.) Each chemical substance has its own characteristic pattern of lines.

[12] It may be helpful to note that the first four sets of evidence were already known even to Aristotle, though not in such accurate detail as we know them now. Something quite analogous to the sixth was known to Avicenna and St. Thomas Aquinas. The fifth, seventh, and eighth depended, for their discovery, on modern instruments and so could not have been known before the discovery of these instruments. But what is important to realize is that,

rial universe, which may be called the hierarchical view. The hierarchical view means that material reality can be arranged in an ascending order of perfection, in which the higher degrees have all the perfections of the lower, and more.[13] Thus, the lowest degree is that of merely material (inanimate) being. The second is that of vegetative life, which has the perfection of material substance and, in addition, the added perfection of life. The third is that of animality (sensitive life); and the fourth, of humanity (rational sensibility). Thus, the highest degree of material being is still material being, has the perfections of vegetative life in common with plants, the perfections of sensitive life in common with animals, and in addition the perfection of rationality.

The eight types of evidence mentioned are really facts, and so an explanation which denies them cannot be valid or complete. But they are not the whole evidence. Not only is there the demonstrative evidence for the unity of any living thing which has already been considered; there is also some evidence to be added precisely with regard to the constituent material parts of man.

First, are the cells of a human body (and of the common plants and animals of our experience) distinct units, in the sense that man is an accidental aggregate or "cell-colony"? [14] The evidence does not warrant this conclusion. It is true that there are cell walls around each cell, and that growth largely takes place by the multiplication of individual cells. This proves only that man is material and organized. To be material involves being quantified (as we

---

though the evidence has become clearer and in some respects enormously detailed, it is not foreign to the philosophical explanation of material reality in terms of matter and form.

[13] This means that what is generically true of material substance will also be true of man, and so on in due proportion of the intermediate degrees. The lower the level, the smaller the specific differences are and the greater the number of species. At the top level, there is only one species; and individual differences are more noticeable at this level than specific differences at the lowest.

[14] A "cell-colony" is sometimes clearly recognizable from this, that each cell has the same structure and function as the others. But there may well be instances in which the biologist cannot tell whether he is studying a closely integrated cell-colony or an imperfect multicellular organism. This fact does not weaken the evidence where it is available and even unmistakeable.

have seen above). To be organized means to consist of parts with a spatial order to each other, parts which differ in structure and function. Nothing so far is proved about the kind of unity man has. We can only judge that from the kind of unity manifested in his operations. Do the cells in a human body act for themselves, like little plants or animals, or do they so work together that when they operate as they should they operate for the good of the whole? The intrinsic finality of the activities of healthy cells shows that they are not distinct individuals; consequently, the cell structure of man and other multicellular organisms does not interfere with their substantial unity.

Secondly, are the chemical compounds in a living body actually distinct, individual substances with their own proper being? The evidence here is that the living body is nourished by special kinds of chemical compounds and after death returns to those same compounds; that the spectrograph derives the characteristic spectrum lines [15] of at least some of these chemical substances from the living body; that "tagged" atoms can be followed through the bodily system and located when they are assimilated. To make this question more concrete: Is the water in the skin of your hand formally and actually water, existing as water? Is the nitrogen present there formally and actually nitrogen?

It is through their activities that we know what things are. Now, a scientist, for the purposes of his own science, may say: "Water, measured by the spectrograph, gives a certain set of characteristic lines. Wherever I find those lines, there water is present." This is all very well, provided the scientist does not attempt to say that water in every instance of this type is a distinct *substantial being*. We know that water, in a relatively pure liquid state, has a set of characteristics all of which belong to it. Does the water in living human skin have, actually, all of those characteristics? If not, then it does not have the formal perfection of water. It actually was water; it actually will be water; it actually *is* a *part* of the human body. The principle of hierarchy will give us a general

[15] See above, footnote 11.

point of view by means of which we can solve this problem in a more positive manner. For we can then add: And this particular part of the human body receives such perfection from its presence in the human substance that it is both a real part of a human body, with a part-structure like that of a molecule of water, and an activity to some extent like that of water, but not wholly so.[16] There is nothing to be wondered at in this: even at the large-scale level of organs, human substance has a different structural and operational perfection in the eye than it has in the muscle.

Thus the chemical compound or element (*a*) is not formal and actual as present in the living body; (*b*) is more than merely present in potency, for it actually shows some of the properties and characteristics of the distinctly existing compound; and (*c*) at some time also was, or will be actually existing as a distinct substance. To cover this special situation, the terms "virtual being" and "virtual presence" have been coined. For example, when we say that water has a virtual being in the living human body, we mean (*a*) that here and now it is not formally the distinct actual substantial supposit, water; (*b*) that it exercises, by being present as this part of a living body, some of the traits and activities of water, but not all of them; [17] and (*c*) that it was once, and will be again, formally and actually water.

A chemist, as chemist,[18] cannot ask the question we have asked

[16] To some extent it is possible to tell what these activities of the part within the whole will be, but largely it is a matter of experience, of finding out what it is.

[17] For example, water as part of the body will react with sodium and other chemicals as water by itself does. On the other hand, water as part of the body is not a clear fluid but part of a firm, opaque, consistent material; its freezing point is lower, and its boiling point higher than that of water by itself.

[18] That is to say, precisely as using the principles and methods of chemistry. For science as such is indifferent to philosophical positions; it does not contain either philosophical questions or answers. A man can be an excellent scientist without raising these questions; he *can* continue to be a good scientist while giving very poor answers to poorly stated philosophical questions. But inasmuch as science is not the whole of knowledge, a man who is also a scientist frequently can and does ask philosophical questions. When a man asks philosophical questions, he must turn philosopher to answer his questions adequately.

here, and cannot find this answer meaningful. In other words, chemistry is not philosophy; the two knowledges do not come into conflict, because they do not even meet.

Thirdly, are the elemental particles in a human body present there formally and actually as distinct substantial existents? Again, we can go only by a man's activities. Does a man look like and act like an electric current? or move about like an alpha ray? Like the compounds, the elemental particles are virtually present in the human body. It is true that the argument for man's unity is considerably stronger and much more direct than the argument for the presence of elemental particles in his body. For the very existence of these particles is arrived at by a long and very involved argumentation. But what science has found about the subatomic structure of matter is sufficiently clear to enable us to say that elemental particles are present in the human body, not in pure potency; what we know about man's unity precludes the presence of these particles in formal substantial act.[19]

*A few remarks about the causality that is working when a part (an element or a less complex compound) is changed from a state of virtual being to actual distinct being may be useful at this point. Take the case of the recovery of definite compounds in the destruction of a living thing. If an animal dies a natural death, or is burned in a furnace, or is killed by a crushing blow, the same basic ele-

[19] Once virtual presence has been found and *proved* in the one clear case of living things, it is possible to ask whether anything similar occurs on the non-living level. The evidence is not altogether clear. It would seem that chemical compounds are substantial units, because they have specific properties, and because the elemental particles in a compound seem to have a different action within the compound than they have as independent existents outside. Hence, the elements would seem to be virtually present in chemical compounds; and in turn, the electrons and so forth would seem to have a virtual presence in both elements and compounds. Perhaps the same explanation should be extended to cover the so-called conversion of matter to energy.

But to the extent that these cases (electrons, matter-energy conversion) involve theoretical constructs (see below, Appendix K) rather than facts, virtual presence is not applied to them. A scientific theory as such is neither in harmony nor contrary to a philosophical statement. And it is quite possible that new scientific theories can arise. Neither present nor future theories interest us here; we are concerned only with evidence.

ments, in the same proportions, are recovered. Clearly, therefore, the various things which kill the animal cannot be the sufficient causes of the actual perfections which are found. Yet there must be a cause proportioned to these effects.

*In efficient causality, there is one case where everything in the effect is due to the efficient cause—and this is creation, wherein God alone is the total cause of the whole being of the effect. In all the cases of efficient causality exercised by created agents, there is a pre-existing subject(When there is a pre-existing subject which undergoes the action of an efficient cause, does the subject itself play any part in the result? In most cases it does.[20] You simply cannot make a good saw out of beeswax, nor water out of chlorine and oxygen, nor derive silver from a hydrocarbon. In such cases, the full perfection of the effect is to be attributed partly to the efficient cause, partly to the dispositions of the pre-existing subject (and the proportion between these two can vary widely). The fewer the dispositions that pre-exist, the more is due to the efficient cause; the more determinate the dispositions, the less is due to the efficient cause.) Now, if we try to determine what type of causality is exercised by these pre-existing dispositions, we must say that it is most like material causality: They are in the line of the material cause.

*The question now is: Are the pre-existing dispositions of the parts of a living thing such that they can account for (cause) the substances which result in its destruction?

*A few analogies may help to clarify the situation. Suppose you have a metal ring in the form of a circle; you squeeze it between your fingers and it becomes an ellipse. What is the cause of the elliptical figure? You *and the previously existing figure,* you as efficient cause, the circle as proximate disposition to an ellipse. (The situation would be different if you first broke the ring,

[20] If elemental particles can be transmuted into each other, or built up out of energy, then apparently the whole formal perfection of the new particle would be due to the efficient cause; the material cause would merely provide a limiting recipient.

straightened it out, and then formed an ellipse from it. You would then much more completely be the cause of the ellipse.) Suppose you take a test-tube full of water at 40° and hold it in your hand until it is 60°. What is the cause of this new temperature? You as efficient cause, and the previous temperature of the water as a proximate disposition. Suppose a man is on top of a cliff; falling headlong over the edge, he is luckily caught by a projecting tree. Someone coming along the bottom of the cliff might wonder how such a steep face of rock was scaled. The lucky mountaineer might well say: "It's easy—if you come down, not up."

*Two conditions must be borne in mind, in order that we can answer the question: Are the pre-existing dispositions of the parts of the living thing such that they can account for (cause) the substances which are found after its death? (a) As in the analogies given, the process must be directly from the more complex to the less complex. It is not supposed that the living body, in being destroyed, is reduced immediately to a whole batch of loose protons and electrons and so forth, and that then specific elements and compounds are formed. The supposition is that in the very action or passion by which the living thing dies these new substances come to be. (b) There must be nothing in the new substance which is not directly derivable by way of a mere change in the dispositions of matter.[21]

*From these analogies, and under these two conditions, we can understand the origin of new substances in the very destruction of a more perfect substance. Precisely which compounds will be found when a more complex compound is destroyed can be completely known only from experience. Experience does show that, where scientists have been able to synthesize very complex compounds, the synthesis and the destructions of these compounds does not take place in a single large leap, but by successive stages.

---

[21] This second condition seems obvious; the reason for making it is that a special problem arises with regard to man; for a full consideration of this, see below, Appendix M, section 3, pp. 410–11.

14. The counter-evidence for plurality: III. The life of parts of the body outside the body [22]

Many plants can be propagated by cuttings or slips. Some one-celled living things multiply simply by dividing themselves. It seems probable that some cells and even tissues of the body continue living after the rest of the body is dead. In a similar way, it is possible to keep skin and various kinds of tissues alive outside the body; in the well-known "Carrel's Experiment" a piece of chicken heart was kept alive for years.

The origin of new plants by cutting and the multiplication of single-celled living things by mere division are one and the same problem: How can that which was a part by mere division alone become a complete, whole being?

The nature of composite units has just been studied, and we have seen that a very complex living thing contains other beings and other perfections *virtually*.[23] In Chapter III we shall find that it is proper to all vegetative beings to have an organized matter or body. This organization differs in different living things. Compare the complex organization of an adult human being with the relatively simple structure of a worm. Human organization at the adult stage is characterized by a great heterogeneity (dissimilarity) of parts, in both structure and function; a worm or tree is almost homogeneous by comparison.

Now, when structure and function are very heterogeneous, the organized parts of the body must be highly specialized, and therefore cannot take over other functions. In other words, such highly specialized parts do not virtually contain the perfection of the whole being. But as parts approach homogeneity, functions are not so highly specialized; and therefore the whole can be virtually present in one or more parts. This virtuality can approach so close to act that mere separation is enough to actuate it. The willow

[22] This is more fully considered in Appendix M, section 2.
[23] For a full definition of *virtual presence*, see below, section 17.

branch virtually contains the perfection of the whole tree, for all it lacks are roots, and these are not greatly dissimilar to branches. So, too, in the division of a one-cell living thing, the nucleus first divides into two parts, and then roughly half the protoplasm goes with each nucleus. Thus each part virtually contains the perfections of the whole and therefore can by mere division give rise to new living things. Hence, also, this virtual multiplicity does not interfere with the actual unity of the living thing.

*In view of what has been said about virtual presence, the life of separated parts is really no problem. A part, even while it is actually a part of one living thing, virtually contains other lower perfections. Among these perfections may be that of a lower grade of life than the one actually possessed by the being of which it is a part. For example, it is perfectly possible that a piece of tissue cut from an animal will live with a kind of imperfect vegetative life.[24] We might classify this kind of vegetative life as "that kind of vegetative life which corresponds to the virtually vegetative perfection of the animal from which the tissue was cut." And, if it is true that hair and other parts continue to grow after the death of the organism, the same solution will hold.

Hence, the evidence goes to show that every material living thing is virtually many things. (a) If it is a homogeneous organism, it is virtually many living things of the same species; (b) it may be virtually many living things of a lower kind; (c) it is virtually many compounds and elements. And so none of this evidence contradicts the evidence given above for the actual substantial unity of the living thing.

[24] "Imperfect," because of themselves such pieces and parts die almost immediately upon removal. By elaborate laboratory techniques the imperfection of function can be supplemented or other functions, completely missing in the separated part, may be added by the experimenter. Note that in addition to being supplied with the missing functions, the separated part depends on an intelligence, that is to say, the intellect of the experimenter.

The kind of unity of such separated parts is not easily determined. It is more probable that a piece of tissue, for example, is an accidental unit, and that the substantial unit in such a part is the cell. The principal reason for this conclusion is the indefinite proliferation of such parts.

15. The counter-evidence for plurality: IV. Evidence from psychological states

Experimental psychologists and physicians have long been accustomed to speaking of "multiple personalities." The basic nature of this type of mental illness must be understood, lest multiple personality seem to be an evidence against the unity of a living being.

Briefly, personality in the psychological sense (hereafter referred to as "psychological personality") is the sum total of past and present experience, attitudes, and ideas as referred to one conscious subject. Personality understood in this way necessarily involves memory. For various reasons which do not concern our present investigation, some people under certain stresses seem to "break up" the unity of their personalities. This dissociation or splitting of the personality may sometimes so manifest itself that at certain (more or less regularly recurring) periods of time a person will be, for example, gay, irresponsible, remembering only a selected group of past experience; while in the other intervals that person will be gloomy, severe, remembering a different set of past experiences. Usually, at least one of these personalities will be ignorant of what the other has done in the past. At times there may be conscious opposition between them. Occasionally, there may be more than two personalities involved.

A careful analysis of this evidence, however, shows that it is not against the unity of the living organism. First of all, the dissociation or multiplicity is largely at the level of memory (under the influence of emotion, and so forth). In other words, one group of actions and experiences is remembered as a group, and is not joined in memory with another. Such a group of experiences, attitudes, and ideas, united in memory, is called a memory-system. It often happens that one of the memory-systems includes the other at least partially. Secondly—and this is by far the more important consideration—as the illness progresses toward cure, the memory-systems are gradually reintegrated, while even during very severe stages of the illness, the systems can be joined by hypnosis and similar techniques. Hence the very evidence of multiple personality goes to show that an underlying unity remains. This underlying unity, implied in the experimental evidence, is founded on the substantial unity of the living being.

Another type of apparent evidence is that found in "personality changes" after certain illnesses, or injuries, or profound emotional experiences. Of such cases we sometimes say, "Henry is a different man since his accident." What we mean is that his ideas and/or his attitudes are different. The difference here refers to psychological personality, while the fact that we continue to call him by the same name implies that he is the same human being.

A third type of psychological evidence is to be found in the experience of distraction and conflict. But in these cases, the evidence points to a simultaneous unity of the human being. We usually say, "*I* was drawn this way and that," "*I* couldn't bring myself to do this," "*I* didn't think of what *I* was doing."

The value and function of this psychological evidence is that the unity of man is to be found at two levels. By being born with a human nature, a man has substantial unity. But that unity is such as to permit a certain multiplicity of action, attitude, memory, and so forth. A man may progress toward greater unity of life and action; he may regress toward greater multiplicity. Therefore, complete unity is an ideal of a mature character, not simply something given us by nature.

16. The evidence for unity: B. From the inside: direct experience and reflection

In section 11, we have considered the evidence for the unity of a living thing (man included) which we obtain by observing that thing. But, in the case of ourselves, we can derive more striking proofs from self-observation.

a. Under normal circumstances, I am aware that every part of my body is mine. I have an immediate, though quite obscure, awareness of my body and its states. I know where my hands and feet are; I can touch my right hand with my left, and so forth. The sum total of this direct knowledge of my body will be called "propriosensation."

b. I am aware that I see, I hear, I feel, and so forth. This kind of knowledge is called self-consciousness or self-awareness and is always obscurely present in all conscious activity, though its intensity varies quite considerably.

c. I am immediately aware that certain concrete sensible things are good *for me* (for example, tastily prepared food when I am hungry) and that others are bad *for me* (for example, being in imminent danger of falling). This is also a direct and concrete form of knowledge of myself; its meaning and significance will be studied later on.

d. In reflection, I am aware of myself as the actually undivided source and term of my known activities. This form of knowledge of myself is called "reflex self-awareness" (self-consciousness).

Therefore, every adult human being who is capable of these kinds of activities knows that he is really one being. Reflection on this evidence makes it clear that though various states, or modifications, or activities change, yet that which acts and exists in all these ways of acting and existing is one. Technically, in reflection, we implicitly experience our substantial unity through all the accidental changes that occur within us.

17. Definitions [25]

One is that which is actually undivided.

Unity is the state or condition of actual indivision.

Simplicity is actual unity which has no potential multiplicity (that is, is such that it *cannot* be divided).

A *whole,* or a *composite unit,* is a thing which is actually one, independently of the way in which it is considered, and is com-

---

[25] The most important terms are italicized, and the student is expected to be familiar with their definitions. Terms which occur more rarely, or are less important, are not italicized.

posed of parts which can be distinguished (either by the mind, or also in reality, at least so that one of the parts can exist without the other).

Accidental unity is the state of actual indivision brought about by something superadded to the nature of the parts in that unity.

Substantial unity is such a unity within a substance that the being is actually one in its substance.

Per se unity is a unity whose parts are by their very nature ordered to each other and to the whole.

Substance is that to whose essence there belongs an act of existing (*esse*) in itself and not in another.

Accident is that to whose essence there belongs an act of existing (*esse*) in another and not in itself.

Act is a perfection of the being.

. Potency is the subject as capable of perfection. (Potency taken abstractly is the capacity for perfection.)

Supposit is a substantial unit; (more fully) a being with a complete nature subsisting in itself, with its own proper act of existing.

Virtual presence (of an element in a compound, or of a lower perfection in a higher) is neither (*a*) the fullness of being in act nor (*b*) sheer potency, but (*c*) presence according to some properties, characteristics, or traits which are like those to be found in the thing (element or perfection) when actually subsistent, which properties flow from the higher substance, and frequently implies (*d*) that the higher substance was formed from the lower and can be resolved back into the lower.

Virtual being is that which has virtual presence.

Personality is an abstract word meaning that by which a person is a person.

Person, philosophically considered, is a supposit which has a rational nature.

Personality, philosophically considered, is the act of existing exercised by (and proportioned to) an individual possessing a rational or intellectual nature.

Psychological personality is a group or memory-system of experiences, attitudes, and ideas linked together by possible recall and related to present actual experience.

Propriosensation is all those types of immediate sense experience which a person directly has about his body, its state and condition and the relative positions and/or movements of his members.

18. Proofs [26]

A. *Every living thing is a substantial unit or supposit.*

That is one supposit (one existing substantial unit) whose parts act primarily and directly for the good of the whole, and only secondarily for their own good.

But: The parts of any living thing (organism) act primarily and directly for the good of the whole, and only secondarily for their own good.

Therefore: every living thing is a substantial unit or supposit.

B. *Elements, intermediate compounds and parts have a virtual presence in the living thing.*

That has virtual presence in a higher substance, which, being in a substantial unit according to some (but not all) properties, may in addition have been the pre-existing subject from which this higher substance was formed and/or the remaining result of the destruction of that substance.

But: elemental particles, elements, intermediate compounds, and parts or tissues of a living thing are in a substantial unit (according to proof A), have some but not all the properties which they would have as distinct supposits, do (or at least may under special conditions) arise in the destruction of living things, and (except for parts and tissues) have been the pre-existing subject from which the living thing was generated and nourished.

Therefore: elemental particles, elements, intermediate com-

[26] The meaning and demonstrative force of these summarized proofs are to be found in the preceding discussions.

pounds, and parts or tissues have a virtual presence in a living thing.

19. Readings

M. M. Desmarais, O.P., "L'auto-perception de la personne psychologique," *Études et Recherches, Philosophie I* (Ottawa, 1936), pp. 11–47. This is the most detailed presentation and analysis of the experience of the unity of the self.

Francis L. Harmon, *Understanding Personality* (Milwaukee, Bruce Pub., 1949), pp. 113–142; 214–215; 229–235, gives a brief and competent account of the evidence concerning the unity of personality and the facts of multiple personality from the viewpoint of the experimental psychologist.

Pierre Hoenen, S.J., *Cosmologia,* 3rd ed. (Rome, Gregorian Univ. Press, 1945), pp. 280–300. One of the outstanding Thomists in the field of philosophy of nature gives the best explanation of the virtual presence of elements in compounds and of the origin of the life of separated tissues and organs.

St. Thomas Aquinas, *The Principles of Nature (De Principiis Naturae),* trans. by R. A. Kocourek (St. Paul, North Central Publ., 1948). This brief work of St. Thomas deals with the notions of matter and form, and the relations of elements and compounds.

Étienne Gilson, *The Spirit of Mediaeval Philosophy,* trans. by A. H. C. Downes (New York, Scribner, 1936), pp. 168–208. This section gives the historical background of the medieval discussions of the unity of man, and a conspectus of further problems to be seen later.

Francis L. Harmon, *Principles of Psychology,* rev. ed. (Milwaukee, Bruce Pub., 1951), pp. 110–145, on the organic basis of human activity, and the dual characteristics of that activity.

K. S. Lashley, "Basic Neural Mechanisms in Behavior," *Psychological Review,* XXXVII (1930), 1–24. Professor Lashley, an outstanding non-Catholic biologist, here presents the evidence for the unifying systems of the body. He seems incorrectly to assume that in this way the entire unity of man is accounted for. But his presentation of the facts is clear, inclusive, and competent.

W. B. Cannon, *The Wisdom of the Body* (New York, Norton, 1939). Another prominent non-Catholic biologist presents manifold scientifically accurate evidence that the activities of the body are for the good of the whole.

D. Nys, *Cosmology,* trans. and adapted by S. A. Raemers (Milwaukee, Bruce Pub., 1942), Vol. 1, pp. 161–191, 218–264; a detailed consideration of the evidence, mostly drawn from the natural sciences, for the substantial unity of chemical compounds.

Christian L. Bonnet, S.J., "The Unity of the Complex Individual Body," *The Modern Schoolman*, XXII (1944), 33–43.

Vincent Edward Smith, *Philosophical Physics* (New York, Harper, 1950), pp. 73, 205–208, 213, 426–427, 452; brief discussions of virtual presence.

W. R. Thompson, F.R.S., "The Unity of the Organism," *The Modern Schoolman*, XXIV (1947), 152–157.

E. S. Russell, *The Interpretation of Development and Heredity* (New York, Oxford Univ. Press, 1930), pp. 166, 173, on the unity of the organism.

Brother Benignus M. Gerrity, *Nature, Knowledge and God* (Milwaukee, Bruce Pub., 1947).

Sir Charles Sherrington, *Man on His Nature* (New York, Macmillan, 1941), pp. 76, 79, 112, 119, 198. These reflections of an eminent biologist are a mixture of insistence on unity and also on diversity; there is a clear realization of the limitations of "science" (e.g., p. 269), but no clear understanding of what form of knowledge takes in the area beyond science. Perhaps this is why, at the end, the author adopts what amounts to a complete dualism of thought and energy.

CHAPTER III

Vegetative Life—the Soul

20. Preliminary

We have just seen that living things are substantial, per se units. Since we learn what a thing is by seeing what it does, the first step in discovering the nature of living things is the analysis of vital activities.

The form or type of life that is most widespread in our visible world is vegetative life, for it is found in plants, animals, and men. Though for our present purpose we are mainly interested in the vegetative (biological) level in man, we will to some extent consider plants, for in them we can find vegetative life unmixed with other perfections. For the most part, however, the consideration of vegetative life will be generic.

First we shall try to see what the proper character of vegetative life is (sections 21 to 24). From this we can decide whether there is a difference between living and non-living things, and determine the kind of difference (section 25). Then we shall analyze the nature of the immanent action (self-perfecting activity) of living things, and try to follow out its implications (section 26). Finally, we shall see that immanent action requires the presence of an intrinsic principle in living things, which is called the soul (section 27).

21. Generic description of vegetative life

Living things *grow*. By their own activity, that is, they take food into themselves, change it into their own particular kind of substance (assimilate it), and by means of this assimilated matter increase in size and develop themselves (for example, they develop organs· leaves of plants, legs of animals, and so forth). Real growth does not take place simply by addition, as a wall becomes larger by adding more bricks. The assimilated food is constructed by the living thing itself into the new parts which the living thing needs for its own complete development. Thus, out of assimilated matter, the oak constructs the leaves, the trunk, the bark, which the live tree has.

Living things *nourish* themselves. During the course of their activity they are constantly wearing themselves out to a greater or lesser extent; they use up energy and discard some of their material components. This loss of energy and matter (catabolism) is compensated for by the food which is taken in, assimilated, and used to repair and maintain the organism (anabolism). The complete cycle of these processes is known as metabolism.

*A particularly striking vegetal characteristic is the healing process, where tissues, parts, and sometimes even whole organs are repaired or replaced by the activity of the organism itself. For example, a gash made in the bark of a tree will be healed over with new bark, just as a cut in the skin of an animal will be healed; animals can, at least to some extent, replace parts of their tissue or flesh that have been destroyed by injuries or disease. In some animals, such as crabs, complete new legs or antennae are grown to replace ones lost.

*Though both growth and nourishment are concerned with the perfection of the living body itself, they differ in the type of perfection they confer. The process of growth aims directly at the extention of the living body to its due size and to the differentiation of the various organized parts out of a relatively simple one-celled stage. Nourishment, on the other hand, is basically a sustaining or conserving process. Many plants exercise growth functions throughout their life span; trees, for example, continue to become larger every year they live. Some plants (for example, annual flowering plants) cease to grow after a definite time, and most animals have a relatively definite limit of growth. Once such a limit has been attained, growth functions ordinarily stop, and nutritional functions continue on alone.

A third vegetal characteristic is generation. Living things *reproduce* themselves; they increase and multiply. Throughout the whole range of material living things, from single-celled organisms to man, we find reproductive activities, by means of which new individuals of the same kind are brought into being. The processes of generation differ widely—being sexual or asexual (fission, budding, spore production)—in accordance with the proper natures of the things that generate. In all cases, and despite all these variations, the end result of generation is a distinct, new living thing of the same species and kind.[1] In generation, a part of a living thing is separated from the parent (or parents) and becomes a new living individual. Nevertheless, the activity of generation is first directed to the body of the parent, so developing and perfecting it (or a part of it) that a new living thing can be produced.

22. Irritability and Adaptation

*In the higher living things, another aspect of vegetal life is easily noticeable. In dealing with non-living things, men have found a constant correspondence between action and reaction; action and reaction, the physicist says, are equal. At first sight, this fact does not seem to be verified in living things. If you step on a dog's tail, there is a violent reaction that is far out of proportion to the external stimulus. The same kind of disproportion between external stimulus and reaction can be found on a less noticeable scale in plants, even in single-celled ones. If a living tissue is scratched or wounded, a very complex reaction takes place which results in the healing over of the lesion. This trait of living things is sometimes called by the general term of "irritability." The proper characteristic of irritability consists in this, that even though living things need some kind of external stimulus to begin acting, yet

[1] The new individual of course has its individual traits. Under normal conditions, however, the specific nature of parent and offspring are the same. For a consideration of what may happen under interfering conditions, see below, Appendix N, section 8, pp. 422–23.

they are also and sometimes largely the source of their own activity,[2] and this activity *leads to their own perfection* (growth, nourishment, repair, and so forth). The inequality of action and reaction wins our attention at first, but it is only apparent, for if we add the activity of the organism to the side of action, then action and reaction are equal even in living things.

Another point of view about living things is brought to light by the term "adaptation." The activity of non-living things is determined by the causes that surround them and act upon them. Living things, on the contrary, react to their environment; and it is peculiar to them that they can adjust themselves to the special conditions in which they are.[3] Living things can compensate for adverse factors with which they are in contact. The tanning of the skin, for example, is a compensation for the excessively burning rays of the summer sun; many animals develop heavier coats of hair during severe winters. In fact, within definite but rather surprisingly wide limits, "living things are the better for being bumped." Hot-house plants have an early start, but their growth is lush rather than sturdy. Domesticated animals often fall victim to diseases which their less fortunately situated wild cousins are easily able to resist.

23. Organization

*A look at the substance of living things will furnish some further information about their nature. From the viewpoint of their material composition, things have sometimes been classified as elements, compounds, and mixtures. By an element (for example,

---

[2] At one time, certain writers tried to explain the activities of living things (especially of animals) purely in terms of stimulus and response and the link between them: everything was to be explained by "S-R bonds." Critical investigation of this attempt led to a modification of the formula: "S-O-R bonds"; where "O" stands for "organism." This is precisely the point that is being insisted on here.

[3] All living things, to some extent at least, can also react upon their environment and modify it. Man in particular frequently is able to modify the circumstances in which he lives and, in fact, sometimes is bound to change them rather than adjust himself to them.

oxygen) is meant a material substance which cannot be separated by ordinary chemical means into substances different from itself, but is directly composed of fundamental units (electrons, and so forth). A compound is a material substance whose immediate parts are the several elements which are virtually present in it and which is produced by their union. Water, for example, is composed of oxygen and hydrogen. A mixture is an intermingling of small particles of different substances which do not form a single new substance. A mixture can be obtained, for example, by stirring together salt and sugar.

*Biochemists find that there is no single chemical formula for any living thing, no matter how small or simple; much less is there any common basic chemical substance such as "protoplasm." A living thing is not an element or a compound or a chemical mixture. In other words, a living thing is not chemically homogeneous. Consequently, on the scientific level, living things cannot be adequately characterized only by their chemical formula; they must be described also physically, that is to say, in terms of the kinds and arrangements of the various material parts.

*A living thing is thus a composite being whose parts have a definite arrangement or structure. For example, even a single cell is composed of a cell wall, protoplasm, and nucleus.[4] Higher organisms show this characteristic of life much more clearly: for example, the leaves, bark, and heartwood of a tree with the arrangement of branches, trunk and root; the skeleton, tissues, and organs of a dog distributed into head, trunk, and legs. This differentiation (heterogeneity) of structure is related to a variety in function: each specialized part has a proper work to do. Digestive organs prepare food material, the circulatory system distributes it, and so forth. For this reason it is possible to compare the living thing to a machine which is also based on the structural arrangement of different parts. But since the living thing is a substantial unit, it is a natural unit of organized matter.

---

[4] The slime molds (myxomycetes) have, as far as is known at present, no cellular structure; nevertheless, there is a textured disposition of parts that is definitely noticeable at least at certain stages of their life.

24. These traits are characteristic only of living things:

A. *Nutrition, growth, reproduction.* Ancient as well as modern writers make use of expressions like "feed the fire." But fire is not a substance; it is an activity or process of oxidation in the course of which heat and light are produced. Since it is only an activity and not a substance, it is not accurate to say that it nourishes it-self; the most we can say is that it is a chain reaction. To say that fire is fed or nourished by combustible materials is to use a per-fectly valid metaphor; but when metaphor is used in the course of an argumentation, the conclusion itself must be understood in a metaphorical sense. On the other hand, the things that burn—fire, wood, a candle—certainly do not nourish themselves; rather they are destroyed.

*Crystals are said to grow and nourish themselves. They cer-tainly do increase in size, and fractures in their surface are re-paired while they are in a saturated solution. But such increase is not growth in the same sense that growth is found in living things, because the increase in size is due to the addition of pre-existing amounts of specifically the same substance in a noncrystalline state, not to the assimilation of different substances. The repair of a crystal, in the same way, is by external addition of the identical substance, not by a redistribution and reorganization of matter.

As far as reproduction or generation is concerned, there are practically no parallels in the nonliving world. Remote likenesses of reproduction might be seen in magnetic and electrical induction and in the transmission of fire from one burning object to another. But even these examples are so far-fetched that no one has seri-ously offered to "explain" the generation of living things by them.

Consequently, when we understand nutrition, growth, and re-production in their strict and univocal sense, we find that they are proper activities of living things alone.

B. *Irritability and Adaptation.* Is irritability not characteristic of all unstable compounds and elements—of an over-saturated solution, of explosives, of the radium atom, for instance? It is true that in these and similar cases, there are a specificity of reaction and a great disproportion between the reaction and its stimulus. An explosion, for example, releases much more energy than the spark which set it off. Some people, impressed by this likeness, have sought the explanation of life in an as yet unidentified "unstable compound." The significant difference, however, is to be found in the *direction* of the response.[5] In the violent reaction of an unstable compound, the reaction precisely leads to (or sometimes even is) the *destruction* or breakdown of the substance. The explosive ceases to be gunpowder; the radium atom turns into a different chemical substance; the over-saturated solution reacts by precipitating the solute and so ceases to be an over-saturated solution. The irritability of organisms, on the contrary, leads to their *own preservation and development* (the good of the whole). We must therefore conclude that irritability is a peculiar and proper activity of living things.

A certain kind of adaptation is to be found in nonliving things. Water is adaptable to the shape of whatever container holds it at the moment. All such adaptability is of a purely passive type, however. Living things actively adapt themselves to their surroundings. Adaptability, too, is thus a proper activity of living things.

C. *Organization.* It has been pointed out that machines and living things are similar in this, that both consist of different parts that are arranged according to some structure or pattern and having specialized functions. Those who try to find a mechanical explanation of life have seized upon this very clear similarity. One could object, of course, that machines are man-made artifacts, while living things are natural in origin. This is, at best, an external difference,[6] and need not point to any real difference in nature. Very clever machines have even been constructed which imitate in some fashion some of the activities of living things.

But to think that living things are merely machines (in the ordi-

[5] See above, section 9, for the significance of finality in our knowledge of the natures of things.

[6] For a further discussion of this point, see below, Appendix N, section 8.

nary meaning of that term) is to ignore a significant and indeed massive, imposing evidence; machines and living things differ in their substantial being. In the preceding chapter, we have studied the evidence which shows that a living thing is one composite *substance*, whose many parts virtually present in it are produced by the living thing itself in the course of its growth. A machine is made up of many substances, joined in an accidental unity.[7]

25. Summary and Restatement

Therefore, living things and nonliving things differ in that the former have a given set of activities (nutrition, growth, and reproduction), while the latter are without them. What is the significance of the difference between having and not having such proper activities? [8]

When one thing differs from another only in degree, we say that one can be reduced to the other. For example, a small particle of iron at a great distance is not able to deflect a magnetic compass, but a large quantity close by can affect the needle. The total effect of the large mass arises through an addition of the particular effects of the individual particles. So, too, a compound activity can sometimes be explained in terms of its components, as when two forces acting at an angle explain the resultant movement. A complete reduction would therefore explain the proper characteristics of one thing in terms of one or more simpler things. A partial reduction can be accomplished when some of the properties of chemical compounds can at least partly be explained by the properties of the constituent elements.

But when the activities of two things differ in such a way that the first has one set of activities which the second does not have at all, then reduction is clearly impossible. In other words, such

[7] It should be evident that a machine is composed of many actually distinct substances. For a fuller discussion of the difference between living things and machines, see also below, section 27.

[8] In the technical terminology of Aristotelian logic, these activities are said to differ as "habit and privation," that is, as having, in the one case, and being deprived of, in the other.

activities differ essentially. Furthermore, things with essentially different activities must themselves differ essentially, since operation follows upon and manifests the essence.[9]

26. Immanent action

We have seen that the three activities of nutrition, growth, and reproduction are characteristic of all the living things that come within our experience and are proper only to such living things. An analysis of these activities should therefore lead us closer to a knowledge of the nature of living things.

Is there a common element in the three activities by means of which we can come to a definition of vital activity? Nutrition is the activity by which a material living thing maintains itself in good working order and replaces matter or energy which was lost through action or injury. Growth is the activity by which a living thing brings itself to its mature development. Reproduction is the activity by which a living thing perfects itself (or a part of itself) so that it can become the principle of a new being in the same species. In all three cases, the living agent is not only that which acts but also that which is affected by the activity and brought by it to a greater perfection. Therefore vital action is defined as the activity by which a living thing perfects itself.

When we say that a living thing perfects itself, we do not mean that a perfection appears from nowhere without any causal antecedents. A living thing is substantially perfect in its species as soon as it comes into being and from that perfection moves itself to its own accidental perfection in act.[10] Obviously, we do not mean to exclude the influence of outside causes (as food and environment); these are necessary either as material or as stimulating causes for the living things, which by means of external influences advance from potency to act.

---

[9] Essence: that intrinsic principle of an existing thing by which it is *what* it is, has its proper perfections, and is in a given species.

[10] In reference to this, substantial being, form, and the act of existing are called "first act," while the consequent accidental perfection (quantity, quality, or action) is called "second act."

It will be helpful to compare vital action with the other actions of things. Action (activity, operation) first of all is the full flowering of being. It is not the same as being (in created things), since a limited being can reach its good only by means of activity. Activity is an act or perfection of being. In the kind of activity which is common to all types of being, living and nonliving alike, there are an agent, an action, and an external effect. There is a builder, for example, an activity of building, and the building that is constructed. In such cases, what precisely is perfected by the activity is the external thing which undergoes the activity (called the "patient"). Such activity is called "transient," for it is conceived of as passing from the agent to the patient. But in reality, it is not necessary that anything "pass" between agent and patient, as is clear from the analysis given. The reality of transient action lies in this, that it is the perfection, not precisely of the agent, but of the patient, in dependence upon the agent.

Vital activity, on the contrary, is the perfection of the agent itself which acts. A distinct patient, or external distinct product is simply not implied in vital activity. It is wholly "in" and ordered to the agent. Hence, vital activity is called "immanent" action. (We must be careful not to jump to the conclusion that only vegetative activity is immanent; we shall see later that knowledge and appetition are also immanent activities.)

*The immanence of a plant is true immanence, for by its own activity the plant perfects itself. At the merely vegetative level, however, immanent activity involves a previous transient action upon the food to be assimilated, and implies a kind of semi-transience, inasmuch as it takes place through the action of one part of the plant upon another. Moreover, the principle and the end of vegetative activity are wholly determined by the plant's nature and thus involve external causes. For the nature of the plant is wholly determined by the processes through which the seed is formed, and the purposes of vegetal activity are wholly determined by this nature.

*In animals, as we shall see, there is another principle of activity besides the substantial nature (that is, the form of knowledge), so that the animal's immanence extends at least partly to the accidental principles of its animal activity. Man, we shall see, also chooses the ends of his human activity, so that man's immanence extends to the action, the principles, and the ends of the action. There are therefore three degrees of immanence.[11]

*Children first learn the difference between living and non-living things when they begin to distinguish between things that move themselves by local motion and things that must be moved. This is a convenient enough distinction, and we often use it. If we come upon a motionless animal, we poke it to see if it will move; if it does not, we think it is dead. Experience soon shows the child, though, that the criterion of "self-motion" in this crude and vague sense is not nearly accurate enough. So, the idea of "motion" is gradually refined and made more abstract and general. When taken up by the philosopher, "motion" is refined, so that it comes to mean "any passage from potency to act." "Self-motion" thus comes to mean "the passage from substantial act to operation (second act) through the causality of the being that acts." By this careful philosophical refining of a rather common notion we come to the same idea of immanent action that was reached by the more elaborate analysis of vital activity.

From this analysis of vital activity as immanence, we can proceed to the definition of life. "Life," as the abstract term derived from the verb "to live," is predicated on three levels. (1) "Life" is used as an abstract term for the vital activity itself, as in the expression "He has a lot of life"; this is its first and original usage. (2) "Life" is used to designate the nature or essence from which flow immanent activities in the material order, and especially in the vegetative order. This is the more common, univocal use of the term; in this sense it almost always refers to the lowest degree of living things, namely, inasmuch as they have vegetative ac-

---

[11] We are considering immanent activity only as it is found in the created beings of our experience. Immanent activity is also to be found in God, but in the special sense that the Divine activity is identical with the Divine Being.

tivities. For instance, we say that an injured man is still alive if he breathes or displays some other vegetative function. (3) "Life" can also be used to designate the mode of being (*esse,* to be, act of existing) proportioned to such an essence; in this rarer and specifically philosophical sense, the term "life" can be applied to God and angels, as well as to men, animals, and plants. Used in this third sense, "life" is an analogous term,[12] which will be found to be most useful in the attempt to understand the nature of God in natural theology.

27. Soul

A living thing is a special kind of thing because it is the source of special kinds of activities, that is to say, immanent actions. Therefore the nature or substance or essence of living things is a specific (or generic) nature.

Living things have traditionally been called "animated"[13] or "besouled" things. As a preliminary definition of soul or animating principle we may say: The soul is that by which the living thing ultimately has the operations of life. In this preliminary and descriptive meaning of the word, everyone knows immediately *that* he has a soul, inasmuch as he knows that he is performing the actions of life.[14]

The first question that immediately arises is this: Is the soul, thus defined, the same as the substance of the living thing?

The premises needed to answer this question are two. (*a*) The living thing is substantially and specifically distinct from the non-living. (*b*) There is an interchange of matter between the living and the nonliving; in other words, nonliving matter is changed into living in the process of nutrition and growth, and living matter is changed into nonliving in death.

A change from one specifically distinct substance to another is called a "substantial change." What, then, is implied by such a

[12] For the meaning of "analogous," see above, Chapter I, section 5, footnote 11.
[13] "Animated," from the Latin, *animatus,* which means "having an *anima,* or soul."
[14] For the investigation of this evidence, see below, section 159.

change? There must be two terms in a change—one at the beginning (the prior term, from which, *a quo*, the change takes place) and one at the completion or end of the change (the posterior term, at which, *ad quem*, the change terminates). Now, change does not mean the successive presence of two totally distinct things. Suppose there is a bottle of ink on a desk, which is removed and replaced by an alarm clock. The bottle of ink has not changed into an alarm clock. Or again, suppose that a chair, presently existing, were to be annihilated (simply and absolutely cease to exist), and in its place, without any lapse of time, a pile of kindling wood were to be created (simply and absolutely begin to be). Again, this would not be a change. What is lacking in both of these cases is a *common element or constituent*. A change, therefore, implies these three considerations: a prior term, a common element, and a posterior term.

To see the implications of this analysis, let us designate the prior term by "*A*," the posterior term by "*B*," and the common element by "*C*." It is clear that the common element, to be really common, must be *in* both terms. It follows at once that the two terms, since they are also essentially different, must be composite,[15] each containing the common element (which in the case of substantial change is primary matter), and each containing also a proper element in virtue of which each has its specific and determined perfection. Schematically: if A changes into B, then $A = (a + c)$ and $B = (b + c)$. Now we have already defined soul as "that by which the living thing ultimately has its proper operations of life." Hence, the soul is that real and really distinct principle of a living thing in virtue of which the thing is living.

What is this soul? Is it simply the structure or arrangement of parts of the living thing? It is of course evident that structure (both

---

[15] Some authors want to say that a substantial change can be accounted for by the composition only of *one* term. But the "common element or constituent" is then itself a complete substance or substances. Hence, any added perfection in the composite term is an accidental perfection, or the composite term is not a substantial unit (see Appendix A on dualism). But we have shown in the second chapter that man or any living thing is a substantial unit. Hence, both terms of the substantial change must be composite.

in the sense of "organization" and in the sense of "complexity") is absolutely necessary for vital activity, as it is for any except the simplest elementary activity. Moreover, chemists and anatomists tell us that structure is specific; a given structure is related and proportioned to a special kind of activity. For example, protein is of different kinds (has a different structural formula) in different plants; chromosome and gene numbers and arrangements vary in the different plants and animals; the gross structures are our easiest ways of identifying living things. We recognize a dog by its shape; we identify a tree by its shape, the form of its leaves, the surface texture of its bark, and so forth. On the inanimate level, the structural formula is the best—and sometimes even the only accurate—way of giving an identifying description of a chemical substance. In this sense, and to this extent, structure is specific and is *a* principle of activity.

Is structure the ultimate principle or soul? First of all, the structure of a living thing is itself (at least partly) produced and is wholly maintained by the activity of the organism. This is particularly evident in the more complicated organisms. Suppose some one were to say that an oak tree can nourish and reproduce itself because of the structure of its nutritive and reproductive organs (leaves, roots, flowers). But these structures are themselves developed out of the acorn by the activity of the little seedling itself. Hence, the oak, throughout its whole life, substantially possesses the perfections which it later exercises through its own developed structures. Similar evidence can be found in the case of animals and men. Even single-celled living things develop themselves to some extent. Even the cell-structure (which some think is the basic principle) is at least maintained by the living thing. Hence, structure cannot be an *ultimate* principle of vital activity. Secondly, structure is a disposition of parts, such that the parts must *be* (exist) before they can be arranged and disposed in some order. Therefore, structure is a perfection of a being already in act (that is, existing as one being) and therefore presupposes rather than explains the being in act. Thirdly, in the previous chapter, it was proved that a living thing is a substantial unit. Suppose that the structure of already existing parts (elements, compounds, organs, and so on) is the ultimate principle of life. It follows at once that a living thing would be an accidental unit, composed of many substances or beings united by a super-added perfection, structure. Hence, since living things are substantial units, the principle of life must itself be substantial. Structure, then, since it is necessary for a living thing (section 23) and different in different kinds of living things, must be a proper accident.

In the analysis of substantial change we concluded that a living thing which undergoes such change must be composite. It must have a common element which can variously be determined, and a proper or specifying element which determines the actual being of the living thing (that is, makes this thing to be alive). Hence this proper or specifying part of the substance of the living thing is the soul.

The soul is a real principle of the living thing. What is its relation to the other principles by which the organism is constituted? The soul is not a complete thing, for it is a principle within a substantial unit; and a substantial unit, though it may be composed of really distinct principles and parts, cannot be composed of things or complete beings. Again, the soul is not an agent or efficient cause with respect to the body. For, when we look for the efficient cause of the body of a living thing, we find that it is first prepared and generated by its parent, and after the offspring is separated and begins its own distinct life, the body is developed and nourished by the living thing itself through the action of its *parts* upon each other and their transient action upon the food it assimilates. Nor is the soul as such necessarily an efficient cause even of the operations of the living thing—with the possible exception of certain distinctively human activities.[16] For the ultimate principle of activity *which acts* is the supposit, the whole thing.

Yet the soul is a cause of the living thing. To understand the nature of this special type of causality, it is necessary to refer to the

16 Namely, of intellect and will; see below, Chapters VIII and **X**.

argument which established the need for a soul. The reason why we assort the real distinction of the soul as a principle from the rest of the living thing is the two-fold evidence that (*a*) a living thing is specifically distinct from a nonliving thing and (*b*) substantial changes occur between living and nonliving things. Hence the function of the soul is to constitute the living thing in its determinate substantial perfection by its presence in the whole after the manner of a specifying principle and so to be the ultimate specifying source of vital activity. Thus the causality of the soul consists in this, that by being received in the potential indeterminate principle the soul actuates and specifies that potency through self-communication to it. The potency, in return, is a cause of the living thing in a somewhat similar manner of self-communication, by providing a subject to be determined and thus limiting and particularizing the act which has been received.

In Aristotelian terminology, the actuating and specifying principle of material substance is called the "substantial form." [17] The potential and restrictive principle is called "first matter" (or "primary matter"). The substantial form of an inanimate thing has no special name; but the substantial form of a living thing is called "soul."

In view of all that has been said, the soul can now be defined as "the first (i.e., substantial or formal) act of a physical, organized body which has the potency of life."

28. Definitions

Vegetative life is that kind of life which is characterized by nutrition, growth, and reproduction.

Life is (*a*) an abstract term for vital (or immanent) activities;

    (*b*) the nature or essence of a being which has vital activity on the vegetative level;

---

[17] The English word *form* is a very poor word philosophically, for it suggests the shape or structure of the thing. It is therefore important to insist on the definition as given above, as against ordinary usage.

(c) the mode of being proportioned to a living nature, at
various levels (vegetative, sensitive, and so forth).

Organ is a specialized structural part of a living thing which has
a particular function or work.

Organization is the arrangement of heterogeneous parts belonging to a being which is substantially one.

Irritability is that aspect of vital activity which consists in the
disproportion between the exterior stimulus and the reaction of
the living thing, and in the finality of that reaction toward the
proper good of the organism itself.

Immanent action is that kind of activity or operation which is
the perfection of the agent itself.[18]

Transient action is the action (in the line of efficient causality)
which perfects a patient distinct from the agent.

Substantial change is the change from one substance to another
substance which is different from the former at least numerically,
or more usually, both numerically and specifically.

Soul is the ultimate intrinsic principle by which the living thing
has the operations of life.[19]

Soul is the substantial form of a living thing.

Soul is the first act or substantial perfection of a physical organized body suited for (in potency to) life.

Substantial form is the ultimate actual specifying substantial
principle of a material thing. This principle is the source of that
being's substantial perfection, and through that substantial perfection of the proper accidents and activities. It is an intrinsic cause,
which causes, *not by an activity*, but by way of communicating
itself to the matter of that thing, specifying and actuating that

[18] As here defined, it refers precisely to the activity of a created material
being; to be applied to other kinds of living things and to other modes of life,
it needs to be defined differently, in accordance with the different natures of
the things in question.

[19] Note these three definitions of soul. The first is a nominal descriptive definition. Hence, it can validly be used as one of the premises of a proof. The
second and third are definitions which are the result (conclusion) of a proof.
Hence, they may not validly be used prior to the proof. The third definition is
simply an expansion or explanation of the second.

matter and, by that communication and composition, *constituting* the being in act.

First matter (primary matter) is the ultimate potential principle of a sensible, changeable thing.

Body (in contrast to soul) is the first matter of a living thing, really distinct from soul.

Body (in contrast to mind, consciousness, and so forth) is a partial consideration of a man or an animal, including primary matter, the soul as principle of substantiality and material activity, and usually structure and other accidents. Body in this sense is not really distinct from soul, but partially includes it.

29. Proofs

A. *Living things are specifically distinct from nonliving things.*

Those things are specifically distinct whose activities are specifically different and irreducible.

But: vital activities (nutrition, growth, and reproduction) are specifically different from, and irreducible to, the activities of non-living things.

Therefore: living things are specifically distinct from nonliving things.

B. *The soul is the substantial form of the living thing; or the first act of a physical organized body suited for (in potency to) life.*

A change whose terms are substantially different requires each of those terms to be substantially composite.

But: the change from living to nonliving is a substantial change.

Therefore: both living things and nonliving things are substantially composite.

But: in a substantial composite, one of the components must be determining and specifying (substantial form), the other potential and determinable (first matter).

But: the ultimate specifying principle by which the living thing has the operations of life is the soul, while the potential principle is the body.

Therefore: the living thing has two substantial components, body and soul.

Therefore: the soul is correctly defined as the substantial form of a living thing; or as the first act of a physical organized body suited for (in potency to) life.

30. Excursus: Are there purely vegetative beings?

Though in the present course there is no investigation into the nature of plants for their own sake, yet some light can be shed upon man's place in the universe if we can establish a hierarchy or order of material things.[20] We have seen so far that living things are essentially different from nonliving merely material things. Therefore, there are at least two levels of being: living things have a greater substantial perfection and can be called the higher, while nonliving things have less and can be called lower.

Are there any levels of perfection among living things? or do they simply differ in degree of perfection? Are there really such things as plants which lack sensation and all forms of knowledge? Note that this question does *not* mean: Is everything which has the shape and external appearance of a plant a plant? For there are animals which are fixed to one spot on the ground. We can only argue that things have knowledge if their activity is such that it manifests knowledge. If such evidence is lacking, we ought to assert simply that we do not know whether these beings have knowledge.

If we know relatively little about the activity of certain beings, we may have to remain content with that negative conclusion. For example, what about the one-celled living things? Some of them seem to have a sense of touch or taste; of others it is almost impossible to say whether they do or do not know their surroundings. To go beyond such a negative conclusion, we need other evi-

---

[20] "Hierarchy" is not a principle from which we *deduce* truths about the things of experience. But the fact that the conclusions which are gained one by one from experience actually find their proper place in an ordered whole is a kind of secondary confirmation of the propositions taken singly; cf. above, section 6.

dence. Of certain things—for example, trees, grass, and the like—we can easily conclude that there is no reason at all to say that they have knowledge. And in some of these cases, we can easily see that sense-knowledge would be both impossible and harmful to them. For example, grass lacks the organic structure necessary for any form of sensation. Moreover, it would be an evil for grass to have either sensation or appetite. These activities would be useless, for grass has no power of external action which could be modified (controlled) by knowledge. The activities would be directly an evil, for they would be a source of great suffering without any compensating advantage. Nature is the source of operations for the good of the being; a nature which by supposition would be the source of operations for its own evil would be a contradiction.

31. Readings

St. Thomas Aquinas, *Summa Theologiae*, I. 18. 1, 2, on the general meaning of "life"; 75. 1, 3, 5, on the soul; 78. 1, 2, on the vegetative soul.

John Wild, *Introduction to Realistic Philosophy* (New York, Harper, 1948), pp. 283–288 on matter; pp. 291–295 on matter and form; pp. 394–399 on the soul; pp. 399–402 on the relation of the soul to the body. Professor Wild is an Aristotelian, but he is also an original thinker. Reference is made to this book, not only because of its excellence, but partly also because he is not a Catholic. Some of the things said in the last two sections suggested for reading are true of the soul as soul, but not of the *human* soul. For the human soul is not just a soul in general, but a specific kind of soul, and so it is to be expected that certain conclusions true of the genus will not be true of the species.

Hans Driesch, *The Science and Philosophy of the Organism* (London, Black, 1908), especially Vol. 2, pp. 153–291. Some interesting and pertinent facts are cited here, though more recent embryologists insist that he has not carried his work far enough. In the interpretation of his facts, Driesch intends to follow Aristotle, but he seems to make the soul an efficient rather than a formal cause.

CHAPTER IV

Knowledge

32. A preview of the chapter

We have seen that every living thing is per se, or substantially, one being. We have then taken up the type of activity common to all the living things of our experience, that is, vegetative activity. We have seen that this activity is proper to living things, because it is immanent, that is, is the self-perfective activity of a per se unit. Hence, we have seen that all living things are essentially different from nonliving things. From the fact of substantial change, we have concluded that living things have a proper substantial form, called a soul.

We now come to another type of activity, which is not common to all living things, but is proper to animals and men. Here, we find a distinct type of activity, conscious activity, which includes, on the one hand, all the forms of knowledge, and on the other, desires, emotions, conscious tendencies, and the like.

In the study of knowledge, we meet with something which is completely familiar to us. It is in a sense better known than the members of our own family, than our home, our clothes, our daily food. And so no one need be told what knowledge is. Every human being experiences it.

Yet for most people knowledge is an uncharted field.[1] It may

---

[1] Often people do not realize how little they know about knowledge till they are asked to define and describe it to someone who is ignorant of that word and all its synonyms.

The reader, unless he is already well acquainted with Aristotelian terminology, will probably not understand either the questions or the answers in this preview. But an outline is not meant to convey a full understanding of the subject outlined.

therefore be useful to give a kind of map before we begin a detailed investigation. Now, when we see a map of a place where we have never been, we do not expect to learn from the map what the roads, cities, or mountains look like. We just want to know where we are going and to be able to tell at any stage of our progress where we are in relation to our starting point and our destination. In this preview we will merely list the questions that we are going to ask, and indicate the answers. The numbers in brackets refer to the various sections of the chapter which develop the point indicated in the outline.

An Outline in Question and Answer Form of the Analysis of Knowledge

[1] How are we going to go about this investigation? The method we will use will be reflection (corroborated and to some extent amplified by observation), distinction, and analysis.

[2] Is there any other element in conscious experience from which knowledge must be distinguished? The first distinction to be made is that between knowledge and appetency.

[3] Which experiences, then, do we designate by the term "knowledge"? Typical experiences like understanding, perceiving, sensing, recalling, thinking, are what we refer to by the term "knowledge."

[4] What does the act of knowledge tell us about the nature of the knower? A being which knows is not entirely enclosed within its own limited nature.

[5] What does this "openness" of a knowing subject mean? A knowing subject is in some sense immaterial.

[6] What do we mean when we say that knowledge is immaterial? Knowledge is a special kind of being: intentionality.

[7] Is knowing, then, a special kind of activity (or operation)? Knowing is an immanent activity.

[8] Does knowledge therefore involve a change in the knowing subject? Knowledge in man involves an intentional change, which is very different from natural or physical change.

The following suggestion provides an example of how this outline can be used. The reader, approaching the subject for the first time, should read through the questions. Then, before working through any given section, he should turn back to the outline and read the question. After he has completed his study of the section, he should have found there the answer which is summarized in the outline. If he has not found it there, or does not see its meaning, this is an indication that he should rework the section again till it has been mastered.

[9] Does intentional change require the reception of a form or per-fection? The requisite for the intentional activity of any creature is the received *species*.

[10] Would it then be correct to say that knowledge is change? No, the act of knowing is not itself a process of change.

[11] What then do we do when we know? We are united with a form, which can be at the same time the form of a distinct object.

[12] Is knowledge sufficiently described as the possession of the perfection of the other? No, for knowledge at least in some of its forms is also self-possession.

[13] Is there then more than one kind of knowledge? Knowledge, even from the viewpoint of its unity, is of many kinds.

[14] Can knowledge be defined? Knowledge, in the strict sense of the term "definition," cannot be defined.

We now take up these points in order.

33. [1] The method: reflection, distinction, analysis

In dealing even with human vegetative life, we were studying something which is not very different from the vegetative life of things outside us. For we experience our own vegetative processes largely by observation. A tree, or an animal, or another person can be observed as well as ourselves, and sometimes better.

When we treat conscious experience, on the other hand, we are dealing with a reality of a different order. When we sense, or imagine, think, feel, or will, these acts are known to us directly, immediately, from the inside as it were. That is precisely what the term "conscious" is intended to point out—that the experience, the very act, is itself known as mine. Each human being is in a privileged position with regard to *his own* conscious experience. We know that we know or feel directly *in* the very knowing or feeling; hence the attending to conscious activities as such is called by a special term "introspection" (*intro* = within, *-spection* = looking), or reflection. In studying knowledge, we must use intro-spection; we must reflect on what we do when we know.

Of course, in the study of conscious experience, we also observe the activity of other persons. However, we cannot directly see or hear or touch an act of knowledge performed by someone else. We can only observe external activities of others and interpret what we see in accord with our own internal experience. Frequently we can obtain help in the understanding of our own activity from what other persons tell us.

To observe ourselves is not an easy or simple thing to do. True, the direct awareness *that* we think, guess, imagine, sense, feel, is not only easy, but is always present to us. But attentive reflection is an art that must be practised before we can accurately observe, distinguish, discriminate, and judge our internal experience.

When we reflect upon our conscious activity, we find that ordinarily it is a unified activity. Usually, only one thing at a time absorbs our attention (even though we can partly attend to several things). And certainly all our conscious activity is unified in that it is ours.

On the other hand, conscious experience is a complex and almost infinitely varied activity. Consciousness is not merely the screen on which myriad pictures flash and move and blend into the seventeen-reel stories of our waking days. That would be to represent our conscious experience as wholly passive. In like manner, conscious experience is not merely the feeling toward, and striving to use and enjoy, the things around us; that would be to represent merely the active side of our life. These two aspects are mingled and blended, now in one proportion, now in another. Experience may be rich and full, or relatively narrow and empty. It may vary in content and in tempo. Yet at almost any given time, it is a unified activity, a single experience. How can we deal with a reality which is so fluid and changing, which never seems to be quite the same as it was, and yet has a real continuity in itself? We must begin by discovering the various elements and processes within experience.

34. [2] The distinction between knowledge and appetency

In the transient activity of sensible things, we find a double movement: motion as coming from an agent (action) and motion as received in a patient (passion). Similarly, there is a double movement in our conscious experience: knowledge, which is an activity that takes its rise from external things (like passion in transient activity), and appetency, in which we take a dynamic attitude toward things (like action). Descriptively, we classify the following as acts of knowledge: sensing (hearing, seeing, and so forth), imagining, remembering, apprehending, asking questions, having opinions, judging (asserting or denying), requesting, reasoning, inferring—even making an error. All these acts, different though they are (and the list is not complete!), agree in being aware of objects. On the other hand, appetency or conscious tendency is a general term for activities like pleasure, joy, sadness, likes, dislikes, valuing, choosing, rejecting. These reactions are all alike inasmuch as they are directed to objects as good, suitable, pleasing to us or evil, displeasing, and so forth. The acts of appetency will be studied later.[2]

Note again that to discover distinctions within conscious experience is merely to assert that one element or part of that total activity is not the other. We would be wrong if we supposed that knowledge, for example, could occur without some form of appetency. The separate consideration to be devoted to each part of conscious activity is merely a tool in order that we may be able to comprehend the total unified activity more clearly.

35. [3] The experience of knowledge

The first step in an attempt to understand what knowledge is must be a consideration of knowledge as it is experienced.

Let us take a proposition: "This whole page of paper is larger than the part which is covered by print." When we read this sentence the experience is not simply that of an arrangement of patterns of black and white; we understand what the words mean. These words mean (a) a concrete sensible thing (the page of paper) and (b) an intelligible relation present in it. Somehow we possess—we speak of *grasping* the meaning and the object—the thing which we know.

A useful comparison is that between knowledge and assimila-

[2] In Chapters IX, X, and XI.

tion. It is a commonplace metaphor to say that "truth is the food of the mind"; it points therefore to a basic and common experience. To understand a doctrine, a thought, a thing, is to assimilate it. Both in nourishment and in knowledge, the human person has need of an exterior object. In both cases, the object is absorbed. But the two cases also differ greatly. In nourishment, the exterior object is assimilated by being destroyed in its own reality in order to feed vegetative life: the food is turned into the living thing. But in knowledge, destruction is not necessarily implied.[3] The knower respects the integrity of the object. Assimilation [4] then must mean the change of the knower so that he becomes united to the thing known.

A peculiarly striking example of this assimilation is to be found in the effort which one must make in order to understand another person. We must, as we say, be prepared to enter into another person's mind and heart, to think and to feel the way he does. Only when we have done that can we say that we know him. That is why a great historian or a great dramatist (or for that matter a great doctor or a great confessor) knows so much about human nature. To know a person is to make his thoughts, his attitudes one's own. I enter into his life to the extent that his thoughts and feelings enter into mine, that my thoughts and feelings are a living reproduction of his. In doing that, I am myself and the other person as well. It is in this sense that we say, "He who actually knows is the thing actually known." [5] In more modern terms, the act of the knower (or the act of knowledge) constitutes a thing actually known. The knower and the known-in-act share one and the same act: the act of knowledge.

Another helpful approach to the nature of knowledge can be

[3] Though in some of the sciences there are procedures which destroy the object (for example, dissection, chemical analysis), they are to that extent imperfect methods; they are only instruments to a knowledge of the object in itself. Moreover, they are supplemented by other methods—of observation and description—which more evidently respect the existence of the object.

[4] When terms like "assimilation" are used, it is important not to imagine this to be a superficial similarity in appearance: knowledge never looks like the thing known. This point is treated more fully below.

[5] St. Thomas Aquinas, *Commentary on Aristotle's De Anima*, Bk. II, lecture 12 (ed. Pirotta, no. 377).

found in the analysis of imitative gesture. To convey to another a knowledge of what we mean, we can and sometimes must use mimetic gesture. The hand, the bodily motion express the object; they model themselves upon some trait or characteristic of the thing known. Here, too, the body remains a human body, and yet simultaneously bears within itself the form of another thing: The hand becomes the circle, the gesture, the length of the fish.

36. [4] The nature of a knowing subject

Thus a knower is as such in contact with external reality. A knower is never a mere subject, never sunken and lost in mere subjectivity (in the derogatory sense of that word).

A subject is a real thing, which exists in itself. Subjectivity is self-centeredness, being limited to one's own finite perfections, being closed in upon one's self. Pure subjectivity is to be found at the level of inanimate being and of merely vegetative life. A plant or a mineral merely is what it is.[6] Of course, it has relations to other things, but these relations are in the order of quantity or of transient activity. A plant can act upon other things, only to the extent of making them like to itself and in the final analysis destroying them to enrich and enlarge itself. Plants and minerals can undergo change from external agents; such change forces the plant or mineral to become other by *losing* a perfection or act which it had formerly; and if the change is pressed too far, it destroys the plant or mineral.

A knower is also a subject, a real being existing in itself. Over and above that, knowing implies an object, and that object can be something other than the subject. We have seen that to know something other than one's self, the knower must become the object known, must take on the form of the object. Hence, in the act of knowledge, the knower attains objectivity.

Consequently, knowledge is far from being a merely subjective

---

[6] This is *not* to say that things which lack knowledge are static, nor that they possess their full perfection from the first moment of their being. Even the most inert of material beings has some activity, so much so that a real being which never acts is a contradiction. Moreover, no finite being is fully perfect from the start; it acts precisely to attain the perfection of its being.

modification. To the extent that knowledge is merely subjective, it is imperfect or even false. When knowledge is perfect, and attains truth, then it is assimilated to and identical with the thing known.

37. [5] The knowing subject is in some sense immaterial [7]

What has preceded has been a description of knowledge; we can now begin to consider some implications of what we experience. We have considered that knowledge of another person or thing means taking on the form, the actuality of the thing known.[8] And yet, we do not know another by way of ceasing to be ourselves. For example, in the expressive gesture by which we signify a fish with our hand, we have seen that the hand becomes, takes on the form of, the fish. Yet it remains a hand, losing none of its real, natural being. It is precisely on the plane of signification that the hand has become a fish. There has of course been a real, physical change: the hand has moved in a wavy manner. Yet this is not the signification, but only a condition of it. The change (or becoming, or being) implied in knowledge is not directly and immediately a physical or a material one.

This point is so important, and yet so difficult, that we must approach it from another angle.

What is implied when we say that a change is not merely material? It means that such a change is not subject to the limitations

---

[7] Some authors speak of "spirituality in the wide sense" when they mean what is here meant by "immateriality." In this book, "spirituality" is used only in its strict sense, the term "immateriality" being kept in a more generic sense.

[8] To take on the "form" of another is to take on that form according to the other's concrete being, that is, as limited and determined by the matter. We should not imagine that a knower takes on an abstract form of a fish, for example—for then he would not be knowing a real fish. The knower takes on the concrete form of the object (fish), but only to the extent that the object possesses act and perfection. As we shall see more clearly later on, potency (and especially first matter) is not knowable in itself, nor is an object knowable to us precisely inasmuch as it is in potency. For this meaning of the word "form" cf. St. Thomas, *In De Trinitate*, q. 5, a. 2 and *Truth*, 10. 5. (Distinguish "form" as used in this paragraph from the "substantial form" as used in the previous chapter; for "form" here includes the "substantial form" plus its concretion in a substance, or the accidental form plus its subject.)

of merely material change. In material (or physical) change, the thing which changes can become other than it was only on condition of ceasing to be itself, on condition of losing one perfection to acquire another. In other words, a merely material being is restricted or limited to possessing only one form at a time, and that is its own physical form by which it is what it is. A material being is necessarily and essentially a singular thing (this chair, this water, this tree); it is limited to a particular time, place, quantity, and so forth. In sum, the conditions of mere materiality are these: restriction to one form at a time, inability to acquire another form without losing its own, restriction to a definite space and time, and limitation to a particular group of individuating characteristics. When we analyze physical change and physical activity, we find that a form is transmitted and begins to be in the subject of the change. For example, when something hot, like a burning log, heats another object, the form, the heat energy is produced in the other.[9] The iron which is being affected by the burning log, itself becomes hot. The result is that the subject of the change has acquired a new form which makes it really to be in a different condition. In all cases of transient activity in material things, the form is received according to its natural physical manner of being and, strictly speaking, informs the matter (the passive potency) of the subject that is being changed. For example, a piece of wood, receiving the form of fire, burns; receiving the form of table, is a table on which articles can be set.

On the other hand, the form received in knowledge does not *of itself* and as characteristic of knowledge have a physical mode of being.

When I know a piece of wood, I do, in truth, *come to be* that piece of wood, and yet I come to be it in a manner peculiar to a knower. I am not turned into wood; I do not take on, for instance, the qualities of the wood which I know. The piece of wood which I know cannot be predicated of me; I cannot say I *am* a piece of

[9] The characteristics of the efficient causality of material things can be stated much more precisely; see below, Appendix L, pp. 402–07.

wood. There is a most intimate *union* between myself and the piece of wood, but, in spite of this union, I continue to exist in my own proper being and the piece of wood continues to exist in its own proper being. This union peculiar to the knower with the known is called an "intentional" union. Consequently a form in the order of knowledge is immaterial in the sense that it does not of itself have the same physical mode of being in the knower as it had in the agent which caused the knowledge: it is not the physical perfection of a matter or recipient.

Thus far the immateriality implied in knowledge has been stated in a negative fashion: knowledge implies a non-material aspect in the act of knowledge and in the knower. *Immateriality*, then, is that characteristic of a being according to which it can receive a form in a different way from that in which a proper matter receives its form and yet not in such a way as to constitute a new kind of nature with its recipient.

But knowledge is a perfection, and so it is not sufficient to define its immateriality negatively. What positive perfection is implied by immateriality?

38. [6] Intentionality

Briefly, to know another is in some sense to be (and thus to have become) another, to take on the form of another. To be another, to possess another's form—though not a material, physical being and possession—is nevertheless real, for we actually have knowledge of various things.

Though knowledge is *in* the knower, of its very nature it puts the knower into union with the thing known. This orientation of human knowledge to things known is in a way a kind of "extending out toward or over, including" (*intendere*) the object in itself. Hence, knowledge is of its very nature *intentional* [10]—it is a dynamic, active identification between knower and known.

Since knowledge is real, that is, is a real event in a world of real

[10] Intentional here means "having the special nature proper to a sign." In popular and legal terminology, "intentional" is "that which is deliberately intended." Distinguish these uses carefully.

knowers and real things known, the intentionality of knowledge is a special mode of being: intentional being. Inasmuch as knowledge is being, we can predicate of it all the things predicable of being as such. For example, we can say that knowledge is one, or good; that if it is contingent, it must have an efficient cause. But inasmuch as knowledge is a special mode of being, all that we predicate of knowledge as being is predicated according to that special mode.

We can come to an understanding of the special nature of intentional being by a further analysis of the sign. By knowledge the thing known is made *present* to the knower. When I possess a thing in knowledge, I possess it in a r*epresentation*. When we think of knowledge as "representation," we should not think of it as a picture, but as a meaning which represents an object meant, or perhaps as a word which represents the object for which it stands—as "tree" represents a tree, or as a calling card represents the person whose name it bears, though it does not in the least look like him.

Thus, knowledge is itself a *sign*. It will be worth while to spend some little time on the notion of sign. A sign is something which refers to and stands for something else. A word is a sign; so are things like traffic lights, a uniform, a fraternity pin, and so forth: they stand for and lead to something else. These are artificial, conventional, or arbitrary signs. On the other hand, there are also natural signs: smoke is a sign of fire; a red sunset, of fine weather, and so forth. In all these various examples (both of conventional and natural signs), the thing or action which is a sign is a reality also in itself: a word can be heard even if we do not understand its meaning, the clouds are visible even when we do not know what the weather will be. A thing which has its own proper being and nature, and in addition also serves as a sign, is called an instrumental sign. In the case of knowledge, we have a sign which is *only a sign:* its whole reality is to make the object present to the knower. This is a pure or "formal" sign. We call it a pure sign, because the being of knowledge cannot be divorced from its signification. Consequently, a pure sign is not arbitrary or conventional, but is a natural sign. Unlike a word (an arbitrary instrumental sign) which can change or lose its meaning, knowledge stands for its object by its nature.

To prevent ourselves from thinking of knowledge as a kind of "little picture" (an easy mistake, to which reference has already been made) it will help to consider a phonograph record. Now, we do not ordinarily think of a record as a sign, yet it will help to clarify what is meant by "representation." In its physical reality, a record is a thin disk on whose surface is inscribed a wavy groove. The wave-patterns of this groove, in relation to a record player, represent the music. The wavy groove does not *look* like music at all. If you did not know by experience, you would never dream that the record can reproduce sound. A record is not a pictorial representation. Yet the patterned groove does represent the music. And the wave patterns are natural representations, in the sense that when used they make the music *present* for us. This example has its obvious defects; [11] and yet, inasmuch as the form of the music in the record does not constitute the physical or material being of sound, the record is a kind of instrumental sign in which the music is "immaterially," "intentionally" present.

Intentionality, therefore, is the mode of being proper to knowledge, or to a sign (or representation) considered formally as such. Consequently, knowledge is intentional being.[12]

39. [7] Human knowing is an immanent operation

Human knowing, of whatever kind, is a modification of a subject or knower. Knowledge as being, therefore, is neither subsistent

---

[11] The major difference lies in this, that the wave-patterns in the phonograph record have a reference to sound only through the record player. Hence, their intentionality lies in the action of the combination "phonograph record—phonograph." On the other hand, the intentionality of knowledge is intrinsic to knowledge itself.

[12] "Intentionality" (in reference to knowledge) always means "having the being of a sign," "putting into the relation of identity," and so forth, as explained above. Frequently, in many stages of human knowledge, it also implies an *orientation* or finality toward the object known or to be known; see below, section 40.

nor substantial. Rather, it is that *by* which the knower comes to exist in a new way: namely, as actually knowing. The technical term for such a reality is "accident" [13] (*ac-cidit:* that which comes to a subsistent reality). The knower himself is a substance, for he is in himself.

Now, accidents as here defined are of several kinds: qualities, quantity, relation, activity, and so forth. Though they are all perfections of substance they are quite different in the way that they modify substance. For our purposes, one important difference must be pointed out and stressed. Some accidents are forms (in a stricter or looser sense); they modify and determine the mode of being of a substance. By quantity, for example, a thing is so long; by figure or shape, it has a certain outline. As against these formal and more or less static modifications, we find that beings also perform activities. Activities themselves are not strictly forms, even though they are acts or perfections. We should rather remember that, as the act of existing is the act of an essence (or nature), so activity is an actualization of the potency of the agent.

The difference between knowing and not-knowing is the difference between act and potency: the act of seeing is an act in comparison with not-seeing. And knowing is not a form like shape or quantity or any other of the formal accidents [14] but rather an activity, a dynamism, an operation.

[13] "Accident" has a much more common meaning: "That which happens by chance; without being foreseen." But as an Aristotelian term of metaphysics it is defined as "any perfection or reality coming to a thing already essentially constituted and subsisting." Note that "accident" in this sense has no reference to chance: it may be completely necessary (a property, for example). *Accidents* are *not things,* but that *by* which things exist with various modifications.

[14] Operation is accidental in the same sense as change is accidental. This does not mean that it belongs to one of the nine categories of accidents. Change (*motus, qui est via ad esse,* as St. Thomas says), and the act of existing, and operation (which follows upon existing) are not directly categorical realities, because they are not formal. St. Thomas very often compares immanent operation to categorical action and passion (as is also done below, Chapter V, sections 54–57). In this way, he remains true to the experienced actuality of knowing as compared to the habitual possession of knowledge (see his distinction between *consideratio* and *scientia*); the latter is formal and directly belongs in the category of quality. However, a philosopher may

In the previous chapter we have seen the difference between immanent and transient activity.[15] We can briefly recall that an activity is transient when it produces an effect outside the agent; when it is in the strictest sense the act and perfection of the patient rather than of the agent. Immanent activity, on the other hand, is the act and perfection of the agent. Which of these kinds of activity is knowledge?

Very simply, it does not of itself produce an effect or product; it does not modify its object. When I know a table or book, these things are not thereby changed in themselves. Quite the contrary: when I know something, I have been changed, so that in this act of knowledge I have been made more perfect. And so, since knowledge is the act or perfection of the knower, it is an immanent activity. (In section 26, we have discussed immanent activity in connection with vegetative life. Knowledge, as immanent activity, is somewhat similar to vegetation, but also different; it is more perfectly immanent.)

We have seen that immanent activity is the special characteristic of life, distinguishing it sharply from non-life. Knowledge is therefore a kind of life.[16] Now, the immanence or interiority of knowledge has an immateriality about it, as we have seen, so that the immanence of knowledge is greater than the immanence of merely vegetative life. One who knows lives more perfectly and fully than one who merely vegetates—more perfectly, because more immanently, and because knowing implies more actuality than vegetating.

40. [8] The difference between intentional change and natural change

We have seen that not-knowing in man is compared to knowing as potency to act. Hence, knowledge in man must be connected

---

legitimately speak of knowing as a quality in order to show that it is an absolute and unmixed perfection of a subject. For us here and now such language would be ambiguous. See also, St. Thomas, *Truth*, XI. 8.

[15] Cf. above, section 26.

[16] See above, section 28, on the meaning of "life."

with a transition (a passage) from potency to act. Such a transition is known as change (passion,[17] suffrance).

Change, as we most commonly experience it in sensible things, involves the loss of one perfection in the gaining of another. For example, when a piece of wax acquires one shape, it can do so only by losing the shape it had previously. This loss-and-gain is change or passion in the first sense.

Now, not-knowing expresses the simple absence of a perfection. In this way, it is something like "darkness" in comparison to light: "darkness" is not an act or perfection of the translucent medium (e.g., the air), but a simple absence of light. Similarly, the change or "passion" involved in coming-to-know is the simple acquiring of a perfection without the loss of a perfection previously possessed.

Of course, in many instances, there will be a change or passion in the first sense (loss of one perfection in the acquisition of another) involved in coming-to-know. For example, in feeling a hot object, the hand itself becomes physically and materially warm. In seeing, the eye receives a colored image, and this physical, mate-

---

[17] The term "passion" has six different particular meanings. (1) The acquiring of a form or perfection in the place of another which was previously possessed, as in ordinary physical or material change [for example, in local motion there is change of place; in blushing, there is the loss of a white color and the gain of a pink one]. (2) A passage from potency to act that involves the loss of a suitable disposition and the violent reception of a new disposition unsuited to the subject [for example, in the phrase "the Passion of Christ," the term "passion" means the harmful and painful violence suffered by Christ's Body]. (3) The simple acquiring of a perfection without the loss of another perfection; this perfection is acquired by the influence of a cause distinct from the patient. (4) A violent, disordered, or excessive act of sensory appetency [for example, in the proposition, "An habitual debauchee is a slave to his passions"]. (5) Any act of sensory appetency (and by analogy, of rational appetency). (6) Any immanent *operation* which has been preceded by a passion in the third meaning above (the simple acquiring of a perfection without any accompanying loss of previously held perfection).

Frequently, passion in the third sense and its consequent operation (second act) are considered together, and simply called a "passion in the most general sense of that word."

Note that we are dealing with knowledge as experienced, and with immanent activity as experienced. The metaphysician, in studying Divine Knowledge, will have to refine this analysis; see below, Chapter V, footnote 4.

rial change sets up a whole series of changes (in the retina, the nerve, the brain).

But such physical changes, though they are ordinarily present in perceptual experience, are not the essence of knowledge itself. For quite similar physico-chemical changes occur in nonliving things. Parallel examples would be: a thermometer which itself becomes warm in registering the heat of an object; a photographic film which undergoes chemical changes in being exposed to light. Hence, we can conclude that such physical material changes *of themselves* have no necessary relation to knowledge. What is needed is an immaterial, an intentional change. For change, like motion, is specified by its term: when a given change leads to a new quality, it is alteration; when it leads to a new quantity, it is growth or diminution, and so on. Since knowledge implies immateriality and intentionality, the change leading to such an act and perfection must itself be immaterial and intentional.

When we say that the change or passion that brings about knowledge is an intentional change, the term "intentional" has a second implication. As before, the word "intentional" designates the mode of *being* proper to a sign as such. But here, it also designates a *process* which is to terminate in the pure or formal sign which is actual knowledge. The word "intention" aptly designates the dynamic *tendency* of this process toward the object to be known.

41. [9] The prerequisite for intentional activity: the *species*

We have seen that the human knower, of himself and prior to the experience of objects, is merely in potency to know. He comes into being, not as actually having all knowledge, but rather without any actual knowledge.[18] Hence, in order to know, man must undergo an intentional change.

The absence of actual knowledge in man is a state (*a*) of potency without act, and (*b*) of indetermination. For example, not only is the human eye in the state of sheer potency to seeing, when

---

[18] This point will need specific investigation with regard to the origin of ideas; see below, section 91.

there are absolutely no visible objects present to it; but it depends on objects also to see this rather than that. Thus, when we look at a piece of white paper, we cannot at our arbitrary whim see it as a brown dog or a sleek black automobile. The nature of the object under the concrete circumstances determines or specifies the act of knowledge.

The human knower has no innate determinate experience. Before his powers of conscious experience can be put into act, they must be determined, specified to some one object. Now, that by which a being or action is specified is called a "form." [19]

What we are speaking of here is something *by which* man's capacity to know is specified to a given object. Because this "something by which" is not a complete being (substance), and is not capable of existing all by itself, but is only a partial constituent of a being in act, we call it a "principle" (*principium quo*). What is the function of this principle in human knowing? It is to specify or determine a capacity indetermined in itself, and so we call it a *formal* principle. We can also call it the inhering formal cause from which knowledge proceeds. The formal principle is a cause, the act of knowing is an effect. Therefore, we cannot directly experience this formal principle, for it is a prerequisite for knowledge, not an object of direct knowledge. Because of its function in *specifying* the act of knowledge, it is called a received (or impressed) "*species*." [20] This function of the received *species* is necessary because of the knower, and hence we can say that it is needed by reason of the subject which knows (*ratione subiecti*).

The *species*, however, has a complementary function: it makes the object actually present or united to the knower; it is thus a "presentative form." Whenever the object known is not actually as such really identical with the knower, then the *species* is necessary also by reason of the object which is known (*ratione obiecti*).

[19] Recall that a form is not a thing, but the principle by which a thing is such as it is; cf. above, section 27.

[20] To distinguish the received *species* from "species" in the logical sense (when the word means "class or group"), it will always be italicized in this text.

Now, as we have seen, an object is possessed by a knower intentionally, the known object is intentionally present to him. Consequently, the *species* whose function is to unite knower and known, is itself in the intentional order.

Of course, the *species* is a real modification of the knower, and to this extent is an accident, a quality of the knower. So the *species* has real accidental being, but to call it an accident tells nothing about its relation to knowledge.

On the other hand, *species,* as means to knowledge, are *pure means.*[21] This is to say that they are not themselves directly known or experienced, but are pure signs or means of knowledge of the object of which they are signs. They are, as it were, the bond of union between knower and known.

We have seen that the mode of presence of the object to the knower is an intentional presence; that the form received in knowledge is an immaterial form; that the object is in the knower in an intentional way. Hence, the *species* as such is not a physical but an intentional form.[22]

We shall see later that there are essentially different kinds of knowledge, namely, sensation and intellection. Consequently, there will also be two different kinds of *species,* sensible and intelligible *species.*

42. [10] Knowledge is not itself a change

The activity of all merely material beings takes place through change in the strict sense. Moreover, we have seen that a material change is connected with all perceptual knowledge as such. Hence, it is quite easy to jump to the conclusion that knowledge not only involves a preceding change from potency to act, but is itself such a continuous change. Yet the immateriality characteristic of all

---

[21] Known as a *"medium quo"*—"a means by which."

[22] Thus, for example, the received *species* in sight is *not* the image which can be seen by another person on the retina of my eye, though the retinal image is a preliminary stage for the act of seeing. Hence, not even the intentional *species* in sight is a "little picture"; much less can this be said of other *species.* Recall what was said above about the way in which knowledge can be said to be "representation."

knowledge should make us pause and examine the validity of the reasoning. Is knowledge a continuous change or process?

Physical, material change is a passage from physical potency to physical act, as when a body that is warm in potency becomes actually physically warm. Since this kind of change is included in all bodily activity, and since the body has a part to play in all perceptual knowledge,[23] it follows that to this extent there is a continuous change in knowledge. This, however, is not the whole story of knowledge, nor is it necessarily a condition of knowledge as such. For there is an aspect of knowledge which is immaterial, and under this aspect knowledge is a purely actual operation. Knowledge is therefore (at least under its immaterial aspect) the activity of a being which has been perfected (by the reception of the intentional form).[24]

*43. [11] Objectivity in knowledge

In the description and analysis of knowledge, we have seen that "to know another" is "to be the other." Hence, we can speak of knowledge as the identity of the knower and the known. This identity of course is intentional and not physical.

Knowledge then, is the identity-in-distinction of subject and object. In all discussions of knowledge both the identity and the difference must be admitted and accounted for. The identity of subject and object in the act of knowledge is due to the *species*, by which the object is made intentionally present to the subject.

---

[23] By "perceptual knowledge" or "perception" (simply so called) is meant the total unified knowledge of a sensible or material object when the latter is present. Obviously "perception" includes both intellectual and sensory elements. Chapter VI will deal more particularly with the part played by the body in perception.

[24] Under this aspect, knowledge as the activity of a being-which-has-been-perfected (*actus perfecti*) is quite different from that type of change which is known as "motion," since the latter is defined as "the act of that-which-is-in-the-process-of-being-perfected" (*actus imperfecti*).

Again, the metaphysician will point out that the prior reception of a perfection is not a necessary constituent of knowledge in itself. He will then say that knowledge is the act of a being which is perfect. More explicitly, he will say: "Knowledge is the act (operation) of a being wholly in act (that is, with regard to substantial, accidental, and existential perfection)."

The distinction between subject and object arises through some opposition between the two and so in its perfect form requires a reflection of the subject upon himself, a self-awareness.

On the other hand, in all knowledge except that of self-awareness, the knower and the known are set in opposition as terms of the relation of knowing and being known. Therefore we can say—except of self-knowledge—that in an act of knowledge something is present to a knower as distinct from the act by which it is known.[25] Thus, for example, when we see something, the thing appears to us as distinct from, and even "opposite to," the one who sees. When we know something, the object of knowledge appears other than the knower. This opposition in relation is summed up briefly in the phrase "to know is to be the other *as other*." Thus, knowledge involves a confrontation of subject with object.

*44. [12] Knowledge is self-possession as well as possession of the other

Human knowledge is not knowledge merely of objects, though it is *directly* of objects. The awareness of objects, as we experience it, contains and includes a self-awareness of the act and of the agent.[26] When we know a thing, no matter what that thing is, we also know *that* we have an act of knowledge. This "knowing that we know" is evident in the act of knowledge itself, as if the act of knowledge were somehow and immediately evident to itself.

Furthermore, the act of knowledge presents itself to experience *concretely*, as being the act of a subject, as being my knowledge.[27]

[25] This descriptive analysis of knowledge shows that the notion of knowledge as a mere subjective "state of mind" is a radical falsification of experience. But it does *not* show that *every* object of knowledge is necessarily a really existing or subsisting thing. As we shall see later on, the relation of the mind to reality is a very complex one, and needs a careful critical consideration. Such critical consideration, however, does not belong to the philosophy of human nature, but to the theory of knowledge.

[26] As we shall see in Chapter VI, adult human beings do not experience sensations as isolated or separate acts. By "knowledge as we experience it," we mean either perceptual knowledge in its lived complexity, or non-perceptual knowledge (see below, next paragraph) which always involves intellectual knowledge.

[27] What is said in the rest of section 44 is asserted only of the human

In the self-awareness of any object there is therefore implied an obscure but very real awareness of the subject or person who knows.

Consequently, every act of knowledge implies not only the possession of the object known, but also a self-possession. The human knower not only exists, like a mineral or a plant; he is also for himself. I not only am; but when I know, I know that I am. And so my being or existence is something special for me, a kind or mode of being in which no one else can share, just as the lived experience and being of another person is his with its own special immediacy and intimacy.

Though knowledge is an escape from the mere subjectivity of the unconscious plant or mineral, it is at the same time a possession of self in a much higher way. The subjectivity of unconscious beings is the possession of a nature that is closed in upon itself. The higher "subjectivity" of a knower is the self-possession of a nature that is simultaneously open to other reality.

In addition to what may thus be called "direct self-awareness," there is the "reflex self-awareness." This reflex self-consciousness occurs when we take another act of knowledge or the knower himself as the object of an act of knowledge. Here of course the self-possession implied in all human knowledge is made explicit.

In human knowledge, the self-possession that is characteristic of knowledge is directly connected with the possession of other beings in knowledge. For every act of knowledge increases the perfection of the knower, makes him more actually and completely be what he essentially is by nature. Hence, the self-perfecting activity of knowing other things increases the actual and active self-possession of the knowing subject.

45. [13] Kinds of knowledge: perceptual and non-perceptual

Before we can define knowledge, we must reflect and see whether knowledge is always one and the same thing. For what

---

knower. In what way it can be applied to brutes, for example, will need special consideration later, cf. section 75.

is not one, can have no simple definition. Now, we noted in the very beginning of our reflection on knowledge,[28] that knowing is a very complex activity and one that varies widely from time to time.

There are various ways of dividing and classifying acts of knowing, and we shall use some of them later on. Our concern at present is not to distinguish the kinds of knowledge according to the principles from which they flow.[29] Before we can distinguish knowledge according to its principles, a whole method of analysis has to be investigated. But without further analysis we are able to consider the various experimental differences, particularly inasmuch as we can directly experience variations in the unity and complexity of acts of knowing. In conscious experience we can look for a twofold unity: a unity of interest and a unity of knowledge itself. The latter consideration is very important from the point of view of epistemology or theory of knowledge. The discussion can be best approached through a consideration of cases.

(1) The greatest unity is to be found in the concentration of all a person's knowing powers upon a single external object. For example, a person is wholly attentive to a flowering meadow on a sunny, breezy day in early summer. All his senses, all his attention are wholly taken up with that single complex object. Such a unified experience is called a perception. When the object of such a perception is beautiful and is so known, we speak of an aesthetic experience.

A second example of a similar type of unified experience is that of interested knowledge. For example, an automobile mechanic is examining a faulty engine in order to readjust it. Here, too, all the powers of knowing are concentrated on a single object, and so this practical knowledge is also a perception. Quite like this is the case of moral knowledge, when a person is, say, attending

[28] See above, section 33.

[29] For example, the distinction between sensation and intellection is established on the basis of their different formal objects, and involves distinct powers. This distinction is of course extremely important, but we are not ready to speak of formal objects or powers now.

to an external action to be done, considering in particular its relations to moral qualities.

(2) A second type of knowledge is by comparison fragmentary and partial. For example, a chemist is testing a solution with a thermometer. The solution, let us say, is pleasantly warm to the touch, is viscous, a beautiful bright pink, and delicately perfumed. Moreover, the day is uncomfortably warm, and there are noises coming in from the street. The chemist knows all this, yet he pays no attention to it—he abstracts from all these various sensible qualities and the sensations of them that he has. His knowledge is directed to that one quantitative report of his instrument and to the significance of that report. Such an abstractive knowledge may be called infra-perceptual, in the sense that almost the whole of the sensory elements are neglected. A somewhat different example: a geometer is working a problem involving two triangles. The paper may be white or green, the lines drawn with pencil or pen, and so forth. These qualities of the object are disregarded as irrelevant; the knowledge of geometry is an abstractive knowledge, and so is infra-perceptual. Most sciences are of this type.

(3) A third type of knowledge consists in an analogous knowledge of a sensible reality: this is philosophy dealing with sensible things. Take the example of a philosopher studying a material change (of color, let us say) which he experiences, and in which he sees manifested the distinction between substance and accident. Such knowledge is supra-perceptual, because substance is not sensible of itself, but only intelligible, yet it is seen in an object which is perceived.

(4) A fourth type of knowledge can be said to be extra-perceptual. For example, a philosopher considers the nature and operations of a spiritual (non-material, non-sensible) being. Here, the philosopher does *not* proceed *without* perceptual, sensible elements; indeed, as we shall see, knowledge in this life is naturally impossible without some sensible elements. No: the knowledge of a metaphysician is extra-perceptual, not in the sense that it is unconnected with perceptual elements, but precisely in this, that

it denies what is perceived and transcends the sensible content of perceptual and partly perceptual knowledge. It is therefore a knowledge which is essentially a negative representation; that which is denied is precisely that which characterizes man's ordinary perceptions. Hence, metaphysics is evidently very different from other types of knowledge.

46. [14] Knowledge cannot strictly be defined

(1) *Knowledge cannot be defined by genus and specific difference.*

Knowledge, therefore, is a complex and varied reality. As we shall see in detail later on, "knowledge" is not a univocal term like genus or species, but rather an analogous term, so that the different kinds of knowledge differ even in that in which they are similar.

A second problem to be faced is that all definition, in the strict sense of the word, implies the expression of the reality to be defined in terms of genus and specific difference, which are simpler than the thing to be defined, and at least one of which, the genus, is common to other things. Now, "knowledge," as we have just seen, has no simple genus to which all the kinds of knowledge can be reduced; much less is there a genus common to knowledge and to other forms of reality. Moreover, knowledge cannot be reduced to more ultimate components. For example, a blind man can never fully understand what seeing is, nor a deaf man what hearing is.

(2) *Nor can knowledge strictly speaking be defined in terms of other types of being.*

One other attempt at definition can be made, and that is to define "knowledge" in terms of something else. Now, this procedure is valid enough, under two conditions: first, that a careful description (at least) of knowledge in its own experienced reality has been given; secondly, that the reality in terms of which knowledge is to be defined be apt to disclose the nature of knowledge. For example, the behaviorists' definition of knowledge as "behavior that is adapted to the environment" is poor, simply because the proper nature of knowledge is thereby obscured, if not wholly denied.

We must therefore conclude that there can be several definitions of knowledge. If in using them we keep in mind the descriptive analysis that has been made in this chapter, they will be valid and serviceable definitions.[30]

47. Definitions

Knowledge (as a general term, descriptively) is any act of sensation, imagination, perception, thought, reasoning (and so forth), inasmuch as these acts are in some way similar.

Knowledge is that kind of immanent activity (life) which perfects its subject through the possession of an intentional form.

To know another is to be the other as other.

To know is to be some thing according to an intentional mode of existence.

Consciousness is a collective term for all those human activities which deal with known objects; in this general sense it includes both knowledge and appetency. In a slightly narrower sense, it is an abstract, collective term for knowledge.

Perception is the experienced whole of the unified knowledge-processes concerned with a sensed object.

Appetency (nominally) is any conscious tendency or inclination.

Appetency (really) is a tendency toward, or adherence to, a known good (and its opposite, aversion from a known evil).

Immateriality is the characteristic of being without the attributes which are proper to merely material, physical being.

Intentional being is representative being; it is that by which a knower is dynamically identified with the known; it is that mode

[30] Knowledge must in the first instance be defined and described as we find it in our own experience. If we know that there are other beings which also have knowledge—for example, God or angels—we must proportionately modify the definition of knowledge so that it will be proportioned to the nature of these beings. For example, it is proved in natural theology that God is a subsistent Act of existing, in whom there are no operations after the manner of accidents. Consequently, knowledge in God will not be an accident, but will be an act and perfection identical with His act of existing.

of being proper to a sign or representation considered formally as such.

A *sign* is that which leads to a knowledge of something distinct from itself.

An *instrumental sign* is a sign, which when *known* leads to the knowledge of something other than itself. It is a real being in itself, as well as being a sign.

A *formal sign* (or pure sign) is that whose reality is to signify, to make another known. Of itself it has no existence other than its being a sign. Hence, it need not necessarily itself be known and, in every case, that which is signified by a pure sign is not known by inferring it from the sign.

Species is the formal inherent principle by which an act of knowledge is specified and determined to be actually a knowledge of this object rather than another.

48. Proofs

A. *Every knower is in some way immaterial.*

That which can extend itself to things outside itself in such a way that both the subject and the outside things remain unchanged in their material reality, is in some way immaterial.

But: the knower, in the act of knowledge, can extend himself to things outside himself, while neither he nor the outside thing loses anything of his or its distinct material reality.

Therefore: every knower is in some way immaterial.

B. *In order to know, man needs a received species.*

Man has actual determinate knowledge of objects.

But: actual determinate knowledge is a second act or operation which proceeds from the agent as possessing a determinate act, for "every agent acts inasmuch as it is in act."

Therefore: man, as actually knowing, possesses a determinate act from which his act of determinate knowledge proceeds.

But: man does not by his nature possess the determinate act from which definite knowledge flows; rather, he is in potency to all knowable objects, and so must be moved to this determinate act.

Therefore: man as knowing is moved from potency to the determinate act from which knowledge proceeds.

Therefore: man, actually to know, must be moved from potency to act by a formal specifying principle of knowledge, which principle is called the *"species."*

49. Readings

St. Thomas Aquinas, *Summa Theologiae*, I. 14, 1–6; 16. 1; 17. 1–2; 54. 1–3; 55. 1–2; 56. 1; 57. 1–2; 58. 1; an important series of articles in which St. Thomas states and applies his doctrine on knowledge to God and the angels; I. 84. 2, an important article on the immateriality of knowledge.

Jacques Maritain, *The Degrees of Knowledge*, trans. by Bernard Wall and Margot Adamson (New York, Scribner, 1938), pp. 134–143. This section is required reading and should be carefully outlined. The student should be able to give a brief resume of Maritain's seven points. Pp. 144–155 take up the theory of signs, with reference to intellect.

John Wild, "An Introduction to the Phenomenology of Signs," *Philosophy and Phenomenological Research*, VIII (1947), pp. 228–233; a brief but clear presentation of the theory of the sign.

A. D. Sertillanges, *The Foundations of Thomistic Philosophy*, trans. by Godfrey Anstruther (St. Louis, Herder, 1931), pp. 1–44. This brilliant account sometimes uses expressions which seem to be idealistic; they should be read in the realist sense which Fr. Sertillanges intended them to have.

Étienne Gilson, *The Spirit of Mediaeval Philosophy*, trans. by A. H. C. Downes (New York, Scribner, 1936), pp. 229–247.

Idem, Being and Some Philosophers (Toronto, Pontifical Institute of Medieval Studies, 1949), pp. 84–89, 92, 169–176, 203–204, on the special nature of acts which are not forms.

Pierre Rousselot, S.J., *The Intellectualism of St. Thomas*, trans. by J. E. O'Mahony, O. M. Cap. (New York, Sheed and Ward, 1935), pp. 17–60.

J. B. D. Hawkins, *Criticism of Experience* (New York, Sheed and Ward, 1935), pp. 11–23.

John Wild, *Introduction to Realistic Philosophy* (New York, Harper, 1948), pp. 436–39, 448–62.

CHAPTER V

Differences in Activity and the Theory of Powers

50. The problem

In the second chapter, we saw that there is some evidence for multiplicity or plurality in human activity. Then we examined that evidence to see whether it contradicted the evidence for man's substantial unity, and decided that it did not. A partial solution was established by means of two distinctions. First, we saw that human activity is an accident inhering in and modifying human substance or nature. From this, we concluded that some of the evidence for multiplicity points to the many accidents (both proper and contingent) which inhere in the one substance. Secondly, we saw that some of the evidence points to the virtual presence of lower beings in the higher. Consequently, a substance may be actually one, and virtually many.

But some of the evidence adduced in the second chapter has not yet been adequately handled. It is easy to see how one and the same substance can be the source now of one activity, now of another. But we experience simultaneous conflicting activities. Temptation and struggle with one's self are gone through by everyone. Conflicts of desires occur even apart from moral situations; for example, a student can have the desire to study a problem more deeply, and also the desire to go to a dance. Then there is the fact of distraction, not only in prayer, but also in study and in conversation. How, if substance (nature) is the principle of activity, can it be in conflict with itself?

In the third chapter, new evidence for some kind of multiplicity has come up, which has been stated and used, but not yet put into relation to substance. This is the fact that all things which have vegetative life also have *organized* bodies. Now, organization means a difference in parts: not a substantial difference, but a difference in structure and function. For example, the leaf of the tree has among its other activities that of freeing carbon from carbon dioxide with the aid of light (photosynthesis), while the root does not. In animals, the difference of bodily organization is greater and more evident. A dog has eyes and ears. And we know from our own immediate experience that seeing is a function quite different from hearing. How can one nature have different kinds of operations simultaneously?

This same problem can be approached from the point of view of man's position in the total collection of sensible, material things. We have already seen that there are three levels of these beings, which differ specifically, and can be put into an ascending order of perfection: (1) the lowest, which are the material, inanimate things; (2) the plants, which have the greater perfection of vegetative activities; (3) the animals and men, which have knowledge. For the moment, in order to complete this picture, we shall presuppose the essential difference between animals and men, which will be proved later on. We shall therefore have to say that the third level is that of the animals, and the fourth, that of men, who have rational knowledge which the animals lack.

Not only do the beings on these four levels have their own proper activities; each level also shares in the activities of all the lower levels. Schematically, this hierarchical order of material things can be presented thus:

	Material Activities	Vegetative Activities	Sensory Activities	Rational Activities
Man				⟶
Animals			⟶	
Plants		⟶		
Inanimate things	⟶			

This situation creates a problem. Not only are these beings substantially different, but they also have activities in common. And these activities are not only virtually, but are actually present. The substantial perfections of inanimate things, plants, and animals are virtually present in man, but man actually performs material activities (he is subject to gravitation, falls, and so forth, just like a stone); actually performs vegetative activities (he grows, nourishes himself, reproduces his kind); actually performs animal actions (sees, hears, and so forth).

To the present data we can add some of the information already discovered in the preceding chapter, and again, temporarily, suppose the further distinctions to be proved in later chapters. In Chapter IV, we saw that there is a distinction between knowledge and appetency; we shall see later on that appetency is divided, like knowledge, into sensory and rational levels. Consequently, we can schematize man's activities in this way.

Inanimate Level	Vegetative Level	Sensory Level	Rational Level
Actions	Actions	Knowledge	Knowledge
Passions[1]		Appetency	Appetency

This is a sufficiently complete table to show the nature and point of the present problem. How can one and the same substance, constituted in one definite degree of perfection, by a single substantial form,[2] be simultaneously the source of seven different kinds of activities? and this, when specifically quite different beings share in some of these same activities?

51. Activity is specified by its object

So far we have been considering the activities of men and of other living things in a rather general and descriptive fashion.

---

[1] See sections 40 and 51 for the meaning of "passion" here.

[2] This point will be explicitly proved later on in the case of man, and the argument can readily be generalized; cf. below, sections 157, 159, 160.

This has been a perfectly valid proceeding, and has enabled us to reach a certain number of conclusions. To go any further, we need a method of approach that will make it possible to discover and define the *specific* nature of an activity.

We have already seen that action or operation is of two kinds: transient action and immanent action. Transient activity is capable of being divided in two ways: we can consider either the action as proceeding from the agent, and then it is "action" formally so called. Or we can consider it as received in a patient, and then it is called "passion." Take the transient activity of heating as an example. As an action, heating is the change in an object from cold to hot, inasmuch as that change comes from some agent, a hot thing. As a passion, being-heated is the same change, inasmuch as it is received in the thing or patient. Thus, transient action and passion are fundamentally identical: transient action is the act or perfection of the patient as coming from (depending on) an agent; passion is the act or perfection produced, as inhering in and modifying the patient.

How do we specify and define action and passion? The most evident case is that of local motion. How do we distinguish one motion from another? Sometimes it is quite easy to see *that* they are different; if we force ourselves to state very clearly and precisely what makes each of the motions to be what they are, we will be able to designate them in terms of the points of departure and the points of arrival (principle and term). This kind of designation can be applied to other transient actions. Suppose we see a man standing, bending down, putting his hands somewhat in front of him, moving them back and forth, stepping a little to one side, and repeating the process. We can see these movements, and we immediately ask· "What is he doing?" Suppose someone told us: "He is moving his arm up three inches with a force of three dynes, moving it forward, and so forth." This description might become very accurate and complicated, and we still might not have the faintest inkling of what he is doing. Then we are told that he is laying bricks. Now the whole thing is clear: we know what the activity is by knowing its term. Another word for the term of an action is "object." We discover the nature of a passion in the same way. We see a happening; for example, we are looking at a white board, and we see several holes appear in it; we look around and see a man with a rifle. Now the happening is clear: the holes are bullet-holes. Thus we know what a passion is when we know what the principle of the happening is. The principle of a passion is also called an "object."

The method of designating an activity by its object can also be used with regard to immanent activities, but with important modifications. In the first place, the living being is the efficient source of its own operations.[3] Therefore, the distinction between action and passion as it occurs in transient action does not apply to immanent action. Nevertheless, a similar distinction is to be found. We call an immanent activity an "action" in the strict sense of the word when its object is a term (or product) of the activity. For example, the vegetative activities perfect their subject by way of inducing a physical change in the body of the subject (that is, by making it larger and more organized in growth, and so forth). Compare this situation with what happens when we see something. When we see something, for example, a page of this book, nothing happens to the book in its physical reality. But something happens to the eye: for (a) a sensible *species* is received in the eye from the book, and (b) the indetermination of the power of sight is specified as by a formal principle. Inasmuch as some immanent operations involve the reception of an act, perfection, or form, and all immanent operations are specified by their objects as by a formal principle, they can be called passive. But note again the difference between immanent and transient activity. The passion correlative to a transient action is the reception of a perfection from an agent,

<hr />

[3] For the argumentation of this paragraph, see St. Thomas Aquinas, *Truth,* 2. 6; 24. 4 ad 15; 26. 3 ad 4; 8. 6; 28. 8 arg. 4 in contrarium and its response; *In De Sensu et Sensato,* lect. 4; *In II Sent.* 36. 2. 2; *Summa Theologiae,* I. 14. 4; 56. 1; 79. 3 ad 1; 85. 2 ad 1; I–II. 74. 1 ad 3; *Q. D. De Unione Verbi Incarnati,* a. 5. The purpose of these references is merely to establish that the explanation given above is really the teaching of St. Thomas.

in place of a perfection formerly possessed. The passive immanent operation (as far as the immediate efficient or eliciting cause is concerned) is from the *patient* itself; the specification from the object does not of itself imply efficient causality; and, when the object has acted efficiently upon the *patient*, the reception does not involve the loss of a perfection formerly possessed.[4]

With this understood, we can use the designation by object also for immanent operations. For example, the vegetative activities are defined and distinguished from each other by their terms or results. Nutrition has as its object the living body to be maintained in proper working order; growth has as its object the living body to be brought to proper and proportionate organization; generation, the living body to be brought to such a level and kind of perfection that by separation or division a new living being of the same species comes into being.

As far as the passive immanent operations are concerned, their designation by object will have to be taken at this point by way of a preview of matter to be seen later in detail. But certain general lines of the argument can be given here. We know, for example, that seeing is a passive operation;[5] when we designate it specifically, we do so by indicating *what* we see. And what we see is determined by the sensible *species* received from the object seen. The same type of designation applies to other acts of knowledge. For the moment, the way in which other *species* are caused will be omitted from consideration. But in various types of perceptual knowledge, the object of our knowledge (that is, *what* we know),

---

[4] In our experience, every passive immanent operation actually implies a prior reception of a perfection. A "pure" immanent operation would be passive only in the sense of being specified by its object. This pure immanence is partly exemplified in the intuitive self-knowledge of the Angels, and entirely exemplified in the Divine knowledge. But to enter into these investigations is beyond the scope of the philosophy of human nature.

[5] On the basis of first impressions, most people would probably agree with St. Thomas's grammarian, "who says that *to know* is active and *to be known* is passive"; as we shall discover more clearly later, "*to sense,* as far as the reception of the sensible *species* is concerned, means a passion . . . , but as far as the act consequent upon the perfecting of the sense power by the *species* is concerned, it means an operation," *In I Sent.,* 40. 1. 1 ad 1. Cf. *Summa Theologiae,* I. 17. 2 ad 1; 77. 3.

is somehow the cause of the *species* by which we know in act. For example, when we look out of the window, and know the various things that are outside, that which we know is the cause of the *species* by which we are put into the act of knowing. Hence, the activity of many kinds of human knowing is designated and specified by its object, which is the cause or principle of the received *species*.

52. Material and formal object

So far we have referred to the object in a general way. For example, in transient action, the cause of a golf ball's motion is a golfer with a club, and what is hit is a ball. In immanent operation, that which acts upon an eye is a building, an automobile, a tree, and these are the objects which are seen. When we refer to objects in this way, we designate them as "material objects." [6]

A little reflection will show us that designating material objects is altogether too general an indication to be of much help. For example, the man who plays golf is somebody's son; he may be a student and a singer as well. Does he hit the golf ball as a student? Clearly not (unless what he is studying is golf!). And the golf ball is hit (passion), not in so far as it is white or warm, but in so far as it has resistance and inertia. Again, in reference to the object of immanent operation, the building which is seen may be an office building, of fireproof steel and concrete construction, with a heavy mortgage on it—but in none of these ways does it affect the sense of sight. A building (and in the same way any other sensible or material thing) acts upon the eye inasmuch as it is the source of radiation upon the eye. And so, fully to designate an activity by its object, we must speak precisely of the object in the way in which it is an object, that is, specifically as object. Object in this strict sense is called "proper object." For example, the proper object of sight is a colored thing; of the temperature sense,

[6] The adjective "material" in this usage does not imply matter. When a man is thinking of the spiritual nature of God, God is the "material object" of that act of thought.

a warm thing; of the intellect, an intelligible thing; of appetite, a good thing. The form or the act (*ratio*, which is sometimes a form, sometimes a different kind of perfection in place of a form) which we explicitly state when we name an object as proper is called the "formal object." The formal object in the proper objects just mentioned are: color, heat, intelligibility, goodness.

Consequently, activity can be designated and determined to some extent by its material object. The full and complete or specific determination of an activity is through its proper object, or its formal object.

53. Application to the present problem

Human activities, descriptively, are of many kinds. Are they also specifically and essentially many? This question, in the light of the previous discussion, can be rephrased thus: Do human activities have many different proper objects? Vegetative activities have as their proper object the living body to be perfected in three various ways. The activities of knowing have as their object a thing as knowable (this very general designation will be studied in greater detail later on). The activities called appetencies have as their object things as good (or evil). Thus, by looking at various human activities, we see that they do have different formal objects. The original question of this chapter can now be asked in this way: How can one substance be the source of many specifically different activities?

54. The distinction between power and substance

A created substance as such is the immediate subject of its formal accidents; for example, the substance of a tree is the immediate subject of its quantity, and its qualities (color, shape, hardness). In general, there is no difficult problem here: the substance or receiving subject is as potency to the accidents which are as act and form. Is created substance also and immediately the subject or principle of activity?

We have already seen, on an a posteriori and experiential basis,

that the activities of a living thing are really distinct from its substance. Now, activity is the ultimate actuality (second act) of any
being. Hence, if the ultimate actuality of any thing is identical
with its substance, then it is wholly in act: it is substantially a full
actuality. But such a being is only God; experience shows us that
the things of our universe are in many ways in potency. Hence,
their activity not only is but must be distinct from their substance.

*Moreover, the activity of a created being is not the same as its
act of existing. This is perfectly clear with regard to transient
activity, for transient activity is the perfection of the patient, while
the act of existing must obviously be the perfection of that which
exists, its subject. With regard to immanent activity, we may consider vegetative, cognoscitive, and appetitive activities separately.
Vegetative activities are not and cannot be the same as the act of
existing, for they presuppose the existence of the living body which
they perfect in various ways. Cognoscitive activities have a certain infinity [7] about them: for man can know all sorts of objects.
Appetitive activities have the same kind of infinity, for man can
desire (hate, and so forth) all sorts of objects. But the being of
man, and of all the other living things of our experience, is quite
limited: man is a man, and thereby at once is not a tree and a stone,
while a tree by being a tree is not a horse. Consequently, in every
finite being, activity and the act of existing are necessarily distinct.

*In view of this, can the substance of a finite thing be the im-
mediate principle of, or potency to, activity? The substance or
essence of a finite thing is a potency to its act of existing and to
the formal accidents which are necessary or possible modifications
and completions of its manner of being. But activity is a different
kind of act than either the act of existing or formal accidents. And

[7] Infinity can either be actual, positive infinity, when it refers to the fullness of being, either absolutely or in a certain order. It can be potential, negative, when it refers to the mere absence of determination, in the way in
which there is a potential infinity of points in a line. Human knowledge is
infinite in both senses: it is positively infinite in the order of knowledge, for
there are no actual limits to it; it is negatively infinite, for its capacity for
knowledge can be indefinitely fulfilled—there is no finite point which marks
its limit.

potency by its nature is essentially related to and ordered to its act. That is why we must say that every limited act has its own proper potency, and every potency has its own proper act. Consequently, since activity is a distinct kind of act, different from formal accidents and the act of existing, there must correspond to it a distinct and proper potential principle: the operative potency or *power*.

A man, in his substantial being, is actually a man. If the substantial being of man were the immediate principle of operation, then that operation would be of the same kind, namely, the substantial being of man. But it is perfectly obvious that the activity of a man is not itself a man: a man does not "do a man"; he does an action, for example, of seeing, of wishing, of walking, of building a house. Since the objects of these actions are not the substantial being of man,[8] their proximate principles likewise cannot be the substantial being of man.

We can therefore conclude, from what has been said, that there are at least several distinct powers in a living thing. Three further conclusions immediately follow. First, the many powers of one being, since they are distinct proximate principles of activity, can give rise to different and even conflicting activities without prejudice to the substantial unity of the being which acts. Secondly, distinct powers of activity can be referred to different parts of one and the same organized body, so that the multiplicity of material parts of the body directly corresponds to the multiplicity of powers, and does not prevent the material living thing from being substantially one. Thirdly, it is possible that beings which are specifically distinct, with proper activities, may also have com-

[8] It might seem that the action of generation has as its formal object the substantial being of a new individual of the same species. Recall that generation as an immanent activity is that perfecting of the living being itself (or a part of itself) so that when separated or divided it will be a new individual. Moreover, this perfecting is done by way of introducing accidental modifications which are the instruments of the substantial change. Hence, generative activity presupposes the substantial being of the agent or parent, and attains the substantial being of the offspring, not immediately, but slowly, through the means of a series of accidental changes.

mon activities which are specifically the same, because specifically distinct beings may have the same powers. For example, a man has specifically the same power of vegetative growth that is to be found in a tree. In brief, the problem of the evidence that points to some kind of multiplicity in living things (the problem with which this chapter began), is solved in principle by the theory of distinct powers. Of course, the entire work of determining what these powers are still remains to be done.

Finally, the multiplicity of powers has a relation to the virtual presence of lower beings within a higher being. When we were considering virtual presence, we discovered that one of the elements of virtual presence is this, that the higher complex being has some of the activities of the lower component beings. The theory of distinct powers enables us to see how this is possible. For the higher being has many powers; some of its powers are specifically the same as those of lower beings, and are referred to certain specialized parts of the organism. However, the theory of distinct powers and the theory of virtual presence meet and reinforce each other only with regard to this one set of facts; each of the theories is related to other sets of facts and problems which do not coincide.

*The conclusion that a living being has many distinct powers is borne out by the results reached through the factor method of treating human activities in experimental psychology. Certain scientists, notably the <u>late C. Spearman,</u> have examined series of tests made on many individuals, and in this way have found that there are in each man's activity both common and specific factors which remain relatively constant throughout a large variety of conditions. These factors are not the powers which we have discovered by our formal-object analysis. Nevertheless, if there were only one principle of activity in man (that is, his one substance), there could be no evidence for distinct factors.[9]

[9] The relation between the philosophical theory of powers and the experimental theory of factors is expressed in a similar way by one of the outstanding authorities in this field, Louis L. Thurstone, *Vectors of Mind* (Chicago, Univ. of Chicago Press, 1935), pp. 45–53.

55. Living things and their powers

The preceding consideration from which we concluded to a real distinction between the substance of a thing and the proximate principles of its activity was largely a metaphysical discussion. We can approach our problem more concretely through the fuller evidence obtainable from living things, especially man. Through this approach we will also learn more about the nature of vital powers.

The substance or nature of man is actually what it is, for it is clearly impossible that an existing substance be simultaneously in potency to be itself. A baby has the specific perfection of being human, and this specific perfection is not increased as the baby grows up to be an adult. An acorn has the specific perfection of being an oak. If this were not so, then growth and development would be a process of substantial change. On the contrary, human nature, or any nature, is not an act (perfection) ordered to a further act of the same order: it is the terminus of generation; and when a nature is brought into being, the process of generation stops. So if a man or any living thing is in potency, this potency cannot be the substance in act.

Now, the living thing is sometimes evidently in potency, for it does not always act. It is clearly evident that many human activities suffer interruption, as in sleep. Some living things seem to be able to suspend vital activity almost entirely (for example, wheat stored in the pyramids centuries before Christ was still able to grow when it was found in recent times; the spores of some plants can remain for long periods of time without any apparent activity if they are kept dry). Yet, during the changes and interruptions of activity, the living thing is actually living substance: the sleeping man is a man; the dormant wheat is wheat.

If substance were the immediate principle of activity, then there would be a change in substance when activity began or ceased or changed. For, after all, a potency which possesses its actuation *is* in a quite different manner than that same potency without its

act. Therefore, since man remains man throughout all his variations of activity, the proximate potency of operation cannot be
identical with his substance, but must be something other than
the substance itself, that is, an accidental quality or modification
of that nature.

56. Activity, power, and substance

A power cannot be discovered directly in itself. Since it is a principle of activity, it can be found only in activity, just as any potency can be discovered only from its act. And as potency, in general, is specified and designated by its act, so, too, a power, which
is a potency for operation, is specified and designated by its act
which is activity. Consequently, any discussion about powers must
begin with an experience and an analysis of activity.

Moreover, a power is discovered when we consider the activity
of a substance. Hence, by its nature it is an intermediate between
substance and activity. It would therefore be completely wrong
to look on powers as if they were substances, or things.[10] It would
be equally wrong to think of a power as *that which* acts (*principium quod*). That which acts is the supposit or existing thing.
A power is the proximate principle *by which* (*principium quo*)
a supposit acts; it should therefore in strictly accurate usage never
be used as the subject of a sentence. To follow this rule sometimes
becomes very complicated, and so by a kind of shorthand we
frequently say, for example, "The power of growth in a plant is
not always acting." Expressions like this are always to be understood to mean: "The plant is not always acting by its power of
growth."

Finally, a power is the potency to perform an operation. But
operations, as we have seen, are specified by their formal objects.
Hence powers are designated and specified by the formal objects
of the activities to which they lead. More briefly, powers are distinguished by their formal objects.

[10] To avoid such misconception, the term "faculty" has deliberately not
been used. Though the term "faculty" is in itself a good and useful term, its
historical connotations are unfortunate.

Hence, the analysis of human activity which is to terminate in the discovery, classification, and so forth, of human powers must proceed by means of the discovery of distinct and specific formal objects. For example, in the previous chapter we considered an activity of knowing which we called "perception." Can we immediately conclude that there is a "power of perception"? No. We must first find out whether this activity has one distinct, specifically determined formal object. If such a single formal object can be found, then we can immediately add that it proceeds from a distinct power. If, however, such an activity involves a complexion of formal objects, then it may be necessary to conclude that there is, properly speaking, no "power of perception," but rather that there are several powers, which, when they work together in a particular way, are the complex principle of perception. To take another example: we frequently speak of the "power of speech." Is this a power in the technical, philosophical sense of the word as it has been given here? A standard dictionary definition of "speech" shows three elements: articulated—sound—to express thoughts. No deep reflection at all is needed to see that at least two different formal objects are involved: one concerned with external movements to be produced, another with knowledge. Therefore, in the philosophical sense of the word "power," there is no single, distinct power of speech. And since most human activities are quite complex, we may, at this preliminary stage of the investigation, hazard the guess that most human activities will be complex, involving two or more powers at once.[11]

*57. Generic classification of human powers

By way of a summary of what has already been discovered and an anticipation of what remains to be done, a classification of human powers can be attempted. This classification will be largely formal and generic.

---

[11] In this way, we can see why the scientific factor theory cannot arrive at results of the same kind as those reached by the philosophical analysis according to formal objects.

Kind of Activity Involved	Relation to Object	Natural or Material Powers	Vegetative Powers	Sensory Powers	Rational Powers
Of transient activity:	active	for example resistance	[intus-susception etc.]	[motor powers]	
	passive:	malleability			
Of immanent activity:	active		nutrition growth reproduction		
	passive:			senses sense appetites	reason [or intellect] will

58. Definitions

Activity is the final or ultimate act of a being, consequent upon its act of existing.

Transient action is the perfecting of a patient by an agent.

Passion in transient activity is the perfecting of the patient considered as recipient of the perfection.[12]

Active immanent operation is an operation which remains in the agent, is the perfection of the agent, and is related to its object as an efficient cause is related to its effect.

Passive immanent operation is an operation which remains in the agent, is the perfection of the agent, of itself and as such produces no physical effect, and in creatures is related to its object as to its specifying principle, and implies a prior reception of a perfection.[13]

[12] In the previous chapter, footnote 17, the term "passion" was given six specific meanings. In the general sense of passion as defined here, the first three of those meanings are included (namely, [1] the acquiring of a form or perfection in the place of another which was previously possessed; [2] a passage from potency to act that involves the loss of a suitable disposition and the violent reception of a new disposition unsuited to the subject; [3] the simple acquiring of a perfection without the loss of another perfection). The fourth, fifth, and sixth of the meanings of "passion" as given in Chapter IV, footnote 17, designate various passive immanent operations; see the next footnote.

[13] Passive immanent operation can be called passion in creatures, and it

Object is that with which an operation deals, or with which an operation is concerned.

Material object is the object in its whole reality.

Proper object is the object considered precisely in the way in which it is an object. It is the object considered as having a particular perfection toward which a power or activity has an essential order.

Formal object is that in the proper object by reason of which the object is precisely proper. It is that in the object which an activity reaches directly and of itself (*primo et per se*), to which the power is essentially ordered, and in function of which the material object is reached.

A *power* is the potential principle whose act is a specific kind of activity (descriptive definition).

A *power* (in creatures) is the proximate, accidental principle by which a being performs an activity which has a specific formal object (essential definition).

59. Proofs

A. *Activities are specified by their objects.*

Activities are either transient or immanent, and each type is either active or passive; both types of action are known and determined by their terms (results); both types of passion by their principles.

But: the principle of passion or the term of action is called the object of the activity.

Therefore: activities are known and determined by their objects.

Therefore: activities are specified by their objects.

B. *Power is an accidental principle of operation.*

Power is the potential principle whose act is a specific kind of activity.

---

will then be one of the fourth, fifth, or sixth specialized meanings given in Chapter IV, footnote 17 (namely, [4] a violent, excessive, or disordered act of sensory appetency; [5] any act of sensory appetency; [6] any immanent operation which has been preceded by a passion in the sense of the simple acquiring of a perfection without any accompanying loss).

But: in creatures, activity is distinct from the substance or nature (because changeable and multiple, and in living things able to be absent or present), and distinct from the creature's act of existing (which is the act of essence or substance).

Therefore: power is a principle of operation which is really distinct from substance, and so is an accidental principle.

C. *Powers are specified by their formal objects.*

Power, being a potency, is specified by its act which is activity.
But: activity is specified by its object.
Therefore: power is specified by its object.
But: an object precisely is an object through a form or formal character, the formal object, by which the object is determined or specified to be an object.
Therefore: power is specified by its formal object.

D. *There are many specifically different powers in man.*

The activities of man have many specifically different formal objects.
But: a power is specified and distinguished by its formal object.
Therefore: man has many specifically different powers.

60. Readings

St. Thomas Aquinas, *Summa Theologiae*, I–II. 22. 1, one of the classic passages on the various meanings of the word "passion," I. 79. 2, is a similar treatment; I. 54. 2; 56. 1; 18. 3 ad 1; 85. 2, a few of the many passages explaining what is meant by immanent action, and showing the differences between it and transient action; I. 77. 1, the distinction between the substance and its powers; I. 78. 1, the five kinds of vital powers, and the three degrees of life; I. 77. 3, the specification of power through act and formal object.

Charles Spearman, *Psychology Down the Ages* (London, Macmillan, 1937: 2 vols.), an excellent historical study of each of the "traditional faculties," from the viewpoint of scientific psychology; the author concludes that the arguments for many of these "faculties" are sound; see especially Vol. 1, p. 183. The same author also has some pertinent observations in his *The Abilities of Man* and *Human Ability* (written in collaboration with Ll. Wynn Jones [London, Macmillan, 1950]).

CHAPTER VI

External Sensation

61. Sensation

In considering knowledge in general, we noted that perceptual knowledge, in which the whole knowing activity has some external, material thing for its object, is a frequent kind of knowledge-experience. This experience is capable of great variation in object, content, and richness. It is therefore a complex experience.

Now, a complex whole cannot be clearly understood unless its elements or parts are each known distinctly. The technique by which we can discover the various part-activities which go to make up perception is the analysis by formal object.

An easy starting point for a breakdown of the complexity of perception is to be found in the obvious distinctions of the organs of external sensation. The eye, the ear, the nose, and the tongue are easily identifiable and clearly delimited structures. For a descriptive definition of sensation, let us say that it is the normal experience we have simply and directly through one of the external receptive organs. For example, when we try to pay attention to just what we obtain by our eyes when we look at this paper, we isolate that part of a perception which is called a visual *sensation*.[1] To pin down still more accurately the nature of this perceptual element, it will help to reflect that a visual sensation is our reaction to rays that impinge upon the retina. Generalizing from this, we may say that a sensation is the immediate knowledge of material

---

[1] The term "sensation" has a general denotation accepted by almost all writers. But specific denotations and connotations differ considerably. Hence, it is important to have a clear idea of the term as it is used here. It is particularly important to remember that a sensation is not experienced as a separate act.

things directly influencing us by their action upon our sense organs (receptors).

The sense organs referred to above were the eye, ear, nose, and tongue. In addition to these four organs, there are other organs which are dispersed over the entire body; these organs are not always easily identifiable, and very frequently accompany each other closely. This group is known as the organ of touch.

Hence, speaking descriptively, there are five kinds of sensation: sight, hearing, smell, taste, and touch. More specific and accurate knowledge of these sensations will require a particular study of each of them by means of an investigation of their formal objects.

*It is possible to ask whether the organ of sight is the eye alone, or the eye together with the optic nerve and the so-called visual center in the brain. For our present introductory study, this further refinement of the question is unimportant. We can come to an understanding of the nature of the five senses by considering the external structures, for they either are the organs of the external senses or parts of those organs. On the other hand, the afferent nerves (incoming nerves, from organ to brain) and the various centers are, so far as we know at present, so similar in structure that nothing about them will help us to understand the differences between various sensations.[2]

*62. The external senses

A. *Sight.* When we pay attention to what we can know by our eyes alone, we observe that what we see is something either colored

---

[2] It is a fact of experience that a blow on the eye or a bump on the head will make us "see stars." Scientific experiments show that electrical or mechanical stimulation of the optic nerve or the visual center causes us to see flashes of light and the like. The facts are quite clear; what is not clear is what they prove. Does the optic nerve have a specific structure (different from that of other sensory nerves), and is it the organ or even part of the organ of sight? or is the special visual character of such non-specific stimulation (a blow or an electric spark) due to the specific nature of the visual center? Scientists differ on this question, and there is no decisive evidence available. Some writers suggest that the special visual character of the experience is at least partly due to the arousal of a retained image of past experience. See also footnote 7 below.

or shining, which is extended, and usually has a discernible (though not necessarily a sharply defined) outline; it may be in motion or at rest with reference to other seen objects. Everyone knows that a perfectly transparent object is not visible; for example, the air, on a clear day and for short distances, simply cannot be seen. A perfect pane of glass under optimum conditions is also invisible. Yet the air is extended, while the pane of glass has a definite shape and size. Consequently, it is possible that a thing be extended without being visible, and so that which is formally seen (that is, as formal object) is not that which is extended (though the seen thing must be extended).

Everyone also knows that in complete darkness he cannot see an external object which is in front of him. Hence, it is evident that light in some way is necessary for sight, and we might be tempted to think that light is itself the formal object of sight. But another fact must be taken into account. It is also known that if a beam of light is passed through a perfectly transparent medium (one that is both non-reflective and non-refracting) at a right angle to the line of vision, that light cannot be seen. Hence, it is not accurate to say that light is the formal object of sight, unless the statement is modified, so as to say that the formal object of sight is light received in the eye from a primary or secondary (that is, a refracting or reflecting) source. And, since this is a roundabout and awkward way of expression, the technical term "actual color" will be used to designate the formal object of sight.[3]

Actual color is the formal object of sight. But we also actually and immediately experience with our eyes extension and its various

[3] A primary source of light may give off a "white" light, if rays of all visible wave-lengths are given off equally, or "colored" (in the popular sense) if rays of one or several wave-lengths predominate. A reflecting surface is smooth; if rough, but reflecting all wave-lengths equally, it will be white; if it absorbs some wave-lengths selectively, it will be colored; if it reflects relatively few rays it will be dark or black. These will be types of "actual color." By "potential color" we will mean a surface capable of emitting, refracting, or reflecting light in the ways mentioned. For further detail on this subject, see below, Appendix O.

modifications (shape, motion, rest).[4] Now, it is quite certain that an object must be extended in order that it may be a primary or secondary source of light. Consequently we may say that quantity (and its modifications) is necessary in order that color may really exist. In the order of knowledge, however, color is required in order that extension may be seen. Hence, though extension is seen, it is not seen as such, but as colored. And so extension is not the formal object of sight, even if it is directly attained by sight.

B. *Hearing.* The sense of hearing is quite easily and briefly treated. Though we can hear many things as material objects (for example, automobiles, people talking, pianos), precisely what we hear them do is make sounds. This is easily seen from the fact that all these things can be recorded and reproduced by a simply vibrating surface as in a loud speaker. And so the ordinary direct cause of sound is a vibrating surface. The actually vibrating surface sets up compression waves in the air. Within certain rather clearly defined limits of speed and size, these waves, once they have been transmitted to the ear drum, give rise to the sensation of hearing. And so actual sound is the vibrating medium in contact with the organ of hearing. A properly vibrating medium not in contact with any organ of hearing would be potential sound. Sound always has three characteristics: intensity, pitch, and timber. The intensity of the sound is due to the intensity of the vibration and the consequent amplitude (amount of difference between the crest and trough of a wave) of the sound wave. The pitch of the sound is due to the number of vibrations and waves per second. The timber of a sound is due to the complexity of the vibration and the resulting wave.

Extension is obviously a condition for the existence of sound, for it is necessary both for the vibrating surface and for the wave in the medium. But this extension is not directly heard. On the other hand, succession in time is directly audible, particularly in

---

[4] Motion and rest are immediately experienced when they are relative to other objects in the visual field. For other kinds (motion of the whole visual field with respect to the one who sees, or conversely, and motion in the direct line of vision), see the next chapter.

the form of regularly recurring variations in intensity, which constitute rhythm. And so succession is audible, not purely in itself, but as a succession of sounds. Hence the formal object of hearing is sound.

C. *Smell*. The sense of smell cannot be treated at great length, because most people make but a very limited use of this power. Ordinarily we attend to odors only in so far as they are pleasant or unpleasant, and so there is no accurately fixed terminology. Very frequently we use the names of things which cause the odor to name the odor itself, as when we speak of the odor of frying bacon, or of roses. Experimental psychologists have found that we really can distinguish a great number of odors, and with sufficient training and the aid of a technical vocabulary can distinguish and recognize them.

Scientific investigation into the nature of odoriferous objects and their activity has shown that the sense of smell is stimulated by the gaseous or molecular diffusion of certain substances in the air. It is not known why other substances, equally diffused in the air, do not cause an odor. Hence, we can give only a very general definition of odor, when we say: it is the gaseous or molecular diffusion of odoriferous substances in contact with the organ of smell. We have only an a posteriori knowledge of the fact that some substances are odoriferous.

All this is summed up by saying that the formal object of the sense of smell is odor.

Odor obviously presupposes extension, inasmuch as the odoriferous substance must be extended in order that it may be capable of diffusion. Apparently quantity does not enter into the knowledge of the sense of smell, though time and duration do enter to some extent.

D. *Taste*. The tongue, as a distinct structure, has two powers of sensation: the power of touch, in common with the rest of the bodily surfaces, and its own particular power of taste. Under ordinary conditions, the experiences of taste and smell join together, so much so that they are indistinguishable, and both pass for taste.

For example, the taste of coffee or of roast meat are, to a surprisingly great extent, matters of smell rather than of taste strictly so called. But if we block the nasal passages (for example, by holding our nose), we can experience taste alone. Taste occurs when certain substances are moistened by saliva and are in contact with the tongue and the end-organs of the sense of taste. When these moistened substances are thus in contact, there is an actual flavor, and this is what is peculiarly experienced by the sense of taste. Hence, the formal object of the sense of taste is flavor.

E. *Touch.* Touch is a name for a group of sensations and sense powers, most of which involve contact between the object and the body, the organs of which are embedded in the flesh. Experimentalists have enumerated various experiences under this general heading. We can safely presume that this enumeration is sufficiently complete to be used as a point of departure for our formal-object analysis.

(1) Temperature sensations give us a knowledge of the warmth or coldness of an object in relation to the warmth or coldness of the flesh surrounding the end-organs of this sense. Temperature sensations have this peculiarity among touch sensations, that they can be aroused by an object not in physical contact with the body, through what is known as radiant heat (for example, the sun or an electric heater). But in all cases, temperature sensations report the relative warmth (or coldness) of objects. Therefore, the formal object of temperature sensations is the relative warmth (or coldness) of external objects.

(2) Sensations of pressure or of resistance are activated by external pressures relative to the body's own internal pressure. That is why atmospheric pressure is ordinarily not felt; however, when atmospheric pressure and body pressure differ (as when a man is suddenly exposed to higher or lower pressure than the one to which he is adjusted), the pressure of the air is sensed. Pressure sensations combined with movement (of organ or object) give surface characteristics like roughness or smoothness; combined with temperature sensations they give experiences like the feeling

of wetness or dryness. Pressure sensations, therefore, constitute a distinct class of sense experiences, whose formal object is the pressure (resistance) of objects.

(3) Kinesthetic sensations are the direct and immediate knowledge we have of the position and movements of our body. Ordinarily, they operate at a very low level of intensity, so that frequently we advert to them only in a general kind of way. Kinesthetic sensations report position and movement by the contact of one part of the body upon another, by the tautness of our muscles. From this it seems quite clear that pressure and kinesthetic sensations have the same formal object, but have different material objects and different locations in the body (pressure organs on the surface, directed to the apprehension of the pressure of external objects; kinesthetic organs within the body, directed to the pressure of other parts of the body).

(4) Organic or intero-ceptive sensations are the obscure knowledge we have of the functions of our own body (such as circulation of the blood, breathing, hunger, digestion, and the like), and the quality of these functions (that they are proceeding well and smoothly, that they are disordered, and so forth). These sensations likewise seem ordinarily to be present at a very low level of intensity, and they seem to be further characterized by a kind of inherent obscurity; it is as if the knowledge thus obtained were massive but also amorphous. These sensations are so obscure that it is very difficult to say what their formal object is, or in what way it differs from that of pressure and kinesthetic sensations except by obscurity.

(5) Sensations caused by electric stimulation are listed by some experimenters as belonging to a distinct class of experiences. But it seems possible to consider the sensation of electric stimulation as a special combination of pain, pressure, and heat. Since the uniqueness of this experience can be thus explained, no distinct formal object is required.

(6) Sensations of pain are well known, and seem to be a quite distinct kind of experience. They are associated mainly with touch,

and yet it seems that they can be mediated also by other senses. For example, a very strong light is painful to the eye, a very loud sound hurts. An injury to any sense organ results in pain, and it is hard to find any difference of quality in various pains, though there is a great difference in intensity. Hence, the sense of pain does not seem to be another sense power distinct from the five senses; rather it seems to be common to all the senses, when they are malfunctioning, excessively stimulated, or physically injured. The same conclusion can be reached by a consideration of pleasure. For pleasure is experienced by all the senses: there are pleasant sounds, tastes, attractive colors, and so forth. Consequently, sense pleasure seems to be a quality found in all the senses, when they are suitably stimulated by objects in the proper dispositions of harmony with the senses.

From these considerations, we can draw the important conclusion that the sense of touch, philosophically speaking, is a genus of sensation through or in the fleshy tissues of the body, with at least two species: the temperature sense and the pressure sense (and perhaps a third, the pain sense). Similarly, the "tangible," the proper object of touch, is not a single proper object, but rather a genus of proper objects, having as their common characteristic the ability to act upon an organ through or in the fleshy tissues of the body.

Chapter Two mentioned a class of sensations which are concerned with the immediate knowledge of our own body,[5] and are called "propriosensations." It will be seen immediately that this is not a classification by formal object, but rather by material object. If then we ask what powers perform the activities of propriosensation, we would have to say: the senses of touch, inasmuch as they have as their material object the body itself.

*63. The basic sense of an animal

What sense is presupposed by all the others, and itself presupposes no other sense power? Or: what sense does the very simplest

[5] See above, sections 16, 17.

kind of an animal have and need? By induction, an animal is always found to have the sense of touch, while any or all of the other senses may be lacking as distinct senses. For example, some one-celled animals respond to pressure, though they show no signs of responding to light or sound. It is practically impossible to tell whether such animals have a distinct sense of taste or smell.

Without the sense of touch, at least, an animal could not be nourished, for without it it would never know where its food was. Strictly speaking, no more than this would be necessary for the animal to conserve its life. Again, all other senses may be considered as developments from the sense of touch. Hence, touch is the basic sense power.

In some of the very simplest animals there does not seem to be any distinct organ of sense; the whole animal would seem to have the power of touch. It would seem also that in such cases the sense of touch would be very vague and indistinct, and capable of responding also in a very indeterminate fashion to light, heat, odor, and flavor. If this is true, their sense of touch would be different from ours; it would be the power of apprehending an object which acts upon the animal in any one of the ways mentioned, and the formal object of such a sense of touch would then be any object capable of acting upon it.

64. The proper sensible object

Each of the senses, then, has a distinct formal object which it alone knows. These distinct formal objects—color, sound, odor, flavor, tangibility (pressure, temperature, [organic state])—specify and formally determine certain material things to be proper sensible objects. They are the specifying objects, which are the moving causes proportioned to the various powers. Because the proper object is specified to be such by the formal object, it is of itself and immediately known by a single sense power. It is that which gives the particular "modality" or "disparate quality" to our different sensations as they are experienced.

65. Common and incidental sensible objects

In addition to their proper objects, various senses also know extension, shape, and other modifications of quantity. For example, extension is known by the eye inasmuch as it is colored extension; it is known by touch inasmuch as it is hard or warm; it is known by taste inasmuch as flavored objects might be tasted on different parts of the tongue. In these cases, extension is actually known by the sense itself. Therefore, it is in some way an object of the sense. And because extension is known by more than one single sense, it is called a *common* sensible object. A common sensible object may be defined as that which is known, of and in itself, by two or more sense powers, but only mediately known (that is, by means of a proper sensible object). The common sensibles are, in addition to extension (size, magnitude), motion, rest, number, and shape (figure).[6] The fact that there are common sensible objects shows that all the senses properly belong to one univocal genus of sense powers.

In our common everyday language, we not only say, "We see a red (thing)," and, "We see a large red (thing)," but also, "We see a large red apple." Other examples of the same kind of language are "We *see* a friend, the sweetness of honey, the softness of a pillow." What does the verb *see* mean in such a sentence? From the preceding analysis of sensation, it is clear that what we know with our eyes is a colored object with a particular shape; we also know (but not with our eyes) that this is the natural proper shape and color of an apple, or of a man, or of something which is also sweet, and so forth. Such further knowledge involves memory and understanding, as we shall discover later on; it certainly is not attainable through the formal object of the eye. On the other hand, we

---

[6] Obviously, all these common sensibles are sensed as *concrete,* not as abstract. Abstract extension, for example, is not a common sensible; neither is abstract or formal number. Further restrictions must also be made: three-dimensional extension is not a common sensible, and only motion and rest with relation to the visual field are apprehensible by vision. For the further development of this latter point, see the next chapter.

never say that we *see* or touch the molecular constitution of matter, for example. In general, whenever a reasoning process intervenes between the beginning of the sense experience and the attainment of the fuller knowledge, the latter is not said to be sensed. In the same way, whenever a notable delay occurs (for example, a delayed memory), we do not ordinarily say that we sense that which we remember about the sensed object. Therefore, such expressions as "I see the apple" stress the unity and immediacy with which, when I see the round red object, I know it to be an apple. And so we may define an incidental sensible object as "an object of knowledge, joined to some object which is sensed, and apprehended immediately (without delay) by some power other than the external sense."

66. Are the senses active or passive powers?

In considering knowledge in general, we concluded that human powers of knowledge are passive powers. We still must consider in particular whether the senses are correctly thus described, and. in what special way they are passive.

First, are the senses powers of immanent or of transient activity? More concretely, does something happen to an object when I see it? Grammatically, of course, verbs of sensing are transitive verbs, as are all verbs of knowing. But does anything happen to a car when I look at it? Do I in any way change a bird when I listen to it sing? There is of course an interchange of action between the senses as parts of a material body and external objects. For example, when I feel the hardness of a table, the wood pushes on me, but I also push on it; when I feel the coldness of water with my finger, the water cools my finger, and the finger warms the water. Note that in all these and similar instances, the change produced in the object may necessarily be a part of the reciprocal interaction of material things. But whether this change be necessary or not, it is not the act of knowing, nor the being-known. Hence, the act of knowing is essentially the perfection of the knower, and, consequently, it is an immanent activity.

Secondly, to which type of powers of immanent activity do the senses belong, the active or the passive? In other words, does sensation involve being acted on by an object? In all the senses, it is quite easy to see some real action of the object. In sight, the objects act through light rays; in hearing, sound waves affect the ear; odors and tastes involve the chemical action of an object on the organs of smell and taste; pressure and temperature senses are activated by the resistance of the object, or by a heat interchange with it.

Thus, the senses are passive powers of immanent operation.

67. The sensible *species*

Passivity means potency of a particular kind, and to be in potency means to be without an act. In what way, or to what extent, are the senses of themselves in potency? If we are in a perfectly sound-proofed room, we do not hear anything. If our nose is closed off from all contact with odoriferous substances (as when we have a bad cold), we do not smell anything. If we are in a perfectly dark room, and our eyes are at rest (that is, no longer retain any images from previous vision), we do not see anything. This being in potency has a two-fold aspect. The eye, for example, not only needs to be changed from the state of not-seeing (but seeing in potency) to the act of seeing; it also needs to be determined to see this object rather than another, to see red rather than blue. The ear not only needs stimulation; it also needs to be determined to hear A♭ rather than C♯. The same is found to be true by induction in all the senses. The sense needs to receive some determination, specification, and actuation in order to act, and to act in this way rather than that.[7]

[7] In the second footnote to this chapter, reference was made to the non-proper stimulation of a sense organ. To these data can be added such things as the buzzing "sound" that is the accompaniment of certain illnesses. Note that even here, the sense organ is being disturbed by an agent other than itself (the physical energy of a blow, of an electric discharge, of body fever and/or toxic conditions). Therefore, an energy-actuation is not lacking. What seems to be lacking is a formal specification which would be the reason why the buzzing is of this pitch rather than that, and so forth.—For one thing, the sensation itself is frequently fuzzy or obscure; for another, see the suggestion advanced in the same footnote 2.

Now, specification or determination to a particular kind of perfection is a formal perfection. The principle by which the sense power is so specified and actuated that it performs a particular act of sensation is called the sensible *species.*

We have seen that the sensible object acts upon the sense organ. It is by this action that the sensible *species* is produced. Now, action follows from and is proportioned to the being and nature of the agent, and the effect follows upon and is proportioned to the being and nature of the action. Hence, the sensible *species* in some way carries the being and nature of the producing cause.

68. The immateriality of sensation

The sensible object causes a physical, material change in the sense organ: the hand becomes warm, the retina of the eye becomes colored, the ear drum and associated structures vibrate, and so forth. But a thermometer also becomes warm, a photographic plate becomes colored, a microphone vibrates, and yet it would be a perverse flying in the face of evidence to say that these inanimate objects sense. So the material change mentioned cannot be the characteristic of sensation, else all things acted on in this way would sense.

There must be another aspect to the passion produced in the living organ, for the passion caused in the living organ of sense is knowledge-producing, and so is also intentional. Under this intentional aspect, the organ becomes not only physically warm but also representatively warm (and this same double aspect is found in the other senses). The change in the organ is a formal sign of the object acting. It is this intentional aspect of the change produced which is the sensible *species,* and which constitutes the immateriality of sensation.

Another way of expressing the perfection which we have named immateriality is freedom from matter. The "matter" referred to in this expression is not the matter of the moving cause or object of the sensation. For it is perfectly obvious that in transitive causality the matter of the agent remains in the agent and is not in the patient.[8] For example, when a hot object like an electric heater warms another object— for example, a dog—the coil, the reflector, and so forth, remain where and what they were; only the formal perfection (here, the heat energy) is caused by the agent in the patient. The warmed dog does not become iron; it just becomes warm. This is what is meant by the axiom, "Every agent acts according to its form."

In ordinary transitive causality, the formal perfection caused is received in the matter of the patient, to become purely and simply the form and act of that matter. It is thus bound and restricted to being the natural perfection of the matter.

On the other hand, when a material thing acts through a sensible quality upon a living organ of sense, the change produced in that organ is not wholly bound up with the matter of that organ. For example, though the organ of touch is made physically and materially warm by the action of the fire upon it, yet that becoming-warm is a representative or intentional change as well. Now, inasmuch as the heat received in the living organ (under its aspect of being sensible *species*) is a formal sign, *not* of the subject which is changed, but of something else, we have, to this extent, a freedom from the matter of the subject. And exactly the same is to be said of the sensation itself which is consequent upon the sensible *species*.

69. The ﹖ ﹖ect of sensation

In the preceding discussion of the immateriality of sensation, it was necessary also to admit its materiality. This other aspect must now be studied. In the first place, the intentional change which terminates in the sensible *species* is always accompanied by a material change, so much so that there seems to be but one real passion, which has both material and intentional aspects.

---

[8] Note that in this respect, transitive action is quite different from generation or reproduction of a living thing, for generation necessarily involves a sharing of the substance (and so of the matter) of the parent.

In the second place, the act of sensation itself has material attributes. It presents itself to us as being intrinsically temporal. If we want to know whether or not it is affected by quantity, we can discover this from an analysis of its object, for activity is specified by its object. Now, we have seen above that quantity [9] enters in as a common sensible object into the objects of all the external senses.[10] In the objects of sight and touch, extension so evidently is present that it merely needs to be pointed out. In sound, number is present at least in all rhythmic sounds. In flavor, quantity can be found quite clearly in some objects—for example, when we taste a very small piece of candy on one part of the tongue. Other quantitative aspects of taste are not easily distinguished from the quantity apprehended by the sense of touch which is also present in the tongue, so that we cannot say much about them. Finally, the sense of smell does not present quantity very clearly, except that it is localized in one part of the body, and that odors are subject to continuous degrees of intensity. Moreover, the sense of smell is more strikingly subject to fatigue than the other senses.

Now, continuous duration (that is, in time) and quantity are characteristics or properties of material being. Since the sensation is intrinsically modified by quantity and time, it must be a material activity. Consequently, sensation must be the act of a being which possesses matter, and so, concretely, it is the act of an organ.

We can now combine the conclusions reached in this and the preceding sections. Since sensation is under one aspect and to a limited extent immaterial, it is the act of a power; since it is also under another aspect material, it is the act of an organ. Hence, this two-fold aspect of sensation requires us to conclude that it is the act of a two-fold principle: the living, or informed organ.

An organ is a part of the body of a living thing, adapted by its composition and structure for the performance of a specific function. As living, it includes the power by which the vital activity is

[9] As extension, duration, or continuous variation.
[10] Above, sections 62, 65.

performed, but usually the word "organ" by itself abstracts from the power and includes only the material substance with the non-vital accidental modifications like structure, color, and so forth.

*Two sets of facts afford a certain amount of confirmation for the conclusion that sensation is the act of an informed organ. The first is that a violent impression from a sensible quality can be harmful to the sense organ and can even destroy it. For example, a very strong light is painful, and under certain conditions can even injure the eye; similar injuries can be caused by excessively loud sounds, very great pressures, extreme temperatures, and by certain strong flavors, such as acids and alkalis. From this we can conclude to an extremely intimate connection between the intentional and the physical changes produced by the sensible object.

*The second set of facts that tend to confirm the conclusion that sensation is the act of a living organ are those which show the relation between bodily states and sensation. For one thing, as a person ages (which is a condition of the body), the senses become slower in their action and less keen in discerning. Again, bodily conditions such as fever or toxic conditions are able to modify the activity of the senses.

*Finally, the fact that sensations seem to be able to be directly measured [11] in their speed and intensity is at least consistent with the conclusion that they have material as well as immaterial aspects. The reason this is not a confirmatory argument is that the fact is not clear: we are not sure just what the physiologist measures when he measures a nerve impulse.

70. "The sensible object in act is the sense in act"

Material things are by their nature sensible in potency, for they really can be sensed. But when they are in potency, they are not yet united to the sense power of an animal. In order to be so united, there must be an effect of the sensible object upon the

---

[11] The measurement of "intelligence" is rather different; see below, Appendix P.

informed organ. In other words, sensible objects are known by the senses inasmuch as they *appear* to, or act upon the senses. Does this mean that by our senses we know things as they seem to be and not as they are?

We have seen that the action of the sensible object upon the sense is a transitive action and consequently that the change produced is of itself (per se) in the patient or organ and not in the agent or the sensible object. What is the relation of this transitive causality to the being of the object? A thing has its first act when it has its substantial act of existing, and without this the thing *is* not in any way actual. Once a thing is in first act (with its substance, its act of existing, and also its necessary formal accidents), it acts or operates,[12] and this is called its second act. But it cannot be called an efficient cause until an effect is produced. For example, suppose you have a flashlight completely in first act: it exists and has all its necessary formal perfections. As soon as it is completely in first act, it shines (and its act of shining is its second act). Suppose it is shining into a vacuum—does it illuminate anything? Then what must be added in order that this shining light may illuminate something? Does the flashlight need any added change or perfection? Not necessarily; all we need to do is to move an object into the light beam. At once, and without any further change in the flashlight, it begins to illuminate this object, and is now an efficient cause. From this and similar examples, it becomes clear that a change from second act or operation to causality is not necessarily a change in the being which becomes a cause; it may merely be in the patient.

Thus, too, a sensible thing can be completely in the first act of existing, and completely in the second act of operation (for example, a meadow on a sunny day), without being actually sensed, because there happens to be no sensitive organism near by to be affected. The approach of such a living organism makes the sensible object to be actually sensed. This change, however, is not in the

[12] Act or operation necessarily accompanies first act only in beings which lack freedom. The human will is an exception, as we shall see in Chapter X.

sensible object, but in the sensitive patient. Consequently, to be sensible in act is actually to be affecting a sense organ. And this action, being a transitive action, is in the patient. Hence, the sensible object in act is the sense in act.[13]

71. Definitions

Perception is the experienced whole of the unified knowledge-processes concerned with a sensed object.

Sensation (descriptively) is a general term for those acts of knowledge which are immediately and directly of actual color, sound, flavor, odor, and tangible qualities.

Sensation is the knowledge of a material quantified thing inasmuch as this latter is an immediate and direct object of knowledge through its transitive action upon a receptive organ.

A sense is the proximate or immediate principle of sensation. It consists of a sense power, which is its accidental form, and the living organ (bodily structure) which is its matter.

Proper sensible object is the object which of itself and immediately is known by one sense; it is the moving and specifying cause of one kind of sensation.

Common sensible object is an object which is known by two or more senses; it is known in itself and of itself, but only through a proper sensible object.

[13] The principle that the sense in act is the sensible object in act has been understood in another way by some Thomists. It has led them to the theory of an "expressed *species*." According to this explanation, the sense power, by its activity of sensation, produces an internal product (really distinct from the sensation) which is a likeness or image of the material thing which is sensed. The reasons advanced are two. First, it is said that every action must have a term. Secondly, it is said that the explanations of light and heat as given in modern physics, and the facts of sensory illusions and hallucinations, require the presence of an intermediate object in sensation.

These questions are too involved to be gone into here. An analysis of our direct experience of sensing does not reveal the presence in awareness of such an object. And since all we are trying to do is to make an analysis of direct experience, we do not need to go into these questions.

Moreover, this text follows the opinion that such an "expressed *species*" really distinct from the act of sensation is neither in accord with experience nor necessary. The reasons for the opinion held here can be found in the analysis of immanent activity (see above, sections 51 and 66), and in the

Incidental sensible object is an object, not known by the sense but immediately by some other power, and found in one material object together with a proper sensible object that is immediately apprehended.

Sensible species is the proximate inherent formal specifying principle of a sensation.

Organ is a specialized structural part of a living thing which has a particular function or work.

72. Proofs

A. *The proximate subject of sensation is the composite of sense power and organ.*

An operation which has the characteristics both of matter and of a mode of being higher than inanimate matter or merely vegetative life is the act of informed matter.

But: sensation has material attributes (of quantity and duration) and yet is in a way immaterial (intentional).

Therefore: sensation is the act of informed matter.

Therefore: the subject of sensation is the composite of organ as matter and of the sense power as form.

B. *The sense needs a sensible species in order to know.*

That which is indeterminate in potency and passes to a determinate specific act must receive a formal specification.

But: sense in itself is in potency, and passes to a specific determinate act.

Therefore: sense must receive a formal specification in order to act; and this form is called a sensible *species.*

73. Readings

St. Thomas Aquinas, *Summa Theologiae,* I. 78. 3, on the external senses; I. 56. 1; 85. 2; 14. 2, on the two kinds of action; I–II. 22. 2, on the passivity of sense; I. 13. 4 ad 3; 85. 1; 54. 5, on the subject of sensation.

---

meaning of "the sensible object in act" (see also Appendix O, which could be taken up in class discussion at this point).

John Wild, *Introduction to Realistic Philosophy* (New York, Harper, 1948), pp. 413–426.

M. Holloway, "Abstraction from Matter in Human Cognition According to St. Thomas," *The Modern Schoolman*, XXIII (1946), 120–130.

Francis L. Harmon, *Principles of Psychology*, rev. ed. (Milwaukee, Bruce Pub., 1951), pp. 213–331 on the experimental work on external sensation and its conclusions.

E. G. Boring. *Sensation and Perception in the History of Experimental Psychology* (New York, Appleton, 1941). This is a classic study; the author's point of view, while somewhat eclectic, is mostly sensist.

CHAPTER VII

Internal Sensation

74. Perception and sense-perception

Our adult experience ordinarily does not contain sensation as such. Our deliberate cognitive experience either is perceptual (total), containing sensation as a really integrated part, or it is extra-perceptual, as its center recedes more or less from sensation in any one of several different directions. For example, daydreaming, remembering, creative imagination, scientific study, philosophizing, are examples of cognoscitive activity that are either abstracted from, or are at least beyond sensation. The question now before us is: What else is contained in cognoscitive experience besides sensation?

This way of expressing our problem is still much too vague. Specifically, what we want to know is this: Are there acts of sense knowledge in addition to external sensation? In asking this question we grant that there are some elements of knowledge, called "intellectual" or "rational," [1] with which we are not at present concerned. We might put the question this way: In the perceptual knowledge of an adult person, is there an element (or elements) which is neither external sensation nor intellectual knowledge?

A preliminary proof that this is a good question is found from an analysis of animal activity. For animals are empirically different from men, and empirically lack the activities specifically called rational or intellectual (whether this empirical and descriptive

[1] For the present we are neither asserting nor denying an essential difference between intellectual (rational) knowledge and other forms of knowledge. We shall have to inquire into such a distinction at the end of this chapter and the beginning of the next.

123

difference involves an essential difference will be investigated in a later chaptor). Hence, if animals have other elements in their knowledge besides external sensations, these other elements cannot be intellectual (rational), and so must be on a sense level. Now, animals do have such elements in their knowledge. For example, a dog knows that its tail is being stepped on; this implies sensations of pressure and pain, and besides an awareness that these are its own activities. Again, a dog can remember, and remembering is not an external sensation. Hence, there are forms of knowledge on the sense level which are not external sensations, and these forms of knowledge are the matter of the present chapter.

In this investigation we will use partly our own experience, partly an analysis of animal activity. And so a word will be in place on our knowledge of the sensory activity of animals. How do we know that animals sense? And how can we tell anything about the kind of knowledge they have? Part of the basis of this knowledge is an argument from similarity: for we see that animals have sense organs more or less like to ours, and so we suppose that the activity of these organs is similar to our own comparable activity. This argument affords a reasonable supposition. Furthermore, we can argue, and this time with certitude, from an analysis of animal activity. Everything that is necessarily implied by a given activity (for example, a dog's reaction to a piece of meat), can be asserted to be present with certitude.

75. Sensory awareness and the unifying sense [2]

A dog sees, hears, feels, as we judge by its activity. In other words, a dog has sensations. Are they present as such, as distinct activities, or are they parts of a larger and more inclusive total activity? The latter part of this disjunction will have to be accepted, if we can show that there is a unifying factor on the level of sense.

[2] The term "unifying sense" will be used to translate the Latin *sensus communis*. Merely to put this term into its nearest English equivalent (i.e., "common sense") would produce all sorts of confusion, so that the use of the cognate English word would be a very poor procedure.

For example, a dog not only feels hungry, but it knows that *it* is hungry, and so it goes about doing something to satisfy its hunger. In other words, the higher animals are really aware that they sense.

There is a difference between "seeing red" and "being aware of [*or* conscious of] red." [3] The first expression states explicitly only the formal object of the act of the informed sense organ. The second implies that the act of seeing red is somehow itself known, and consequently that the subject which sees is known.

Now, by which of his senses is a dog conscious? and by which sense does a human being experience sensory consciousness? Or could perhaps this awareness be a common sensible, since I know that I am seeing, and that I am hearing, and so on? If we examine the formal objects of the external senses one by one, we find that awareness is not any of them. For example, I see a book, and I know that I see a book. Can I have this latter knowledge by my eye (as proximate principle)? The formal object of sight is actual color. But the sensible *species* and the sensation of color (for example, the intentionally representative aspect of the color-impulse in the optic nerve) are not themselves actually and physically colored, but only intentionally colored. So, by a complete induction of all the kinds of sensation, we can see that awareness is not the act of any of the external senses. It is therefore not a proper sensible.

Nor is awareness a common sensible object. For, as we have seen, the common sensible objects are apprehended by the external senses by means of, or through, proper sensibles. For example, extension is known by the eye inasmuch as it is colored; it is not immediately visible in itself. Is then an act of sensing known through a proper sensible? For example, is an act of sensing, though not a color, still visible inasmuch as it is colored? or audible inasmuch as it is carried by a sound wave? Clearly this is not

[3] As we pointed out above (sections 61 and 74), sensations do not ordinarily occur as separate activities. The present distinction is not experienced, nor descriptive; it is arrived at only by an analysis of formal objects. Hence, it would be incorrect to attempt to verify it in concrete experience.

so. Consequently, awareness is not the act of any of the external senses, either immediately by way of a proper sensible, nor mediately by way of a common sensible object.

Moreover, to know its own act, a sense power would be reflecting on itself; its own activity would have to be its object (or a part of that object). Now, that which is the proximate principle of sensation is the informed organ. Hence, as we have seen, the activity of sensing is under the conditions of matter which are time and quantity. Under these conditions any distinction between agent and patient, subject and object, is also a spatio-temporal distinction. Now, one material thing can act upon *another,* and one part of a material thing can act upon another part of the same thing (for example, I can touch my left hand with the tip of my right index finger). However, it is impossible that one and the same material part of a material thing can act upon itself (for example, I cannot touch the tip of my right index finger with that same finger-tip). As we have seen, the senses are passive powers, and their objects are related to them as agent to patient. Since the sense cannot act upon itself, it cannot know itself. Consequently, the sense power is not reflective. And so none of the external senses can be the principle of sensory consciousness. Consequently, in any and every act by which we are aware of an external object, we can distinguish at least two elements, one of which is the act of a particular external sense, and the other of which is the knowledge of that act. Now, to see, to hear, to touch, and so forth, differ specifically according to their proper and specifying formal objects. Nevertheless, they do agree (generically) inasmuch as all of them are acts of sense powers. Further, the act of a sense power is not reducible to any of the proper objects of any of these powers. Hence, it requires a distinct formal object, and so specifies an activity and a power. This power, which has as its proper object the act of a sense (a sensation as activity [4]) is called the unifying sense.

[4] Which St. Thomas Aquinas calls *intentio sensus;* cf. *Summa Theologiae,* I. 78. 4 ad 2.

Sensation (the sense in act) is the sensible object in act, as we have seen. Because of the formal identity between the sense in act and the sensible in act, the unifying sense apprehends not only the sensation as activity, but simultaneously the sensible object as actually sensed. It is therefore possible to say that the proper object of the unifying sense is the acts of the other sense powers, and the acts of sensible objects, inasmuch as the two acts are identical.

In apprehending the acts of all the external senses, the unifying sense is simultaneously the principle of the first unification of experience. For in grasping sight, hearing, and so forth, as sensations, and concretely as *my* sensations, it grasps them under one common form, as acts of the one subject.

Because the unifying sense is the principle by which we know the acts of all the external senses, and of the external sensibles, it is the power by which we know immediately and concretely (sensibly) that seeing is different from hearing, that "red" is different from "warm." We have such an immediate, direct knowledge, though we may find it difficult if not impossible to express. This knowledge is not a knowledge of what "seeing" is, nor of what "color" is, nor of the nature of the difference between seeing and hearing. It is the same type of knowledge as the sense knowledge we have by our eyes of "red," and of the difference between red and blue.

This concrete and direct experience of the fact that "red" is different from "warm," and "seeing" different from "hearing," is perhaps the nearest we can come to an experiential evidence of the existence of a distinct power called the unifying sense.

*It is on the basis of the unification and discrimination of sensations by the unifying sense that we make such transfers of attributes as "a warm color," "a bright tone," "a rough voice," "a loud color." The intelligent use of language in this way implies first that we have an experience of these qualities in their direct signification, and secondly, that we have a direct way of comparing (and thus of unifying) our various sensations. Thus, "a warm color" means "a color that is to the whole field of visual experience as warm objects are to the field of touch."

*Because the unifying sense is the organ of sensory awareness, it is the power whose activity or partial inactivity is the difference between waking and sleeping. And in like manner, it is the power by which we know concretely and directly that we are awake and really sensing.[5]

*The organ of the unifying sense is somewhere in the brain, though in the present state of our knowledge it is very hard to say just where. But for our present purposes, it is enough to know that it must have an organ, for the sensations which are its object are themselves material inasmuch as they are activities of informed organs.

The unifying sense, then, is the power by which we know that we are actually sensing, and because it is one power which has as its object all our sensations, and the acts of the sensibles as identical with sensation, it is that by which we unify and combine our acts of external sensation into one experience, and compare and contrast these sensations and their objects among themselves.

76. Imagination

It is a matter of immediate experience that we can recall ("live again") at least some of our past experiences, even when the objects that originally caused these experiences are no longer present. Therefore, it is immediately evident that we have a power of retaining sensory experience. This power is called "retentive imagination," or, in our more ordinary language, "memory."[6]

---

[5] On the other hand, the dreamer need not necessarily know that he is dreaming (though in some dreams we know that we are dreaming). Note that we are not here talking about a rational judgment on our experience, but about the concrete and sensory knowledge of waking and dreaming.

[6] Both of these terms "imagination" and "memory" have many meanings. In ordinary language, "imagination" very often means the more or less uninhibited or uncontrolled use of recalled images. In this book, it will be used to designate the "power of retaining and recalling images."

"Memory" has two meanings in ordinary usage. When we say that a stu-

Do we retain and recall objects and experiences by the powers of external sensation? The external senses, as we have seen, are passive powers, and must be moved to their act by objects. This motion or passion, received in the external senses from the object, may last for a short time after the object has stopped influencing the sense; [7] nevertheless, this passion is still due to the object. But both reason and experience tell us that such motions or passions remain only a limited time. Hence, the external senses do not know in the absence of a sensible object.

Is then retentive imagination the same as the unifying sense? The proper object of the unifying sense is the act (activity, operation) of the external sense. What we retain and recall are not only past experiences, but also the objects of those experiences. What we imagine and recall is an image of a sensory object. Hence, because of the differences of their proper objects, imagination and unifying sense are distinct powers.

*Experimental evidence seems to indicate that the retention of visual experiences takes place in one part of the brain, of auditory images in another (visual center, auditory center), and so forth. Moreover, it is found that some people excel in visual imagery, while others have a very weak visual imagery and a good retention-recall of sounds, and so on. Of course, training and experience may have something to do with this, but native ability seems to be involved as well. The most likely explanation is that, since the imagination has a bodily organ consisting of various parts spread throughout the brain, one part (for example, the part for retaining visual images) may be more perfectly developed than the others.

---

dent has a good memory, we usually mean that he *retains* knowledge easily and accurately; in this sense, memory means the same as imagination (in ordinary experience, this retention of images in the imagination is accompanied by a retention of understood meanings in the int.llect). When we say that a maître d'hôtel has a good memory, we usually mean that he can easily and accurately *recognize past* patrons, refer to their previous visits, and so forth.

[7] Technically, this is called an "after-image." The after-*image* does not prove that an expressed *species* existed as distinct from the act of sensing. The after-image occurs because seeing is the operation of a material thing; it is something like the inertia manifested in local motion.

Retentive imagination is a purely sense power, for its proper object, like the objects of the external sense, is a material singular thing, known according to the way in which that thing has acted upon the external organs. This argument is corroborated by the fact that imagination is found in some animals. There seems to be evidence that some animals dream (for example, dogs growl in their sleep). Moreover, some animals go about looking for various objects, as food, that are not present to them in actual sense experience, so that they must retain the images of the objects for which they are looking. Finally, some animals can be trained, so that they must be able to retain past sense experience.

So far we have been speaking of the simple retention and recall of past experiences and their objects, as these occurred to us, with all their observed characteristics. For example, any one of us can recall that yesterday he saw a blue automobile on a particular street at a definite time. Images of this type, which are simply the impressions of past experience, are called memory-images.

But images can be retained and recalled in more complicated ways, even on the sensory level.[8] The images we have may be combinations of several experiences, or they may just be parts of one experience.

*The combination of images can take place in three ways, according to the three laws [9] of the association of images: that is, according to similarity (a *dog* walking, a *dog* barking, a *dog* sleeping); or dissimilarity (black is more noticeable on a white background); or nearness in space or time (the class that you always remember as having been so long, because you were hungry at that time). It is evident that human experience is cumulative, even on the sensory level; that the enrichment of images is not necessarily deliberate, and that in many cases we are not aware of any effort

[8] We are speaking here of the purely spontaneous activity of the imagination, as a sense power acting as such. There is another activity of imagination under the guidance of reason or intellect, which will be discussed below, at the end of this section.

[9] These laws do not express the reasons for the association of the images, nor for their recall, but rather the ways in which association occurs. See also below, section 79.

of active association. Most frequently we are not aware distinctly of all the elements that have entered into a given complex image. Sometimes, in fact, special techniques are necessary to separate and identify these elements. Complex images (image-groups) form of themselves by the simple retention of past images according to similarity, dissimilarity, and nearness.

The same process of retention by repetition also leads to an inverse result: that of the separated, or abstract, or divided image. A useful analogy here is the technique of taking a composite photograph; by exposing a film 1/10th of the proper time on each of ten men, we can obtain a picture in which the dissimilarities of each are blurred and faint, while their similarities are clearly represented. Somewhat in the same way, the repeated impression of similar objects can result in what may be called a general image. In such an image, the variable features are reduced to a state of very weak presentation, while the constant, invariable characteristics stand out, and are as it were separated, abstracted from the others. When this is done by the imagination according to its spontaneous movement, the result is usually a vague and relatively useless image.

There is, however, one important type of image, which arises by this kind of spontaneous abstraction. We have seen that along with their proper sensible objects, the external senses attain directly but only mediately a group of common sensibles. Because, for example, all sensible objects, no matter how much they may differ in all other respects, are quantified (extended), the mere repetition of experience will give us an image of quantity that can be free of most or even all sensible qualities. The same will be true of figure, number, motion, and rest.[10]

A study of the origin of the image of three-dimensional space will clarify this situation, and at the same time lay the foundations

[10] Such abstract images are important, because of the frequency with which they are used in perception, and because of their functions in relation to mathematical sciences. On the perception of the common sensible, see St. Thomas, *In de Memoria et Reminiscentia,* I, lect. 2 (ed. Pirotta, No. 319); *Truth,* XV. 2.

for some later conclusions about perception. Most people who have not reflected very carefully on their experience think that they directly *see* visual objects in three-dimensional space. Experimental psychologists have shown that this is not true, though it is true that we do *perceive* objects under three dimensions. The retina of the eye receives the impression of objects on its curved, two-dimensional surface. Because of the slight difference in the images of the two eyes we know or experience the third dimension of depth. This is true enough, but how does it happen that such a difference of images is spontaneously known as "depth"? [11] (*a*) Space as acquired by touch can be three-dimensional, for our hand can grasp a small object. (*b*) We can walk forward into the visual field. Now, by abstractive repetition, the visual, tactile, and kinesthetic qualities can be separated from the extension which is first known through them. Separated from these qualities, the various extensions become one unified image of three-dimensional space. Through this abstract image, the differences in the visual sensations of right and left eyes are spontaneously translated into a perception of depth. Because visual space is not of itself three-dimensional, we are able to "see" a drawing on a flat surface as a picture of a three-dimensional scene. Such an habitual experience would not be possible, if the depth dimension of perception were immediately seen by the eyes.

Both combinatory and abstractive functions of the imagination

[11] A stereopticon will afford a convincing proof of this. An indirect and negative proof is afforded by the fact that errors and illusions of third-dimensional "vision" are frequent.

Some cases of persons with congenital cataract seem to confirm and illustrate these conclusions. Several patients after operation thought that all the objects they saw were immediately in front of them; one thought they were pressing on his eyes. All the cases that were questioned about the matter showed that they had to *learn* visual depth perception (but they did not have to learn color). Similarly, these patients were not able at once to correlate visual shape with familiar tactile shapes; identification came through abstract shapes. See the data reported in Thomas Verner Moore, *Cognitive Psychology* (Philadelphia, Lippincott, 1939), pp. 313–321. (Father Moore's data do not always distinguish between the ability to recognize shapes and the ability to *name* them; furthermore, what he ascribes to the "synthetic sense" we have ascribed partly to the unifying sense, partly to the imagination.)

can be placed under the guidance of intellect. In this way, useful general images can be formed, for example, of a man, a dog, a four-footed beast. Such general images are often the tools which we use to recognize and classify objects. For example, we see a distant object, and we say "It looks like a man," because of its similarity to the general image of man which we have built up. When images function in this way as intermediaries between our rational understanding and particular sensed objects, they are called "schematic images."

*Much has been written about the "creative imagination." Strictly speaking, this is a shorthand expression for "the creative use of the imagination." When we look at the results of such activity (a great poem, an original painting, a new invention, and so forth), we can see that at least two factors are involved: understanding and imagery. Consequently, "creative imagination" is not a new, distinct power, nor either the imagination or the intellect used alone. There is therefore no present need of going any further into this question.

The external sensation is directly *of* the physical, sensible object, for the object which is known is causally present to the sense that knows it. But in imagination, the case may be quite different. Suppose that I imagine a hippogryph (the fabulous winged horse of the Greek myths). What do I know when I know a hippogryph? This is a real question, because there neither is nor ever was such an animal. Now, knowledge, that is the act of knowing, is essentially related to an object; all knowledge is knowledge of *something*. It is clear that when I imagine a hippogryph, I am not imagining my act of imagining, because, though this latter can be done, it is quite a different sort of knowledge, namely, the remembering of an act of knowledge. Nor am I imagining my impressed *species* in the imagination, for the *species* is not known except by reflection and reasoning; it is not directly imaginable at all. Consequently, the only object I can be said to be imagining is the image itself; in this case, an arbitrarily constructed image which is the hippogryph which I imagine.

And so, in the imagination, we must distinguish (*a*) the power, (*b*) the impressed *species*, (*c*) the operation, the act of imagining, and (*d*) the image itself, which is a kind of substitute, intermediate object. This image, though it is related to real sensible things (in the case of an arbitrary image, at least in its various elements), is still an object, to which my imagining is directly referred. Some authors call the image a *medium in quo*, but it is really very imperfectly like the mental word which we will discuss later. The proper object of the imagination is the sensible thing as absent, and so the image is not a formal sign but rather a substitute or intermediate object.

77. Instinctive activities and the estimative power

Some activities of animals can be accounted for on the basis of powers already discussed or at least mentioned. That an animal should know sensible objects is due to its powers of external sensation: a dog sees red meat by its power of sight. That an animal should take pleasure in, and seek, sensibly pleasant goods, and attempt to avoid sensibly unpleasant things, is explained by its external senses and its sense appetites: a dog tries to get the meat it sees, and takes pleasure in eating it; it tries to escape from a painful beating. That an animal should be aware of its own sensation is due to its unifying sense. That an animal should seek absent goods is due to its imagination of the absent good and its desire for it: a dog goes out hunting for food which it does not see at the moment. Now, if these were the only types of animal activity, we would have a complete explanation of all animal activity in terms of external sensation, the unifying sense, the imagination, and appetite.

But over and above the kinds of activities just mentioned, there are other activities which are characterized negatively by this, that their objects are not pleasurable and yet sought, or are unpleasant and sought, or are not unpleasant and yet avoided. For example, a bird hunts for the straw with which it builds its nest; it will run a great risk of injury and death in protecting its young;

a chicken will run from the shadow of a flying object. Moreover, activities of this kind are positively characterized by (*a*) uniformity within a species, (*b*) specificity, and (*c*) relative independence from learning. By *uniformity* within a species is meant the fact that all members of the species perform these actions in about the same way: all swallows build their nests in the same way, all larvae of the Bombyx moth spin their cocoons in the same way, all honey bees construct the same kind of honeycomb. By *specificity* is meant the fact that different species have characteristic activities and products: crows' nests are quite different from orioles'; some kinds of spiders weave webs, others set traps; some animals know how to stalk their prey by ambush, others pretend to be dead to discourage their enemies from attack. By *independence* from learning is meant the fact that these actions, taken as a total series, need not be learned: [12] a honey bee knows how to build a honeycomb without ever having seen one; a tiny kitten practices pouncing on objects without ever having seen a mouse caught before. In some species, the previous generation is dead before the next is hatched, and yet the young go through the same activities as their progenitors did. Activities which have these three characteristics are called instinctive.[13]

There is no need to multiply examples of instinctive activity, but a very careful analysis is necessary. In an instinctive act there is

[12] The total series is composed of movements of feet, wings, head and so forth, as the case may be, and these actions may have been learned by practice, individually and at different times. Moreover, the total series is guided by knowledge as it is carried out: the bird looks at the straw, the kitten does not close its eyes when it jumps. It is only the total series as a whole that needs to be independent of past experience.

[13] Another way to describe instinctive activity is to say: it is the organized behavior of the whole organism, goal-orientated and conscious. For the first approach to the problem, the more purely descriptive definition given in the text is preferable.

The noun *instinct* is deliberately avoided in this discussion for two reasons. Either "instinct" is taken in a very general sense as "a natural impulse," and then it adds no particular explanation (though it may be useful as a term to contrast with "deliberate" or similar words). Sometimes people think they give an adequate explanation when they say, "This happens by instinct." Such a statement is meaningless, for "instinct" is not a substance.

some knowledge of the sensible qualities of an object, an appetency, and a series of external actions. The end result of the whole series is a necessary good of the individual and/or the species.

The first and most striking point about instinctive activity is the lack of correlation or proportion between sensation and appetency. In one type of instinctive action the animal acts with evident enjoyment concerning a sensible object whose sensory qualities are not directly pleasant to the external senses; for example, a bird picks up straw (without any special regard for its color and without being attracted to very large objects of the same color), a hen eats gravel (without selecting stones of a particular chemical composition by which flavor is determined). In a second type of instinctive action opposite examples are found: chickens are afraid of hawks flying overhead (nothing unpleasant about the sight), the sheep is afraid of the wolf (nothing necessarily unpleasant about the smell). In these cases an object which is not unpleasant to the external senses brings about an action of avoiding or fleeing. In a third type of instinctive action, an unpleasant or even painful object is actually approached instead of being avoided; for example, most animals will fight for their young in spite of pain, many birds will remain on their nests in spite of hunger, and so forth.

Now, as we have seen in general, and will see in greater detail later on, appetite is moved to act only by knowledge. But the knowledge of things that is given by the external senses cannot account for these cases, as we have seen. Consequently, imagination cannot account for them either, since it can do no more than reproduce sense experience or its elements combined or separated. The only other sensory power of knowledge which we have discussed so far, the unifying sense, is likewise unable to perform the necessary task, since it deals directly, not with sensible objects, but with sensations themselves.

To discover what kind of activity is being performed by animals in these cases it is necessary to go back and analyze the data. Appetite, as we shall see, is moved by a known object, in such a way that it tends toward or rests in a known good, and flees from or rejects a known evil. Therefore, in instinctive activity, the animal must actually know that sensible object or action as good for it (or harmful), by a kind of knowledge other than sense, imagination, and unifying sense,[14] and this kind of knowledge must be predetermined specifically, to account for the specific uniformity and necessity of these actions.

Now, good and evil are relative terms, and imply their correlates, appetite or tendency.[15] Therefore, the knowing of an object as good implies knowing both an object and that for which that object is good (in this case, the subject).[16] The individual object in which goodness is to be known (for example, straw), is presented by the external senses or the imagination. The subject (for example, the bird itself) is known by the unifying sense and propriosensation. What is precisely unaccounted for so far is the knowledge of the goodness of the object for the subject. Consequently, an animal must perform an act of knowledge in which it apprehends concretely, here and now, an object [17] as good (or harmful).

The proper object of such an act of knowledge is the sensible

[14] St. Thomas calls the object of this kind of knowledge *intentio insensata*, which might be translated as "a non-sensible object of knowledge."

[15] This merely means that *good* is always "good for some being, or many beings, or all beings." It does not necessarily mean that goodness is arbitrary, or changeable from day to day and from individual to individual, or any of the other derogatory meanings of "relative."

[16] By analyzing the nature of relation we can find out what elements must be present in the knowledge of a relative term. This does not mean that the animal which knows a relative term also knows the relation as such, abstractly, or that it makes a similar analysis. As we shall see, there is no evidence for this latter.

[17] Some psychologists think that they say enough if they say that there are innate neural links between certain sensory areas of the brain and the appetitive-motor areas. But they forget that an appetite is moved by a *known good*, which in the case of instinctive activities is not known either by the senses or the imagination. Now, there may be such neural links; but if there are, they are insufficient. A special power of knowledge is required.—A still more inadequate explanation (in terms of reflex action) would disregard the animal's appetency as well as its knowledge. But disregarding facts does not explain them. (A reflex action is a stereotyped response to isolated stimuli on the part of specific muscles or other delimited structures.)

object as good or harmful (*conveniens et nocivum*). This proper object is distinct from the proper objects of the external senses, of the unifying sense, and of the imagination. Hence, a distinct power is needed to perform this special kind of activity. This power is called the estimative power (because by it the animal estimates an object or situation as good or harmful).

In summary, instinctive activity is concerned with objects and actions that are not sought for their immediately sensible pleasure or avoided for their sensible painfulness, but are sought or avoided for the good of the individual and/or the species; instinctive activity is characterized by uniformity, specificity, and relative independence of experience.

Consequently, the estimative power must be a power that is innately determined to recognize some object-subject groupings as in harmony (as containing the relation of good), and certain others as in conflict (as containing the relation of evil). Only if the estimative power is specifically determined by nature and structure to certain definite and specifically characteristic acts of knowledge can we explain the uniformity, specificity, and perfection of instinctive activity. The estimation (or appreciation of good and evil) can be suited to the advantage of the animal itself or its species in the same way that nature is ordered to an end: by being the kind of power that it is.

*The function of propriosensation as part of the subject's knowledge of itself is to account for periodic and maturation changes in instinctive activity. For example, the bird's desire to pick up straws in the spring involves a change in the bird's own bodily condition at that time of the year, and only when it is in that condition does it estimate that straw is good. Another example: very young chicks instinctively follow almost anything (the mother hen, the farmer, and so forth); after a few days of growth (maturation) this no longer happens; the chicks follow whatever they have become used to following, but no longer take up with new leaders.

*One further consideration will help to understand instinctive activity. There is no need for supposing that an animal knows clearly and precisely the end result of its action from the beginning. All that is necessary is that it wants to do just the next step (for example, to pick up the straw). Once that is done, a new situation is present, and so it has a new, further desire (for example, to carry the straw to its nesting place). This interlocking of action, result, and further action continues till the work is done. The fitting-together of these stages is done, not by the knowledge of the animal, but by the nature of the situation, and the specific character of its innate estimative judgments. In the higher animals, which are capable of more flexibility in their actions, the estimation often leads, not so much to a complete action, as to a kind of readiness to act which is further guided by external sensation and imagination. Such a readiness to act can be called "situation-set" or "goal-set." [18]

78. The memorative power

Animals obviously can be trained to recognize some things as good and others as evil by experience. Therefore, an animal must have the power of retaining past estimations for future recall. This power is called the memorative power.[19] The relation of the memorative power to the estimative is like the relation of the imagination to the external senses.

*In the concluding discussion of the imagination, we argued that the act of the imagination involves an immanent object, really distinct as term from the operation which produces it; this immanent object is called the image. Can a similar argument be used to show that the memorative power also has an immanent object (namely, the concrete relation of good or evil)? [20] Now, the argument that

[18] Section 85, below, on the "intelligence" of animals, may be taken up at this point.

[19] Some authors call this power "memory." To avoid confusion, the power of retaining estimations will always be called the memorative power, and the term "memory" will be kept for the two usages already pointed out.

[20] Many Thomists, following John of St. Thomas, *Cursus Philosophicus Thomisticus*, Part IV, q. 8, a. 4, maintain that imagination, estimative power and memorative power each produces an immanent object. The argument

the image is an immanent object has two parts: (*a*) an appeal to the direct immediate experience of the image; (*b*) an argument that in the cases of absent or nonexistent sensibles (for example, the hippogryph), there must be something which we imagine. In the case of the memorative power, it does not seem that an immanent object is experienced. The retention of past estimations is sufficiently explained by the retention of an impressed *species*. In those cases where we remember the estimations about absent objects, the object known is perhaps the image in the imagination. A difficulty against an immanent object in the memorative power is this, that it is very hard to see how concrete relation (that is, good or evil) can be expressed without its terms—and the terms are evidently in the imagination. Because of the obscurity of this problem, we will leave it unsolved.

79. Memory as recognition

At least some of the higher animals can recognize objects and events of their past experience. Dogs can recognize their masters, friends, enemies, and so forth; birds can recognize their nests, bees their own hive, ants the members of their own colony.

These facts (and many others of the same kind) need explanation. Such recognition as animals do show involves first of all the retention of the images of past experience; secondly, the actual recall of these images at the time of the renewed experience; and thirdly, to some extent at least, a concrete knowledge of the image as of a past experience. Now, the retention of the image, and the knowledge that this image is similar to a present experience, are both functions of the imagination (together with the unifying sense) as a power of retention. The two points that need

---

for the immanent object of the imagination is demonstrative; for the other powers, the arguments are unconvincing, and the position involves great difficulty. As far as St. Thomas is concerned, it would seem that he thinks there is only one image or phantasm with which all three of the powers are concerned, each in its own way; cf. St. Thomas, *Comm. in libros Ethicorum,* Bk. 6, lect. 7 (ed. Pirotta, nos. 1214–15), lect. 9 (nos. 1247–49); Bk. 2, lect. 11 (no. 381).

special consideration are the actual recalling of the image, and the sort of "dating" of the image as past.

When we inquire about the animal's knowledge of the past, we have no right to suppose that it has any abstract knowledge of pastness. All that we can legitimately look for is a concrete awareness of the past. To be able to know the past means to be able in some way to sense time. Now, all material activity is intrinsically temporal; it is a motion with an irreversible direction. All, or at least the higher, animals have an awareness of their own activity. This in itself is not enough; the animal's attention must be able to span some appreciable length of time. But if an animal's imagination is perfect enough so that it can retain a former stage of its activity while it is experiencing a later one, it can have a concrete awareness of time, and so it can as it were "date" some actions. And since experience involves objects, to this extent an animal can recognize a past object, that is, as involved in a past experience.

*We must next ask why a particular image is recalled to actual awareness. Many images are retained; some of them come to awareness at one time, some at another. The reason for this difference cannot lie in the imagination itself, and so we must seek outside the imagination for the efficient cause of the recall, that is, of the motion or passion produced in the imagination.

*This motion can happen in three ways: [21] (1) as the direct result of a present sense experience; (2) or from an estimation or appetency; (3) from some physical (chemical, etc.) excitation of the brain-organ of the imagination. The third is quite easy to understand; it is usually accidental and random (for example, in fever-delirium, drug-induced dreams), except in the case of hormone stimulation, particularly in the working out of the sex cycle (for example, some animals show sexual desire only during a mating season; desire for an absent object presupposes an image; the periodicity of the mating season is partly governed by the endocrine system). It would be a sheer accident if this source of

[21] For a helpful diagram, see below, section 134.

the recalled image had anything to do with recognition. The second way of recalling begins with a present experience, goes on to an estimation (new or recalled), and thereby goes back to a past image. For example: a dog is hungry; this experience arouses the image of food; food recalls the image of the owner who fed it; the master then is estimated to be that from which the food is to be obtained, and consequently the animal seeks him out: the dog has remembered. The first way of recalling an image passes from a present experience to an image which recalls an estimation from which appetite and action follow. For example: a dog sees its master. This present sense experience actuates past images of his goodness, perhaps in feeding it; this past image actuates a retained estimation; hence the dog is pleased at the sight of its master: the dog has remembered.

To sum up. Animals can remember, inasmuch as a present experience can, either directly or by way of an estimation, bring to awareness a retained image of a similar act or object, which by way of estimation leads to appetency and action.

80. Human instinctive activity; the discursive estimative and reminiscence

Man belongs to the genus of animals, and so he has the same essential sensory powers as other animals. In external sensation, man is quite similar to many of them, and inferior to some in keenness and power (to the eagle in sight, the dog in smell and hearing, and so forth). The only evident differences here are differences of degree.

As far as the unifying sense is concerned, there is no reason to suppose any great difference between man and other animals. In imagination, one striking difference of degree is almost immediately evident. Animal imagination is quite limited in retention, and extremely limited in ability to compose and divide images. Human imagination, on the other hand, shows a very great range and suppleness of activity, though there is no evidence for an essentially different kind of act here. In addition to this difference, the human imagination is subject to the guidance and control of the intellect, and in this way it is capable of constructing types of images (for example, symbolic images) that are quite beyond the capacity of brute animals.

Human instinctive activity, however, is radically different from that of animals. Animal instinctive activity is characterized by specificity, uniformity, and relative independence of experience. Human instinctive activity is (a) specific only in being a vague and indeterminate sort of thing: (b) it is very complex and variable, and (c) it is essentially tied in with experience and rational control. In view of these almost opposed characteristics, is it necessary or even possible to speak of human instinctive activities? The answer to this question will be possible only after a brief look at human activity.

While animal instincts are completely predetermined when the organism is adequately developed, and lead to a number of very specific and quite narrowly determined actions, human instincts are few, very generic, and lead only to the most general kind of activity.[22] Studies on very young children show only three types of cases which could be considered instinctive. (1) The infant shows pleasure and delight, not only in being fed and kept in a sensibly pleasant situation, but also in being petted and cared for. The infant's reaction is rather indeterminate: he makes various sounds, and random movements, none of which attain any definite biological results. (2) Infants naturally show fear at sudden noises, and in falling. They react by crying or shrinking, which activities are again not immediately useful. (3) Infants show rage or anger at being restrained. Their reaction is a wild, aimless flinging about of body, arms, and legs.

Secondly, in adult persons, these reactions are enormously modified and developed under the guidance of reason. By "guidance"

[22] The indetermination of these reactions persists even after the development of the central nervous system. A sign of this is the panic reaction of adults, when the sensory impulse escapes from the control of reason. In animals, any imperfection of instinctive response manifested at birth is removed automatically in the growth and development of the organism.

we do not necessarily mean "moderation," nor does "reason" always mean "*right* reason." (1) Thus, men learn what objects to love, and those who are properly mature express their appetency for sensible things in one way (for example, miserliness, or provision for old age), their friendship in another, marital love in still another, and so forth. (2) Men can learn what objects are properly to be feared, and they learn the effective responses which are appropriate to various situations (for example, that an impending threat of war is guarded against by military preparedness, that elevators need safety devices, that job security can be reached through organization). (3) Men learn what things suitably arouse anger, and their reactions are directed to very particularized results (for example, they learn to lead with their left).

Thirdly, these developments and modifications of primitive reactions take place by means of experience. This experience may be partly personal, but it is largely the accumulated experience of the race as contained in the tradition and culture of the group.

Nevertheless, in all the varied patterns of human activity, the three basic movements of sense appetite can be discerned. Human activity is necessarily rooted in the sensory drives for goods and against evils. And, though we can and must learn what objects are good, and what are evil, we cannot learn that the good is to be sought; such knowledge is a *starting point* for action.[23]

The obvious point of this imperfection and indetermination of the estimative power in man is to leave room for (as well as to demand) control by intellect and will. The great perfection of the intellectual nature of man requires that his external activities be not completely innately predetermined—else what would there be for intellect and will to do?

Consequently, all except the basic estimations of man must be arrived at under the guidance and impulse of reason. In other

---

[23] Nor will intellectual knowledge substitute for the necessary innate estimations. (*a*) What about the years when intellect is not yet able to direct action? (*b*) A sensory appetite must be moved by a sensory good; it cannot be moved by an abstract good; cf. below, Chapter XI.

words, all our specific practical estimations are reached by reason-and-estimative power. Now, in such composite activities, the lower or instrumental power shares in the movement of the higher. Hence, this composite activity of estimation manifests the discursive movement of reason. It works through a rationally guided assembling and comparison of experience to definite concrete estimations. For this reason, the estimative power in the man who has the use of reason is called the discursive estimative, or simply, the discursive power.[24]

The variability and discursive movement of human estimation are paralleled in human sense memory, which is sometimes called reminiscence.[25] Man does have the sudden, direct recall and recognition which we called memory, and which we studied in animals. But in many cases, recall for us takes place through a syllogistic (discursive) process. For example, to recall a man's name, we sometimes go from the present sensation (or image) to the first time we met him, and then to the man who introduced him to us, and thus we remember the name.

*81. Attention. The "unconscious"

Consciousness or awareness admits of many degrees of intensity; we could compare it to a ray of light which is bright in its center, and dims off gradually to its circumference. Attention then would be the bright center of awareness. Now, the power of sensory awareness is the unifying sense, and so attention is the act of the unifying sense. But what determines where the center of consciousness is to be?

There are two types of attention: object-directed, and subject-directed. Object-directed attention may be seen, for example, in the act by which we turn to look for the source of a sudden loud noise. In object-directed attention, the center of attention is deter-

[24] The *vis cogitativa* of St. Thomas. For another function of this power, see below, section 97.
[25] This term has a quite different meaning in scientific psychology.

mined by the intensity, or novelty or other attractive characteristic of the sensation or image. Subject-directed attention can be
seen in the dog which unswervingly follows a trail in spite of other
possibly distracting sensations, or in a man who lets nothing dis-
tract him from the work he is doing. It thus appears that the
deciding factor is the interest which the object holds, and in its
correlative appetency. In object-directed attention, it is the sensed
quality of the object which moves the appetite to its act. In subject-
directed attention, it would seem that ordinarily the sense appetite
is moved to its act by an estimation. Therefore, subject-directed
attention is usually a function of the estimative or discursive
powers.

The direct contrary of attention is that which is unconscious.
That is said to be unconscious which (a) is not and cannot be
directly and immediately known, like many of the functions of
nutrition and growth; (b) that which was once conscious, but is
not now, as an image while it is merely retained; (c) that which
is on the fringe or border of attention—in other words, the relatively unconscious; (d) an activity of a knowing power which is
not a conscious act. The first three meanings of "unconscious" are
quite clear and should need no further explanation. What about
the fourth (d)? Can there be an act of a knowing power which
act is not itself known? [26] Or, in other words: can there be acts of
the senses, or the imagination, or the sense appetites which are
not known by the unifying sense? There is some evidence that
in abnormal states such acts are possible. Of course, the person
himself who is supposedly performing them would not know that
he is, but it seems to be possible to discover them by certain very
technical methods of investigation. On the other hand, there
seems to be no ground for thinking that "unconscious" acts are
performed by normally developed, mentally healthy persons.

---

[26] Some writers take the attitude that this question means: "Is there an
unconscious consciousness?" Now, Freudianism contains many mistakes (see
below, Appendix F), but it is not absurdly self-contradictory. We may thus
ask whether such acts may be truly called "knowledge" or not; but we should
at least not so phrase the question as to make it look silly.

82. Reconstruction of sense perception

This chapter began with a question about the existence of sensory elements in perception over and above external sensation. The investigations which followed have shown conclusively that internal sensations enter as elements into perception. Are these elements unified into one perception only by the act of understanding? Or are these elements partly unified by their very nature and order to each other? [27] Clearly, the unifying sense is such a unifying factor for all sense knowledge. Again, estimation is a unifying factor in the order of practical knowledge and action. For this reason, we can legitimately speak of "*sense* perception" as a unified activity, though when we speak of sense perception in man we are making an abstraction from the more closely knit and complex unity that we call "perception" without qualification. Sense perception, therefore, can now be defined as the total, unified awareness minus the meaning (that is, without the acts of intellect and will).[28]

To see how the various powers that we have studied enter into one single act of sense perception, it will be helpful to analyze an example. Suppose I am looking out of my window at a car on the street. My eyes bring me knowledge of a black and shiny extended thing on the background of a dull black extended strip.[29] At the same time I hear a low-pitched pulsing or purring sound. This sight and sound are unified as one act of mine through the unifying sense, by which I am aware of these acts as my sensations. To this immediate sensory data, memory-images are added by the

[27] Cf. Chapter II, section 16. Experimentally, it can be said that "all our percepts interact with each other" (that is, are not independent fragments), and that "perceptual organization will always be as 'good' [that is, complete and unified] as prevailing conditions allow." Cf. Francis L. Harmon, *Principles of Psychology*, rev. ed. (Milwaukee, Bruce Pub., 1951), p. 176.

[28] To prevent misunderstanding, let it be insisted again that we do not mean that sense perception exists as a separate act in man.

[29] Gestalt psychology rightly insists that even the simplest sense datum, taken abstractly, still has some order in itself, notably (especially in vision) the structure of figure and (back-) ground.

imagination, by means of which I perceive the sound as being the noise of the car's motor, I guess the distance between me and the car, I remember the pleasure of driving, and so forth. This whole experience is localized outside me and in a set of spatial relations, through the abstractive image of space [30] which is my normal frame of reference for sense experience. Through the discursive estimative, I know this shaped-colored-sounding-in space as an object of sense knowledge, and as an object concerning which I can act, either externally, for example, by using it, or internally, for example, by coming to understand it.

It is well to remember that the progressive stages in the reconstruction of the complexity of perception are not *now* separate stages. They are known by me here and now as stages by reflection and analysis. Nor are the elements of this perception gathered together by any deliberate activity or even by any conscious process. Rather, what is given in perception is the whole with which we began our consideration. The parts of that whole are not distinct as parts before reflection. At one time, of course, these parts were given more or less separately; the combining of these parts was partly conscious (though not necessarily deliberate), partly spontaneous (as in the super-posing of the image of space around all sensible objects). In the adult, all these things are in the state of custom or habit, and therefore perception easily and smoothly presents itself as a unified experience.

Notice the important parts played by the imagination and the discursive power in the unification of the object of sense perception. The first step is the uniting of the color and the sound around one area in space. How do I know that that which I see is making the noise? Partly because I remember (that is, retain in my imagination) that a sound heard equally by both ears is either in front or back of me, but not to one side; partly because I remember hav-

---

[30] See above, section 76, on the abstract image; not that three-dimensional space is more abstract than two-dimensional extension, but that three-dimensional space cannot be directly seen, and therefore can enter into a perception only by way of an abstraction from various sense experiences.

ing been very close to cars, and so traced the particular noise to them. Because I remember this, I perceive the sound as coming from the same point in space at which the color and shape are located. To do this, I must have a common frame of spatial reference, which is neither auditory space nor visual space, but an abstract image in which neither of the qualities is actually present, so that I can identify the auditory and visual experience within it. Moreover, pure visual space is directly only two-dimensional, as we have seen; yet I perceive the automobile as not only having length and height, but also as being at a distance from me. I do this by locating, through various remembered signs (such as that of the size as seen), my visual experience on a "projected" three-dimensional continuum. The second step is the addition, by way of memory, of the smoothness and hardness of the car's surface, and of other remembered sensible qualities which enrich the present experience.[31] A third step is the perception of the car as a distinct object. It is very difficult to realize how this takes place on the sensory level, because of the fusion of intellectual elements into our adult perception. But if we proceed analytically, we can discover how and in what way sense perception is of a distinct object. At the stage of external sensation, the sensed quality is not explicitly sensed as in a distinct object (though it is not therefore sensed as a mere subjective modification). It is distinct merely as an object of knowledge as far as explicit knowledge is concerned. Nor does the imagination necessarily add an explicit objectification, except by way of adding the memory that the automobile can drive away, or something similar. As far as direct knowledge is concerned, the first part of perception in which, by analysis, we find the explicit knowledge of distinction between subject and object, is at the practical level of action and passion. This almost always involves a prior estimation. For I act concerning things inasmuch as they are good or bad for me. And in the concrete apprehension of an object as good, I obtain implicitly the two

[31] See above, Chapter VI, section 65, on incidental sensible objects.

terms in relation, that is to say, as opposed to each other in being subject and term of this relation. Hence, every sense perception of a thing as a distinct object involves also an act of the estimative power.

83. Definitions

Internal sense is a sense power which deals with an object already known by one or more of the external senses.

The unifying sense is the power of sensory awareness, which unites the various sensations, and thus unites, compares, and contrasts the proper objects of all the senses. Its proper object is sensation: as an activity and as sensed object.

Imagination is the power of retaining and recalling the images of sensible experience.

Memory (1) is the retention and recall of the past sensible experience as it was. In this meaning of the word, memory is one of the functions of the imagination.

Memory (2) is the retention, recall, and recognition of past experience concretely as past. This is a composite function of imagination and the estimative (or discursive) and memorative powers.

Instinctive activity is such animal activity as is characterized by specific uniformity, invariability, and relative independence of experience, and which leads to the good of the individual and/or the species.

Estimative power is the innately determined power of apprehending objects, concretely and directly, as suitable (or harmful) for the individual and/or the species.

Memorative power is the power of retaining estimations.

The discursive (estimative) power is the human estimative when, under the control of reason, it acts in a discursive (syllogistic) way, that is, by combining and comparing individual experiences.

Reminiscence is the memory (2) when, under the guidance of reason, it attains the past as past.

84. Proofs

There are as many internal senses as there are different proper objects (in addition to those of the external senses) to be found in an analysis of sense perception, and as are necessary for the life of a perfect (highly developed) animal.

But: by an analysis we find four proper objects, which are needed for perfect animals:

(a) sensation as an activity and as sensed object—which is needed to explain the animal's awareness of itself, and its ability to compare and contrast sensations and their objects.

(b) the sensible object retained—because animals act concerning objects which they experienced in the past, and which are not actually present to external sensation.

(c) sensory good (and evil)—because animals act, not only through present pleasure and pain, but also for objects which are useful for the good of the individual and/or the species.

(d) sensory good (and evil) retained—because animals can to some extent at least learn, through the experience of pleasure and pain, to go beyond their natural store of innate estimative judgments.

Therefore: there are four internal senses: (a) the unifying sense, (b) imagination, (c) estimative, and (d) memorative powers.

85. Excursus: the nature of brute sensibility

In the beginning of this chapter it was noted that though we have no direct experience of the inner or conscious activities of brute animals, we can arrive at some knowledge of these activities by arguing from similarity of structure, and, more importantly, by an analysis of their external behavior.[32] By this latter argument we can discover that animals have sensation, even when their sense

[32] Cf. above, section 74.

organs are different from ours (for example, the antennae of certain insects are organs of touch), or not readily discoverable (as the organ of hearing in snakes).

Because of the very special way in which we know the conscious activities of brute animals, we are justified in asserting only as much about them as a reasonable or necessary argument conveys to us. The value of this investigation will be twofold: practically, it will protect us against the misleading statements of some who wish to prove that man is *only* an animal; speculatively, it will, by contrast, make clearer the special rational nature of man. The discussion will have three parts: first, a consideration of the arguments by which some writers wish to prove that a brute animal has more abilities than those which we have assigned to it in this chapter; second, an argument to prove that animals have only sensory cognition; third, a brief summary of the nature of brute sensibility.

The arguments by which some wish to prove that animals have intellect or reason can be summarized under the following heads.

(1) It is said that finality (or purposiveness) of activity proves intellect. It does indeed—but where is the intellect which is implied by finality? It is either in the nature which acts purposively, or in the author of nature. For even inanimate things act for an end (because their activity is determinate), and yet they do not possess an intellect. In order that purposive action (finality) be an adequate criterion of the presence of intellect, the purpose of the action must be preconceived by the being which acts. And this precisely is what is to be proved, not assumed as a medium of proof.

(2) Animal activity, even when it is instinctive, is guided by cognition. For example, a crow looks for twigs with which it builds its nest; it does not just pick up anything which can be picked up, like pebbles. This proves that such activity is not a mere reflex [33]

---

[33] A reflex is an automatic, of itself unconscious, reaction of a muscle or organ to a stimulus; the stimulus proceeds from receptor to ganglion to motor nerve without necessarily going through the brain. This is at least the ordi-

or a chain of reflexes. Instinctive activity is usually begun by an act of knowledge, and is to a certain extent guided by knowledge so that there may even be a kind of adaptation, at least within the limits of sensible similarity. But all the facts which are brought up in this connection can adequately be explained by the external senses, the unifying sense, imagination, estimative power, and appetite.

(3) Animals learn. First of all, as we shall see,[34] learning is of many different kinds. The evidence here is precisely the kind of evidence that led us to affirm the existence, in animals that learn, of imagination and memorative power. Secondly, the capability that an animal has of learning a complicated series of external actions does not prove that the animal *understands* what it is doing, even though the experimenter or trainer may understand. Nothing that would require a power beyond the sensory level has yet been adduced.

(4) Animals perceive relations and use tools. Certainly animals perceive that which is related; in fact, the perception of objects as good and evil, suitable and harmful (which involve relations), is the reason why we concluded to the existence in animals of an estimative power. However, these relations are apprehended only concretely (therefore, not formally as such), and only concerning sensible objects.

Further, animals with a sufficiently complex imagination have the abstract image of space, and therefore the concrete knowledge of spatial relations within that framework.[35] The "insight" that some experimentalists claim to have discovered in the actions of some monkeys clearly involves the knowledge that a certain set of spatial relations concretely obtains, and can be useful. The sudden improvement in the animals' activity can be explained

---

nary physiological explanation. Examples: sneezing, the dilation and contraction of the iris.

[34] See below, Chapter XII.

[35] For the experimental evidence that spatial perception occurs in two forms, one of which is purely imaginative, see Charles Spearman and Ll. Wynn Jones, *Human Ability* (London, Macmillan, 1950), pp. 70–71.

by the abstract image of space and the knowledge by the estimative power.

Finally, all the tools which animals use involve spatial relations, and/or experienced, concrete suitability. For example, they use tools to reach an object which is placed beyond the reach of their arms; or again, they can be taught to use tokens ("money") to obtain their food. These activities can be explained by imagination, estimative, and memorative powers. There is no evidence that animals use tools which are not merely spatio-temporal, nor that they understand the relation of means to end, or grasp the nature of relation or of space.

(5) Animals are said to be intelligent. With the late Professor Spearman,[36] we are inclined to say that the term "intelligence" is scientifically useless. It means any or all of the four types of activity just mentioned, and/or intellectual ability, strictly so called. An argument which rests on the use of an equivocal term is simply useless.

From these considerations we can conclude that there is no positive evidence that animals have the power of intellect. We can reach the same conclusion by another consideration of instinctive activity. For instinctive activity is consistently, and over centuries of time, without improvement or progress. Moreover, in some unusual cases, instinctive actions fail of their purpose, or are even harmful. In such cases we can clearly see that the purposiveness is innately determined, and not preconceived by the animal. For example, a setting hen will try to hatch china eggs as well as real ones; a bird will continue trying to fly through a window pane; a wild duck, with its wings clipped, will exhaust itself trying to fly at the time of migration. Finally, "brilliant" achievements in one line are joined with extremely "stupid" activity in another: for example, a bee builds an astonishingly perfect hexagonal honeycomb, and will continue to pour honey into it even if the bottom is knocked out; birds collect food for their young even when they have seen them killed.

[36] *Ibid.*, p. 67.

Hence, there is no proof that animals possess an intellect, and some very strong indications that they do not possess such a power. Activities which would be unequivocal proofs for intellect, such that they could not be interpreted in any other way, are: the use of a real language; [37] the invention of tools of a kind which involve more than merely spatial relations; learning by independent originality; appreciation of beauty, morality, and so forth; freedom of choice; culture, and a progress in it. None of these are had by animals; in some instances (freedom as contrasted with uniformity and specificity of response), their activities are directly contrary to activities which imply the possession of intellect.

To sum up this section, we conclude that there is no proof that animals possess an intellect, and there is positive proof that they do not.

The whole direction of animal sensibility is practical. Appetite, of course, is ordered to action. In animals, even their knowledge is ordained to action. They have nothing like speculative knowledge, no contemplation of the beautiful. The conscious life of an animal is a continuous stream of sense experience (sights, sounds, and so forth), in which the only *objects* that stand out distinctly are the objects of action and being-acted-on. Thus, the final organization and peak of animal sensibility is the estimative power, which is a power of practical knowledge.

86. Readings

St. Thomas Aquinas, *Summa Theologiae*, I. 78. 4, the classic summary of his teaching on the internal senses; *Truth*, 15. 2; *Summa Theologiae*, I–II. 11. 2; 12. 5; 13. 2; 17. 2, a series of texts on brute sensibility, and the difference between man and brute.

L. Bernard, *Instincts, A Study in Social Psychology* (New York, Holt,

[37] Not every use of words constitutes a real language. A phonograph or radio produces articulated sounds; they have no real language, for they do not understand the sounds they make. The use which animals make of articulated sounds (parrots "talk"; dogs and other animals "obey commands"), can be explained by experience and association (imagination and memorative power). Even in man, one element of language is non-intellectual; see Spearman and Jones, *op. cit.*, on the "verbal factor."

1924). This is a comprehensive review of the varied concepts among psychologists and others, with the conclusion that there are no instincts.

Raymond Cattell, "The Discovery of Ergic Structures in Man in Terms of Common Attitudes," *Journal of Abnormal and Social Psychology*, XLV (October, 1950), 598–618. A report on the first application of factor analysis to "instinctive activity," and a conclusion that certain "structures" are to be found in human activity.

Julian Péghaire, C.S.Sp., "A Forgotten Sense, the Cogitative, according to St. Thomas Aquinas," *The Modern Schoolman*, XX (1943), 123–140, 210–229. An excellent article, which however occasionally tends to exaggerate its importance, and at times to leave the impression that it is in some way a power of speculative knowledge.

Eric Wasmann, S.J., *Instinct and Intelligence in the Animal Kingdom* (St. Louis, Herder, 1903). A classic account of instinctive activities, and a rejection of "the intelligence of the brute."

Mark Gaffney, S.J., *The Psychology of the Interior Sense* (St. Louis, Herder, 1942). Contains many fine examples, but is somewhat marred by the anecdotal method.

Dom Thomas Verner Moore, O.S.B., "A Scholastic Theory of Perception," *The New Scholasticism*, VII (1933), 222–238. An interesting rapprochement to Gestalt psychology. The author wishes to assign the perception of wholes to the common sense, whereas in fact, the apprehension of wholes is done partly by external sense, largely by imagination, and partly by the estimative power.

Cornelio Fabro, "Knowledge and Perception," *The New Scholasticism*, XII (1938), 315–343. A useful article. But it intellectualizes the functions of the discursive estimative, and its historical interpretation of St. Thomas by Averroes is false.

G. P. Klubertanz, S.J., "The Unity of Human Operation," *The Modern Schoolman*, XXVII (1950), 75–108. A textual study on composite operation, which doctrine is used in this and several of the following units.

Robert S. Woodworth, *Psychological Issues* (New York, Columbia Univ. Press, 1939), pp. 149–162, "Situation-and-goal Set" [taken from the *American Journal of Psychology*, L (1937), 130–140], shows the function of a "set" (anticipatory attitude) in perception; pp. 179, "How the psychological mechanism works" [taken from *Psychotherapy*, I (1909), 68–84], deals with the different degrees of memory possessed by various animals, and shows that no animal gains an insight into the conditions of success.

J. J. Gibson, *Psychological Bulletin*, XXXVIII (1941), 781–817. This is a critical review of the concept of "set."

John Wild, *Introduction to Realistic Philosophy* (New York, Harper, 1948), pp. 426–430.

Leland B. Alford, "Cerebral Localization; Outline of a Revision," *Journal of Nervous and Mental Diseases* Monograph No. 77 (1948).

Hubert Gruender, S.J., *Experimental Psychology* (Milwaukee, Bruce Pub., 1932), pp. 286–300; 245–252. The former passage presents a theory of instinctive action called the "sensitive-impulse theory," which stresses the part played by appetency; the latter discusses the reflex-theory of instinct.

Vincent V. Herr, S.J., "Gestalt Psychology, Empirical or Rational," *Essays in Modern Scholasticism*, Anton C. Pegis, ed. (Westminster, Maryland, Newman, 1944), pp. 222–243. Discusses the arguments and evidences offered by Gestaltists.

Edmund J. Ryan, C.Pp.S., *The Role of the Sensus Communis in the Philosophy of St. Thomas Aquinas* (Carthagena, Ohio, Messenger Press, 1951). A textual study of St. Thomas's doctrine of the *sensus communis*, and a discussion of the experimental data relating to it.

Dom Thomas Verner Moore, O.S.B. *The Driving Forces of Human Nature* (New York, Grune and Stratton, 1948), pp. 231–42. A discussion of human instinctive activity under the terms "impulse" and "impulsive activity," showing that there are no instincts in man like those of animals, and that reflexes cannot account for this activity.

Francis L. Harmon, *Principles of Psychology*, rev. ed. (Milwaukee, Bruce Pub., 1951), pp. 148, 149–50, 176, 179–93.

G. P. Klubertanz, S.J., *The Discursive Power* (Saint Louis, The Modern Schoolman*, 1952); Chs. V to IX contain a detailed textual analysis of St. Thomas's doctrine on the *vis cogitativa*.

N. Tinbergen, *The Study of Instinct* (New York, Oxford Univ. Press, 1951).

CHAPTER VIII

The Intellect

87. The choice of a point of departure

Between men and the other animals there are a number of obvious differences, as we have already noted. Important among human traits and activities are language, art, culture, the invention of tools, freedom, social organization, and law. It now becomes necessary to see what sort of differences these are, and what they can tell us about the nature of man. In a textbook it is impossible to make a full analysis of each one of these differences; we must rather select one of them for special investigation, and more or less neglect the others, interesting and helpful though they might be.

Language, taken in a wide sense to include all external (usually arbitrary) signs that carry a meaning, seems to be peculiarly suited for our purpose. It is something with which we are familiar, and yet something which permits a very rigorous and careful investigation. Perhaps we are so used to language that its importance escapes us. Here we can be helped very much by recalling certain privileged cases, those of persons deaf and blind from their birth, or so afflicted before the awakening of their understanding. In *The Story of My Life*,[1] Helen Keller (who lost sight and hearing at the age of nineteen months), tells of the dark,

---

[1] (New York, Grosset, 1904), pp. 1–24.
Compare also the quite similar case of Ludivine Lachance in Canada; see Corinne Rocheleau, *Hors de sa prison*, 2nd ed. (Montréal, Thérien Frères, 1928). The experience of Miss Lachance is instructive because of her great physical weakness, and because there is an explicit treatment of the way in which she attained knowledge of spiritual realities: the idea of charity, her soul, God.

cramped, and fearful world in which her reason awoke. Her body
grew, like that of any other child; but her mind remained scarcely
developed. Other children who have been similarly afflicted frequently impress observers by their almost animal-like behavior.
But into Miss Keller's dark and silent world there came the patient
influence of a teacher. At first even her constant solicitude and
attention made little difference. Then came the day when Miss
Keller learned her first "word," a manual sign for water, and *recognized this as a sign.* By this, the possibility of communication was
opened up, and by it also the power to grow in understanding.
From then on, her mental growth was rapid, until as an adult she
reached a very high level of learning and culture. The turning
point in her case was the acquiring of language as a medium of
expression and of attaining knowledge and thought.

88. The analysis of language

An external sign consists in a bodily movement (gesture or
sound, and secondarily in the more or less arbitrarily chosen signs
of bodily movement: printing, writing, to some extent art, and
so forth), which designates something other than itself, and simultaneously indicates the consciousness which the maker of the sign
has of the object. The sign doubles for the object, and in many
ways can replace it. Thus it represents an object distinct from itself.
It unites consciousness and object, yet without confusing them.

What makes a language to be what it is, is not merely the performance of certain activities which in fact represent other objects, but, with that use, the recognition that the movements (or
their signs) are formally signs. Language begins with mimicry
(of sounds by sounds, of shapes and movements by gesture and
movement). There seems to be a natural mimicry that is based
on things themselves and the nature and functions of our body
(for example, the beckoning finger is understood by everyone).
But mimicry does not become language till it is conscious mimicry,
and is used for purposes other than itself, a purpose which is chosen
and expressed in the sign itself.

It is this recognition of the sign as sign that differentiates human language from the cries and movements of animals, and the mechanically acquired "speech" of parrots. For these cries are purely natural signs, limited to a definite object or situation (generally to an emotional state, or to purely biological needs). A proof of this can be seen in the fact that animals do not extend the field of representation of these signs. For its part, the acquired speech of birds shows no initiative on their part; they can only imitate. Hence, it is peculiar to man that he makes use of signs, in the knowledge that they are signs.[2]

The initiative, which demonstrates the mastery over the sign as such, is demonstrated most clearly in the construction of a new sign, or in the extension of the field of representation of a sign already in existence. Examples of this are to be found in ordinary experience—not merely in the original invention of the various languages that are or have been spoken. Even young children, not necessarily budding geniuses, invent languages of their own, sometimes surprisingly elaborate ones. Another important evidence is the use of slang terms and of figures of speech. Metaphor particularly shows the disengagement of the sensible sign from its original material limitation, and even from what might have been its natural function as mimicry or imitation. Along the same lines, the fact that language can be cultivated for itself, for the manifold enrichment of its meaning, as in poetry, again demonstrates the disengagement from material limitation which the bodily movement undergoes in becoming language.

Under the various particular languages which men have formed for themselves, there is a universal characteristic of all languages. This trait is that a material element (originally a movement of the body, then its sign) is charged with a meaning and intention, so that movement becomes expression.

[2] That is why some modern writers speak of man as a "symbol-forming animal."

What the higher animals evidently lack is not the material means, nor the organs, but the power to use them. In other words, it is not that they do not have the elemental materials for constructing a language, but that they have nothing to say.

What are the characteristics of the act which generates language? As movement, or the representation of movement, the sign is extended in space and time. In order to understand a sign it is necessary to grasp it as a whole in its vital or in its meaningful context. For example, to make a statement, and to arrange the words properly to form a sentence, it is necessary to have the whole meaning of the sentence in mind throughout each of its parts. Therefore, the act which generates language is a unifying, synthesizing act, which exists as a whole throughout an entire series of material activities. Throughout the sentence, the understanding of the meaning must be identical and total. The act which dominates the successive must itself be without succession. The kind of unity that the sentence (or other complete expression of thought) has as a meaningful sign involves a unifying act which is extended neither in space nor in time. But that which is not extended in space or time is in no sense material.[3] Therefore, the very use of true or formal language involves a wholly immaterial, spiritual act of understanding. And, since a power is known by its activity, the act of understanding is the activity of a spiritual power, which is called the intellect.[4]

89. Confirmatory proofs for the existence and nature of the intellect

Another analysis of language selects for consideration words which are universal (for example, *man, running, gold, hydrogen*), or abstract (*humanity, causality, force, wave motion*), or which refer to negatively or positively immaterial[5] realities (examples

[3] In contrast to the immateriality of sensation, or of knowledge in general, which are immaterial only under one aspect; cf. above, sections 39 and 68.

[4] Synonyms for the term "intellect" are "understanding" and "reason," though the three terms have their own proper connotations. The term "intelligence" will not be used here as a synonym for "intellect"; cf. Chapter VII, section 85 (5).

[5] By a "negatively immaterial" reality is meant something which is found in our experience as material, but whose perfection does not necessarily and intrinsically involve matter; theoretically, at least, it can be found without matter. By a "positively immaterial" reality is meant a perfection which cannot be found in a material substrate.

of the first: *substance, activity, power;* of the second: *God, angels*). Obviously these words themselves (as printed signs, or sounds, and so forth) are not universal, nor abstract, nor immaterial. The adjectives refer to the function and meaning of these words. This meaning is not carried by the external senses, whose knowledge is particular, concrete, and material ("this red thing"). Nor is it carried by any knowledge of the internal senses, or any combination of it (images or association of images). Images are particular, of a determinate color, size, and so forth; frequently sketchy and vague, fluctuating, variable (from person to person for the same object, in the same person from time to time). Even the "abstract" and "general" images spoken of in the preceding chapter are abstract and general in function and meaning rather than in themselves; in any case, they are always of matter or material objects. Therefore, the act by which we know the meanings of words—that is, intellectual knowledge—must be abstract, not particularized, and immaterial.

Now (*a*) quantity, temporality, (*b*) concretion in a subject, and (*c*) materiality are necessary attributes of matter and material things, and of their activities. If an activity has attributes directly opposed to these, it must be said to be a non-material or immaterial activity. But an activity is a real being, and a real being which is non-material (does not have just a non-material aspect) is spiritual. Hence, the activity of understanding is spiritual.

Again, intellectual knowledge not only includes terms, but judgments and reasoning. But judgment and reasoning are not the functions of any external nor internal sense, nor of any variation or complication of their functions. This will become quite evident if the formal objects of the various sense powers are considered. And even though the composite activity of these powers in sense perception is elaborate, subtle, and capable of great variation, there is nothing in it which could be confused with judgment (affirmation, negation) or reasoning. Therefore, intellectual activity is distinct and different from any sense knowledge.

The same conclusion can be reached by the consideration of

another characteristic of all sense knowledge. If we compare the eye with the organs of heat and cold, we see a noteworthy difference. The eye is acted upon through a series of colorless media (air, the lens, and so forth), the organs of heat and cold through the medium of the skin which has a temperature of its own. The eye, having no actual color in itself, can respond to and discriminate all the colors within its range of power. The organs of heat and cold, having a temperature of their own, report the temperature only of those bodies whose temperature differs from that of the skin. Furthermore, if a colored glass (for example, a filter) is put into the visual process, some colors can no longer be seen. So, too, the sense of hearing offers a good illustration. The organ of hearing contains no actual sound. In addition, the diaphragm of the ear is aperiodic; if it had a period of its own, we could hear only one, or very few sounds. Thus, by induction, we arrive at this general principle: Any power of knowledge which is the form of an organ attains to material qualities in the proportion in which neither it itself nor its organ has these qualities.[6]

The human intellect knows (at least in an inchoative and general way), not only what it means to be affected by a color, but what a color is; not only what it means to be warmer or colder, but what heat is; not just what it means to be hard or soft, light or heavy, but what resistance, weight, and the like mean. It can therefore have none of these material qualities. Furthermore, the human intellect knows what matter is, and what (at least in general) material things are (if this sounds too ambitious, let us say that the human intellect can speculate about and be aware of material things). Therefore, the human intellect can neither be affected by material qualities nor be of a material nature, nor possess a material organ; in other words, it is spiritual.

In sum, therefore, a power of knowing whose activity is spiritual must itself be spiritual in its being and nature. In contrast to the sense powers, which are the accidental forms of sense organs,[7]

[6] This paragraph presents and exemplifies St. Thomas Aquinas' principle: *"Intus apparens exterius prohibet."*

[7] See above, Chapter VI, section 69.

the intellect is an abstract or separated principle of operation.[8]

Another proof for the spirituality of the intellect will be found below, section 93D.

90. The object of intellect (I) *in itself*

In order to find the nature of a power, we must examine the acts which man performs by means of that power. It is *man*, the agent, who acts by means of a power; the power is only a principle *by which* an action is performed. But for the sake of more convenient expression, we will say, for example, "The intellect knows . . . ," using this as a shorthand phrase for the more awkward "Man by his intellect knows. . . ."

Every power is by its nature the power to perform a particular kind of act, and the kind of act is determined (specified) by its object. Consequently, to pass from a description of intellectual activity to an analysis of the nature of the intellect, we must discover the material and proper objects of understanding. Here a special problem arises. For, though the intellect is by its nature separated, it naturally acts together with, and in relation to, some sensory activity. Hence, a complete consideration of the proper object of the intellect must include two points of view: (1) the proper object of the intellect considered as a power of knowing in itself, and (2) as a power of the man who knows, in relation to his sensory activity. At present we will discuss the intellect only from the first point of view, leaving to a later section the discussion of the intellect in relation to sensory activity,[9] after we have seen the reasons why there is such a double point of view.

The material object of the intellect is most easily found by listing the various objects which men can know intellectually, or speculate about, or even ask questions about. Men have known or thought about things within sense experience, and things which are beyond; material things, and spiritual things like God or pure

---

[8] This is just a preliminary statement, giving one side of a picture that needs completion by other statements; see below, especially sections 91 and 96.

[9] See below, section 96.

spirits; creatures and their Creator; real beings and intentional beings; beings which actually exist, and those of fiction and imagination; substances and formal accidents and activities. Is there any common reality in all these things by reason of which we can designate them by a single term? There is nothing univocally common,[10] for univocation applies only to things which have the same nature (generically or specifically) in exactly the same way. Yet the real order presents them as alike in some way, as having in some way a common make-up. This community is not a community of formal identity, but of analogy.[11] Now, that which is, according to any manner of existing, is a being.[12] Consequently, the material object of the intellect is all beings.

The proper object of the intellect can most easily be approached negatively, by answering the question, What is that which is strictly and from every point of view completely unintelligible? Surely, the completely unintelligible is the self-contradictory. Now, the self-contradictory, and only that, is absolutely impossible—it cannot be, it is non-being absolutely. Hence, every thing which at least can be, is, to that extent, able to be understood. Hence the proper object of the intellect is being.

Positively, we can argue to the proper object of the intellect by analyzing intellectual knowledge. No matter what thing we know, nor what we know about it, or are seeking to know about it, we can always find, as the basic element of our knowledge (or our question) the fact that what we are thinking of, in some way, *is*. But that which is basic or first [13] in any form of knowledge is the

[10] By "univocally common" is meant "universal in the strict sense." That is universal in the strict sense which is capable of realization in exactly the same way in each of many individuals. Cf. any textbook of logic, for example, Andrew H. Bachhuber, S.J., *Logic* (St. Louis, St. Louis Univ. Bookstore, 1952), pp. 19, 192–93.

[11] The community of analogy is found wherever a perfection is present in many individuals, not in the same way, but in different ways.

[12] Being is properly *that which is*, or, *that which has an act of existing*. The full consideration of this descriptive definition belongs to metaphysics (philosophy of being).

[13] Not necessarily first in time, but *analytically first*, as color is the first object of sight.

proper object of that knowledge. Hence, the proper object of the intellect is being.[14]

Once we know what the proper object of a power is we can discover its formal object. We have seen in Chapter V that the formal object of a power is that by reason of which its material object pertains to, or is related to, the power. In other words, the formal object is that by which the proper object of a power is precisely a proper object. For example, the visible (or colored) is the proper object of sight. What makes a thing visible? Actual color. Similarly, the proper object of the intellect is being. What makes a thing an object for an intellect? Precisely that in a being by reason of which it is intelligible, namely, the very intelligibility of being itself (*ratio entis*).[15] The intelligible is being; and all being is intelligible, at least potentially.

[14] Since the intellect is able to know anything which is in any way, the proper object of intellect must be something which is (analogically) common to all things. Now, in metaphysics, the analogically common (transcendental) perfections are found to be *being, unity, truth,* and *goodness* (to which may be added *beauty*). These transcendentals are so related, that *being* is the first or most basic, to which the others add either a negation (of actual division, for *unity*), or a relation (to intellect, for *truth;* to appetite, for *goodness;* to both simultaneously and in an eminent way, for *beauty*). Of this group, the only candidates for the position of proper object of intellect are clearly *being* and the *true.* Since the *true* is here taken as "being with a relation to intellect," we can say indifferently, as St. Thomas does, that the proper object of intellect is being or the true (see for example, St. Thomas, *Summa Theologiae,* I. 55. 1, 82. 4 ad 1, I–II. 10. 1 ad 3). But if we take the *true* in an emphatic sense (or also in a reduplicative sense, that is, *as true*), then it must be said to be the object of the act of judgment, and is no longer the object of intellect without qualification. Moreover, the *true* can be taken in a stricter sense (referring to logical truth or truth as known), and in this way it is also not the object of intellect without qualification. Hence, for present purposes, we prefer to designate "being" as the proper object of intellect.

[15] Cf. St. Thomas, *Truth,* XV. 2.

If it were not seriously misleading, it would be convenient to coin a word to express the quasi-formality by which being is being and is intelligible (but this would imply that there is an indefinite subject which is constituted a being by the "form of being"—an implication which is to some extent true of material things which "become being" through form or essence and the consequent act of existing). Since a being is being "all through," it is possible to say briefly that the formal object of intellect is being, as well as to say that being is the proper object of intellect. However, further specification can be made concerning the human intellect; see below, section 94.

Being, which is the proper object of intellect, is analogous. But an analogous reality or perfection is not simply *one* perfection; it is found in many different ways, or according to many different forms.[16] Consequently, we must ask whether the intellect of man is ordered to all these various beings equally, or whether perhaps some difference can be discovered. For example, is God, Who is a being, the object of the intellect in the same way as sensible things, which are also analogically beings? In order to answer this question (which is but another form of the second question put at the beginning of this section), we need to consider how the intellect of man comes to know. This analysis will be based on the object of intellectual knowledge and our experience of intellectual activity. Then, in section 94, we will try to find the answer to the question just proposed.

91. The process of knowledge (Origin of ideas)

Every man has to acquire intellectual knowledge either by his own effort alone, or with the help of others. If the intellect were outfitted with knowledge by its very nature,[17] every man would have that amount of inborn knowledge, and error and disagreement about its objects would be impossible. Hence, the human intellect is first in potency, and actually has knowledge only later. Moreover, like other powers of knowledge, the intellect does not change the thing which it knows by knowing it, but rather, the object somehow puts the intellect into act. Hence, the human intellect is a passive power.

It is immediately evident that our intellectual knowledge takes its origin somehow from sense experience. By careful analysis, we can state this relationship with much greater accuracy. A man who lacks one sense (for example, sight), can never acquire intellectual knowledge of the formal object of that sense as such (a blind man

[16] In metaphysics, the analogical perfection is found to be one only by a proportional likeness.

[17] The theory which holds that man is born with a certain fund of knowledge is called the "theory of innate ideas." This theory is not widely held today.

can never know what color is in its own terms). There is, therefore, a strict dependence of intellect upon sense in the origin of
knowledge. Furthermore, when one man wishes another to understand something, he (a) either shows him a sensible object, or
(b) by means of sensible signs helps the other in discovering the
idea he wants him to know.

This same truth can be proved indirectly. Although the intellect
has no organ, as we have seen, intellectual operation can be hin-
dered or suspended by an injury to the brain (organ of the internal
senses). Again, sleep is an affection of sense life as such, and at
least in the higher animals, an interruption of the activity of the
internal senses. But sleep also stops intellectual activity.

Hence intellectual knowledge is derived from sense, and depends for its use on sense. More accurately still, as we conclude
from the indirect proof, intellectual activity arises from and depends on sense perception, and in that complex activity, depends
immediately on the elaborated images (phantasms) [18] of the imagination.[19]

Intellect is in potency to know, before it is in act; it needs to be
moved to its act, and it needs a formal determination to know
this rather than that. Hence, by reason of the indetermination of
the intellectual subject (*ratione subiecti*), there must be an intelligible *species*, since a *species* is always necessary whenever
there is an indetermination on the part of a knower. Moreover,
the objects of human knowledge are often evidently not united
with the intellect according to their real being. Hence, the *species*

[18] "Phantasm" is the term used for the image, when we are considering
it in relation to intellectual knowledge (cf. St. Thomas, *Summa Theologiae*,
I. 79. 4 ad 4).

A simple image is one that merely retains a previous sense experience. An
elaborated image is a developed or complex image, such as we usually have
in adult life. In the development of this elaborated image, many sense experiences may concur; the estimative and memorative powers may also take
part. Frequently, an elaborated image has a present sense experience joined
to it; it is then equivalent to sense-perception.

[19] After we have proved that (a) man is a substantial unit, and (b) that
the human soul is the substantial form of the body, we can then argue that
the only reason why the intellect is thus *in* a body is that it may acquire
knowledge from the bodily senses. See below, Chapter XIV, section 174.

is also necessary as "presentative form," as that in which knower
and known are united. And, as we shall see more clearly in the
course of this chapter, the human intellect is not actually identical
with any actually intelligible object. Hence, for human knowledge,
a *species* is always necessary as presentative form (*ratione obiecti*).

The *species*, to fulfill its functions as formal determiner of the
act of intellectual knowledge and as the form which makes the
object present and united to the intellect, must inhere in the intellect as an accidental, qualitative modification. But the intellect
is a spiritual power in its nature and being. Hence, the intelligible
species, because it is the modification of something which is spiritual, must itself be spiritual.

Intellectual knowledge takes its origin from sense, and in particular from the elaborated image or phantasm, and so the phantasm must be the cause of the intelligible *species*. But here a
problem arises. The intelligible *species* is immaterial, while the
phantasm is material. Can this be? (*a*) An effect cannot be more
perfect than its cause. But the intelligible *species* is spiritual,
while the phantasm is material. Therefore, the phantasm cannot
be the cause of the intelligible *species*. (*b*) All causation by a
material thing takes place under the conditions of space and time,
and through material dispositions. But the intellect, being a non-
organic power, is *not in space* of itself, so that a material cause
cannot reach it, nor does it have any material dispositions through
the change of which the form (that is, the *species*) could be
educed. Hence, an efficient cause which is material cannot produce
any effect in the intellect, and so the phantasm cannot produce
the intelligible *species*. Hence there is a dilemma: the intelligible
species is caused by the phantasm, and yet the phantasm cannot
be the direct efficient cause of it.

Let us look at the situation again, and see what the data require.
The phantasm can account for the intelligible *species*, under the
aspect of the latter's being the image of a determined object—
if some way can be found in which the phantasm can causally
determine the *species*. The spiritual and intelligible characters of

the *species* can be accounted for *passively*, inasmuch as they are received in the intellect (technically called the "possible intel-

The characteristics of phantasms:	The characteristics of intelligible species:	?
of a definite object——(cause)——➤ of a definite object.		A cause is still needed for each of these aspects, as yet unaccounted for.
material	spiritual◄——————————	?
in the order of sense knowledge	(No causality here) in the order of intellectual knowledge◄———	?

lect"). The possible intellect is a passive power, and so cannot be the efficient cause of the *species*. Hence, something other than the phantasms and the possible intellect is needed,[20] which is in

[20] A different point of view on this whole matter may clarify the argument. The data are: (1) knowledge is a formal identity; (2) formal identity can be guaranteed only by causality; (3) intellect is spiritual, sensation and phantasm are material as well as immaterial; (4) the material cannot directly act upon the spiritual, what is material cannot cause a spiritual effect. Various theories of knowledge meet this situation in one of three ways: (a) By denying the spirituality of intellect and understanding, thus making it possible for sensation and phantasm to influence the intellect causatively. (b) By reversing the causality, so that the object known is as such the effect of the intellect—Kantianism; this denies that we know the real world. (c) By introducing some cause other than sensation and phantasm and the possible intellect. This other cause can be (1) distinct from the man who knows— God or some other separated spiritual being—and ensuring the formal identity of knowing and object known by being the cause of both. This theory has various minor forms: innate ideas, infusion of ideas, illumination, Platonic participation. Or, (2) this other cause can be a power of the one who knows: the agent intellect. Now, theories (a) and (b) deny one or more facts of experience; theory (c), (1) skips over the order of secondary causality to take refuge in the power of God. But the First Cause should not be made to substitute for secondary causes. And, as St. Thomas says, when God makes a nature, He makes it able to operate, to act by its powers; He does not constantly interfere with it, like an inefficient mechanic who cannot quite succeed in making a machine that works.

the same order of being as the effect to be produced and as the other causes which enter in (namely, phantasms as somehow specifying cause, possible intellect as receptive cause)—that is, it must be a power of the soul. This efficient or active power [21] must be (a) spiritual; (b) in the intellectual order, causatively, not formally; (c) itself in act; and (d) really distinct from the possible intellect. To express the characteristics of this power, which is productive of the intelligible *species,* the term "agent intellect" has been invented.

For a clearer understanding of what the agent intellect is and does, we can examine its four characteristics more closely. (a) The agent intellect is a spiritual power, because its effect, the intelligible *species,* has a spiritual being. We can put this reason in another way. The agent intellect is spiritual, because its proper patient upon which it acts is spiritual. Now, an agent or cause must be at least as perfect as its corresponding patient or effect.

(b) The agent intellect must be in the intellectual order; that is, if it is to produce the intelligible *species,* then this production is its proper and proportionate function. It is called "intellect," not because it knows, but because it makes the intelligible *species* which are the formal principles of intellectual knowledge.

(c) The agent intellect is of itself in act, not a power which needs to be moved to act. This trait of the agent intellect is also known from a study of its proper function. For we conclude to the existence of such a power because there must be an efficient cause of the intelligible *species.* Now, an efficient cause must itself be in act. And the agent intellect must always be in act—otherwise there would have to be another spiritual power to put it into act, and still another for the second; or God would have to work a miracle every time a man learns something. Moreover, the agent intellect must be equally ready to produce any intelligible *species,* otherwise there would be some things we could never know.

[21] It is important not to forget that the activities and causes we are speaking about here are not independent substances. An expression like "this power causes" is a kind of mental shorthand for "man by this power causes."

We experience this act of the agent intellect, obscurely but really, whenever we work through a difficult problem and finally come to an understanding of (insight into) it. In this experience, we can discover both the *activity* of knowing and that special character of active understanding which we express under the metaphor of *light*. For, just as light makes a material thing actually visible, and can be considered as using that object as its instrument to cause vision, so the agent intellect makes an object actually intelligible, using the phantasm as its instrument to cause understanding (by impressing the intelligible *species* in the possible intellect). As we shall see later on in this chapter, we can clearly express the production of intelligibility only by the ways of metaphor and analogy.

(*d*) The agent intellect must be really distinct from the possible intellect, because it is impossible that one and the same power be at the same time agent and patient in regard to one and the same object.

So there are two efficient (active, productive) causes of the intelligible *species*. But two efficient causes cannot have one and the same indivisible effect unless they are in relation to each other. Moreover, each of these causes accounts for some aspects of the effect. Hence, agent intellect and phantasm cannot be two independent, or coördinate, causes (compare the relation of two painters to a painted room with the relation of the painter and his brush to the painting). Therefore, they must be causes subordinate one to the other. Of two subordinated causes, one is the principal, the other the instrumental cause. And it is obvious that the agent intellect must be the principal cause, while the phantasm can only be the subordinate or instrumental cause. Thus, the series of causes in the production of intellectual knowledge has these essential stages:

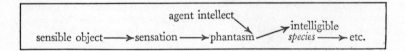

The human intellect is first of all in potency. In order to know, it needs to be put into act by means of the intelligible *species*. These *species*, since they are in a spiritual power as in a subject, are therefore themselves spiritual. Now, the principle of individuation in material things is, as we know, matter with quantity.[22] Therefore, the material thing which is intentionally, immediately, and causatively represented in the intelligible *species*, is represented according to its *absolute nature* only, and not as individuated. The same conclusion will follow, if we consider the way in which the phantasm causes the intelligible *species*. For the phantasm is the instrumental cause of the *species* only according to the formal nature of its object. We have seen that a material cause as such cannot act upon a spiritual power. Since the phantasm instrumentally acts to produce the *species*, but not in the way proper to a cause which is material, it cannot produce an intentional representation which is materially individuated.

92. The acts of the intellect

Once the intellect has been put into act by receiving the intelligible *species*, it performs its own proper acts or operations. Whereas most other powers have only one kind of act, the intellect has three, as is explained in logic.[23] These three acts are apprehension,[24] judgment, and reasoning. To have an adequate understanding of what the intellect is, we need to study these three acts somewhat in detail.

(A) *Apprehension (conception)*. Apprehension is defined in logic as the operation by which we lay hold of a thing, making the thing present in and to our intellect, but without affirming or deny-

[22] This proposition is not proved here, but is assumed from metaphysics (or from the philosophy of nature), and see below, section 93, B.

[23] Strictly speaking, these are the acts of the intellect which occur in the line of speculative knowledge. In addition to them, there is another quite different kind of act, called the "imperium" or "command." This will be treated later: see section 125.

[24] In popular usage, the first meaning of "apprehension" is "a state of fear or anxiety." In its second meaning, it refers to an act of knowledge. The technical meaning in logic is developed from the second meaning.

ing. Apprehension rarely exists as a distinct act, except in the form of definition or division. But implicitly it can be found as a part of both judgment and reasoning. Roughly speaking, apprehension is to the other acts of the intellect somewhat as nouns or terms are to the rest of language.

Let us first consider what the intellect can do, simply inasmuch as it is informed by the intelligible *species,* that is, without receiving any other influence. The intelligible *species,* as we have seen, contains intelligibly the absolute (that is, neither as particular nor as formally universal) nature or essence of a thing, according to a greater or lesser degree of determination. As informed in this way, the intellect therefore knows, understands a thing according to the thing's essential characteristics more or less clearly and explicitly expressed. In other words, by the act of apprehension, we know *what* a thing is. Of course, in the beginning of our intellectual life, we know what a thing is only with extreme vagueness or generality; for example, we know that it is a thing, or a substance. To say that we know an essence is by no means the same as saying that we know what a thing is completely and clearly according to its specific determinations. To arrive at specific differences (and even intermediate generic differences) study and experience are required, and these involve the elaboration of a phantasm by way of getting as many accidental determinations, and particularly as many activities of the object, as we can. The most fully developed form of apprehension is the act of definition.

*Because the act of apprehension, considered as simply dependent upon the reception of the *species,* is the simplest act of intellect, it is frequently called the "first act." [25] This name of the "first act" also implies that apprehensions are found as implicit parts of both judgments and reasonings.

In addition to apprehensions which are simply acts of laying hold on essences ("simple apprehensions"), there are also similar acts (that is, which are neither judgments nor reasonings) which

[25] The adjective "first," applied to apprehension, usually does not mean "first in time"; it necessarily refers only to the kind of priority that any part has in relation to the whole of which it is a part.

necessarily presuppose judgments or reasonings. These kinds of apprehensions will be discussed after we have considered judgment and reasoning.

(B) *Judgment.* Judgment is the act by which we mentally affirm or deny. From the logical point of view, judgment is sometimes defined as the act of mental composition or division—the logician considers that two apprehensions are put together (composed) in affirmation or separated in denial.

What do we do when we judge? In affirmation, we say that a thing is (was, will be, either simply, or according to some mode of necessity, possibility, and so forth); [26] in negation, that a thing is not (was not, and so forth). Hence, a judgment differs from a simple apprehension, in that judgment is the knowledge of a being whose existence is affirmed or denied. By judgment, we know the being as a whole: we know its essence inasmuch as the judgment virtually contains an apprehension of the subject (and of a predicate if the judgment contains a second term), and we know the subject as actually existing, when we assert (or deny) that it is. Consequently, we can set up this proportion: As essence is to being (= an essence with its act of existing), so simple apprehension is to judgment.

We have seen, in considering the simple apprehension, that the intelligible *species* as formal principle gives rise to the apprehension of a thing according to its essence. Now, we learn in metaphysics that the essence of a finite thing and its act of existing are really distinct as two co-principles within the existent (or existing being). Consequently, the intelligible *species* by itself as formal principle cannot give rise to a judgment (in which existence is affirmed or denied). And so something more than the intelligible *species* as formal principle is needed so that the intellect can make a judgment.

What is this something more? Again, going to metaphysics, we learn that the real act of existing necessarily belongs to a singular,

[26] Questions should be looked on as the beginnings of, or movements toward judgments, and therefore, from the viewpoint of our present classification, they are reduced to judgments.

concrete subject. And we shall see that the existents we meet at first hand are the objects of sense. Consequently, in order to make a judgment, the intellect must not only possess an intelligible *species,* but also be in contact with sense.[27]

This contact of the intellect with sense needs some explanation. "Contact" here cannot mean "juxtaposition in space" since judgment is a spiritual activity; it must therefore mean "influence or causality of some kind." Here, we can recall that the role of the phantasm + agent intellect in relation to the activity of the possible intellect is twofold: (*a*) it produces a formal determination, which is the intelligible *species,* and (*b*) simultaneously moves the intellect to its act. This motion is in the order of *efficient* causality. Now, efficient causality carries within itself (that is, is like the agent because produced by it) the existential act of the efficient cause. Consequently, we can suppose two cases: (*a*) The phantasm includes present sense experience, and so contains virtually the existential act of a sensible object, which acts upon the sense by efficient causality. (*b*) The phantasm does not include present sense-experience, but it formally includes past experience by way of memory. Here, the contact is only with existents in past time, but still real existents. Therefore, through the efficient motion (contact) of agent intellect and a phantasm of either type *a* or *b* upon the possible intellect, the latter is able to make a judgment about real existence.

Some judgments are preceded in time by a distinct act of apprehension, but most of the judgments of ordinary experience are not. As an example of the first, we may consider a proposition from physics or history, which we first understand without affirming, and then afterwards affirm when we have considered the evidence. As an example of the second kind of judgment, we may consider direct judgments of perception like "That dog is growling at me"; "This was a good meal." In these acts, we do not first have a distinct

[27] This holds good for all judgments involving real existence; cf. St. Thomas, *Summa Theologiae,* I. 84. 8. But since existing material things are singulars, we cannot push this analysis further till we have looked into our intellectual knowledge of singular things.

apprehension of "dog" or "meal"; we make the judgment immediately in the experience. The apprehension is only implicitly contained.

*From the point of view of the existence which is affirmed or denied, there are three kinds of judgments: (a) those which directly and unqualifiedly assert existence (or deny it), for example, "God exists"; (b) those which assert existence in a given way, or according to some form, for example, "John is a man," "John is white"; and these are called the real attributive judgments; [28] (c) those which assert intentional being, as "animal is a genus." To this third class belong the judgments made in logic, and many of the judgments of mathematics.

(C) *Reasoning.* Reasoning is the operation by which we proceed from known truth to new truth [29] distinct from the previously known truth but implied in it. In order that we may do this validly (legitimately), the objects of the two acts of knowledge must be connected or related.

Acts of reasoning may be classified in many ways; some of these ways are discussed in logic.[30] As reasoning is studied in logic, it

[28] For our present purposes, the further divisions of these judgments into *per se* and *per accidens* judgments, and the consideration of the various modalities, are not necessary.

Because judgment is either immediately or mediately an affirmation (or denial) of existence, the logician's definition of judgment as composition or division is incomplete from two points of view. In the first place, the logician is dealing directly only with attributive judgments which have a real predicate. In the second place, he has not sufficiently distinguished judgment from a composite apprehension. For example, "white house," and "The house is white," are both composite; both contain plural terms which are put together or compared. Consequently, when we begin by saying that judgment is composition, we must say that judgment has two "parts" (or better, "aspects"): the composition or comparison of terms, and the "assent." By the word "assent" we then wish to indicate precisely the affirmation or negation of the composition.

[29] The "newness" of the conclusion need not be new *information;* most often what is "new" about the conclusion is the insight gained into its necessity; cf. above, section 6.

[30] An important classification of reasoning is that according to the connections between the objects of the component judgments. According to this way of classifying, reasoning can be *a priori* (from cause to effect) or *a posteriori* (from effect to cause). And since there are four kinds of causality, reasoning can take place according to any one of them.

appears to be a very formal and rigorous procedure, and sometimes it seems to be artificially explicit. But, psychologically speaking, syllogistic reasoning is far from being the only example of
reasoning that we experience. Any time that we move from one
intellectual knowledge to another, we perform an act of reasoning. For example, the process we go through when we pass from
a question to its answer, the building of a definition, the accumula-
tion of evidence in science or in judicial procedure, the charting
of the possibilities of future action, the construction of a persuasive presentation according to the rules of rhetoric, the discovery of an instance in poetry or the construction of a metaphor,
are all of them examples of reasoning. In a word, any progress of
the intellect from one knowledge to another is an act of reasoning.
Consequently, we can say that reasoning is to judgment and apprehension as movement is to its term.

(D) *Complex apprehensions.* We have already referred to complex apprehensions in contrast to simple apprehensions. Now that
we have considered judgment and reasoning, we can return to
consider complex apprehensions which are essentially dependent
upon a preceding judgment or reasoning, and retain something
of the character of those preceding acts.[31]

The most important complex apprehension that is consequent
upon reasoning is the real definition. A real definition aims at de-
fining a thing, while a nominal definition defines a term, that is,
gives the meaning of a word. Examples of real definitions will
occur in Chapter XII, when we come to consider the nature
of man and of his soul.

Since the most evident of the causes is the efficient cause, and since this
cause exercises its causality through operation, we can set up the following
proportions:

$$\frac{\text{essence}}{\text{apprehension}} \quad : \quad \frac{\text{being}}{\text{judgment}} \quad : \quad \frac{\text{causality and operation}}{\text{reasoning}}$$

[31] We can call apprehensions essentially dependent upon a judgment or
reasoning *per se* complex apprehensions. For there are some complex apprehensions, like "white house" or "gold mountain" which in fact arise through
judgments, but retain nothing of the character of the judgment. These latter
we might well call *"per accidens* complex apprehensions."

Of the apprehensions which are consequent upon a judgment, one of the most important and interesting instances is that of being. Let us suppose a baby, whose internal sense powers are for the first time sufficiently developed,[32] so that he has for the first time a phantasm (image) in his imagination to which his attention is drawn (most probably by pleasure or pain and the consequent affective response). No matter how crude and undeveloped this phantasm may be, and no matter what the sensible object may be from which it has arisen, it still contains a potentially intelligible essence. The agent intellect, using this phantasm as its instrument, produces an intelligible *species* intentionally representing a very incomplete essence: that of something sensible (*sensibile quid*). Because this first apprehension of essence takes place in the presence of sensation and the sensible object, the intellect passes at once to the judgment, "This ([*implicitly*] sensible thing which I touch, or see, and so forth) is pleasant." It is impossible to tell what precise form this first judgment will take in a particular case, but, whatever it is, there is implicit in it the judgment, "This (sensible thing) is." Immediately following upon this judgment there can be the first apprehension of being (which is "a [sensible-material] thing having an act of existing").[33] Whether this apprehension is explicitly made in these precise terms after the first judgment, we do not know, but such an apprehension of being is implicit in any apprehension following the first judgment. These three stages (apprehension within judgment, judgment, complex apprehension) follow each other without any delay, and so the very first activity of the intellect terminates in the apprehension of being. Being is thus the first permanent possession of the intellect, and is therefore called the first conception.[34]

[32] Biologists tell us that the central nervous system of man does not usually reach its full development until some time after birth.

[33] This first apprehension of being is called by St. Thomas *ens primum cognitum* or *ens commune*. Being in this sense is not being with which metaphysics deals.

[34] Can there be an apprehension of the act of existing (*esse*)? It is clear that there can be no simple apprehension of that act, because all simple apprehensions are of a form or nature. Can there then be a complex apprehension of

The baby's knowledge of the real existent entails a complex process, but of course the youngster knows little or nothing of this process. The baby does not know the terms "material," "sensible," nor is he explicitly aware that the being which he knows is sensible and therefore material. Nevertheless, his knowledge of being is in the first instance limited to the being which he actually has experienced.

93. The various material objects of the intellect

Completely to determine the formal object of the human intellect we must find out whether any of its material objects bear any special or favored relation to it. For this reason, it is necessary to consider the various kinds of material objects which man can intellectually know.[35]

A. *Material things known directly.* The intellect is put into act by an intelligible *species* derived in the first instance immediately from the phantasm of a sensed object, and directly related to the

---

the act of existing? Not in the ordinary sense in which there is a complex apprehension of *being*. And yet we use "existence" as a noun; we talk about it without reference to any particular nature; we seem to be able to handle it just as we handle an abstraction like "humanity." Ordinarily, a noun or term stands for an apprehension or conception. What then do we have in our mind when we understand the meaning of the term "existence?" What seems to have happened is this. Instead of having abstracted the act of existing (which is impossible), we have abstracted the *is* of the existential judgment. Compare St. Thomas, *Summa Theologiae,* I. 3. 4 ad 2; *On the Power of God,* VII. 2 ad 1.

[35] For the sake of complete coverage of the material objects of the human intellect, some may find it useful to have a few very general remarks about the object of mathematics, which will serve as a preliminary orientation to this very difficult problem. Mathematical knowledge begins with a special kind of phantasm, that is, with the separated phantasms of the common sensibles (cf. Chapter VII, section 76). The mathematical object, as such, in its basic elements, is the intelligible essence seen in such separated phantasms. The remaining mathematical objects are purely intelligible objects constructed by definition and reasoning (cf. St. Thomas, *Comm. in Metaphys.,* IX, lect. 10; ed. Cathala, nos. 1888–1894; *In Lib. Boethii de Trinitate,* 5. 1, ed. Wyser, p. 28, lines 14–15; *Summa Theologiae,* I–II. 57. 3 ad 3; I. 12. 9 ad 2; cf. also P. Hoenen, S.J., "De problemate exactitudinis geometricae," *Gregorianum,* XX [1939], 349–350), and seen in special phantasms constructed by the imagination under the guidance of the intellectual knowledge.

absolute [36] nature of that object. Consequently, when the intellect, acting only and simply with what it has thus received, knows a thing, it apprehends it according to its absolute and abstract [37] nature (for example, substance, horse, dog, man, rational animal). Furthermore, judgments which flow from these same intelligible *species* will have to be abstract and absolute (for example, "man is a rational animal").

The nature which is known in direct apprehension and in the absolute judgment is neither formally universal nor particular. The reason for this is the nature of the material thing and of the mind as a spiritual power. Hence, there is no "problem of universalization" as far as the most generic of direct apprehensions and judgments are concerned, for the passage from the particular of sense and imagination to the absolute in the concept and the judgment (for example, the statement of a simple physical law) is in no way accidental, or contingent, or arbitrary.[38]

B. *Singular realities, especially material singulars.* According to the analysis which we have just made, it would seem that we can know material reality only universally, since the intelligible *species* which is the formal principle of our intellectual activity is of the absolute nature. Yet, on the other hand, it is absolutely evident that we do know singular material things. And note that

[36] The absolute nature is the nature considered without reference to universality or singularity.

[37] "Abstract" here means "separated from matter and material conditions." Because the nature contained in a direct apprehension is abstract in this sense, it is also absolute. [Distinguish this meaning of "abstract" from the meaning it had in the previous chapter, as well as from the meaning it has in grammar and rhetoric, where it means "separated from a subject," for example, "humanity."]

[38] The problem of universalization never occurs when the object of apprehension is a substantial unit (a *per se* unit). Cf. St. Thomas, *Summa Theologiae*, I. 85. 1 ad 1.

A problem does occur when that which is apprehended is complex (whether it be the union of substance and accident or operation, or of essence and property, or of cause and effect). Each element of that complex group will still be naturally and necessarily (and therefore validly) universal. But is the complex group itself universal? To answer this question a very complex induction and reasoning is often necessary.

this knowledge is not merely sensitive, but also an intellectual knowledge of the singular. For (*a*) on the one hand, we do make singular judgments about singular things (for example, "John is a good man"), and judgments, in this strict sense of the word, are always intellectual activities; and (*b*) on the other hand, we choose singular things with our will. Now, as we shall see later, an act of will is an act of rational appetite, depending on and flowing from intellectual knowledge. Thus, it is clear that we do intellectually know singular things. How can this be, in view of the preceding explanation? Or, conversely, how can the preceding explanation hold, in view of the fact that we do know singulars?

Note that the former inquiry concerned *direct* knowledge of material reality. Direct intellectual knowledge of material things was defined as that knowledge which arises from the intelligible *species* as from its sole and formal principle. Hence, in such knowledge, the intellect is acting as a *separated* power, though not without dependence on sensory activity.

But in addition to this separated (infra-perceptual [39]) knowledge, the intellect is also capable of acting in union or composition with the activity of other powers.[40] The phantasm is material, singular, here and now. Hence, if the act of the intellect is *joined with*, and united into one complex act with the act of the imagination, the knowledge thus obtained will be the knowledge of a singular material thing.[41]

---

[39] See above, section 45.

[40] We have already seen that there are composite but unified activities on the sense level, namely, sense perceptions; see above, section 82.

[41] What is the relation between the universal and the singular material nature? What is the principle of individuation in material things? Since act is not limited in its own order except by a potency in which it is received, the universal is the nature as act and perfection, the singular is that *same nature* limited by matter-and-quantity to a particular being. (Though it is true that the nature as act and perfection does not exist separated from the singular except in the mind, this does not change the argument—for if the nature of man could subsist as such, it could not be multiplied and would be completely perfect as a nature.) This then is the relation between the (absolute) nature and the individual in the order of real material being.

In the order of knowledge, the universal is the absolute nature, while the singular is that same nature as *here and now* (that is, under the conditions of

That this way of explaining the intellectual knowledge of singular material things is correct can be seen by examining our knowledge of material singulars. For example, we know individual persons, Socrates or Peter. We know that they are men, and we understand that they are distinct in their individuality. But the only way we can designate Socrates with unmistakable clarity is to point him out in sense experience (and/or memory). We know Socrates intellectually, it is true. But though the human nature in Socrates can be apprehended with considerable clarity, his individuality ("Socrateity") cannot be penetrated, but only grasped at as a kind of transcended limit.

Thus the intellectual knowledge of the material singular is experientially different from the direct knowledge of material reality. In this act, which we call "indirect" to distinguish it from the universal knowledge, the intellect is not acting according to its full limit of abstraction, but precisely in composition with the act of an organic power. Moreover, the intellectual knowledge of the singular must be in the first instance a judgment, since material singulars are not found except as existing. After this judgment has been made, we can form a complex apprehension or conception of the singular.

*A universal *judgment* need not have preceded the judgment by which we know the material singular, but only a universal apprehension. And even the universal apprehension necessarily precedes the singular judgment only in the order of nature (not in

---

quantity and matter). Hence, the passage from the absolute (or universal) nature to the singular is not an addition, not an increase of perfection, but is a limitation, in the way in which potency limits act, and matter limits form. Now, intellectual knowledge has its origin in the phantasm, which is the material, sensory counterpart of the intellectual knowledge, and this phantasm is limited, singular. When the act of intellectual judgment is joined with a phantasm in a composite operation, the intellectual part of this composite act is as form, the sensory part is as matter. Thus, the composition of the knowledge by which we know material singulars corresponds to the composition of the thing, that is, to its matter and form.

For a textual study of the doctrine of St. Thomas on contact and the knowledge of the singular, see G. P. Klubertanz, S.J., "St. Thomas and the Knowledge of the Singular," *The New Scholasticism*, XXVI (1952), pp. 135–66.

the order of time), and therefore need be found in experience only as a virtual part of the judgment. This is the way in which the first judgments take place—for example, such a judgment as was mentioned when we spoke of the apprehension of being.

C. *The act of intellect. "Direct consciousness."* Intellectual knowledge, as has already been mentioned in Chapter IV, is of its very nature and necessarily conscious. This direct consciousness is simply the known presence of the act of understanding; it does not reveal the nature of the act, but simply that it is present. Experience indeed gives us this fact; what we already know about the nature of the intellect will show why it is and must be so. The intellect is a spiritual power, separated from matter. When, therefore, it is put into act, it is actually intelligible, because it fulfills all the conditions of being actually intelligible, that is, it is (*a*) immaterial, (*b*) actual, not merely potential, and (*c*) immediately united to a knowing subject. Thus, direct consciousness is not an act distinct from the act by which the intellect knows any object. It is simply the actually intelligible presence of a spiritual act to itself. Therefore, no intelligible *species* is needed for direct consciousness (apart from the *species* of the object which is known).

D. *The intellect itself, the soul. "Reflex consciousness; self-consciousness."* The intellect is of itself and at first in potency. Hence, it cannot be known immediately as a power, since potency is never known to us except through act. To know the nature of its act, or itself, or the soul, the intellect must take these things as its direct object. For this, a distinct act is required. But in order that the intellect may pass into act, there must be an intelligible *species* to serve as formal determination of that act. Here there is a difficulty. All intelligible *species* are derived from phantasms. And, as we have seen, all phantasms directly represent material reality. Hence they cannot adequately (univocally) represent non-material reality.

That is why, in the knowledge of itself and of the soul, the intellect must employ analogy. First, the intellect must guide the imagination in the formation of a phantasm which is suitable for the abstraction of an appropriate intelligible *species*. Then it must proceed by way of affirmation and negation to judge the existence of the non-material power which performs the act of understanding, and through the existence of such a power, to derive an apprehension of that nature. Hence, the intellect's knowledge of itself is extraperceptual.

These acts of knowledge, wherein the intellect takes its own activity and its own nature as its direct object, are called acts of reflex consciousness. These acts are truly called "conscious," because they are the knowledge of the subject by itself.

The same thing must be done in order that a man can come to know his soul. In itself, the soul of a man is the form of a body, and, as such, is not actually and immediately intelligible. On the other hand, in so far as man acts through his soul in every one of his intellectual acts, man knows by direct consciousness *that* he has a soul. But *what* the soul is, is a knowledge won only with great and prolonged labor. Man can come to it, only by studying his own operations, among them the operations of intellect and will. Hence, a man's knowledge of his soul will be an analogous knowledge, a knowledge of the soul in terms derived from sensible experience. The direct self-awareness that is contained in all intellectual knowledge is called "self-consciousness."

From the direct consciousness of intellectual activity and from direct self-consciousness, as facts of experience, an independent and striking proof can be developed for the spirituality of the intellect. When we studied sensation, we saw that no sense power can have itself as object in any way, because the spatial, extended character of material reality completely precludes self-reflection. The fact of intellectual awareness, and the possibility of reflex consciousness, prove the total self-presence of intellect to itself. But that which is wholly present to itself cannot have parts outside of parts; in other words, it cannot be quantified. That which is not quantified in its operation cannot be material, nor can it be the form of a material organ. Hence the intellect is a spiritual power.

E. God and other spiritual realities. A spiritual being, since it is wholly in act with regard to its essential perfections (it is a pure form), is therefore wholly intelligible—to itself. Is it intelligible to another being? The answer to this question will be clear if we consider again what knowledge is. To know is to be or to become the other, through intentional possession or union. Do we by nature possess the intelligible substances in an intelligible *species?* Obviously we do not. Can we directly acquire such intelligible *species?* We have seen that the natural process of acquiring intelligible *species* includes the activity of the agent intellect and the instrumental causality of the phantasm. But phantasms directly represent only material things. Consequently, from phantasms the agent intellect cannot abstract the intelligible *species* of an immaterial substance. Therefore, the pure intelligibles, such as God and the Angels, are not directly intelligible to us. Our knowledge of them is something like the knowledge we have of the nature of our own soul.[42] There is this difference, that of course we can have no immediate consciousness of God.[43] Hence, the only natural knowledge of God we can have under present conditions in this life is a knowledge in terms of material sensible reality, and this is an analogous knowledge.

F. The object of metaphysics. The object of metaphysics is said by the metaphysician to be "being as being" (what is, inasmuch as it has or possesses an act of existing).[44] How do we reach being as being? We have seen above that we reach the apprehension of being by way of an existential judgment ("something is"). We

[42] On the negation of the represented content in the judgmental knowledge of God which we derive from sensible things, see St. Thomas, *In Boethii de Trinitate,* 6. 2 ad 5; *Summa Theologiae,* I. 84. 7 ad 2, and also I. 13. 2, 3.

[43] By way of an exceptional favor, some persons experience the action of God in their souls. This is not a direct intuition of God, but of a created (even if supernatural) effect—"the action of the agent is in the patient." Among such rare experiences are the graces of mystical prayer.

[44] We are assuming here that the Thomistic metaphysics has established its claim to be metaphysics. Obviously not all philosophers admit this; but all who accept metaphysics in any sense must admit that somehow it transcends sensible reality.

have also seen that this first apprehension of being attains being as it is found in sensible reality.

By a reflective inspection of the being of material things, aided by an analysis of conflicting philosophical positions, we arrive at an understanding of being as "something having an act of existing." This is a per se complex apprehension, and consequently rests on a prior judgment. The judgment on which the conception of being as being rests is a difficult and (at least implicitly) double judgment. When, looking at any thing of our immediate experience, we judge, "This is," we have made the judgment that is the basis of the conception of "common being" (*ens commune, primum cognitum*), which is the proper object of the human intellect. Now, the beings of immediate sense experience are material-sensible beings. Suppose we ask ourselves, when we judge that this material-sensible *is*, whether this judgment really says anything or not. By inspection of the being and a philosophical analysis, we come to see that "is" in such a judgment does not mean "is material," "is sensible," "is something," "is in a definite place and time," but simply asserts an act of existing. Understanding this meaning of "is" in our judgment, we at least imply another judgment, namely that the act of existing does not necessarily involve materiality, sensibility, a specific sort of essence, or location in a definite place and time. By this implicitly double judgment we attain an apprehension of being as being. Consequently, though we can as yet deal only with sensible being, when we consider it as being, we are exercising a supra-perceptual knowledge, which, though it occurs in connection with sense perception, yet transcends it by virtue of the negative judgment.

By a still further inspection of the being of sensible things, we come to see that the act of existing is limited, not of itself, but by being received in the material thing whose act it is. For example, because we experience many different kinds of sensible being, we are led to see that the act of existing is not restricted to any one sensible being, or any one kind of sensible being. We see, therefore, that to exist is not the essence of any sensible being, and that *to exist* is related to the essence of material things as act to potency. In this same study of beings, we come to see that the existence of all the beings of our sense experience is limited by the material essence of those things (for example, that the act of existing of a man is limited by the essence of that man).

Following upon this analysis, the metaphysician enters upon an investigation of the causes of these limited beings. And at the end of this investigation, he arrives at a cause in which essence and the act of existing are one and identical. In this second moment or stage, the negative judgment (expressed or implied) denies not only the limitations of merely material being, but the whole of the represented content of perceptual experience. At this point the metaphysician possesses an extra-perceptual knowledge. What remains of positive knowledge in this case is the judgment as such, inasmuch as it affirms the act of existing of a subject whose essence is determined (over and above its relation to existence) only negatively, by the denial or removal of limitations, and relatively, that is, through its causal relation to its directly known effects.

94. The formal object of the human intellect (II)

We saw above that the proper object of the intellect is being: *what is*. In the discussions which followed, we saw that our intellect is put into act by an intelligible *species* instrumentally caused by sensible things, that what we directly apprehend in the first instance is the absolute nature of sensible things, and that we reach all the other material objects of understanding by complex processes which positively and/or negatively rest on this first knowledge of material reality, and on the judgments we make about sensible things in the concrete.

Consequently, in order to designate the proper object of the intellect as a power by which man knows, inasmuch as he is a composite of body and soul, we must say that it is "being as it is directly found in the natures of sensible things," or, more accurately, "being (first) as it is proportioned to the natures of sensible things and consequently being as it is reached through the analogy which all beings have to sensible things." The proper object of the human intellect, considered in this complete way, is called the adequate, proportioned object.[45]

To find the formal object of the human intellect, we must answer the question, What makes a being intelligible for man? Considering the complex way in which man comes to know intellectually, we can answer briefly, The essence (quiddity or intelligible form) of sensible things. More accurately and completely, the formal object of the human intellect is "the very intelligibility (*ratio*) of being itself (first) as it is proportioned to the natures of sensible things, actual in them through essence and the act of existing, and revealed through operation, and consequently, being as actual through essence and the act of existing, made known to us through the causal implications of sensible being, and understood through the analogy which all beings have to sensible things."

*95. Intellectual memory

We have studied the acts of the intellect. On the sense level, we found that sensations were retained, and that, by a power distinct from that of the external senses. Is there anything similar to be found on the intellectual level?

Do we retain intellectual knowledge? It might seem that we do not. Given an actual intelligible in the intellect, it is understood (the intelligible in act is the intellect in act, as the sensible in act is the sense in act). And yet, it is a fact that once we have learned something, we do not have to re-learn it every time we want to use it. If we have really grasped a proof once, we can see it again in a flash when it again occurs to us to think about it.

Again: phantasms are destroyed when the organ of imagination

---

[45] By the terms "adequate and proportioned" we mean that we are considering the object of the intellect, not merely as the power of understanding, but as the power of understanding of a man, who is himself a concrete, sensible being composed of body and soul. Thus, the phrase is to be understood as "the proper object, adequate (equal) to, and proportioned to, man's composite nature."

is seriously injured. Doctors find that in some types of brain injuries, complete loss of some formerly acquired knowledge results —for example, the knowledge of spoken language. But in such cases, provided enough of the brain is intact to serve as the organ of imagination, re-learning takes place in a fraction of the time it took originally. Understanding is present without effort as soon as the phantasm is restored. Hence, there obviously is retention of intellectual knowledge. How about the difficulty, that whatever is in the mind is actually intelligible? It is true that the intelligible cannot be retained in full act, or it would be by that very fact actually known. Nor can the intellect be returned to the state of sheer potency in which it was before learning, since then nothing would be retained. Hence, what is retained must be in a state intermediate between potency and act. This intermediate state is called the state of habit.

In acquiring knowledge, the intellect is at first in potency. It needs to be determined to a given object, and to be moved to act. In other words, it needs both a formal and an efficient determination. The formal determination permanently inheres, the efficient determination is a motion from the agent intellect. Hence, in the state of habit or memory, the formal determination of the *species* remains, but the motion of the agent intellect is not present. Hence, the form is present, but not actively, and so the intellect does not act through it.

Is intellectual memory distinct from intellect? On the sense level, imagination, the retaining power, is distinct from the external senses and the unifying sense. The reason for the distinction on the sense level is ultimately the limitation of the formal objects of sense powers. But the formal object of the intellect is being, and this formal object is not limited to "being received into intellect as acting on intellect," nor "being recalled"; neither "being present" nor "being absent." Hence, there is no ground for a distinction between intellect and intellectual retentive memory.

If, however, we take memory in the sense of recognition, of explicit reference to the past as past, the solution is somewhat different. For the past as past is the knowledge of a singular, and the singular knowledge of the singular material thing cannot be explained by the intellect acting alone, as we have seen. Hence, intellectual memory of material objects and sensible events is a complex act, involving intellect (with its retained *species*) and the group of sense powers that are needed to explain sense memory-recognition. However, we do experience a singular, actually intelligible event, namely, the act of intellect. Therefore, we can intellectually remember our past intellectual activities, not only in the sense that we retain their *species*, but also in the sense that we can recognize them as past.

96. Relation between intellect and phantasm in the use of knowledge

We saw that for the acquiring of the intelligible *species* the intellect depends on the phantasm as on the instrument of the ˉagent intellect. We have also seen that the intelligible *species* remains in the intellect in the state of habit. But the *species*, as habitually possessed, is only a formal principle of action, not a complete and sufficient one. A motion from an efficient cause is still needed, and that efficient cause is the agent intellect.

But this motion cannot be from the agent intellect alone. For the agent intellect is always in act with regard to all intelligibles; and so, if it were the only reason why any one retained intelligible *species* was actuated, it would have to be moving all intelligible *species* equally at once. Moreover, as long as the soul is in the body, the agent intellect is ordered as cause to the phantasm. Hence, the motion of the agent intellect upon the possible intellect must take place through an actual phantasm. This is seen from experience, in that when we wish to understand something, we form for ourselves a phantasm in which we see it; it is also seen from the facts adduced above in the discussion of intellectual memory. Hence, the phantasm is a permanent foundation for intellectual knowledge.

Not just any phantasm will serve as the foundation for a given concept (judgment, reasoning). Thus, it is easy to see that the concept "rational animal" could be founded in any phantasm from which the original argument for this definition was or could have been drawn, and that it could not be founded in a phantasm of a dog, for example. As far as the direct phantasms of sensible things are concerned, this is quite evident.

But what about symbolic phantasms—for example, the phantasm of the appearance, sound, feeling of the verbal symbol "m a n"? The phantasm serves as a real, instrumental deter- -mination (limitation) of the action of the agent intellect. Hence, it seems evident that a direct phantasm of a man talking and a symbolic phantasm representing the letters "m a n" cannot function as real determinations for the actuation of one and the same intelligible *species* of man, considered as a real and natural being.

Yet it seems to be clear that we do work at times with just symbolic phantasms, which are usually words (as heard, seen, or spoken). What are we actually thinking of, when, for example, the *only* relevant phantasms in our imagination are the sounds or appearance of the words: "Man has an immortal soul"? Suppose that we have at one time really understood the meaning of this proposition; then, when we use the symbolic phantasms of the words in which it is expressed, we are at that moment intellectually understanding not the real being, *man,* but most probably, in a kind of unanalyzed way, our former knowledge of this real being. Thus, we might be presently understanding that this subject, *man,* correctly receives a certain definite predicate, *having an immortal soul.* To know this is of course to have a real and true knowledge, which, because it implicitly contains the understanding of a real being in its own real terms, is frequently quite sufficient.

*But suppose that the meaning of a proposition has never really and fully been understood, that is to say, in its own proper terms. Some real understanding is of course always present; for example, even the most unintelligent memorizer will have understood that *man* is "that thing in my sense experience which is characterized by a special shape." But he may then go on from there to add:

"and this thing with this shape is called *man*." When a person, who has understood the meaning of the terms he uses only in this superficial way, has present in his imagination the symbolic phantasms of the words, "Man has an immortal soul," he may be actually thinking something like this: "A specially shaped thing, *called man*, has something, *called a soul*, which is endowed with a quality, *called immortality*." We may say that such a person, with the aid of purely symbolic phantasms, has gained an understanding merely of someone else's predication.[46]

*This solution is borne out by the fact that there are sciences of symbols which are quite different from the sciences of that which they symbolize. For example, arithmetic is the science of numbers. Algebra, which is a distinct science, is the science of symbolized numerical properties and relations. The two proofs of the Pythagorean principle illustrate this difference in another way. For we can prove that the square of the hypotenuse of a right-angled triangle is equal to the sum of the squares of the other two sides either directly by constructing figures (with the aid of a compass and a straight-edge) or algebraically (with the aid of symbols).

Thus far we have been speaking of the dependence of the intellect upon phantasms (direct and symbolic) inasmuch as the latter are causes of intellectual acts. Is there any dependence in the order of knowledge itself?

We have already seen, in studying the nature of judgment, that every judgment about real existence involves a contact of the intellect with present experience or memory, since our first and only direct contact with existents is through sense.[47] That is why,

[46] Very little has been done by Thomists concerning the distinctive nature and function of symbolic phantasms. See Peter Hoenen, S.J., *Reality and Judgment according to St. Thomas*, trans. by H. F. Tiblier, S.J. (Chicago, Regnery, 1952), p. 27, for a brief statement.

Understanding gained with the aid of purely symbolic phantasms may be what is referred to by Cardinal Newman when he speaks of "notional assent." Modern psychologists and educationists may be speaking of this same thing when they attack "book learning," "formalism," "verbalism."

[47] See above, section 92.

In addition to real being, there is also intentional being. Intentional being is the kind of being that an object has as known, and so is to be found in the

in the absence of sense experience or memory (in most dreams, as well as in periods of unconsciousness), a person is unable to make an intellectual judgment in which he would affirm or deny real existence.[48] That is also why our judgments are intrinsically affected by time (grammatically, every verb has a tense), even when we know that the object of which we are speaking is itself not in time (for example, God and the Angels are not in time, but in eternity).[49]

We have also seen that there is a contact in the order of knowledge itself between the act of the intellect and the phantasm whenever we make judgments about singular material things.[50] These singular judgments are composite acts, in which the strictly intellectual part of the act is limited by the sensory part (the phantasm), in the way in which form is individualized by the matter-and-quantity which receives the form. In these judgments, the intellect in second act (that is, in the order of knowledge itself), makes a dynamic contact with the act of the imagination as containing present sense experience or as a memory-image strictly so called.

Finally, as far as the act of apprehension is concerned, experience itself shows us that we understand real things as concretized, expressed, exemplified, in a phantasm. In other words, we cannot completely understand the nature of any real being without reference to sense.[51]

Thus, in all intellectual knowledge the phantasm is needed (a) as the instrumental cause and permanent foundation of all in-

---

acts of the intellect even when the latter is acting in separation from the sense powers. Hence, judgments about intentional being (the judgments of logic, and those which occur in a merely logical treatment of any object) are separated, not composite, not in contact with the operation of any sense power.

[48] See St. Thomas, *Summa Theologiae,* I. 84. 7, 8; *Truth,* XII. 3 ad 2, 3.

[49] See St. Thomas, *Contra Gentiles,* II. 26, "Palam."

[50] See above, section 93, B.

[51] See St. Thomas, *Summa Theologiae,* I. 84. 7, 86. 1. With regard to the apprehension of material things, the phantasm positively illustrates the concept. In the apprehension of immaterial things, the phantasm, inasmuch as it is a *representation,* serves as that which is denied (in the preceding positive-negative judgment; see above, section 93, D, E, F).

tellection, and (b) in all judgments about real being, as illustrating and/or joining that being to the world of sensible existents, and (c) in all singular judgments concerning material things, as entering into operative composition with the intellectual act, materially limiting that act to the concrete particular. From this point of view, though the intellect of man is not an organic power (is not the form of an organ), it may well be called a "co-organic power." [52]

In the construction of a science of symbols we can see that the intellect, in addition to receiving intelligible *species* from the phantasms, can also (with the aid of the will) combine or separate phantasms in accordance either with the laws of logic or of the association of images. A still more important function: the intellect, in the presence of a phantasm which is so incomplete as not to be intelligible in any detail, can direct sense experience to enrich the content of the phantasm. This is what a scientist or a philosopher does when he looks for new information (data). In this work, the other internal powers are also concerned; the memory is used by intellect-and-will to bring latent phantasms to awareness, the discursive estimative is used to focus interest and to enlist the sensory appetites in the effort (in the service of speculative knowledge the discursive power is not concerned with the content of experience).

97. Practical knowledge

So far, the discussions of the intellect, its operations and its objects, have been concerned almost entirely with the order of speculative or theoretical knowledge. But we also have intellectual knowledge which is intrinsically ordered to acting or to making something, and this is called practical knowledge. Though practical intellectual knowledge is essentially the same as the speculative, there are some additions and precisions which need to be made.

[52] Cf. A. D. Sertillanges, O.P., *S. Thomas d'Aquin* (Paris, Flammarion, 1925), Vol. 2, p. 158.

The object of practical knowledge is something which is to be done or made by the knower.[53] This object is still *being*, and consequently the practical intellect is not a power distinct from the speculative intellect; there is but one intellect which knows either speculatively or practically. Nevertheless, the thing which is to be done is not something which pre-exists in order to be known, but something which is foreknown in order to exist or to be obtained. Practical knowledge, therefore, is a final cause of the thing to be done or made. And so we have left the order of being as true, and entered the order of being as good as well as true.

Because the object of practical knowledge has a relation to what is good, it presupposes actual tendency (appetency).[54] In other words, an act of the practical intellect presupposes an act of the will, by which the person who knows has adhered to the good, and thus made it his own. In general, therefore, practical knowledge takes place in the following way. First, there is an act of the speculative intellect by which a man knows that something is good in itself (that is, is possible, useful, pleasant, obligatory, and so forth). Secondly, man adheres to (tends toward, accepts) this good as his own good by an act of his will. Thirdly, there follows the act of practical intellect. As we shall see, there need be no time interval between these acts, and so they may not be able to be discovered as separate acts by introspection.

*The phantasm, in which practical knowledge is illustrated and concretized, must itself be a "practical phantasm." Now, as we

---

[53] Distinguish this carefully from knowledge about practice (making or doing). In knowing how to do something (technology) or how to act (moral science), one may be exercising speculative knowledge about production and action.

[54] In an intellectual being, which has the power of choosing what its last end shall specifically be (as we shall see), a distinct act of choice and adherence is required. In brutes, whose specific end is actually determined by their nature, and whose tendencies are limited to particular goods, practical knowledge is preceded only by the end imposed by their nature. Hence, the estimative in brutes, though it is a power of practical knowledge, does not presuppose a distinct appetency, but only the end determined by nature. Hence, the estimative is only analogously practical, and involves the determination of the whole species to a definite end, rather than a special determination or orientation of the individual to an end.

have seen, there is a special power on the sense level, which is the power of knowledge-ordered-to-action: the discursive estimative (or the simple estimative in brutes). Hence, the phantasm for practical knowledge involves the activity of the discursive estimative in order to be constituted as such. For the sake of signalizing the distinctive character of the phantasm of practical knowledge, it is frequently said that in such knowledge the intellect depends on the discursive estimative (without any explicit mention of the imagination).

An example of the working out of practical knowledge may clarify the relations between the intellect and the internal senses. Suppose that a man, while driving down the road, has come upon an injured person. He apprehends what has occurred, and sees that it is a good thing to give aid. He wills to help. After this act of the will, the acts of knowledge are practical. As he considers whether it would be better to bring the injured man to a doctor, or a doctor to the injured man, he tries to picture to himself the two sets of actions (compositive imagination), and tries to discover which of the two would be the more suited under the circumstances to accomplish the end (discursive estimative). At the same time, he is intellectually weighing the intelligible characteristics of the two actions, as manifested in their images. His final judgment, both sensory and intellectual, will lead to his choice of action.

98. The mental word

We have seen so far that in intellection there are (a) a power, the intellect, (b) an intelligible *species*, and (c) an operation. Is there anything else necessary in the account of the activity of intellect? In our very way of talking, we seem to show that we have a direct experience of something more; we say, "I know this thing," but also, and perhaps more frequently, "I know this truth," and we say, "I have this knowledge about this thing."

We have discussed human language before; it needs still more analysis. Some language "stands for" or "represents" things (for example, "book"), but some language does not (for example, "more," "truth"). In addition to this, language never immediately stands for things (except in so far as it is a natural sign, onomatopoeia), else (*a*) there would be only one language, (*b*) there would be only one meaning for words, and (*c*) language would not have to be learned, nor invented in the first place. Language directly, immediately (of course by agreement) stands for knowledge, and through knowledge stands for things. But a spoken or written word (for example, "book") does not stand for the power of intellect, as is obvious; nor for the intelligible *species* (for the intelligible *species* is something we discover only by analysis and reflection, and we have been using language for a long time before this); nor for the *act* of knowing, which is a personal activity, but for the known object.

Again, there are such things as logical relationships: the relation of genus, or predicate, or logical accident. These are not the relationships of intelligible *species*, nor of acts of knowing, but of things as known. In other words, logic is about things according to their intelligible being.

Hence, what we mean primarily and ordinarily by the term "intellectual knowledge" is the intellectually known object—the object produced in and by the act of understanding. This immanently produced object is necessary because the really existing object (or the object that can exist) is (*a*) sometimes absent, and (*b*) sometimes does not exist in exactly the same way as it is known, as in the universal knowledge we have of singular things.[55] Hence, that which we know about something is a medium which is itself known, and in which the real or existent object is known. Such a medium is a pure or formal sign, whose whole reality lies in its reference to the thing that is known. This formal sign is called the "mental word." Being produced by the act of understanding,[56] it is really distinct from that act, as the efficient cause is always

---

[55] Compare this argument with the argument used for the existence of the image as substitute object, Chapter VII, section 78.

[56] The mental word is produced only when understanding is finally reached, and so is not present when we are working for an understanding of something.

really distinct from its effect. It is the mental word which is directly referred to by, and is the meaning of, the external word (which is spoken, heard, and so forth).

This analysis applies not only to the understood knowledge which we have in apprehension and which is expressed by a term, but also to the understood knowledge which we have in a judgment which is expressed in a proposition. In the previous analysis of the acts of the intellect, we concluded that apprehensions occur most frequently as implicit parts of judgments and reasonings. In like manner, the mental word which corresponds to a term most frequently occurs as an implicit part of the mental word which corresponds to a judgment. In other words, the mental word produced by an act of judging (affirming or denying) is actually one undivided mental word, even though analysis can discover within the word of judgment two or more apprehended words.

99. Definitions

Language is an arbitrary sign or system of signs for expressing and communicating knowledge and other mental states, as emotions.

Intellect is the power by which we know things as beings.

Intelligible species is the intrinsic formal determination by which the intellect is determined to know this rather than that.

Phantasm is the image of the imagination (which may have been elaborated by the coöperation of the other internal senses) considered as the starting-point of intellectual knowledge, as the instrument of the agent intellect.

Agent intellect is the always active power (i.e. ready to act, without being moved to it) of the soul which is the principal cause of the intelligible *species*, and moves the possible intellect to its act.

Possible intellect is the intellect which first is in potency to knowledge, and then is the actual subject of that knowledge.

Apprehension is the intellectual operation by which we lay hold of a thing, grasp its essence, without affirming or denying.

Judgment is the intellectual operation by which we combine or separate two terms or a term and its act of existing, affirming or denying that a subject is modified in some way, or simply is (was, will be, and so on).

Reasoning is the intellectual operation by which we proceed from known truth to new truth distinct from the previously known truth but implied in it.

Spirituality is that quality of a being or of a power by which it is able to be and to operate without matter.

The *mental word* is the object as known which is produced by the act of understanding.

100. Proofs

A. *Man is essentially (specifically) distinct from other animals.*

Beings are really and essentially different when one of them has an operation that the other does not have at all.

But: man has a true language, whereas the other animals do not.

Therefore: man is really essentially (specifically) different from other animals.

B. *Intellect is a distinct power.*

A distinct power exists where there is a distinct operation with a specifying proper object.

But: there is a distinct operation manifested in the use of language, and the proper object of this power is being.

Therefore: intellect is a distinct power.

C. *The formal object of the intellect is being.*

That is the formal object of a power which is the common aspect under which things are known, which is first attained by a power, and in terms of which everything grasped by that power is grasped.

But: the common aspect under which things are intellectually known is being (that is, *something having an act of existing*); that which is first attained by intellect is being; everything known by intellect is ultimately known as being.

Therefore: the formal object of intellect is being.

D. *The intellect is a spiritual power.*

That power is spiritual which is not the form of a bodily organ.

But: that power is not the form of a bodily organ whose operation manifests characteristics opposed to those of matter.

But: the operation of intellect manifests characteristics opposed to those of matter, in the total and simultaneous comprehension of a sentence, in the understanding of universal, abstract, and immaterial objects, and in its concomitant consciousness and its power of self-reflection.

Therefore: the intellect is a spiritual power.

E. *The adequate and proportioned proper object of the human intellect is being as manifested in sensible things.*

That is the adequate and proportioned proper object of the human intellect which is known directly and through which other things are known.

But: because the human intellect derives all its knowledge from the phantasms of sensible things, it knows these things directly, and all other beings in terms of sensible things.

Therefore: the adequate and proportioned proper object of the human intellect is being as manifested in sensible things.

F. *Intelligible* species, *which are necessary for intellectual knowledge, are produced by the agent intellect* (*principal cause*) *and phantasm* (*as instrument*).

The (possible) intellect needs an intrinsic formal determination in order to know, and this is called the intelligible *species.*

But: whatever is intrinsic to the intellect is, like the intellect, spiritual.

Therefore: the possible intellect needs a spiritual determination in order to know.

But: the only adequate cause of such a spiritual determination is a spiritual active power (and as such distinct from the possible intellect) as principal cause, and the phantasm as instrumental cause.

Therefore: for intellectual knowledge, intelligible *species* are necessary, and their adequate cause is a spiritual active power, the agent intellect, as principal cause, and the phantasm as instrumental cause.

G. *The agent intellect is necessary as a cause for the intelligible* species.

The intelligible *species,* which are spiritual determinations of the possible intellect, require a proper cause.

But: the proper and proportionate cause of the intelligible *species* is either something material, or a spiritual being outside of man, or the possible intellect, or a spiritual active power in man (agent intellect).

But: Nothing material can cause the intelligible *species* which are spiritual, nor is it reasonable to invoke a separate spiritual substance to substitute for a natural activity of man (since every man directly experiences that *he* knows, and we learn the nature from its activities), nor can the possible intellect cause the *species,* since it is a passive power.

Therefore: the agent intellect is necessary as a cause of the intelligible *species.*

H. *The human intellect, in understanding, produces a distinct mental word.*

An intellect, whose knowledge is distinct from its act of knowing, and whose directly known object differs from its existent object as universal from particular, must produce an internal term as the formal sign in which it knows its existent object.

But: the known internal formal sign, being the formal meaning of the external word, is called the mental word.

Therefore: the human intellect, in understanding, produces an internal formal sign, the mental word, which is distinct from the immanent activity which produces it.

101. Readings

St. Thomas Aquinas, *Summa Theologiae*, I. 79. 1–7, on possible intellect, agent intellect, intellectual memory; 84. 6, the origin of knowledge from the senses; 85. 1–8, the order and progress of knowledge; 84. 1–5, on our knowledge of material things; 87, on the knowledge of itself; 88, on the knowledge of God and the Angels; 84. 7–8, on the permanent relation between intellect and phantasm; (89, on the knowledge which the soul has after death); 34. 1, on the mental word; I–II. 50. 5 ad 2, on the agent intellect; also *Commentary on Aristotle's De Anima*, book III, lect. 11 (ed. Pirotta, no. 158).

Helen Keller, *The Story of My Life* (New York, Grosset, 1904), pp. 1–40, 315–16.

André Marc, S.J., *Psychologie Réflexive* (Bruxelles, L'Édition Universelle, 1949), Vol. 1, pp. 17–57; a brilliant analysis of language, which shows that all important philosophers agree about the basic facts involved; pp. 179–89, on reflection.

Jacques Maritain, *The Degrees of Knowledge*, trans. by Bernard Wall and Margot Adamson (New York, Scribner, 1938), pp. 144–55, on the concept; pp. 252–58, the objects of intellect; pp. 258–78, knowledge of the objects of metaphysics, pp. 278–84, our knowledge of God.

Étienne Gilson, *Being and Some Philosophers* (Toronto, Pontifical Institute of Mediaeval Studies, 1949), pp. 154–215, on the nature of metaphysics, the knowledge of being, of the act of existing, the difference between apprehension and judgment.

Robert S. Woodworth, *Psychological Issues* (New York, Columbia Univ. Press, 1939), pp. 80–88, "Non-sensory Components of Sense Perception" [taken from the *Journal of Philosophy, Psychology and Scientific Method*, IV (1907), 169–76]; pp. 103–27, "A Revision of Imageless Thought," [taken from *Psychological Review*, XXII (1915), 1–27].

G. P. Klubertanz, S.J., "The Unity of Human Operation," *The Modern Schoolman*, XXVII (January, 1950), 85–89, 102–103, 75.

Étienne Gilson, *The Spirit of Mediaeval Philosophy*, trans. by A. H. C. Downes (New York, Scribner, 1936), pp. 229–268.

Francis L. Harmon, *Principles of Psychology*, pp. 356–403, on intelligence; pp. 202–04, a fine summary of the work of Michotte on the perception of causality in experience.

Charles Spearman, *The Abilities of Man* (London, Macmillan, 1927), part 2, Ch. 12; *Nature of 'Intelligence' and the Principles of Cognition* (London, Macmillan, 1928), pp. 63–107, 262–301. A classic work on the "self-notion" in every percept; the second book has a long and detailed examination of the irreducible nature of the "knowledge of relations and correlates."

Louis L. Thurstone, *Nature of Intelligence* (New York, Harcourt, 1924); *Vectors of Mind* (Chicago, Univ. of Chicago Press, 1935).

Thurstone and Spearman give the best over-all picture of modern points of view, unbiased by behaviorism or sensism.

Charles Spearman and Ll. Wynn Jones, *Human Ability* (London, Macmillan, 1950), pp. 68–72, 92–93.

Kurt Goldstein, *Human Nature in the Light of Psychopathology* (Cambridge, Harvard Univ. Press, 1940), Ch. 2, 3, esp. p. 60.

John F. Peifer, *The Concept in Thomism* (New York, Bookman, 1952); a detailed study.

CHAPTER IX

Appetency and Appetite

102. The fact of conscious tendencies and attitudes

When we first began to consider conscious activities, we realized that they form a closely-knit, though not a static, unity. So intimately are these actions intertwined that it requires a difficult and very careful investigation to isolate the part-elements within the unified structure.

The first distinction we made within conscious activities was that between knowledge and appetency. Now that we have completed the analysis of the former, we need to spend some time on a similar analysis of the latter.

In our preliminary look at appetency, we discovered that it includes such things as emotions, attitudes, desires, affections, likes, dislikes, and so forth. Psychologists classify these conditions or states as (a) feeling tone, or affective tone; (b) emotions and sentiments; (c) desires, and their opposite, aversions. To these we will add a fourth, (d) choices.

(a) Feeling or affective tone is a kind of satisfaction (or dissatisfaction, or neutral, indifferent state) with the condition of our environment, and especially our own (bodily) condition (temperature, atmospheric pressure, humidity; and the condition of the body, reported obscurely by propriosensation). Because these facts are reported continuously, and because they usually do not occupy the center of attention, the affection resulting is almost continuous, usually very moderate, and quite indeterminate, so that it can be described only as an indeterminate happiness or sadness.[1] In fact, feeling tone is ordinarily so obscure an activity,

---

[1] Affective tone is sometimes spoken of as if it were a purely sensory af-

that it takes some reflection to discover that it has an object. From the analysis just given, we can see that its object is the good state of our organism and its environment. Hence, it is an activity directed toward a good.

(b) By emotions and sentiments are meant more noticeable affections, whose causes can be pointed out more clearly and easily. Of the two, emotions are stronger and relatively transient, while sentiments are weaker and longer lasting. It frequently happens that an emotion fades off into a sentiment; consequently, we can see that there is only a difference of degree between them. Both emotions and sentiments have definite bodily activities connected with them: changes in respiration and pulse; changes in motor activity; changes in external expression; variations in external and particularly internal secretions (tears and perspiration are examples of the former; adrenalin of the latter). These bodily activities connected with affective states are called "the bodily resonance."

It is evident that these two classes of affective states are similar, and that they differ mainly as continuous and somewhat indeterminate (sentiments) from the discontinuous and sharply defined (emotions). In both cases, they are the reactions of the sensory-rational being to the things it knows. As reactions, or activities, they will be specified by their object, according to the principle that all activities are specified by their object. When the object is a good known to be possessed, the reaction is happiness, joy, satisfaction, and so forth; when that object is an evil known to be present or a good to be absent, the reaction is unhappiness, sadness, dissatisfaction, and the like. The proper object of emotions and sentiments, therefore, is a good known to be possessed (and this proper object includes its opposite, as we shall see).

(c) Desires, aversions, and impulses constitute the third class of conscious reaction-states. In general, these are conscious tenden-

fection; it does not usually occur that way, but is ordinarily penetrated by rational motives and our reaction to them. Some psychologists would say that affective tone is frequently "sublimated" (that is, raised).

cies to action (or away from it) for the sake of acquiring some good or avoiding some evil. Hence, the group of desires, aversions, and impulses is related to the group of emotions and sentiments as movement to or from a term is related to the term attained. Similarly, the proper object of desire (namely, the good to be obtained) is related to the proper object of emotion, sentiment, and attitude (good possessed), in the way in which the term to be reached, and the term, in itself, are related. But motion to a term, and rest in that term, do not require different powers. For example, gravitational attraction is that which causes the stone to move toward the earth, and also keeps it resting on the earth's surface. Hence, these three classes of activities are all the activities of the same kind of power, which is called "appetite."

(d) Choice appears to be quite different from the three classes of activities just mentioned, which are easily seen to pertain to one and the same kind of power. We shall see later that choice is not simply an appetitive activity. But it must be an appetitive activity in some way, for choice is selection, and selection is the movement or adherence to one of several alternatives. Now, desire or adherence is quite clearly appetitive in character. To this extent, at least, choice must be related to appetite.

We know that we ourselves have such activities, for we experience them in ourselves. We see that they are manifested (externalized) by certain signs, and so we judge that when other men show such signs, they experience the like affections. But when we look at brute animals, though they seem to have feelings, emotions, and desires somewhat like ours in a general way, we find that we cannot say much about animal appetency beyond the fact that it occurs. Hence, we will not be able to use it to throw light on human appetency.

103. Appetency is properly called *passion*

So far, the term "appetency" has been used to designate the acts of appetite. What kind of power is appetite? First of all, is it a power of transient or of immanent operation? Clearly, nothing happens to the object we like or dislike merely by the fact that we like or dislike it—though our like or dislike may well cause us to perform other actions which do by their very nature modify the object. Hence, appetite is a power of immanent operation. Secondly, does the object act upon the appetite, or the appetite act upon the object? It is equally clear that the appetite is a passive power, and that somehow (for the present we are not concerned how), the object moves, stirs the appetite. This fact is recognized by our ordinary way of speaking—we speak, for example, of a "moving scene," because it *"affects* our emotions."

We have seen that a passive power must undergo a change to pass from potency to act. We have also seen that any change from potency to act can be called passion. In addition to this, many acts of the appetite involve a physiological change, the "bodily resonance." Experimental psychologists tell us that, with the aid of sufficiently delicate instruments, they can discover bodily changes accompanying even the slightest and mildest appetitive reaction, and that these scarcely noticeable bodily changes are like those that accompany the more violent emotions and sentiments. Because the acts of the appetite not only involve changes in the power itself, but also bodily changes of a more or less noticeable character, they are properly called "passions." [2]

In itself, this term "passion," as used in the philosophy of human nature, has no derogatory connotations; hence, it may be used to designate acts of the appetite which are morally good as well as those which are morally evil, and may as properly denote acts which are mild or weak as acts which are intense or violent. All are acts, and as such are metaphysically good (that is, are perfections of the acting subject).

104. Passions and the bodily resonance

Many passions involve some physiological changes in the body (over and above the corporeal change in the organs of appetite). For example, the passion of anger is accompanied by an increased flow of adrenalin which increases the speed of the pulse and the

[2] On the meanings of the term "passion," see above, Chapter IV, footnote 17.

rate of breathing. The passion of fear is accompanied by shivering and visceral changes ("knots," a fluttery or a cramped feeling). The passion of sadness is accompanied by a general slowing-down of all physiological functions, while the passion of joy has an expansive and exhilarating effect.

*Taken as a whole, and in context, the bodily resonance of one passion is different from that of another. But under careful examination, we will find that the kinds of physiological change are fewer in number than the kinds of passions. Some examples may clarify the relationship between passion and bodily resonance. Anxiety and despair involve practically the same bodily conditions (decrease of bodily activity), while passions as different as anger and violent desire have indistinguishable bodily accompaniments.[3] Hence, the bodily resonance is at least to some extent indeterminate in itself, and is capable of specification by the presence of a definite psychological passion.[4] For this reason, the bodily change is said to be material in the total experience of passionate states or activities, while passion itself is formal. (These terms are derived by a *remote* analogy with the matter and form which constitute material things, and should not be pressed beyond the meaning just given.)

In addition to being related as the material and formal elements of a total experience, the bodily resonance and the passion itself are related also as effect and efficient cause. Because we are angry, we become flushed. This link is partly natural, partly learned.

---

[3] If this seems to be at variance with ordinary experience, let the reader consult the experimental evidence on this point, and on the recognition of the "expressions of emotion"; cf. for example, C. Landis, "Studies of Emotional Reactions: General Behavior and Facial Expression," *Journal of Comparative Psychology*, IV (1924), 447–501; "The Interpretation of Facial Expression in Emotion," *Journal of General Psychology*, II (1929), 59–72.

[4] Note here also that chemical stimulation and the toxic effect of certain diseases can bring about a bodily "resonance" without the passion. People who have gone through such experiences report that they feel as if they were sad or angry or happy. In a sluggish or depressed condition of the body, people readily think of the evils which they suffer or are about to suffer, and thus really become sad. On the other hand, when the body is brimful of health, it is easy to think of pleasant things, and thus really to have the passion of joy. Thus, there can be a kind of reciprocal influence between passion and the bodily resonance.

Some persons do not show their anger mainly because their dispositions do not incline them that way; others, because they have learned to keep their bodily resonance to a minimum. Some persons naturally express their emotions openly; actors learn to give vivid expression to an emotion which is scarcely felt. But underneath these variations of degree, there is a basic natural relation between the passion as cause and the bodily resonance as effect.

Finally, the bodily resonance enters in as a *known* or *experienced* constituent of the total conscious activity. For, as we have seen, the condition of our body, and its functioning, is reported to us by propriosensation. An important element of our experience of being angry is the feeling of the rapid pulse, the short breath, the muscular tension. So, too, part of the experience of being afraid consists in the felt tension of the muscles of the stomach region. And so too in the passion of love, the propriosensation of the bodily resonance may become a large part of the total experience.[5] But no matter how large a part these propriosensations play within the total experience, it is very important to realize that they *are not* the passion itself.

*Moreover, the bodily resonance of its nature tends to be short-lived. The more violent a bodily change, the more quickly fatigue and reaction set in. Everyday experience shows us that a violent bodily excitation is exhausting. Hence, sheer weakness and the natural tendency of a living thing to react against a destructive state bring about the cessation of a violent bodily resonance.

*On the other hand, there is clear evidence that an affective response can continue to be an actual response for a long period of time, though the bodily resonance which was present at the beginning may recur only at intervals, or not at all.

[5] So noticeable is this evidence, particularly in a young and active person, that some psychologists thought that appetency consisted in the propriosensation of the bodily resonance (James-Lange theory of the emotions). But this opinion is (*a*) based on an incomplete account of our actual experience, (*b*) would conclude that a paralytic could experience no passions, and (*c*) overlooks the indetermination of the bodily resonance, for a particular form of the latter (for example, excitation), can enter in as an element into several quite different passions, as we have seen.

105. The basic passions: love and hate [6]

To obtain a philosophical understanding of the passions, we must try to see the relationship between them. For this purpose, a psychological or a descriptive analysis will not be sufficient; we will try to find out whether any causal relations exist between the various passions.

By basic or primary acts of appetite are meant those acts of appetite which arise immediately from the object of appetency and in some way give rise to other acts of appetite. In order that an act of appetite may be said to arise immediately from an object, two conditions are necessary, first, that appetite and object have a *per se* (or essential) relation, and secondly, that the appetency arise without any intermediary. Now, the act of love arises from the good inasmuch as it is good, and without any further qualification.[7] Other acts concerned with the good either arise from the good as qualified in some way (for example, to be possessed), or they arise incidentally (*per accidens*) from the good inasmuch as it presents some aspect of evil. Contrariwise, the act of hate arises from the evil inasmuch as it is evil, and without any further qualification; while other acts concerned with evil arise from it as qualified in some way (for example, aversion from an evil which can be avoided), or incidentally (*per accidens*) from an evil inasmuch as it presents some aspect of good.

We have already seen, in a preliminary way, that the proper object of appetite is the good; and the metaphysical analysis of

[6] This analysis is adapted from St. Thomas Aquinas, *Truth*, XXVI. 5. Note that this analysis is being made prior to the establishing of the distinction between sensory and rational appetites. This is done, because descriptively, our experience of appetency does not manifest this distinction with any great clarity. Moreover, philosophically, we shall see that, whereas sensation, though it occurs only within perception, nevertheless is not radically modified by the presence of intellection (and thus is not under rational control), sensory appetency in adult life ordinarily occurs as intrinsically modified both by the actual control of intellect-and-will, and by the presence of habits which take their origin from reason.

[7] Qualifications which occur are, for example, "the good not yet *possessed*," and "the good *possessed*."

the good reveals that the good is being inasmuch as it is sought, and that good, of its nature as good, attracts things to itself. Hence, love, which is the appetency inclining *toward* a good, is the act which derives *per se* from the good. In the same way, it is the proper characteristic of evil as such to repel the appetite, and so hatred, which is the movement of appetite *away* from an evil, is the act which is aroused by an evil *per se*. Therefore the *per se* and basic acts of appetite are love (toward the good) and hatred (away from the evil).

In the order of means and ends, the more ultimate something is in the order of execution which leads to the actual attaining of the end, the more directly the appetite tends toward it. Briefly, that which is last in the order of achievement is first in the order of ends. For example, a student who studies well and intelligently will do well in an examination, and will receive a high grade. This is the sequence of events in the order of execution. In the order of appetite, it may happen that a student first desires a high grade; because the high grade depends on the examination, this student then intends to do well in it, and because this requires study, the student finally comes around to desiring to study. Consequently, the acts of appetite which are directly concerned with the possession of the end are prior (with the priority of final cause) to all other acts, while these other acts presuppose them.

Thus, joy and sadness which are the appetitive reactions to the end possessed (good and evil *present*) are the completed acts of appetite. Love and hate, the appetitive reactions to the *per se* objects of appetite (good and evil without qualification), are the basic and primary acts which by their nature culminate in joy and sadness.

GOOD		EVIL	
joy	1	sadness	completed acts
desire	2	aversion	
love	3	hatred	basic acts

106. The remaining principal passions: hope and fear

Sometimes the good which we desire comes to us without any effort at all, or without any notable effort. Then the love and desire which the good arouses in us becomes joy when it is possessed. And similarly, an evil which we dislike comes upon us to sadden us, without any change on our part, or any possibility of avoiding it.

At other times, the attainment of the good we desire involves a notable difficulty of some sort, whether this difficulty lie in the strenuousness of the effort required to possess it, or in the length of time that the striving for possession will consume. And similarly, an evil which we dislike may demand an effort in order that we may escape being saddened by it. In both of these cases, it is no longer the simple good or evil that gives rise to the passion, but a good or evil to which some difficulty is attached. What is needed is a passion which will tend toward the good or away from the evil, in such a way as to enable us to transcend or overcome the difficulty that stands between us and the approach to the good or the escape from the evil. The movement toward the difficult good, such that we are led to overcome the difficulty, is the passion of hope. And the movement away from a difficult evil, such that we attack the difficulty to escape from the evil, is the passion of fear. Because these passions are directed toward the overcoming of a difficulty, they are sometimes called the "aggressive" passions.

Fear and hope are principal passions, for they in turn give rise to other, consequent passions. But they are not strictly primary, for they presuppose that the good has exercised its attraction upon us, or the evil repelled us. And they are principal also in this sense, that they are movements toward a good or away from an evil.

*107. An outline view of the simple passions

Obviously it would be a very difficult task to enumerate and classify all the various passions (feelings, emotions, and sentiments) which men can experience. And it is not at all clear that the amount of insight gained into human nature by such an investigation would be at all proportionate to the effort. Moreover, it is almost universally recognized that many affective states or activities are complex, compounded in some way out of simpler elements. On the other hand, there are some simple movements of appetite, which are either primary (basic or principal), or are derived from the principal passions, though without being compounded.

By carrying further the kind of analysis that has already been conducted, we can discover the secondary [8] as well as the primary and principal movements of appetite. From the passion of joy, which is the primary passion of appetite directed toward the good, other passions spring as steps in the attainment of the good. Joy is the act of the appetite in the presence of the good possessed. This primary act can be preceded in time by the act of desire, which is the movement of the appetite toward the good not yet possessed. And the act of desire presupposes in time an appreciation of the good as good, and this appreciation of (or complacency in) the good is called love (in the restricted sense of that term).

From the passion of sadness, which is the primary passion of appetite directed to the evil, other passions similarly spring as moments in the moving away from evil. As desire is the movement toward good, so aversion is the movement of the appetite away from an evil not yet present. And presupposed in this movement away from evil is the passion of hatred, which is the dislike, rejection, repugnance to an evil.

Hence, the passions derived from joy and sadness can well enough be considered after the analogy of motion to or from a term. For first in any movement there is a beginning of motion, and to this there corresponds love and hatred; then there is the movement itself, desire or aversion; and finally, there is the attainment and rest in the term, joy and sadness.

The passions derived from hope and fear cannot be derived in

---

[8] "Secondary" does not mean "of minor importance"; they are of equal importance with the primary passions, but they are derived from the latter.

the way in which the passions just mentioned have been derived from joy and sadness. For hope and fear are themselves stages between desire and joy on the one hand, and between aversion and sadness on the other. But it is possible to derive other passions from hope and fear by way of opposites. Thus, hope is the movement of the appetite toward a difficult good. Because a difficult good is still a good, the *per se* movement of the appetite will be towards it. But inasmuch as the difficult good is difficult, it is under that aspect an evil, and so accidentally the difficult good can move the appetite away from itself. The movement of the appetite by which it turns away from and rejects a difficult good is called despair.

In like manner, a difficult evil is an evil, and so the *per se* movement of appetite will be away from it, in fear. But the element of difficulty in the difficult evil can move the appetite toward itself, accidentally, inasmuch as the victory over an evil can appear as a good. Directly opposed to the passion of fear is the passion of boldness or daring, by which we move toward an evil that can be overcome. And if the evil in question is an evil in the sense of an injury (or an injustice), the appetite can approach it in the passion of anger.

The relations between these various passions can be summarized schematically.[9]

GOOD			EVIL			
joy 1						sadness 1
↑	↑ hope	despair ↓	fear ↓	daring ↑	anger ↑	↓
↑ desire 2						↓ aversion 2
↑ love 3						↓ hatred 3
per se	*per se*	per acc	*per se*	per acc	per acc	*per se*

[9] It may be advantageous again to remind the reader that appetite is still

108. The philosophy of love

A deeper understanding of appetite and its various acts can be derived from a particular analysis of the act of love. For the passion of love is in one way or another at the root of all appetitive activity, and what is true of love is true, with proportionate modifications, of all the passions.[10]

Love is an act by way of being a passion and a movement toward the good, a tendency toward the good. Inasmuch as this good is not explicitly possessed, love is an imperfect act, whose completion lies in the passion of joy.[11] Love is a complex act, and its complexity is of two kinds. First of all, love is the act of an *animated* organism [12] and so it includes a formal element which flows from the appetite as a power of the soul as well as a material element which is due to the organ. Secondly, in addition to the complex passion there is also the element of bodily resonance. As we have seen, the bodily resonance is an effect of the passion, while the propriosensation of the bodily resonance enters into the total experience of love as a kind of material complement of the passion. As cause of the bodily resonance, the act of passion is a mover or

---

being treated as analogically one, that no division has as yet been made into sensory and rational appetites. For those who think that the *schema* given above is not valid for appetite in general, but only for sensory appetites, it may be helpful to read these passages of St. Thomas, *Summa Theologiae*, I. 59. 4 ad 2, 3; 82. 5 ad 1, 2; I–II. 22. 3 ad 3; II–II. 18. 1; applications of the principles can be found in I–II. 26. 1 ad 1; 30. 1 ad 2; 31. 4; 35. 1; II–II. 20. 2, 4; 22. 2; 162. 3.

[10] The passion of love is selected for analysis rather than joy, because, though joy is the primary movement toward the good, the primacy of joy is in the order of the perfection of appetite. On the other hand, though love is not the primary passion in the sense of being the most perfect, it is the primary passion in the order of time and generation. And because it is first in the order of generation, it is included in all the movements of appetite toward the good. The entire discussion of section 108 follows very closely the analysis of M. Corvez, O.P., *Les Passions de L'Ame*, Somme Théologique, I–II, qq. 22–30 (Paris, Desclée et Cie, 1949: "Éditions de la Revue des Jeunes"), pp. 280–289.

[11] This statement of course is true only where the acts of appetite are distinct and successive acts. In God, where the act of love is identical with the act of joy, the act of love is perfect and complete in itself.

[12] At this point we are considering appetite as a genus; we have not yet made the differentiation into sensory and rational appetites.

moving cause, that is to say, a cause in the order of efficient causality. Moreover, the act of appetite is a moving cause in the line of efficient causality with respect to the executive powers (that is to say, the powers of external activity, the powers of transient action).

The energetic or dynamic element of passion is, however, only one aspect. Though passion is active in relation to other powers, it is passive with respect to its object, as we have seen. The cause of the act of appetite is the known good or end which is the *object* of love. As object, the known good specifies the act of appetite, according to the general principle that the specification of any activity is through the object of that activity.

In addition to being a formal cause of passion, the known good is also a final cause. We frequently express final causality by terms like "attraction, drawing, charm." It is necessary here to be on our guard against thinking that a final cause exercises a physical "pull" —as if a team of horses in front of a wagon were a final cause of local motion, while a team pushing the same wagon were an efficient cause. The "pulling" is an exercise of efficient causality as much as "pushing" is. So, too, though magnetic or gravitational attraction may be an interesting analogy for final causality, it really is (in modern physics) a simple efficient causality.

Final causality is a unique kind of causality—the good causes by being known as good, that is, simply by being presented to the will as the will's object. The efficiency is only on the side of appetite itself. Appetite, by its nature, is a first cause in a particular line of efficiency.[13] Under the attraction of the known good, a living being produces in its power of appetite the vital response, which is the act of passion or appetency. Therefore, appetite is a power of immanent or vital action.

*A still deeper understanding of appetite and its act will be gained if we try to consider the *being* of an act of love. As an act

---

[13] As a created cause, it is not a First Cause, absolutely speaking, but a first secondary cause in a particular line of efficiency. In creating a being, God gives it an appetite, and so the appetite is not an unmoved mover, absolutely speaking, even in the line of efficiency.

or operation, it is a perfection of the power by which it is produced. Because the power of appetite in us is a passive power, its act involves a change from potency to act, and is a passion, as we have seen.

*The appetite is changed by the object loved. What kind of change is this? It is a change which sets up an adaptation, or order, or proportion between the appetite and the object loved. The act of love is precisely the adaptation of the power, its harmony with the object. The act of love is the act by which we *take* pleasure in a good (not *feel* pleasure, which is an act of knowledge), and so we appropriate and unite the loved object to ourselves. The act of love is a union between agent and end, which springs from the intentional union of the knower with the known good, and by its nature leads to an immediate union, to a possession of the loved good. Because of its (logically) intermediate position between the intentional union in knowledge and the immediate union in possession, the union of love between lover and loved may well be called "tendential." [14] From this point of view, we may call the change which occurs in passion a tendential change, and we may even speak of the act of love as constituting a "tendential presence" of the loved object in the one who loves. For the loved object is in the one who loves by the harmony, or adaptation, or proportion, or bias of the appetite to the thing loved.[15]

*In calling the union of love "tendential," we stress the inherent dynamism of love. For the proportion between lover and loved which is love is an active and living sharing in the loved. It is not

[14] This union could be called "intentional," in a sense analogous to the intentionality of knowledge. For the sake of clarity and simplicity, this usage is here avoided.

[15] Many authors ask: "Is there anything in the total act of love which is distinguished from the operation of love, in the way in which the produced mental word is distinguished from the operation of understanding?" A large number of Thomists say that there is a "produced love" which is really distinct from the "operation of love." (For a brief listing of opinions, see J.-P. Dallaire, S.J., "Une nouvelle psychologie," *Sciences Ecclesiastiques*, III [1950], 205.) But such a distinction is not to be found in experience (cf. Marc, *Psychologie Réflexive*, Vol. 2, p. 39), while the arguments for it are not cogent (cf. Bernard Lonergan, S.J., "The Concept of *Verbum* in the Writings of St. Thomas Aquinas," *Theological Studies*, VIII [1947], 404–08).

like a state of rest (to which knowledge may be compared from
one point of view), but more like a movement or motion. In love,
the lover so to speak goes out of himself to the thing loved ("love
is ecstatic"). Whereas in knowledge, the knower has in himself
the form of the thing known, in love, the lover is wholly carried
out of himself, borne towards the thing loved. That is why love
can be called an inclination, or a transport. Because love is a motion toward the object loved as a real being, love can be called
"realist," in the sense that it is a tendency toward a thing according
to the object's proper reality (actual or realizable).

A further understanding of the nature of love can be obtained
from a more accurate analysis of the object of love. We have said
above that the object of love is the known *good*. But it is a clear
fact of experience that we know many things to be good in themselves which do not move us to love them. I know, for example,
that a mouse is a being, and so is good in itself; and also that it is
good for a cat as being its food; I do not for that reason love mice.
On the contrary, I love only those things which are good *in relation to me*. That is why the object of love is frequently said to be
"the good for me" (*bonum mihi*), or the "suitable good" (*bonum
conveniens*). I must, in other words, know a thing, not only as good
in itself, but as at least able to be a good for me (it becomes *actually my* good in being actually loved).

From this point of view, the object of love has two aspects: it
is *good*, and it is good *for me*. These two aspects are necessarily
related, but they are not identical. Moreover, in any act of love,
one of these aspects will be emphasized at the expense of the other.
When the *goodness* of the object is stressed more than its relation
to me, we are said to love that object with the love of benevolence
or with a disinterested love. But if, on the other hand, we subordinate the goodness of the object to ourselves (good *for me*),
we are said to love that object with the love of concupiscence.[16]

---

[16] Note the special meaning of "concupiscence" in this particular phrase.
The so-called "problem of love" arises when the two aspects or sides of the
good ("good—for me") are split into two ends. This division would involve
not only two radically irreducible acts ("ecstatic and physical love"), it would

109. The levels of tendency

So far we have been investigating the nature of appetency or conscious tendency according to the way in which we experience it. But tendency is not just a characteristic of man; it can be found on all levels of being. For, as we see much more fully in metaphysics, each being, in its own way, seeks its proper perfection, strives for it if it does not already possess it, adheres to it when possessed.

Now, when we say that each thing seeks its good in *its* own way, we are pointing out that tendency follows from nature or form. Form is for the act of existing, existing is for acting, acting is for the good. The principle "action follows the act of existing" (*agere sequitur esse*) means (*a*) a thing cannot act until or unless it is; (*b*) the kind or type of action is proportioned to the being of a thing; (*c*) if a thing is sufficiently in act according to the kind of act it can and should have, it is inclined to act. All three of these meanings are pertinent here, but particularly the second and third.

The first, commonest, and simplest kind of tendency follows from substantial form or nature. In this way, material things have their tendencies, and, given the proper conditions, their activities. Tendency which flows from substantial form is identified with power as principle of activity. Usually we pay no attention to it, except when a thing is prevented from acting by some external

---

seem to involve two different powers (not to raise the question of the meaninglessness of a "good" which by definition is unrelated to an agent).

But if the relation between the love of benevolence and the love of concupiscence is properly understood in terms of a varying emphasis on the two aspects of the object of love, no such problem exists. Can there be a pure or disinterested love? Yes (if one does not invent the fiction of a necessary conflict between the lover and the object of his love). Can a person love another more than himself? Clearly, for *more* is a matter of emphasis. And it is characteristic of the rational creature that he can love God more than himself, for he can know that God is the greatest good, and that his own personal goodness is precisely an effect of the Divine Goodness.

But the "problem of love" is a real practical problem: Which objects should we love for their own goodness? Which beings should we prefer to ourselves?

impediment or restraint. Otherwise, natural tendency leads immediately to activity for an end. Thus, a thing has tendencies inasmuch as it has a nature and powers; if unimpeded, these tendencies lead to activities by which the end of the nature and of the powers is obtained.

Natural tendency is found in every being. In nonliving things, natural tendencies are few in number, and are either general (like gravitational attraction) or specific (like the tendency of iron to unite with oxygen). In living things, there are the same generic tendencies, plus the specific tendencies of their vegetative powers. In things that have knowledge, the same tendencies are present, plus the tendencies which are inherent in their powers of knowing (the tendency of the eye to see, of the ear to hear, and so forth). Note that these tendencies go directly to the act and object of the power as such.

But in things that have knowledge, a new situation arises. Things which do not have knowledge have only their own forms (substantial forms as ultimate principles of activity, accidental forms, that is, powers, as proximate principles) which belong to their natures. In things that have knowledge, there are not only the natural forms, but also the forms received in knowledge. This new kind of form is the principle of a new kind of action with a new finality. For example, a dog looks at a piece of meat—and the tendency of its power of seeing is fulfilled in the act of seeing. But over and above this natural tendency of sight, the dog tends to (desires, wants to) eat the meat; it tends, in other words, to an action which is for the good of the whole dog, and not just of one of its powers. This kind of tendency is (a) a different tendency than the natural tendencies, because it has a different end and object; (b) it is a conscious tendency, as we know by direct, introspective evidence; (c) it is consequent upon knowledge. This conscious tendency is not only an act, but a power, because it is not always acting; the animal or man sometimes desires, sometimes not; sometimes has one feeling tone, sometimes another. It is a power distinct from other powers, natural, vegetative, and cognoscitive, because (*a*) it has a special cause which puts it into act, namely, the known good; and (*b*) it has its own object, the good which is good for the whole being. Hence, the power of conscious tendency or appetency is a distinct power, which is called appetite.

110. The two kinds (genera) of conscious appetite

In the second chapter, when we were discussing the evidence for some kind of plurality or multiplicity in man, we noted that we actually and concretely experience a conflict of tendencies which are simultaneously present.[17] For example, there are times when we know that we would very much enjoy doing something that we do not intend to do, or that we want to do something which causes feelings of repugnance. Now, one and the same power can act in different ways at different times, or with regard to different objects; obviously, one power cannot act in contrary ways at the same time concerning the same object. These facts of experience prove that there are distinct conscious appetites within us. But from them alone we cannot discover the nature of these powers, nor the way in which they are distinct from each other.

To find out whether powers are of different kinds, we must examine their formal objects.[18] Now, the appetite is a power which is moved to its act by a known good, and is therefore a passive power. We have already seen that a passive power is specified by its moving cause which is its proper object.[19] Therefore, the proper object of appetite is the known good. Furthermore, in the chapters immediately preceding we have seen that there are specifically different kinds of knowledge: sense and intellectual knowledge. Hence it follows that there are specifically different formal objects in the "good known by sense" and the "good known by intellect." Hence, there can be two kinds of conscious appetite in man: sen-

[17] See above, Chapter II, section 10.
[18] See above, Chapter V, section 52.
[19] See above, Chapter V, section 51.

sory appetite, which follows the good known by sense, and the rational (or intellectual) appetite, which follows the good known by intellect.

Do we in fact experience the acts of both sensory and rational appetite? We can answer this question in a preliminary but nevertheless certain way, if we rephrase it in terms of proper object. Thus: do we experience appetencies which have as their object (a) a good indisputably known by sense, and (b) another good clearly known only by the intellect? (a) People are evidently moved by sensory goods apprehended by sense; for example, they experience at least indeliberate movements of desire for some sensibly pleasant goods, as when in the state of hunger they desire attractively prepared food; they experience similar movements of fear or aversion in the presence of physical danger or violent suffering and destruction. (b) People are also evidently moved by goods which can be known only by the intellect; for example, they are moved by the desire of serving their country, or of doing their duty, or of serving God. We conclude therefore that in fact man does have two kinds of appetite, sensory and rational.

But we must not expect to find sensory and rational appetency as completely separate and isolated acts in our concrete experience. Ordinarily, our acts of love or hatred or desire or anger are complex, composed of both sensory and rational elements. We have noted before that the experience of appetitive reaction is complex, composed of the appetency strictly so called as formal element, and the bodily resonance as material element. We must now add that ordinarily the appetency itself is composite, since it contains sensory elements which are material and the rational element which is formal. Consequently, the experience of appetitive reaction usually contains these elements: (a) the bodily resonance as the material, determinable element; (b) the sensory appetency, which in relation to the bodily resonance is formal, but in relation to the rational appetency is material; and (c) the rational appetency, which is formal to both the bodily resonance and the sensory appetency.

A further study of appetency and appetite must give a separate consideration to the rational appetite and to the sensory appetite, while remembering that they are frequently found intermingled, and always are present together with the acts of knowledge by which their objects are known. The order of procedure will be to take the will first, and then the sensory appetite. The reason for what may seem to be an inverted procedure is that in our adult life, sensory appetency is rarely found in a pure state; ordinarily it is deeply permeated by reason and will (though not always right reason and good will).

111. Definitions

Appetency is conscious tendency.

Feeling tone or affective tone is an obscure, relatively continuous satisfaction (or dissatisfaction, or neutral state) with the condition of our environment, and especially our own (bodily) condition.

Emotion is a relatively strong and short-lived appetency, with a marked bodily resonance.

Sentiment is a relatively weak (in feeling tone) and usually long-lasting appetency.

Bodily resonance is a quality of bodily functioning (excitation or depression) which is connected with, and vaguely corresponds to the quality of appetency.

Love is complacency in the known good.

Hatred is the repulsion from the known evil.

Appetite is the power of tending toward a good or rejecting an evil.

Tendency is the power of and inclination to strive for a good and rest in it or to avoid an evil.

Natural tendency is the tendency due to a thing as having a nature or form; it is identical with form or power; it does not presuppose knowledge in the agent.

Conscious tendency is the experienced striving for or rest in a known good.

112. Proofs

A. *Appetency is a distinct kind of activity.*

We have direct experience of feelings, emotions, sentiments, desires, and choices.

But: these acts all deal with objects under the aspect of good (or evil), which is a proper object distinct from that of other activities, notably knowledge.

Therefore: there exists a class of conscious activities, distinct from all others, notably knowledge.

B. *Appetite is a distinct kind of power.*

Appetency is, like knowledge, sometimes present, sometimes not; sometimes present in one form, sometimes in another.

But: an activity which can be present or not, and can have different objects, requires a power as its proximate principle.

Therefore: there is a distinct power of appetency, called **appetite**.

C. *Appetite is a passive power.*

A passive power is one which does not immediately affect its object, but is moved to its act by its object.

But: appetite does not affect its object, but is moved to its act by its object.

Therefore: appetite is a passive power.

D. *The proper object of conscious appetite is the known good.*

The proper object of a passive power is its moving cause.

But: the moving cause of appetite is the known good.

Therefore: the proper object of appetite is the known good.

E. *There are two kinds of conscious appetite: sensory and rational.*

Passive powers are distinct and multiplied, if there are several distinct proper objects.

But: the known good which is the proper object of appetite, is of two essentially different kinds: the good known by sense, and the good known by intellect.

Therefore: there are two kinds of appetite—the sensory, whose proper object is the good known by sense, and the rational, whose proper object is the good known by intellect.

113. Readings

St. Thomas Aquinas, *Summa Theologiae*, I. 80, on appetite and its division into sensory and rational; *Truth*, XXVI. 5; *Summa Theologiae*, I–II, 22 and 23, introductory questions on the passions.

Robert S. Woodworth, *Experimental Psychology* (New York, Holt, 1938), pp. 234–41, the experimental evidence that appetency is a distinct kind of activity.

William McDougall, *Body and Mind*, 5th ed. (London, Methuen, 1920), pp. 312–29. McDougall is an outstanding psychologist, and one of his major efforts has been to show the importance of appetency in all varieties of conscious life. McDougall is not a Catholic, and the little philosophical background he has is of a dualistic sort. He is honest, very competent, and widely recognized.

————, *Energies of Man* (London, Methuen, 1932). Contains his revised views near the end of his career.

Dom Thomas Verner Moore, O.S.B., *The Driving Forces of Human Nature* (New York, Grune, 1948), pp. 105–14, on appetition in general; pp. 115–44, on bodily resonance; pp. 165–77, on sensory emotions and the will.

Clifford T. Morgan and Eliot Stellar, *Physiological Psychology* (New York, McGraw, 1950), pp. 340–56; excellent background material for paragraph 104.

CHAPTER X

The Will

114. The fact of rational appetency and appetite

In considering the affective-appetitive side of a nature that has knowledge, we have already noticed distinct acts of rational appetency. When we reflect on our own experience, we can directly and immediately observe (by direct self-consciousness) *that* we tend toward, or rest in, or choose rationally-known goods and reject or hate rationally-known evils. But this direct introspection merely enables us to see clearly and unmistakably that we perform these various actions. The nature of these actions cannot be found by such investigations; as we have already seen, the nature of an activity and of a power is discoverable from an analysis of its formal object.

First, then, we must be sure that we perform acts of rational appetency. Examples of rational appetency are rational affections and sentiments, such as patriotism, sympathy for the underprivileged, love of beauty; rational desires for honor, virtue, knowledge and power, desires to serve God and to save our soul; and choices, like the reasoned and deliberate adherence to an act of self-sacrifice out of love of God. Though in our concrete experience of these activities the passions of the sensory appetite usually are present, yet the sensory appetite cannot account for the entire appetitive experience. In patriotism, for example, we love our country. Now, though many things about our country are sensible facts (the land, the climate, the people and their customs of action and dress, flora and fauna, the material dispositions of our cities), our country as such is not sensible—it is an intelligible reality, with a formal structure, an authority, and a common good. Our country as an intelligible reality is what we love in patriotism. Since we experience an appetency whose proper object is an intelligibly known good, we can be sure that there is a distinct class of human activities. These acts are acts of willing.

Now, rational appetency, or willing, is not always being exercised; for example, it is ordinarily interrupted during sleep. Moreover, we do not always experience the same appetency: we desire one thing at one time, at another something else; we love or hate different objects as they come within our experience. This evidence proves that there must be a power of the soul which is the potency to these various acts.[1] And because will acts (acts of rational appetency) have a proper object distinct from the proper objects of the other powers of man, the rational appetite must be a power distinct from all others; the rational appetite is called the will.

Furthermore, the will does not immediately, by its action, produce a change in another being. In other words, a thing is not changed in itself because someone loves, desires, hates it. On the contrary, it is a power of tending toward, choosing, adhering to and taking pleasure in a good known by intellect. We must know a thing, at least obscurely, before we can will it; what is totally unknown is not desired. Therefore, the will is a passive power of immanent activity.

115. The nature of will

When we investigate the nature of the will, we must remember that we are not studying a distinct, independent agent, but a power of a rational being *by which* that being performs acts of rational appetency. But for the sake of clarity and convenience, we will use expressions like "The will intends . . . ," "the will chooses. . . ."

The will is a *rational* appetite. One of the distinguishing characteristics of intellectual knowledge is that it can be universal.

[1] Cf. above, Chapter V, sections 53–56.

Hence, the will also can be moved by a universal object. That this actually occurs is clear from such facts as these: that a man can choose a general course of action (for example, always to be kind); can love or hate a class of people or all men; can make and accept universal laws. In this way, man escapes from the confining limits of the immediate present and the material, sensible world. On the other hand, it is also clear that a man can will singular acts and objects: he can will a particular act (for example, to obey this command, to give this alms); he can will to work to acquire this house, that painting.

The will is an appetite, a tendency. A tendency is always and necessarily a tendency toward a good, for good and tendency imply each other. Now, all the other appetites (natural tendency as well as the sensory appetites) are directed to, and naturally specified by, a particular kind of good. The will (which follows upon intellectual knowledge) is directed to the good without qualification, the good as such. Empirically, we can verify this, when we reflect that in everything which we will there is some good, and that because of its goodness we want it. This is true, even when we will particular acts and objects. For example, when we will to eat, to give this alms, to take this job, we desire each of these things because they are good. Thus, the good as such is the aspect under which a thing becomes an object for the will. In other words, the formal object of the will is the good as such (the good in general, the good without qualification).

When we were considering the nature of appetite generically, we saw that the more ultimate an end (or good) is in the order of execution, the more it is primary and inclusive in the order of appetite.[2] Now, the good without qualification (the object of the will) is more ultimate and more inclusive than any sensible good (the object of the sensory appetite). Hence, in man, the will is his primary appetite or tendency, that is, primary in the order of appetite itself.

Because the will is primary in the order of human appetency,

[2] See above, Chapter IX, section 105.

it is the tendency or appetite of man as such. This same conclusion is reached by considering the power which presents to the will its object. We have seen that, whereas man shares his sense powers of knowledge with brutes, man's power of knowing inasmuch as he is man (his *proper* power of knowing) is the intellect. The object of the sensory appetite is a good as known by sense; the object of the will is a good as known by the intellect. Hence, the power of appetite that is proper to man as man is the will.

Again, a consideration of the levels of tendency [3] as they are found in man will serve to bring out the priority of the will. The natural tendencies of any being are directed to the operations and objects of its powers; only indirectly do these tendencies aim at the good of the whole. Appetency, on the contrary, is in one way or another directed to the good of the substantial nature. Sensory appetency, being on the sense level, of itself operates for the good of a sentient being. Now, though man is a sentient being, he is more than that. Hence, the sensory appetite in man is the appetite of his nature, though not of his whole nature. But the will is a power of human nature inasmuch as that nature is completely specified and perfected. Consequently, man's will is his primary appetite, his proper appetite as man, and his appetite as a whole or entire being—in other words, as a person.

Because the will is the primary and proper appetite of man as man, it is the power by which man establishes the ultimate direction of all his activities. For, in any finite being, all activity is for the production or acquisition of some good or end. In its turn, activity springs from some appetite. Now, the particular appetites (sensory and natural) are directed to particular ends, and lead to activity which is directed to particular, intermediate goals. On the other hand, the will is in a sense the universal appetite, and gives the over-all orientation to the whole activity of a man.

*The interrelationships of the various appetites can be illustrated from the functions of a well-run army. There is an over-all direction of the army's movements that is determined by the com-

[3] See above, Chapter IX, section 109.

mander-in-chief. He lays down the plan, and arranges the various divisions so as best to attain his purpose. At the head of each division there is a subordinate commander, who disposes of the forces he commands to suit the particular task assigned him. Finally, there are the non-commissioned officers in charge of the smallest groups. These last, too, within their own area, determine the movement of their men. For example, a corporal directs his group in the capture of a building. In doing this, he attains his end, and also does his part in reaching the goal of his division which is to take a city. When the division captures the city, it is fulfilling the end of its commanding general, and at the same time working toward the end of the commander-in-chief, who plans the strategy that is to win the war. Here there are three sets of movements enclosed one within the other. The most inclusive movement (that of the army as a whole) is the direction or tendency of the army as such. The particularized movements within that over-all movement take their ultimate, unqualified direction from the movement of the whole. This is somewhat similar to the way in which we must conceive the order of ends and activities of man. Consequently, it is also an illustration of the interrelationship of the appetites or tendencies of man.

116. Some preliminary distinctions

A distinction that is absolutely necessary is that between acts which are done by the will itself, and the acts of other powers which are performed by them under the influence of the will (I will to walk, and then I walk willingly). Both acts are "voluntary" (willed): the will to walk is the act performed by, elicited by the will; the walking is voluntary inasmuch as it is commanded by the will and performed under its influence. We shall be considering mainly the acts which are performed by the will—voluntary acts in the first sense.[4]

---

[4] Any and every act of the will is *voluntary*, whether it be free or not. Hence, every free act is voluntary; not every voluntary act is free. In ordinary usage, "voluntary," "voluntarily," "willingly" are used loosely in the sense of "free" or "freely."

Whenever we are talking about activity, we can distinguish two considerations of it. For example, in the act of seeing a chair, we can consider the "seeing" and the object of that act, the chair. The seeing depends on the subject (for example, he must be alive, awake, have his eyes open). This is called the "order of exercise." But what the subject sees depends on what there is to be seen, namely, on the object. This consideration is called the "order of specification." In regard to the will, if we ask in the order of exercise why a particular act of willing happens, we mean to ask why the person wills rather than not willing at all; if we ask the same question in the order of specification, we mean to ask why he wills this object rather than another.

When we study the various activities that are called will-acts, we place their source in a power whose nature is manifested in these acts. This nature is "to tend toward the good as such." Now, as we have seen, the will is not always actually willing; it has a starting-point as a nature (when the person begins to be), and its activities, though they fall into certain continuous series, have at least some new beginnings after each interruption of consciousness. In each beginning of a series of will-acts, we must find the source in the presentation of an object.[5] This makes it necessary to distinguish the various acts of will in a series. And to discover the various acts of the will and their order, we must consider their objects and the relation of their objects to each other.

The object of the will is the good; and that which is good in itself is an *end*. Things which are good in relation to ends are called *means*. The goodness of means lies precisely in this relation to end. Among ends, one is ultimate; the others are intermediate. The ultimate end is the one which is completely and adequately such; it is the first cause in the order of finality. Intermediate ends are ends, in so far as they have some goodness in themselves (and as such they may be the term of some means); they are means in so

---

[5] To discuss the relationship between primary and secondary causes (God and created nature) is not a part of the philosophy of man, but of the philosophy of being in a general kind of way, and of natural theology in particular.

far as they lead to further, more ultimate, higher goods. An intermediate end can therefore be considered in two ways: (*a*) simply in itself, without further qualification, and then it will be an end; (*b*) in relation to the further good, and then it will be a means.

The act in which the will has as its object *a good in itself* is called a "will-to-end" or the "will as nature"; when the object is an end *as obtainable* by some means, the act directed to that object is called "intention." When only one means is presented, we speak of "the acceptance of a unique means." The simple approval of one among several means is "consent" as a terminal act; the *selection* of one means with a view to action is "choice" or "election." Choice and election are also called "the will as reason." After choice, there is the command to other powers, if what is willed is an act or object external to the will; this command is called "imperium," and this is followed by "use" and "enjoyment" which occur as the act is being accomplished, and attains its object. Between the will-to-end and choice there is "deliberation," the reflection, planning, or counsel about things to be done.

By necessity is meant the condition or qualification of a being by which it is what it is, and cannot not be. Necessity is of two kinds, antecedent (predetermining, *de jure*), if it is in any sense prior to the being; or consequent (*de facto*), if it is not in any sense prior to the being. Thus, everything which is, as long as it is and as far as it is, is necessary, with consequent, *de facto* necessity. When Socrates sits, he sits necessarily—but with consequent necessity. Consequent, *de facto* necessity is compatible with complete lack of antecedent, predetermining necessity.

Antecedent necessity is of two kinds, intrinsic and extrinsic. By intrinsic necessity is meant the necessity of nature or essence (a triangle must have three angles, three sides, and so forth). The intrinsic necessity which pertains to the essential structure of a being is absolute (sometimes called "metaphysical"). The necessity of the proper or specific activity of natural beings (by which an apple tree produces apples and not grapefruit, a stone falls to the ground), is also predetermining and intrinsic, but no longer absolute (sometimes called "physical"). Extrinsic predetermining necessity is the necessity imposed by an efficient cause. Thus, the necessity imposed by a carpenter upon the wood which he makes into a table is an extrinsic, predetermining necessity.

Opposed to predetermining necessity there are contingence and freedom. Contingence means the lack of intrinsic necessity, but implies extrinsic necessity or the possibility of extrinsic necessity. Possibility implies both contingence and lack of act. Before the wood becomes a table, it has the possibility of becoming such. After it is made into a table, it is a table with *de facto* necessity— and contingently. Freedom, on the other hand, means lack of both intrinsic and extrinsic necessity, and implies act. Possibility is called freedom only in an improper sense (if we say "This book is free to move in any direction" we mean "There is no necessity for it to move at all, and no movement"). So, too, the lack of external constraint or extrinsic necessity alone, which is called "spontaneity" is only improperly freedom. Freedom is found only when in the absence of both intrinsic and extrinsic necessity an *act* occurs.

117. The will and extrinsic necessity

No power of a person can act on his will by way of efficient causality. For if these powers are organic, they must act and produce their effect according to the way in which a material thing causes —that is, by modifying the material dispositions of the subject of their action. But the will, because of its object and its relation to intellect, is a spiritual power which has no organ, and so has no material dispositions. And the intellect, which is the only spiritual power a man has besides his will, is not, by itself and of its nature, in the order of efficient cause at all. In other words, when we know, we do not by that very action produce a change either in an external object or in a distinct power or part of ourselves. For intellect is a power of life and of knowledge, and therefore its operation is immanent, perfecting itself and its subject, the person, by its own operation. But because the intellect is a knowing power, it can provide a formal and/or final cause in knowledge.

No created cause can act directly on a human will by way of efficient causality. For if this created cause is a material thing, it also causes by way of modifying material dispositions. Hence, the efficient causality of a material thing cannot reach the will. If the created cause is itself spiritual (an Angel or devil) it still cannot act directly on another's will, because willing is by nature and definition the operation of the one who wills. But a created cause cannot make a nature or give it its efficacy.[6] A will-act of one creature caused by another is therefore a contradiction. Hence, the will is not subject to efficient causality from any created cause, and so is not subject to extrinsic necessity. Hence, the will-act is always spontaneous.

118. The will-to-end

When an end is known as end, it is an object in which the intellect sees goodness without any further qualification. Such an object fulfills, contains in itself, the formal object of the will. In the presence of such a thing, which contains its formal object and nothing else explicitly, the will can only love it. When only the knowledge of the goodness of a thing is present to the intellect, the will cannot hate or reject it. Hence, in willing an end as such, there is intrinsic necessity in the order of specification.

It should be noted that the formal object of the will is not a subsistent thing. "Goodness as such" or "what 'goodness' means" is strictly and formally an analogical apprehension of the intellect. But though we can apprehend and understand goodness as such without any subject which is good, we never will it. The formal object of the will is and remains that in the object by reason of which it is an object of the will. But various material objects (be-

---

[6] God, Who is the author of human nature as such and in particular, as we shall see in considering the origin of the soul, gives its natural efficacy to the will, and so can intrinsically change the will, and put it into act. But when God so actuates the will, the will act is a grace (*gratia operans, inspiratio*), and a necessary act. (Obviously, this proposition does not say that this is the only kind of grace, nor that man is not free when he coöperates with grace.)

ings, and beings as known) can realize and have the formal object in various ways.

The supreme, infinitely perfect good, if directly known in itself, would present itself as fully good, as meeting all the requirements of goodness, as being nothing but good. Such an object presented to the will would necessitate the will to accept it in the order of specification. Further, in the initial moment of its presentation, the will not only could not hate (reject) it; it would adhere to it necessarily in the order of exercise. For, since this is what the will is made for, it would find in this object its perfect never-cloying satisfaction. And, since nothing would be between the intellect and its object in this knowledge of vision, the adherence of the will to this object remains a permanent spontaneous intrinsic necessity of nature.—But this supreme Good, which is God, is never naturally known to us directly, while our present analogous knowledge of God does not meet these requirements. It only shows God as good in terms of particular goods; [7] and though God is judged to be good without limit, the positive infinity of this perfection is not seen. Consequently, in our present knowledge of the supreme Good, we can always switch our attention to the act of knowing that good. Now, the act of thinking about God in this life does not present itself to us as fulfilling the whole of what "goodness" means. Consequently, there is no necessity to adhere to it in the order of exercise.

The secondary ultimate end is the possession of the perfect good, which possession is happiness, the complete satisfaction of all our desires. To say that we act for the good, or for happiness, is to speak in terms that mutually imply each other. The good is that which is to be possessed, and when possessed brings happiness. Happiness in turn is the possession of the good. Happiness is perfect when the good is perfect, and imperfect when the good is imperfect or partial. Consequently, happiness as known necessitates the will in the order of specification, for it, too, as a state of possessing the good without qualification, completely fulfills the

[7] Recall what was said about our intellectual knowledge of God.

requirements of the will's formal object. But even though when we think of happiness we cannot hate or reject it, yet, clearly, thinking about happiness is not good without qualification, is not happiness itself. And so in this case, too, the will is not necessitated in the order of exercise.

These things (God and perfect happiness) which are simply good, ends without qualification, occasionally occur to our thoughts. But most frequently our will-act series begins with something else which is presented to us as good in itself. As good in itself (note: neither explicitly wholly good nor explicitly partially good), it is sufficient to be an object which moves the will toward itself as end. In fact, our ordinary experience tells us that this is what usually happens. For example, if we are sick, health presents itself to us as a good. Or again: we observe that we are hungry; food therefore presents itself to us as a good, and we accept its value for us. These and similar starting points, which are naturally ends for us, are presented to us simply as good, and so our will necessarily acts to embrace them as ends. However, objects once chosen can, in virtue of that choice, become starting point for future will acts.[8] For example, once a man has chosen a job, it is possible for him to begin from that point as an accepted end for days and years. In this kind of situation, the starting point is necessary with *consequent* necessity.

The act of simply willing an end must be initially necessary (with either antecedent or consequent necessity) both in the order of specification and in the order of exercise. Why? Because, before the will acts, there must be an adequate reason why it comes to act. Nor can we normally have an extrinsic necessity by way of an efficient cause, as we have seen. Suppose that a limited (finite, particular, mixed) good is known by intellect as such, as a first knowledge in a series. Such an object under one aspect contains the formal object of the will; but under the aspect of "being limited (mixed, particular)" it does not contain that formal object. More-

---

[8] Just as in reasoning, where we do not always begin with the first principles, we can, and in fact more often do, begin by taking as premisses the conclusions of other reasonings.

over, inasmuch as it is limited or partial, it excludes at least some other partial goods, and so can be called "evil" (in the modified sense in which the word "evil" denotes an absence of good). Therefore in itself it is simultaneously good and evil, and so it is in itself only a possible object. But with an object that is possible, and a will that is in potency, we cannot begin. Consequently, the first act must be, in its beginning, an act which is naturally necessary. (There is, of course, a way to get at a possible object; we will consider it later under the heading of choice.)

We must look briefly at the relations of intellect and will in this first act, the will-to-end. In considering appetite in general, we have already seen that appetite and cognition are related as tendency and object. Cognition presents the object which actuates the appetite by way of final causality. But there are several precisions which we can make concerning the intellectual appetite.

In the first place, both intellect and will are non-organic, immaterial powers. Consequently, there is no spatial distinction between them: the only distinction is that of nature (definition) and order. Hence, will is *in* intellect; that is, it is on the same level; it is the appetite corresponding to intellect; it is not "separated" from intellect; it is ordered to intellect, and intellect to it. And so the relations of intellect and will are purely qualitative relations of order and dependence.

Intellect is the most universal knowing power in man. As knowing power it is on the side of form and specification. Therefore, the first, simplest relation between intellect and will is that wherein intellect presents an object, and will tends simply and directly to that object. The relation here is that the will depends on the intellect in the line of final causality.

Will is the most universal appetite in man, and all appetite is in the order of efficient cause. Hence, the will is the ultimate, most universal moving power in man. And so, apart from the initial dependence of will upon intellect, the will can move the intellect to the exercise of any one of its acts.[9] In this second relation, the

⁹ The will can move the intellect to consider this or that particular good;

will is as efficient-principal cause, the intellect as patient-instru-
ment.[10] The will is mover, the intellect is the power moved. In a
later section (number 124) we will consider this relation more
closely.

119. Intention [11]

The simple will-to-end is an act of love (complacency, approval,
and the like) which arises spontaneously and necessarily in the
will when the intellect understands that something is good for me,
simply and without any further qualifications. As such, this act
does not necessarily and directly lead to any other act.

But suppose that when the intellect understands that something
is simply, unqualifiedly good for me, it simultaneously understands
that I do not actually and physically possess that good. For, though
an object is intentionally possessed in knowledge, what we possess
in knowing a thing is its intelligible form (or essence), not the
thing itself according to the thing's own proper act of existing.
And yet, good and evil are in things (whereas truth and error are
in the mind in relation to things). And so, when the will adheres
to an unqualified good which is known to be able to be possessed
in reality, the will *intends* the good thing. Loving the good possessed as known, the person wants to possess it really. This act of
the will naturally leads to a series of other acts.

Intention, as it is here defined, is very similar to the will-to-end,
differing (*a*) in the kind of knowledge which precedes (good
able to be obtained, in contrast to *good*), and (*b*) in the fact that
intention naturally leads to further acts. Consequently, like the

---

but can move it to the *specification* of its act only when the object is not presented as known with rational necessity. In case of ignorance, of truth known
probably, and in the case of what are called "free certitudes" man can fully
command his intellect to accept one or the other side of contradictorily opposed propositions.

[10] As we have seen, analogies drawn from external, sensible reality are defective when applied to the soul, its powers and their activities.

[11] This is *not* the "intention" of which we speak when we use phrases like
"a good [*or* bad] intention." "A good intention" is always a free act directed
toward the ultimate end, or at least to some relatively ulterior end.

will-to-end, intention is spontaneous and necessary with the necessity of specification and exercise.

120. Deliberation

Under the impulsion of the intention of the will, the intellect begins to seek for means to gain physical possession of the end. This action of seeking for means is an act of the practical intellect, and is called "deliberation" or "counsel" or a "practical syllogism."

The action by which the intellect seeks for means by which an end may be gained is a process, and therefore a kind of reasoning. In practical reasoning, the starting point (principle or first premise) is the end, for example, good health. In considering this as an end to be gained, the intellect will work toward more and more proximate means—for example, consultation of a doctor, following his advice, taking this medicine now. These intermediate steps are means to the end intended.

The act of deliberation is an inquiry, and so it is an act of the intellect; yet it deals with good, ends, means, and so it is also related to will. Hence, deliberation is a complex or composite act, in which the will stands as moving cause and the intellect as power moved.[12]

121. The acceptance of a unique means

In deliberation, the intellect discovers the means to an end. One of two possibilities can occur here. Either there is but one means (or one series of means) to the given end, or there are alternative means. It makes no difference for our present consideration whether the intellect correctly apprehends the plurality of means —sometimes the intellect sees but one means where there are several alternatives; at other times it sees alternatives where there

---

[12] This kind of act happens only when a person thinks over what he himself will do. Planning the course of action of another person is a work of purely speculative intellect in which the will is not directly and necessarily concerned. These two kinds of planning look quite similar on the *intellectual* side; they differ in that in deliberation the will is necessarily and intrinsically concerned; in planning for another, not so.

are really none. Since it is only the good as known, and the means as known, that have a relation to the will, we need not here consider whether the understanding is true or false; the workings of the will are psychologically the same.[13]

Suppose then that there is but one means (or one series of means) to a willed end. Obviously then the will to the end involves the will to the means. Once it is clearly seen that there is but a unique means to a willed end, the acceptance of those means [14] is as necessary as the original intention. For a unique means, clearly and evidently seen as such, is merely the end known more explicitly, more comprehensively. Consequently, the acceptance of a unique means is usually an act distinct from the intention which brings it into being. The nature of this act will be considered together with the nature of the act of choice.

122. Consent as a terminal act

In the course of deliberation, one of the means discovered can turn out to be in some sense a good in itself, which solicits the adherence of the will. The clearest instance is that of a moral evil which is sensibly good or pleasant. For example, suppose that a man considers that it is a good thing for him to have security and comfort in his old age, and that this good is something still to be procured for himself. When he sees this, his will spontaneously intends to acquire the good which he knows. Under the impulsion of the intention, his intellect begins to search out suitable means. The first remote means that occurs to him is money. And then he considers that money may be gained in various ways: by gift, by luck as in gambling, by hard work, by dishonesty in a business in which he is a partner. Dishonesty appears to him to be the easiest way to acquire a large amount of money; he knows it is morally

---

[13] "Psychologically" is an important word here. Obviously the real effects of a choice based on an error may be disastrous. Then, too, the moral evaluation of such an act which we make in ethics will be affected by the truth or error of the premises. Error does not make for moral goodness, no matter how earnestly, sincerely or piously that error is accepted.

[14] The acceptance of a unique means is sometimes called "consent"; for example, St. Thomas Aquinas, *Summa Theologiae*, I–II. 15. 3 ad 3.

wrong, and he suspects that he would be caught if he tried embezzlement. And yet dishonesty appeals to him as a very fine way to get money in spite of its evil. Considering the attractive feature of dishonesty, his will moves to embrace it as an idea, or as a possibility. This movement of the will is known as consent. At other times, consent takes the form of accepting and taking deliberate pleasure in merely thinking and mulling over an action which one might have no desire to perform.

Consent as a terminal act also is given to an object or action that is morally good. But a good consent (because it is in harmony with reason) is more easily overlooked than the morally evil consent. The nature of the act by which we consent to or approve of a particular means in the concrete will be investigated later, when we study the act of choice.

123. The act of choice

Usually, deliberation uncovers alternative means to the willed end; these may be single alternatives or alternative series. And the original intention, from which deliberation has sprung, is of its nature directed to the physical acquisition of the willed end. Consequently, we must consider the case in which the original intention will not be sidetracked by a consent as a terminal act.

The intellect, then, has arrived at alternative means to the end. Of course, not all these means are always equally effective as means to the end. Nevertheless, as long as consideration reveals a plurality of means, there is no necessity in any one of them. In the case of alternative means, any one of them is only contingently related to the end. This means that if it is chosen, it will lead to the end. In such a case, there is neither necessity of specification nor necessity of exercise.

Nevertheless, in such cases, a man does make a choice. Choice is an appetitive reasoning, or, more accurately, a reasoned adherence to a means. In this kind of deliberative process, the will has before it an object which can be good (because it can be a real means to an end), and yet is not wholly or necessarily so (because its choice would exclude other means which also could lead to the end). It is thus an object which from one point of view verifies the will's formal object (it is good as related), but from the point of view of being only a partial good, and thus exclusive of other goods, it does not contain the will's formal object. And such a good, as we have seen, cannot be willed in itself. But when it is considered as leading to the end, it is good.

A comparison with the activity of the intellect will help to clarify the relation of intention and choice. In the case of intellect, there are some truths ("enunciable propositions") which do not contain any evidence in themselves. A true conclusion, presented to the intellect without its proof, cannot be an object of understanding. But if the intellect is put into act by the evidence of the proper premisses, it can actuate itself to the knowledge of the conclusion. So, too, the will, once it is put (necessarily) into act with respect to the end, can actuate [15] itself to adhere to one of several means; it can choose among means.

Is the act of choice free or necessary? Apart from the action of God upon the will, there is no extrinsic necessity imposed upon the will, because apart from the preternatural or supernatural motion of God no efficient cause can act upon the will. Is then the act of choice necessary with the necessity of nature (with intrinsic necessity)? There is a necessity of nature (both in the order of specification and of exercise), when an end is presented as good without further qualification, and when a necessary means to a willed end is presented as such. But the deliberation which precedes choice usually reveals several means, none of which are exclusively necessary. Hence, if choice does take place—and all of us are immediately aware that we do choose—choice is an act without any predetermining necessity, a free act.

Indeed, in the act of choosing following upon a real delibera-

[15] When the will moves itself a choice of means or to consent, this self-motion is not a change from passive potency to act, but from active potency to act (that is, "second" act). Some authors put it this way: This change is from virtual act to formal act. The terminology is not a happy one, but the idea is the same.

tion, we experience obscurely and concretely the *fact* that our choice is free.[10] During the deliberation, we know that we are really able to choose among the means that we are considering, In putting an end to deliberation and actually choosing, we experience the active interposition of the self (Ego), we experience the actual dominion (control and domination) which we have over the act we are performing. In such an experience, we see freedom in act, even though the nature of, and the reason for, freedom become clear only upon analysis.

The act of choice is an active adherence, a conscious tendency. Moreover, it is an act which manifests order and relation, for it tends to means-because-of-end. Consequently, both intellect and will must be involved in this act, for the nature of both intellect and will are revealed in it. Now, it is clear that intellect is on the side of form, and that order and direction are on the side of form and finality. Tendency, in the act of choice, is that which is ordered by the means-to-end relation. Hence, in the complex act which is choice, the intellect is as form, the will as matter.

From this deeper point of view, the freedom of choice becomes still clearer. The union of matter and form in any given composite being is only *de facto* necessary, for the essence of a form does not include its information of a particular matter, nor does matter of itself include the reception of a particular form. The only necessity by which this form informs this matter is the necessity imposed by the efficient cause which united them. Now, choice is a complex act, having a material part (the adherence of the intellectual appetite) and a formal part (the understood order to the end). The efficient cause uniting the two parts is the will, which has already been put into act when it performed the first act of the series, the intention. And so, the choice is reasonable when made, but its making is wholly dependent upon the will, which moves itself to be determined in this way.

[16] Note that in our adult life, we very often act because of a previous deliberation, and sometimes even we choose because of a choice made previously. In such cases, the experience of freedom will be vague and extremely brief, sometimes absent, because the roots of the present free act are in the past.

٩   *Our choices do not always take the full and complete form which has just been analyzed. Sometimes a choice which has once been made after explicit and full deliberation is repeated. At other times, a choice freely made in the past appears as an unquestioned end in relation to further sets of means and further choices. In both cases, there is an indirect or mediate freedom—that is, not here and now, but in the original choice.[17] It is possible for a man to go through a whole day or more, merely repeating the results of former deliberations and choices. On such a day, a man could not discover his freedom in experience, unless he remembered at least this much, that he had previously deliberated and freely accepted the original choice.

١٠   Choice, then, is a very clear example of the composite activity of intellect and will. Both consent as a terminal act and the adherence to a unique means are similarly composite acts. The consent as a terminal act is most like the act of choice, from which it differs only in not leading to the actual performance of the activity contemplated, but in an approval or a disapproval of the activity as known. The adherence to a unique means differs from both choice and consent as a terminal act in that it is not directly free. Yet inasmuch as it is an adherence or acceptance, it is an appetitive act; while inasmuch as it is directed to a means because of an end, it manifests the order of reason. Consequently, even the adherence to a unique means is a composite act, whose formal part is the order and conclusion of reason, and whose material substantial part is the tendency of the will.

124. Complex processes of willing

Thus far we have considered the will-to-end, intention, choice, and consent in their simplest forms. These acts can become immensely complicated and involved. Two of the many possible combinations need special consideration.

---

[17] Responsibility for an act performed in virtue of a previous deliberation and choice depends partly on the preceding foresight and acceptance of the acts that would follow upon the original choice, partly on the person's "virtual intention"; see Chapter XII, section 145.

(1) A regressive movement in deliberation is possible, and occurs in several fashions. It has been pointed out that the ends which usually occur to us as the beginnings of will-series are really only intermediate ends. Now, in the course of deliberation about means to such ends, something may occur to us which causes a conflict. For example, one stage of the means may seem excessively difficult or painful; one of the means may conflict with a contrary habit, or sensory passion, or choice which we have made in the past and still adhere to. At any rate, for whatever reason, a conflict in the elaboration of the series of means halts the process from means to end and throws it into reverse.

Such a reversal of movement is quite similar to something which can happen in the order of speculative reasoning. Suppose we begin with a set of unquestioned premises, and work to a conclusion which seems to conflict with a fact or with another conclusion. When this happens, the normal thing to do is to go and check the reasoning and the premises; if these turn out to be themselves conclusions, we go back until we reduce the argument to really first principles.

So, too, in the order of means and ends. A means in the process of deliberation shows up as one which we know from other sources to be bad, or which we dislike, and so forth. Its goodness lies precisely in its relation to the end already willed. Then, what about that end? is it simply an end, or is it itself a means to a further end? For example, in time of sickness, recovery of health appears simply as a good; deliberation reveals a serious and painful operation as a necessary means; the sick man may then ask himself: "Is health that important?" Such a process of searching and testing will go on till we reach an end which is unquestioned; from the nature of the case, it could go on till we reach the consideration of the ultimate end. In this way, any intermediate end, though it begins as an object that necessitates the will in the order of specification and exercise, can always turn into a non-necessitating object.

This regressive movement can always be used to ensure that the intermediate ends which occur to us for acceptance as ends are the right ends. But the process is laborious and time-consuming. There is another way in which the rightness of such proximate ends can be guaranteed, and that is through good habits. Hence, a successful, happy, and morally good life is largely dependent upon right habits.

Another way in which this regressive deliberation may occur is the situation in which we come to know some object as a mixed good. As such, it cannot move the will to act, either to accept it or to reject it. Circumstances may be such that some action is necessary. In order to be able to choose our course of action, we can check to see whether or not it fits in with some true end. When its relation of means is discovered, it can be freely chosen. For example, I am offered an opportunity to earn some extra money and an answer must be given today. I could use extra money, but I would have to sacrifice some leisure time. I then reflect to see whether there is something I want; in the course of reflection I recall I wanted to buy a present for my aunt, but did not have the money. When I see that this extra work would bring me the money to buy the gift which I want, I can freely choose to take the opportunity.

(2) So far we have been speaking mainly of choice as a choice between two positive alternatives. However, the alternatives can be of another kind, namely, acting and not acting. For where action is in any way difficult, refraining from action may appear as a good. Thus, the "freedom of exercise" (to act or not to act) rests upon the freedom of specification. And so, even in cases where no two positive alternatives present themselves, there is always (except in the case of the Beatific Vision) an alternative: to act or not to act. Hence, the acceptance of a unique means can become free.

This is important for the understanding of how we are free in those cases where the object of consideration is a necessitating one. We saw that even when the object is necessitating, the thinking of such an object is usually only contingently related to the object itself. The alternative to thinking about it is not to think about it. And thinking about a necessitating object might appear difficult, or unpleasant, and so forth; hence, as not being a part of the perfect good, not necessarily leading to our happiness, not perfectly verifying the formal object of will. And so, by way of a shift from the object to the thought of it, there can be freedom, secondarily and indirectly, with regard to objects which directly and initially necessitate in the order of specification [18] (exception being made, as always, for the direct knowledge of God in Himself).

One more remark must be made. We have been speaking of the good as such, of goodness. This goodness need not at all be moral goodness; it can be goodness of any kind: self-perfection, pleasure, honor, material goods. This explains how sin is possible. For the sinner does not and cannot choose the sin from the viewpoint of its leading away from his ultimate end; from that point of view he must reject it. But from the point of view of being pleasant, or useful for honor, possessions and the like, it is a possible object of choice.

125. The imperium and the commanded act

When a choice has been made (or a unique means accepted), the end remains to be accomplished (unless there was question of willed complacency). The power which is to execute the chosen deed or activity needs to be moved. And all the powers of man are moved in the attaining of the end desired by an impulse which manifests the efficiency of will and the order of reason (means-to-end). This directive impulsion is called the "imperium." The imperium is an act of intellect, translating the order of choice (end-to-means) into the order of action or execution (means-to-end). Because the imperium is an act of ordering, it is an act of intellect; because it is an impulse to action, it manifests the nature of will as tendency. Hence, the imperium is a complex or composite act of both intellect and will.

After the imperium comes the commanded act.[19] The com-

---

[18] The thinking about a good thing can not of itself be an object that begins, initiates a will-act series. Of itself it is a partial good, which can begin a series only by way of regressive deliberation.

[19] There need be no time-interval between the imperium and the com-

manded act may be any activity of any of the powers, or any group of powers (for example, walking, talking, manual movements, thinking, further willing, and so on). In the commanded act, any or all the other powers act as the instruments of reason-and-will. This is so, because in the order of action the end is first and ulti- mate, and so, in the order of action, the will is as form to all the other powers (whereas in the order of cognition, the intellect which is the higher cognitive power is as form). From the point of view of the metaphysics of action the same conclusion follows. It is always true that the operation of the principal and the in- strumental cause (strictly so called) is one complex operation, and that all true composition implies the relation of matter and form among the parts.

Finally, the complex unity of imperium and commanded act shows itself directly to us. When I will to move my hand, and move it, the will and the motion flow one from the other without any break, or perception of separate activities. And all my volun- tary acts show themselves to me as mine, as human, as being good or bad. But clearly, walking is not human walking, nor mine, nor good, because of the local movements of legs and feet which proceed from a separate act of the will (else the movements of my typewriter would be human, too). It is because my external move- ments, and indeed the movements of all the powers which admit of voluntary control, are joined in a unity of operation with the imperium, that they show in themselves my specific nature. As willed, chosen, the activity of man has its highest and most intimate unity. In this unity of the imperium and the commanded hu- man activity, the substantial unity of man is most clearly mani- fested.

126. Diagrams of the will acts

NOTE: ACTS NAMED IN BOLD-FACE type are the essential acts of a given series. Acts in regular type are such as can be explicitly put

---

manded act. "After" may mean only the posteriority of dependence in causal- ity. But inasmuch as the external activity of man is performed by material powers, such activity takes place in time.

in, or left implicit in the essential acts. Acts in small italics indicate where choice could have replaced consent, or where consent could have terminated a series which in fact issued in another activity. Solid lines show the sequence and influence of the essential acts; dotted lines point out where additional, supplementary acts come in.

ACTS OF INTELLECT   ACTS OF WILL

I

Acceptance of a unique means

[Apprehension of a good-for-me ⟶ will-to-end, love, complacency]

Apprehension of what is good for me simply, and is yet to be procured (by means)

Intention

Deliberation

Conclusion-judgment   Acceptance of unique means

Imperium   Use, enjoyment

ACTS OF INTELLECT   ACTS OF WILL

II

Free consent as a terminal act

[Apprehension of a good-for-me ⟶ will-to-end]

Apprehension of what is good for me simply, and is yet to be procured (by means)

Intention

Deliberation
Discovery of means - - - - - acceptance of or consent to means in general

Conclusion-judgment ⟵ Consent to a particular means

choice

imperium   use, enjoyment

III

Choice

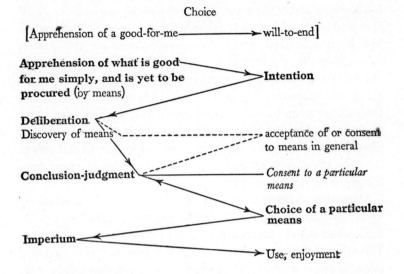

NOTE that in Series I, the acceptance of a unique means simultaneously takes the place of both the possible act of acceptance or consent to means in general, and the consent to or choice of a particular means (Series II and III, respectively). Note also that the acceptance of a unique means is a necessary act as long as the intention remains unchanged, necessary.

127. The will and the other powers

All the lower animal powers of man are the instruments of his will, but in different ways. On the other hand, the vegetative and natural powers are not subject to voluntary control.

*The senses have their own definite moving causes. Thus, the external senses are moved to their acts by sensible objects. Though we have some control over sight—we can usually close our eyes or turn our gaze away—the only other control we have over external sensation is to move ourselves out of the vicinity of the sensible object, or block its activity from reaching us. We do have, however, some control over our attention to external sensation, which is another matter.

*Internal sensation is somewhat more under control. The unifying sense as power of awareness is not directly controllable at all. Imagination, on the other hand, submits to a good deal of control. We have a limited power to arouse phantasms deliberately (though no direct power to repress them). But, as we have seen, there are also other causes independent of will which can arouse phantasms, namely, external sensation, organic modifications, and the estimative and memorative powers. Our control over phantasms aroused by any of these causes consists in (a) arousing other phantasms and (b) diverting our attention to this second group, whereby attention is naturally and necessarily directed away from the previous independent phantasms.

*Attention seems to consist in (a) the presence of a relatively vivid sensation or image and (b) the greater or less absorption of the limited act of sensory awareness by this sensation or image. The external sensation is vivid or weak, depending on the relative strength of the stimulus. The image (phantasm) seems to become vivid or weak depending upon estimation and sensory appetite. Consequently, the control of attention would seem for all practical purposes to reduce to control of estimation (and/or memory).

We have already seen that the human discursive estimative is directly and by its very nature subject to the control of intellect-and-will. With the exception of the generically predetermined estimations with which we are born, all other estimations of man are discursively arrived at, and are under the imperium.

The sensory appetites are directly put into act by sensation or by sensation-image plus estimation (and/or memorative power). Experience shows us that we have no direct control over the passions. If the sensation-image and the estimation remain constant, the will can do nothing with the passion. For the sensory appetites are not merely potential; they are in us independent principles of activity, passive only with respect to their object. But because the sensory appetites are passive with respect to their object, it is possible to control them by controlling their object. This is done, either by changing the estimation (if it is an acquired one), or by controlling attention. Hence, it is clear that the voluntary control of our sensitive animal nature functions directly through the discursive estimative, so that this power is the pivotal center of our unified voluntary action. This control can be developed into a habit, as we shall see.

Finally, we must consider the control of intellect-and-will over external movements of our members. Most of our external members are directly subject to voluntary control through imagination. These same external members can of course be moved also by sense appetite, just as they are in animals. Consequently, as long as the sensation-image is at all under the control of reason, external action is under control. If, however, the image is released from control, or gets out of control through turbulence of passion or disturbance of the imagination, then external activity flows from sensation-image and appetite.

What about the influence of other powers upon the will? We have seen that no external efficient cause (except God) can act upon the will. We have also seen that the will is moved by intellectual knowledge in the line of object and final cause. But do not our passions move our will? Is it not the case that many men are wholly influenced by their passions? The fact is true, but note that in such cases we speak of "men yielding to their passions." The passions move the will by way of object. For under the influence of passion, sensory perception is changed. For example, under the influence of anger, a man may perceive mainly the good aspects of taking revenge. Hence the intellect would understand this as a good and an end. In so far as it is possible to control this apprehension, and make it present not only the good but also the evil aspects of taking revenge, the will is not moved by anger, and remains free. Also in other situations the knowledge which at first is adequate, presenting both the good and the evil of the object, tends to shift under the influence of passion which acts directly on the phantasm, to an emphasis on the good (e.g., the pleasure in a sinful act), or the evil (e.g., the difficulty of fasting). Hence, what was presented originally to the will as a mixed good changes under the influence of passion to a simple good or end. It is during the course of this change that freedom is exercised; once there is only good or evil present in the intellect, the will is moved with the necessity of specification. That is why ascetical writers advise us to resist the beginnings of temptation, and explain that we fall into sin by letting (consenting freely) our attention dwell on the sinful object.

128. Definitions

The *will* is the rational appetite which tends to the good as such; whose formal object is goodness as such.

Order of exercise is the consideration of an activity which views it as being in act rather than in potency.

Order of specification is the consideration of an activity which views it as having a definite object.

A *voluntary* act is an act that is willed.

A voluntary elicited act is an act that is directly performed by the will.

A voluntary commanded act is an act that is performed by some power other than the will under the impulsion of the will.

An *end* is a thing which is good, desirable in itself.

A *means* is a thing which can serve to obtain an end for us, and so whose goodness lies in its relation to an end.

An ultimate end is an end which is simply and absolutely good in itself, and serves no end beyond itself.

An intermediate (proximate) end is a thing which is, in some way at least, good in itself, and also serves to obtain another end.

The *will-to-end* is the simple acceptance (love) of an end as good in itself (without any further qualification).

Intention is the love or acceptance of an end in relation to means of obtaining it.

Consent (*a*) is the acceptance of a unique means to a willed end.

Consent (*b*) is the approval of, or taking pleasure in, a particular (limited) good for its own sake, or approval of the thought and imagination of that good.

[Consent (*c*) sometimes means the simple acceptance, in general, of the means which lead to an end.]

Choice (or *election*) is the reasoned adherence to a contingent means to an end. It is the will-act that follows deliberation.

Imperium is the act by which we voluntarily move a power to action.

Deliberation is the act of inquiring about things to be done, or about means to an end.

Necessity is that condition or qualification of a being by which it is what it is and cannot not be.

(Essential necessity of being is that necessity of being by which God exists, inasmuch as in Him essence and the act of existing are identified.)

Antecedent (*predetermining, de jure*) necessity is necessity which is prior to the being to which it belongs.

Intrinsic antecedent necessity is the necessity of nature, essence or property.

Absolute intrinsic necessity (metaphysical) pertains to the essential structure of a being.

Relative intrinsic necessity (physical) is the necessity of the proper or specific activity of natural beings.

Extrinsic antecedent necessity is the necessity imposed by an efficient cause.

Consequent necessity (de facto) is the necessity which is posterior to the being to which it belongs.

Contingence is the lack of intrinsic necessity which however can be or is affected by extrinsic necessity.

Spontaneity is the lack of extrinsic necessity, usually implying intrinsic necessity.

Freedom is the condition or qualification of a being in *act* which has no antecedent necessity, neither intrinsic nor extrinsic.

Freedom is the power of self-determination in act.

A *free power* is one which is actively indifferent with regard to a contingent means to an end,[20] or which actively determines its own act in relation to an end.

Freedom of exercise is the power to perform or to omit an act.

Freedom of specification is the power of choosing one of two or more alternative means to an end.

Free will is the power of tending to and adhering to an intelligibly grasped good, which, even when all the conditions and causes of action are present, ready, and unimpeded, can act or not act, can do this or that act (choose this or that means).

Free choice is the act in which the will determines itself to one of two or more alternative means according to the formal relations discovered in deliberation.[21]

129. Proofs

A. *There is a rational appetite.*

Appetite is specified by its proper object.

But: we have acts of appetency whose object is an intellectually known good (intellectual affections, desires, choices, whose object is an abstract or universal, or unqualified and unlimited, or immaterial good, and so an intelligible object).

Therefore: there is a rational appetite.

B. *The rational appetite (will) is a spiritual power.*

The nature of a power corresponds to its proper object.

But: the proper object of will is an intelligible object, and as such has a spiritual mode of being.

Therefore: the rational appetite is a spiritual power.

C. *The will is not subject to any efficient causality except from God, and so is not subject to external necessity.*

The will is a spiritual power whose act is the tendency or adherence of the person.

But: such a power cannot be affected by any efficient cause

---

[20] "Active indifference" is *not* a failure to be interested in, or to care about, but is absence of constraint and natural necessity together with self-dominion.
[21] Recall that the alternatives may be to act or not to act.

which is a material thing (because it is spiritual), nor by a material power of the person, nor by his intellect (because the intellect is not an efficient cause), nor by an Angel or devil (because willing is the act of the person, not of some other co-ordinated cause).

Therefore: the will is not subject to any efficient causality except from God, and so is not subject to extrinsic necessity.

D. *The will-to-end is necessary with natural, intrinsic necessity.*

The will-to-end is the act by which the will tends to, or adheres to, an object simply as good.

But: an object as good simply and actually verifies the formal object of the will.

Therefore: the will-to-end is necessary by natural intrinsic necessity.

E. *In choosing, we sometimes experience the* fact *of freedom.*[22]

Before choosing, we experience deliberation about various acts which we really could do; in choosing we experience the active interposition of the self (Ego) and the actual domination we exercise over our act of choice; after choosing, we may experience satisfaction or regret over the way we have acted.

But: in this experience, we have our own self-determination, our own originative activity, our own responsibility.

Therefore: in choosing, we experience the *fact* of freedom (the *experimental* proof of freedom).

F: *Choice is a free act.*

That act is free which actually occurs without any predetermining necessity.

But: choice actually occurs, and without any predetermining necessity, neither extrinsic (for no created cause can touch this case, and there is no reason nor necessity for asserting a non-predetermining motion from God at this precise point), nor in-

---

[22] Some psychologists are of the opinion that we do not experience freedom in act. For a presentation and analysis of the evidence, see Hubert Gruender, S.J., *Experimental Psychology* (Milwaukee, Bruce Pub., 1932), pp. 427–39.

trinsic (for choice is directed toward means which are presented by intellect as only contingently related to willed end).

Therefore: choice is a free act. (The analytic proof of freedom).

G. *Those who admit the experience of obligation, and the moral responsibility of men for their actions, should admit free choice and free will.*[23]

Those who admit the experience of obligation and maintain man's moral responsibility for his fully human actions should admit that which alone makes obligation and responsibility intelligible.

But: obligation and responsibility are intelligible only if man has free choice (and so free will), for (*a*) obligation is such a necessity as in fact can be resisted, and so can be laid only on a free power, for if it were not necessity there would be nothing wrong in refusing it, while if it could not be resisted it would be physical, not moral; and (*b*) responsibility implies that a man acts, not because of physical compulsion from an external cause, nor because of a necessity of his nature, but because of his own self-determination, and a self-determined act is a free act.

Therefore: those who admit the experience of obligation and and the moral responsibility of men for their actions should admit free choice and free will.

130. Readings

St. Thomas Aquinas, *Summa Theologiae,* I. 80. 2, on the distinction between will and sensory appetite; 82. 1–2, on the will-to-end and the conditions of necessity and freedom; 82. 4, on its relation to will; 105. 4, on the Divine motion of the will; 106. 2; 111. 2; 114. 2 ad 3; 115. 4, on the impossibility of a created cause acting directly on the will by

[23] Note how this argument is put. In fact, obligation and responsibility are consequences of freedom. Logical thinkers who deny freedom say that obligation and responsibility are illusions, or really nothing more than social pressure, or custom, or the result of childhood experiences, and so forth. Against these latter thinkers this argument is worthless. It has its value against those who see and admit the intrinsic personal and social value and even need for responsibility. From this insight, they can be led by this argument to see the point of freedom.

efficient causality; I–II. 8, on the nature of the will; q. 9, on the things that move the will; q. 12, on intention; q. 13, on choice (add q. 10 on the movement of the will); q. 14, on deliberation; q. 17, on imperium and the commanded act.

Hubert Gruender, S.J., *Experimental Psychology* (Milwaukee, Bruce Pub., 1932), pp. 427–39 on the experience of freedom.

G. P. Klubertanz, S.J., "The Unity of Human Operation," *The Modern Schoolman*, XXVII (1950), 85–89, 94–102, a textual study of St. Thomas which establishes the notions of choice and imperium used here.

Étienne Gilson, *The Spirit of Mediaeval Philosophy*, trans. by A. H. C. Downes (New York, Scribner, 1936), pp. 269–323.

John Wild, *Introduction to Realistic Philosophy* (New York, Harper, 1948), pp. 475–93. The explanation of freedom is well done, but its application seems unduly restricted, perhaps because the import of non-action as an alternative is not emphasized, nor sufficient stress laid on the retrogressive deliberation.

Francis L. Harmon, *Principles of Psychology*, rev. ed. (Milwaukee, Bruce Pub., 1951), pp. 573–90. The experimental considerations of volition (willing); and interesting discussion of determinism, showing how the denial of freedom is the result of philosophical prejudices.

J. Donceel, S.J., "Psychology of the Will," *Mélanges Joseph Maréchal* (Bruxelles, L'Édition Universelle, 1950; 2 vols.), Vol. 2, 223–34.

Michael Maher, S.J., *Psychology*, 9th ed. (New York, Longmans, 1933), pp. 394–424. One of the classic expositions of Thomistic psychology, particularly valuable here for the great number of difficulties which it explains and solves.

J. Lindworsky, S.J., *Training of the Will* (Milwaukee, Bruce Pub., 1929); *Psychology of Asceticism* (London, Edwards, 1936). Excellent treatment of the nature of the will, and its relation to other powers.

F. Aveling, *Personality and Will* (New York, Appleton, 1931).

Gerard Smith, S.J., "Intelligence and Liberty," *The New Scholasticism*, XV (1941), 1–17.

Robert P. Sullivan, O.P., *The Thomistic Concept of the Natural Necessitation of the Human Will* (River Forest, Ill., Pontifical Faculty of Philosophy, 1952); a systematic study of the will-to-end and its necessity.

CHAPTER XI

The Sensory Appetites

131. The fact of the sensory appetite

The fact of sensory appetency has already been referred to. The conflict of simultaneously present tendencies within man proves that man must have at least two appetites, in other words, that he must have some other conscious appetite in addition to his rational appetite or will. Secondly, the fact that man has sense knowledge of sensible goods indicates that he can have a conscious appetency on the sense level. But we have yet to consider sensory appetency in detail.

To know the nature of a power, we must look at its formal object. An appetite is a power which is moved by a known good, and in that sense it is a passive power. We have seen in Chapter V that a passive power is specified (and distinguished from other powers) by its moving cause which is its proper object. The proper object of appetite, then, is the known good. But we have also seen that man has two specifically different kinds of knowledge: sense and intellectual knowledge. Hence, it follows that there are specifically different formal objects in "goodness known by sense" and "goodness known by intellect." Hence, an appetite which is moved by a good known sensibly is specifically different from the will, which is moved by a good known intellectually.

Moreover, man experiences in the concrete unity of conscious activity an element of sensory appetency. This is evident from the fact that we feel ourselves inclined to certain sensibly known goods like food, under the proper conditions. It is also evident from the fact that sometimes we feel ourselves drawn toward objects which are sensibly good (pleasant), though under the concrete circumstances they are intellectually known to be evils and are rejected by the will.

Again, we have seen that appetency in man is frequently accompanied by a noticeable bodily resonance. A quite similar bodily resonance can be observed in some animals, and so we can, with great probability, conclude to the presence of appetency in those animals. In addition, some animal activity cannot be explained without the presence of appetency.[1] Since animals have no intellect, they can have no intellectual appetite. Hence, animals have a power of sensory appetite.

It is important to remind ourselves again that we must not expect to find sensory and rational appetency as separate, isolated acts in our concrete experience. Just as there is no intellectual knowledge without a phantasm, so there is no rational appetency without some corresponding sensory appetency (though, in the cases of conflict, there may be sensory appetency without any corresponding rational one).

132. The two kinds of sensory (animal) appetite

We have already seen that those acts of appetency which differ as movement (impulse, desire) from rest (joy, sadness) do not require a different power of appetite, because no intrinsic difference of formal object is involved. Similarly, the movement toward a good and joy in its possession do not require a different power from the power which is the principle of the movement away from evil or sadness in its presence. This will be clearer if we remember that evil, taken abstractly, is defined as the absence (privation) of a good which ought to be present ("privation of the good which is due"). Good and evil, taken concretely, are therefore contraries, and contraries are functions of one and the same power, as for example, true and false judgments are both found in the intellect.

Are there then only two appetites, the sensory and the rational? We can answer this question by looking at animal nature. In all

[1] See above, Chapter VII, section 77.

animal natures we find actions whereby they seek food and other sensible pleasures, and avoid sensible pain. In addition to this kind of activity, there is another by which animals resist harmful objects; this is seen in the fights of animals, and their defense of their young, and so forth. Now, the appetencies which are the sources of these two kinds of activities cannot be reduced to one and the same proximate principle or power. For in the former case, the good which is sought (or evil which is avoided) is a pleasurable good, while in the latter what is sought is a painful or difficult good. This is a difference in the kind of good as such, and therefore a difference in formal object.

Moreover, it frequently happens that the one kind of reaction will conflict with the other, as the desire for a sensible good will diminish anger, and anger tends to diminish the desire for a sensible good.

Because of their characteristic acts, the two sensory appetites are called "concupiscence"[2] (desire) and "irascibility." If the terms are correctly understood, we could speak of "pleasure-appetite" and "aggressive-appetite."

If we look at the nature of the irascible appetite, and the evidence which leads us to conclude to its existence, we can summarize its activity in these two phrases: to protect a good against a menacing evil, and to acquire a good in the face of difficulty and resistence. Hence, on the purely sensible level, the irascible appetite serves the concupiscible. In other words, every act of the irascible appetite takes its origin from an act of concupiscence, and, if it is successful in attaining its object, leads to another act of concupiscence.[3]

*133. The organ of the sensory appetites

Because the sensory appetites are powers on the sense level (animal powers), they must have an organ. Frequently we speak

[2] From the Latin word *concupiscentia*, "strong desire." As this term is used in the philosophy of human nature, it has no derogatory implications of any kind.

[3] See the diagram above, Chapter IX, section 107.

figuratively of the heart as the organ of love, but it seems quite clear that this is not literally true. What is true is that circulatory changes are among the most apparent of the bodily resonances to an emotional state. Since the sense appetites are moved by sensibly known good, it seems natural that they should be close to the organs of the internal senses. In view of our scanty knowledge of this whole problem, the best that we can say is that the organs of these appetites are associated with the lower part of the brain, or the rear part (or perhaps both).

*134. How the sensory appetite is put into act

Appetency follows upon knowledge. But because there are many different kinds of sense knowledge, and because they combine together in various ways, the origin of a particular sensory appetency will be slightly more complex than the general principle might seem to indicate. To understand this situation, a few cases presented schematically will be of great help. (This discussion will not be an analysis in the terms of experimental psychology, but a philosophical analysis in terms of object and cause.)

(1) A directly sensible good or evil, that is, one that causes

Originating Knowledge	Intermediate Knowledge	Appetency
1. Sensible good (pleasurable) →	unifying sense → imagination	→ concupiscence
2. Sensible good (useful) →	unifying sense → imagination → { estimative / memorative }	→ concupiscence
3. Image of either good → / → unifying sense	{ estimative / memorative }	→ concupiscence
4. Difficult good →	unifying sense → imagination → { estimative / memorative }	→ irascibility
5. Image of difficult good → / → unifying sense	{ estimative / memorative }	→ irascibility

pleasure or pain, is known as such by the external sense (for example, tasty food). This movement in the sense of taste passes into the unifying sense and continues on to the imagination, where its direct motion ceases. But upon this perception of pleasure, concupiscence is put into act. Such a sensible good (or evil), first grasped by external sense, and presented to appetite by the unifying sense and imagination, is a sufficient cause for the appetency that follows.

(2) In studying instinctive activities, we saw that there are certain concrete goods (the suitable and the harmful) which are not grasped as goods by any external sense. Such objects, which are known by external sense, unifying sense, and imagination through the proper and common objects of these powers, are presented to the estimative (or to the memorative), and by this last power are grasped as good for the individual and/or the species. The estimation of suitability (or unsuitability) is now sufficient to move the concupiscible appetite to act.

(3) An image, beginning in the imagination, is not of itself (that is, as mere image) sufficient to move the sensory appetite, for we can imagine the most terrible scenes without fear, and we *can* imagine a sensible pleasure without desiring it—that is, as long as it is regarded as a mere image. Yet sometimes an image does move the sensory appetite. This movement, therefore, can only occur because the image is apprehended as real, that is, as past by the memorative power, or more commonly as future, as attainable, and then the estimative (together with the memorative, if past experience is necessary for such an estimation) comes into play. For the characteristic of being past or attainable does not belong to the image as mere product of the imagination.

(4) The irascible appetite is moved by a difficult good. This formal object is entirely beyond the grasp of the external senses, the unifying sense, and the imagination. Hence, the act of the irascible appetite always involves the apprehension of the estimative or memorative powers.

(5) The image of a difficult good is not formally presented as such by the imagination. Consequently, the image of an object, which is a difficult good, can move the irascible appetite only after an act of the estimative (and/or memorative) power.

These are the simplest possible schemes. But the whole process could begin with a sensation of an object which of itself would not be appetible, but to which an image of an appetible object has been associated by past experience. Or there could be a complex series of images, of which only the last would be an image of good. And in addition to this kind of complication, we must recall that the image itself can be brought to awareness in several ways, one of which already involves appetency.[4]

In these cases the sense appetite is moved precisely as appetite, that is to say, by the known good. The proper mover of appetite is therefore a final, not an efficient cause. Appetite is as such passive (responsive) to final causality.

However, the sense appetite is not just appetite; it is also an animal, that is, an organic power. Consequently, it can be put into act by an organic stimulus, for example, by a hormone, or by a chemical, physical, or electrical agent. Such an act of the sense appetite would appear artificial and violent to the person who experiences it, because its proper object (that is, the known good or evil) is absent; and if it led to action, would not lead to any determinate, definite action. Such are the irrational (that is, groundless) fears that are experienced in certain types of illness (for example, involutional melancholia), or the excitation and physiological disturbance, similar to rage, felt by persons who have large amounts of adrenalin injected into their system. However, in such cases, it is quite possible that such a really groundless act of sense appetite call up in imagination a substitute ground, which would then appear as the reason for the feeling.

Cases wherein the sense appetite is put into act by the material modification of organic dispositions are to be distinguished from

[4] See above, Chapter VII, section 78.

instances where the image that really moves the sense appetite does not appear in clear consciousness. If we look at the schemes of causality of the image, it will be seen that the image could be actualized and could arouse the appetite, while its line of causality to the unifying sense would be blocked. In such a case, the appetite would have a proper cause in fact, though that proper cause would not be discoverable by simple introspection. It is not clear that such cases really occur; it may simply be that apparent cases seem to have an "unconscious" memory-image as their cause, because that image remains at the very fringe of attention.

135. The classification of the sensory passions

We have seen that the acts of appetency are properly called "passions," and that the more appetency involves corporeal (physiological) changes, the more aptly it is so called.[5] Because the sensory appetites are the acts of bodily organs, bodily change is necessarily associated with them.

We have also seen that bodily change—the bodily resonance—frequently accompanies appetency. Since the sensory appetites are themselves organic, it follows that the bodily resonance is most immediately connected with sensory appetency, and only mediately with rational appetite. Hence, the acts of the sensory appetite are more properly called passions than the acts of the rational appetite, the will.

When we discussed appetite and appetency in general, we found that there are four basic passions: love, hate, hope and fear. Now, on the sensory level, there are two appetites. Love and hate, which deal with good and evil, clearly belong to the concupiscible appetite, while hope and fear, whose object is a difficult good and evil, just as clearly pertain to the irascible appetite. On the basis of the formal object, and the relation of the subject to that object, the passions can easily be arranged in a simple scheme.[6]

---

[5] For the meanings of the term "passion," see Chapter IV, footnote 17.
[6] In this scheme, the words in a small type indicate the formal objects of the appetites and passions. Solid lines indicate direct, *per se,* relationships;

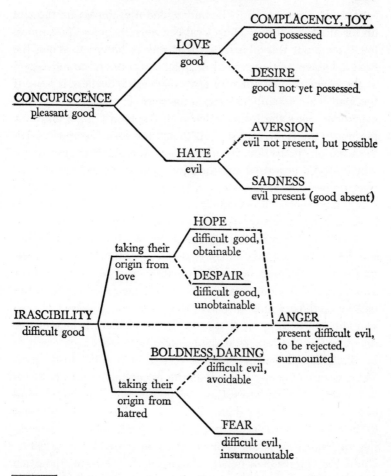

dotted lines, indirect and *per accidens* relationships (for example, despair accidentally flows from love because the difficult good is thought or found to be unobtainable, though this fact is accidental to a difficult future good).

Notice that these divisions are not exactly parallel. Desire and joy are not opposites, but related as movement and term; while hope and despair are opposites. Boldness and fear have a special opposition, in that the former leads one to attack the evil, while fear leads one to avoid or flee it. Anger is closely related to hope and to hatred (sometimes it seems to arise from despair, but this seems to be by way of *r*eaction). Anger has no opposite passion (or counterpart), because it directly involves *both* evil (injury) and good (victory over evil, vengeance).

*This diagram can easily be understood if examples are thought up for all the divisions. Thus, food is a sensible good (presupposing throughout this illustration that one is hungry). When the food is known (either sensed or imagined), the basic movement of the concupiscible appetite toward its attractiveness is love. If the food is not actually present to the sense of taste, then the love concretely takes the form of desire; if the food is here and now present to the sense of taste and touch, the love concretely takes the form of satisfaction. From such an example, it is easy to see why the good possessed and the good to be possessed are not distinct proper objects specifying different appetites; it is also easy to see how such experimentally different appetencies as striving and adherence can flow from one and the same power.

*An example carried through the diagram will help us to understand how the passions of the irascible appetite begin from the passions of concupiscence, and ultimately are directed toward the same, particularly and finally to complacency or satisfaction. Let us take up the example of food at the point where desire has been aroused. Let us suppose that sensation or memory brings up the difficulty that the food is at the top of a high hill which needs to be climbed, and that the climb is very tiring and the road dusty. The pleasure of eating is less than the discomfort necessary to obtain the food. Then the estimative power adds its innately and experientially determined judgment that food is not only pleasant to the taste, but also necessary for life. Such a good is worth working for, and the passion of hope arises in the irascible appetite. Under the impulsion of hope, the difficulty is overcome, the place where the food is located is reached. But in the meantime, a selfish and well-fed thief has taken the food under his "protection." As the injustice of the act, our deprivation, and the possibility of removing these evils dawn, the passion of anger arises against this difficult evil, a struggle against the thief ensues, and he is vanquished. Then as the food is obtained, the passion of satisfaction arises as the final movement of the concupiscible appetite.

*136. Classification of the passions and classification of emotions, desires, and feelings

According to the classification of the acts of the sense appetites on the basis of formal object and relation, the passions are relatively few in number, and the consideration of the material object of the passion is quite irrelevant. In this way, the desire for food and for sexually gratifying objects are specifically the same act of one and the same appetite.

But our experience seems to present us with a great variety of appetency. Likewise, the classifications of the psychologists are numerous and involved. How are these apparently different facts to be reconciled? Ordinarily, we classify feelings, emotions, and sentiments, and desires, partly in terms of their act, partly in terms of their material object, and sometimes also partly in terms of the activity to which they lead. For this reason, the two kinds of classifications are frequently at cross purposes, and should not be expected to come out the same. Some examples may make this clear.

These are various examples of two different kinds of passions.

OBJECT as known by sense (and estimation)	APPETENCY	BODILY RESONANCE	EXPRESSION	NAME
useful object	desire	?	gathering up	hoarding avarice
food	desire	watering of mouth, etc.	reaching, chewing, etc.	desire for food
drink	desire	"		thirst
sexually stimulating object	desire	organic excitation	fondling, etc.	physical love
food	aversion	visceral disturbance	rejection	disgust
unpleasant people	aversion	visceral disturbance	?	dislike

If we classified them experimentally, we would list them according to the way in which they present themselves, as whole reactions. In reference to the above diagram, we could say that this classification is "horizontal." But in the philosophical analysis of these experiences according to their formal object, we find only two different kinds of passions, because we are considering them "vertically," that is (in this diagram), according to their formal object alone.

In animals, the knowledge which initiates the series from object to activity is determinately linked with the desire and a definite exterior act or series of acts, as we have seen in the consideration of animal instinctive activity.

In man, such a determinate linking of knowledge with appetency and definite exterior expression and activity is not innate. Yet it is present in a normal adult person. How such determination and limitation is accomplished will be the partial object of the next chapter (on habits). Let it simply be noted here that in a normal adult the sensory appetency and the expression and activity are proportioned to the object known. When an adult fails to act in a way proportioned to the thing known, we speak of emotional immaturity, or of unbalance or insanity depending on the degree of disproportion. Such disproportion can be a failure to act at all (apathy), or an excessively violent reaction, or an over-flowing into powers that are irrelevant to the situation.

137. Definitions

Sensory appetite is the power of conscious tendency consequent upon sensory knowledge.

Concupiscence (concupiscible appetite) is the sensory appetite whose proper object is the good of sense or the pleasurable good—"pleasure-appetite."

Irascibility (irascible appetite) is the sensory appetite whose proper object is the difficult good—"aggressive-appetite."

Passion (in the context of animal appetite) is any act of the sense appetite. It is the same as sensory appetency.

138. Proof

The sensory appetite is of two kinds: concupiscence and irascibility.

The sensory appetite has as its proper object the good known by sense.

But: the pleasurable good known by sense is different from the difficult good known by sense, because of the limited scope of sense knowledge.

Therefore: the sensory appetite is of two kinds, one whose object is the pleasurable good (concupiscence), the other the difficult good (irascibility).

139. Readings

St. Thomas Aquinas, *Summa Theologiae,* I. 81, on the sense appetite.

Dom Thomas Verner Moore, O.S.B., *Dynamic Psychology,* 2nd ed., (Philadelphia, Lippincott, 1926), pp. 132–33, summary of the experimental evidence on appetency, and some conclusions.

John Wild, *Introduction to Realistic Philosophy* (New York, Harper, 1948), pp. 469–74.

Francis L. Harmon, *Principles of Psychology,* rev. ed. (Milwaukee, Bruce Pub., 1951), pp. 534–35, 545–74, on emotion and feeling.

Clifford T. Morgan and Eliot Stellar, *Physiological Psychology* (New York, McGraw, 1950), pp. 340–56, on the physiological correlates of the passions.

CHAPTER XII

Habits

140. Introduction

There can be no doubt that what we learn stays with us some-how and to some extent. The simple fact that we can memorize words proves that we can retain and possess images of sensible things even when we are not attending to them. On the intellectual level, too, the fact that we can recall proofs, arguments, problems is an evidence that we can retain intelligible *species* in the "state of habit." [1]

Other repeated experiences also leave some traces upon us, and these traces, in the form of habits and acquired dispositions, are evident, because they modify activity. We can think of such acquired modifications in widely different areas of human activity: the acquired skill of a mechanic is a habit; cursing is a bad habit of speech; meekness is an habitual control of a tendency to anger; a scientist habitually approaches his intellectual problems from the data of experimentation.

Thus, a superficial glance at human activity reveals a number of acquired modifications in various areas or fields. As philosophers, trying to understand the nature of man and his activity, we must investigate and try to understand these acquired modifications. We should not, however, assume from the start that all the facts concern a single and simple problem, or that they do not. We can conclude to the nature of the problem only after a thorough analysis.

[1] Chapter VIII, section 95.

141. Habits of motor activity

Everyone is aware that he can and does acquire certain perfections in external activity. For example, before you learn to write, it is a slow, difficult job to form letters, and the results are awkward and fumbling. But after you have learned to write, writing is rapid, relatively easy, and the results are consistent and good, at least in comparison with the original efforts. Notice that the result of a habit does not have to be morally good, nor even good in the sense of "being what it ought to be," but good in the sense in which we can say "a perfect mistake." For example, a man may become accustomed to put the accent on the second syllable of Calgary, or always type "adn" for "and." Other habits of motor activity are playing a musical instrument, walking, dressing one's self, talking, eating, athletic skills.

In such cases, there is a set of differences between one who has the habit and one who does not. The musician plays easily and rapidly, the beginner with difficulty and very slowly. The musician moves his fingers accurately and consistently; the beginner makes many mistakes. We can say that the musician has a determinate activity, so that one definite result is accomplished in a definite way, instead of just any one of the many movements that are possible. One result of these differences between the one who has a habit and one who does not is that the former enjoys doing what he does. Thus, ease (speed), accuracy (consistency, success), and pleasure in action are the characteristics of a habit. Finally, in all these cases, there must be a power, which at first has many possibilities, all of them practically equal, and through training is determined to act in a particular way.

*What is the subject of motor habits? In other words, precisely what power is made more perfect by them? At first sight, it might seem that the muscles are improved, strengthened in the acquiring of habits. But reflection will show that the muscular strength is only a condition—if it is not sufficiently present, it will have to be acquired. Take the old story of the man who "learned" to lift a bull by daily lifting a growing calf. In the muscular growth there was no determination to lift a bull, or even to lift at all. The skill in balance that was acquired is another matter, and is not related to muscular growth. The accomplished typist does not have to develop finger strength in order to play the piano, but she must acquire the skill or habit.

The important thing in external activity is control, "coördination." And such control is quite evidently an improvement in the dispositions (and so forth) of the nerve centers that initiate and regulate the muscular movements, and in the accuracy of the kinesthetic sensations and images.[2] This type of control is peculiar and specific to motor habits.

Control implies first of all the accuracy of the result. In this meaning of the word, we can speak of temperature control and similar things. But as used of human action, control implies voluntary direction. Now, all habit aims at success and accuracy; and in this sense, all habit is equally a controlling, directing perfection. But in so far as habit implies voluntary initiation, direction, and mastery of activity, not all habits are of the same kind. For example, when we begin to write, each little movement of fingers, hand, or arm needs separate attention and voluntary direction. As our writing improves, our attention is directed to larger groups of movements: whole letters, then words, then sentences are attended to. Finally, our voluntary direction initiates the movement explicitly, but then merely continues to will it as a whole. Thus, motor habits are partial automatisms: they turn into groups of movements that, once started, tend to continue of themselves. For example, in walking we merely will to walk in this direction or that; and provided that we keep this intention in a partially-willed state (called "virtual"), we are able to give all our explicit attention and will to other matters. How thoroughly automatic motor habits can become is clear from such things as sleep-walking, talk-

[2] A kinesthetic image is an image of the position and movement of the parts of our body. These images are developed out of the sensations of movements which are begun spontaneously and are not directed or controlled—"random movements."

ing during sleep, automatic mannerisms like scratching one's head, and so forth. In the automatic stage, these motor habits are actuated by (sensation +) image + estimation + appetite. Other habits differ most clearly from motor habits in that they always remain in some contact with rational and free control. Some habits can only be used freely and deliberately.

If, then, we try to see what is the nature of habit, as we see it exemplified in motor habits, we can discover its characteristics and build a definition of habit. A habit has a special cause that brings it about: a plan or order in intellect (conceived more or less vaguely) and an impulse of the will, in other words, an imperium. An element of plan, order, or arrangement is always present in a habit. Moreover, a habit is something you can use when you want to, and as long as it is a habit remains under rational control. Finally, a habit is acquired by acting: you must actually do the things which you want the habit of doing. A habit flows from act, not from potency.

Therefore, a habit is an accident, not a substance or part of the substance, for it is acquired. It is a quality, for it makes a man different from what he was. It is relatively stable; once acquired, a habit remains, at least for a while. It perfects an individual in a certain way, though not necessarily in a moral way, or even in a desirable way. Finally, it is a determination of an operative power, and so is ordered to action.[3] Therefore, a habit may be defined as a stable or permanent quality which determines a power to easy, accurate (sure, steady, consistent), and pleasurable operation under the control of intellect and will.

[3] There is also a kind of quality that inheres directly in the substance, and makes it to be of a certain kind in relation to being and not directly to action. Not innate, but permanent, and relating to the state of being in which the subject finds itself, it is called an "entitative habit." Examples are: health, illness, physical beauty, sanctifying or habitual grace.

So-called "physiological habits" (like smoking, alcoholism, drug addiction) are habit-groups (see below, section 149) which contain operative as well as entitative factors. The entitative elements of a physiological habit are, for example, modifications of organs and tissues, narcotic poisoning. The operative factors include both appetitive modifications and associations of images and ideas. Physiological habits easily become partial or complete automatisms.

142. Habits of the senses

We have seen that the external senses and the unifying sense are not directly under the control of intellect-and-will. Their activity is wholly accounted for by the nature of the power and by their active objects. There is no indetermination of these powers in the concrete, and therefore no place for a habit; there is no direct control by intellect-and-will, and therefore no cause of a habit.

The remaining internal senses can be considered in two ways: (a) as sense powers leading to animal appetite and action, and as steps leading *to* intellectual knowledge; or (b) as under the control of intellect. Considered in the first way, the internal senses can have no true habits, because all that goes on in them is naturally determined; in this way they are like the external senses. The retained images in imagination and the retained estimations in the memorative power are of course in the "state of habit"—that is, they are a perfection of the potency midway between mere potency and act, and are acquired by act. But their nature is to be formal determinations; they are principles of action, it is true, but not of *improved* action. They lead to one definite action by way of formally determining its *object,* not by modifying the disposition of the subject.

As under the control of intellect, the imagination, the discursive estimative, and the memorative power are capable of improvement and control. For example, the imagination can be developed so that it readily retains and re-presents in the proper order a series of words—a habit of memorization. Again, the imagination can be developed so as readily and properly to supply images for poetic writing, for scientific study—habits which are connected with and subsidiary to the intellectual habits of poetry, science, and so forth. The discursive estimative can be improved and controlled so that by it man judges readily and correctly of the concrete value of concrete sensible situations—a habit subsidiary to prudence. The memorative power can be developed, perfected, so that it readily supplies the experience of the past that is necessary for prudence. For example, a competent military leader grasps, without explicitly weighing, the many relationships between the terrain, the state of his supplies, and the attitudes of his own men and of the enemy. Such a concrete estimation frequently cannot be analyzed into fully rational factors (we sometimes call an estimation of this type "almost instinctive"); though it involves imagination, experience, and foresight, it also contains a concrete evaluation of a concrete situation. Similarly, in the area of personal prudence, a well-disciplined man will judge concretely that because of the nature of his work today, his present bodily vigor, and his state of mind, a small luxury in the way of an especially appetizing dessert is the appropriate way of practicing temperance here and now. Such an evaluation, too, involves memory and foresight, but is immediately and proximately an activity of the discursive estimative and memorative powers.

143. Habits of the sensory appetites

Through the discursive estimative and the imagination, the sensory appetites obey reason. Experience shows us that habits of these sensory appetites are very important and fairly numerous. The most obvious of such habits are the moral virtues of temperance and fortitude, and their opposites, the vices of intemperance, cowardice, and uncontrolled anger. Evidently, these are determinations, perfections of a power which result in ease, speed, and success (accuracy, consistency) of action.

Most of the habits [4] of the sensory appetites consist in a modification of the way in which they move to their act. In studying the sensory appetites and human instinctive activity, we saw that by nature the basic acts of these appetites are few in number, and indeterminate and generic as regards object and mode of operation. Concupiscence, for example, simply goes toward the pleasurable good. In animals, there is a built-in limit to this tendency: the animal tends toward the pleasurable good according to the limit

---

[4] Not all, because virtues such as celibate chastity and total abstinence are directed to the complete non-use of a given pleasurable object.

that is proportioned to its nature; for example, under its natural conditions it eats what is good for it. In man, on the contrary, there is a kind of insatiability about the appetite taken in itself. Virtue, therefore, usually consists in this, that the tendency acquires a limitation according to the measure which reason, rightly informed and rightly used, discovers to be suitable to human nature. Vice, on the other hand, consists in an acquired determination of the tendency to a measure determined by reason (but not rightly), which is not suitable to human nature.

144. Habits of the will

Can the will acquire habits? Yes, for one (subsequent) act of the will can be commanded and controlled by a previous imperium. This much is true: to decide more accurately just what these habits are, we must consider the various objects of the will. Toward the good as such, which is the proper object of the will, there can be no habit, for this is the very nature of the will. In loving the good, simply (even the highest good), there is no natural habit,[5] because this object falls directly under the proper object of the will.

There can be will-habits wherever there is the possibility of choosing in various ways with regard to a special or particular object which in some way goes beyond, or particularizes the formal object of the will. Thus, with regard to the good of other persons, there is a special object: not just the good, but the good of another, as distinct from us, or as united to us; and a possibility of acting according to various orders of reason, justly or unjustly, as a friend, or as an enemy. Hence justice and injustice, friendship

[5] In loving a supernatural good, a supernatural, divinely given habit is necessary—namely, charity.

The natural habits of friendship and enmity are not toward the good simply, but toward the good of another as united to us (or opposed to us). These habits are often overlooked, but they should not have been after Aristotle's lengthy treatment of friendship (love of our fellow-citizen, fellow-man, and so forth). Of course, friendship involves other habits than those of the will, but a habit of the will is definitely included.

Is there a natural habit of the love of a personal God? It would seem not, since without revelation we could not know that we are called to be friends, even children of God and sharers in the Divine Nature.

and enmity, are habits of the will. Likewise, with regard to one's own good, there are various ways of acting: selfishly or unselfishly; proudly or humbly.[6]

145. "Virtual intention"

In the case of the will, there is a special kind of act which seems to have no parallel with the other powers. For example, when we decide to walk downtown, we make an act of choice concerning that object. Here the act of the will moves the powers that carry out the local motion. But this walking takes a while, and during that time we may be thinking about wholly different things: how much money to spend, what to do when we get home, what course to take next semester. If we examine ourselves at such a time, we can find no trace in our consciousness of the act of willing to walk. Yet the act of willing to walk continues to influence the walking, as is clear from these two facts: (a) if we decide not to walk, we stop walking; (b) if our distraction becomes too concentrated, if we become wholly wrapped up in our thoughts, plans, and so forth, we also stop walking. Therefore, there is such a thing as a continuing influence of the will, which is called a virtual intention.

The virtual intention is something like a habit, something like a retained intelligible *species*. It differs from a habit in that it is an exercise of causality, and so is the continuation of an act in a somewhat reduced state.

The virtual intention, though most evident in cases of distraction, is most important where the virtual intention is a general one, covering a whole series of actions, and the explicit attention and willing are devoted to parts of the series. For example, I decide to study a mathematical problem, and in virtue of that act of will, I begin to study the data, the proof, and so on. Or again, I decide to clean the car or tidy the house; in virtue of that general inten-

[6] Our general attitudes toward the goods of the body, or toward material possessions, concerned with the use or non-use of these objects, are also habits of the will rather than of the sensory appetites; for example, "poverty of spirit," which consists in not having any affection for material possessions at all, pertains to concupiscence only negatively.

tion, I take up part after part of the job, think about it, make decisions, and carry them out.

Certain general intentions are a necessary part of our grown-up, reasonable life. The more ultimate the end to which the initial act of the will is directed, the more far-reaching, inclusive, and enduring is the influence of the virtual intention to that end. Since the act by which we choose our ultimate end [7] orders and includes all the activities that can lead to that end, the virtual intention to that end influences all our acts which are deliberate and not deliberately withdrawn out of that order.[8] For example, suppose that a person has the virtue of charity by which he is rightly ordered to God as to his true last end. In all his deliberate acts which are not sinful, the virtue of charity is in a state of virtual act.[9] Only during the commission of a venial sin (a deliberate act in some way withdrawn from the order of charity but not against it), or during sleep, dreams, delirium, and so forth, is the virtue of charity in the state of mere habit. Of course, the influence of a virtual intention can be greater or less. The intensity of its influence will depend directly on the perfection of the virtue and the intensity of the act which began that intention. Indirectly, the intensity of the influence of a virtual intention may depend on a repetition of the acts which actually initiate or renew it.

[7] That is to say, the thing or person in which the perfect good and our perfect happiness is to be found. The perfect good and happiness are natural *ends,* not subject to choice, as we have seen; but, because of our way of knowing these, *that which is* in fact the perfect good and in whose possession we expect to find happiness is subject to choice; cf. above, Chapter X, section 118.

[8] Thus, if we accept that which is in reality the supreme good as the supreme good—in other words, if we accept God as our last end—then the virtual intention of that acceptance orders and directs all our deliberate activity which is neither venially sinful (withdrawn from that order) nor mortally sinful (against that order).

[9] That is why, in ethics, theology, and religion, we speak of merit and meritorious activity even when there is no explicit advertence to God and no conscious, distinct act of charity. That is why the acts of a man who has deliberately chosen, and still adheres to, a wrong last end (who is in the state of mortal sin) are themselves evil, even when he is not acting with deliberate malice, unless such acts are equivalently withdrawn from that order of evil by being conformed to right reason.

146. Habits of the intellect

In the intellect, intelligible *species* are retained in the state of habit (that is, midway between sheer potency and act). Like the retained images and estimations of the internal senses, these retained *species* are not true habits.

But the intellect, in some of its activity, is under the control of a previous act of the intellect, the imperium. From this control and order a habit can be produced in the intellect. The fact that there are intellectual habits is most commonly and clearly seen in men who have acquired definite habits of reasoning. For example, a mathematician knows how to approach a mathematical problem, even if he has never seen it before; in reasoning mathematically, he consistently and easily reaches true conclusions. A biologist's reasoning is different; habitually, he looks for facts on which to build his theories; consistently and successfully, he uses methods which a mathematician could not use (for example, that of controlled experimentation). Both mathematics and biology are examples of demonstrative habits.[10] Other intellectual habits are wisdom, prudence, the habits of first principles (and opinion and faith).

*Wisdom is the habit of judging all things according to the highest cause(s). A wise man is one who knows how to order all things on the basis of their degree of perfection in relation to the ultimate end. A wise man need not necessarily be a learned man, nor a well-informed man; essentially, he is a man who judges correctly of the reality, significance, and value of the things which he knows; he can locate them correctly in the order of being, and he knows, at least in general, how they are related to the ultimate end. Hence,

[10] The term "demonstrative habit" is used to translate the Latin *scientia* in so far as that term designates a habit of the intellect. The English word "science" is used so consistently to designate a particular group of demonstrative habits that it seems no longer worth while to insist on the older English usage, where "science," like its Latin ancestor *scientia*, meant any demonstrative habit.

For a further discussion of demonstrative habits, see Appendix K.

though wisdom is essentially a habit and virtue [11] of the speculative intellect, its influence overflows into the order of action. Clearly, if a man knows the order and value of things, he would be acting very irrationally if he did not measure his actions by that knowledge. That is why it is sometimes said that wisdom, though it is a speculative virtue, is eminently practical. In relation to the other intellectual virtues and habits, wisdom is a master-virtue. It gives an over-all order and direction to the activities of the intellect. Wisdom, then, can be found in the unlettered and unlearned who are not in possession of other intellectual habits. But it can be found (and should be found more perfectly) in a man who has other intellectual habits. Ideally and in its full perfection, the virtue of wisdom should be also the habit of philosophy. In a philosopher who has exercised his intellect, not only in reasoning philosophically, but in judging and ordering the things he knows, his habit of philosophy has become also his habit of natural wisdom.[12]

*A demonstrative habit is the habit of reasoning, of proceeding from principles to conclusions in a way that is proportioned to the formal object of that habit. Among demonstrative habits there are philosophy, the natural sciences, the social sciences and history, and mathematics. In the first and primary sense, all these are habits. A science, for example, is clearly not the printed book alone, for science is first of all knowledge. And in the primary sense of the term "science," it is not even the conclusions retained in the intellect; for these conclusions, in so far as they are retained

[11] The intellectual habits can be called virtues for this reason. A virtue is the proper perfection of a being according to its nature. Understanding is the specifically proper perfection of man. Hence, those habits which make understanding perfect are virtues. However, virtue usually implies a relationship to the last end. Among the intellectual habits, wisdom is the only one which naturally treats of the last end. Hence, wisdom is more truly a virtue than the other intellectual habits.

[12] Many Thomists say that "natural speculative Wisdom" and metaphysics (first philosophy) are one and the same. This is true if a man has so developed and perfected his habit of metaphysics that it is capable of dealing, not only with its own proper, material and formal objects, but also with all reality and all other forms of knowing—indirectly of course and mediately.

at all, are retained as intelligible *species.* Science, mathematics, and philosophy, in their strictest sense, are habitual ways or types of rational procedure,[13] for it is only the perfection of acting correctly that brings ease and speed, accuracy and consistency into reasoning and investigation. In its fullest or widest sense, "science," in addition to its direct denotation (demonstrative habit), primarily implies an organized and interrelated body of conclusions (as retained intelligible *species*), and secondarily, under our present conditions, implies the symbolic representations of the principles, reasonings, and conclusions in printed or otherwise recorded forms.

*Demonstrative habits are many in number. In general, they are distinct habits in virtue of the principles which specify and distinguish habits in general, namely, their acts and formal objects. But because a demonstrative habit involves reasoning, demonstrative habits can be recognized to be distinct by a consideration of their proper principles and conclusions.

*Prudence differs from the habits already considered, in that it is a habit of the practical intellect; that is, it is a habit of reasoning and judging correctly about the things we have to do from the viewpoint of the relation of these actions to ourselves, and thus of specifying our choices to be good and proper under particular circumstances.

*Art is also a habit of the practical intellect. It differs from prudence in that it is a habit of judging correctly and reasoning about the things that are to be made from the viewpoint of the things themselves.

*There are two innate habits of the intellect, called the "habit of first principles" (*intellectus principiorum*) and "synderesis." The habit of first principles is that perfection of the speculative intellect by means of which every man, upon sufficient experience, easily, rapidly, and accurately forms the first indemonstrable prin-

---

[13] "Science" differs from "scientific method," in that the former term includes the latter, and in addition implicitly contains a formal object and a principle or principles, and virtually contains conclusions.

ciples of speculative reasoning. Examples of these indemonstrable principles are the principle of non-contradiction, the principle of causality, the principle of sufficient reason (the principle of intelligibility), as well as more particular principles, such as "an extended whole is greater than any of its parts," and even "a spiritual being does not have a location." These principles really flow from a habit, because the intellect, considered in itself as a power, is truly the power to perform these acts, and yet, merely as a power, contains no guarantee that they will be done as easily, rapidly, and accurately as men in fact do perform them. The habit of first principles is innate,[14] because it is found universally, and is effective prior to any experience. Synderesis is the habit of the practical intellect which attains to the first principles of practical reasoning and action. These principles can be expressed thus: "good is to be done"; "evil is to be avoided."

*It is well to remember that the first principles of both speculative and practical intellect are usually not enunciated explicitly except after mature reflection. But they are implicit in all understanding, and in that sense are prior to all other principles and to all conclusions.

*In addition to these natural and acquired habits, there are other less important acquired habits, such as opinion and human faith; there is also the infused habit of faith.

147. The nature of habit

The very name, "habit," has been aptly chosen to indicate the real nature of a qualitative modification of a power. "Habit" is derived from the verb "to have." To have something is to stand in relation to something. Now, a relation has two terms. On the one hand, habit is an adaptation and modification of the nature

---

[14] The habit of first principles is innate as a disposition or tendency. But before experience neither subject nor predicate term nor the affirmable union of both terms is present in the intellect. The mind, as we saw, has no innate content; all that can be innate in the human mind is the power itself, and an inclination to see certain very simple and obvious truths when they are presented in experience.

to an activity. But habit also refers to the subject in which it inheres; as a modification of the nature, habit implies as well a way of "having myself." In this way, habit implies possession as well as adaptation.[15]

The three signs by which we can recognize that action has been modified by habit are then: ease in the performance of the action; consistency, accuracy, or firmness in the action (and its results, if any); and pleasure. From these three characteristics, we can draw several conclusions about the nature of a habit.

It is obvious, first of all, that habit is something added to a power. Habit modifies action, which is its principal intent, by modifying the principle of that action.[16] This modification is a relatively permanent and intrinsic perfection of the power, and so is like a form which gives determination, actuality, and perfection. Yet a habit is not wholly an act, since it is still a potency in comparison to a further act which is operation. In this, habit is something like the power in which it inheres. For a power is an accidental, qualitative perfection of a substance, and so it is an act in comparison to substance; yet a power is at the same time a potency in comparison to activity. A habit, too, is an act or perfection, inasmuch as it is a qualitative modification of a power; yet it is still a potency in comparison to activity. However, a habit is closer to act than the power, which is a pure potency in the order of activity. To express the perfection of a habit in relation to activity, as well as to power, habit may be called a *first* act.

*When we say that a habit is a principle of action, we imply that habit has a causal influence upon the action which it modifies.

---

[15] Cognate uses of the root bring out some interesting similarities. The word "habit" itself is used to designate a specially adapted manner of dress, as in the expression "a religious habit" (compare the striking analogy of the terms "custom" and "costume"). The word "habitation" implies a two-fold or mutual adaptation, that of the environment as well as of the person who lives in that environment.

[16] St. Thomas Aquinas plays on the words "facility" and "faculty" to illustrate the difference between habit and power. Cf. for this, and for the development of the entire section, R. Bernard, O.P., *St. Thomas, Somme Théologique,* I–II, qq. 49–60 (Paris, Éditions de la Revue des Jeunes, 1933), pp. 381–97, 312–18.

This causal influence partakes of both efficient and formal causality. Inasmuch as a habit inheres in and modifies the power which is the originating principle of an action, the habit itself partakes of the efficient causality of the power. It may be slightly more difficult to see the formal causality of a habit. In the argument by which we concluded to the existence of a habit, we noticed that one of the characteristics of habitual action is its firmness, or sureness, or consistency, or accuracy. Clearly, this is an effect (modification) along formal lines. How, then, can a habit exercise formal causality upon activity? With regard to immanent action, the formal causality of a habit is exercised inasmuch as an immanent action remains in the power of which it is the perfection. With regard to transient action, the habit exercises its formal causality, inasmuch as the transient action proceeds from the agent.

*Habit, as we have seen, is a quality. The meaning of this conclusion can be considerably enriched by a comparison with other qualities. Quality, in general, touches substance very closely, and modifies substance internally. Quality is to the development of a being what essence (especially the specific difference) is to the being taken simply.[17] Qualities are of four kinds, according to the Aristotelian analysis: (1) figure ("form") or shape, (2) potency and its opposite, (3) passion and the qualitative dispositions which are like passion, and (4) habit. The difference between figure and shape on the one hand and habit on the other are evident, for figure and shape presuppose quantity, and are directed toward being rather than operation; habit on the other hand does not presuppose quantity, and is directed toward operation. The difference between habit and potency we have already considered. The difference between habit and passion lies in two characteristics. Passion (and related dispositions) depends entirely on an exterior cause for its being; for example, "being warmed" depends on an external source of heat like a fire, or upon some distinct cause like food, or disease; when the influence of these exterior

---

[17] Aristotle distinguishes predication *in quale quid* into substantial and accidental.

distinct causes stops, the passion comes to an end. Secondly, a passion is never wholly one with the power in which it is received. But habit becomes connatural, it adapts the power to itself, it enters into a very close union with the power in which it inheres. The reason for this is that habit does not depend for its being on an external cause. Passion, we say, "carries a man out of himself," [18] it lessens self-control on the one hand, and on the other may even tend toward the destruction of the being upon whom some violence is being inflicted. Habit differs from passion in this characteristic. Habit leads to self-mastery, an increase and concentration of power and effective action. The more the initiation and control of action is centered in reason, the greater the dynamic unity of the person, and the more his substantial unity is reflected in his unified and successful activity. Moreover, as we shall see, habit is developed by personal activity. Hence, it does not depend on an external cause.

148. Distinction of habits

A habit is the perfection of a definite power, ordered to a special kind of act; and this act has its own definite and proper object. For example, the habit of reasoning correctly can only be the perfection of a power that does the work of reasoning; the habit of desiring moderately can be the perfection only of a power whose nature is to desire. Therefore, the habits are first classified, generically, according to the powers of which they are the perfections.

Habit, though it is a determination and as such act and form, is nevertheless not yet fully act, because it is for operation, activity. Hence, it cannot be known immediately, actually, directly in itself, but must be found in its act. Now, as we have seen in the fifth chapter, acts are distinguished and specified by their objects. Restrictions of the formal object specify classes of acts; and when a given class of acts is performed easily and accurately, we know that a habit is present. For example, the imagination is the power

[18] St. Thomas says that passion is *ecstatic*, playing on the basic meaning of *ex*, out of.

of retaining sensible experience, and so its proper object is the sensible object as absent. Its act is to re-present, to image the sensible object. Suppose that a man acquires the facility of imaging seen words according to the order in which he has seen them. The proper object of such an act is an absent visual object according to the order in which it was seen. His habit therefore would be the habit of memorizing seen words. Another example is the intellect. This is the power of knowing things inasmuch as they are, as we have seen. Things are in different ways; they are by various causes, they manifest themselves to us in different ways. Suppose that a man knows that kind of being which is abstract quantity, and knows it according to its formal constitution (formal cause). To know a thing according to any kind of causality is to know it by demonstration, by reasoning. Hence, a man who does this easily and accurately has the habit of mathematics. Suppose that a man knows material living beings according to the manner in which they are differentiated and related in physical structure and externally observable organic function. When he does this easily and accurately, he has the habit of biology.

Therefore, habits are distinguished generically by the powers of which they are the perfections, and distinguished specifically by the special objects of their acts.

149. Habit-groups

Thus far we have considered various kinds of habits, power by power. But when we come to experience, we do not find such habits in isolation. For example, the good artist shows a special cast of understanding, a special kind of imaginative activity (usually together with special emotional reactions), and in most kinds of art special skills (motor habits). The habit of science involves at least a special way of proceeding intellectually together with one or more habits in the imagination, of having on ready call the appropriate images in the right order, of sorting and selecting appropriate sense experience to form phantasms suitable for further abstraction, and so forth. Prudence involves a habit of practical reasoning, and subsidiary habits in the discursive estimative and memorative powers, by which the universal judgments of practical reason are particularized and concretized. Friendship—to take a different kind of example—is an even more complex group of habits, including habits both of knowledge and of appetite. Married love includes habits of knowledge (ways of understanding things), a habit of the rational appetite, habits of the internal senses (shared memories, for example); habits of the sensory appetite, and motor habits. The kinds of activities which are referred to as "social instincts" or "complex instincts" in man are either wholly or in part habit-groups.

150. The inter-relationships of habits

In a habit-group, it is necessary that the two or more habits be somehow related and ordered to each other, otherwise no unified action can result (for action follows upon being, and being and unity are convertible). As habits, such related habits must of course be distinct, since they are in really distinct powers. And yet they must be so related that when they pass into act, they form one composite principle of action. Now, wherever there is a unity of composition, there the parts are related as matter and form are related.[19] And so, in a habit-group, there must be at least one principal and one subordinate habit (principal = formal part, subordinate = material part). In more complex groups, there will be intermediate habits, which are formal in regard to the lower, and material, determinable, in regard to the higher.

Some habit-groups are natural and necessary, as for instance the habit-group of science, with its formal essential part in intellect and its material counterpart in the imagination; prudence as a formal habit also has its material counterpart in the discursive estimative and memorative powers. Thus also, there seems to be a habitual formal order in intellect itself, which is the counter-

[19] Obviously, matter and form in activity and the principles of activity are used analogously to the matter and form which are the principles of substantial composition.

part of the essential habits of fortitude, temperance, and justice. These habit-groups are necessary in order that the complete habit exist and operate.

Another kind of habit-group consists of the three moral virtues of justice, fortitude, and temperance together with prudence. These virtues are so related that the three appetitive habits cannot be had perfectly without prudence, nor prudence without them. For example, mere temperance without prudence will simply restrain the sensory appetite according to the measure of reason, but will not be able to make allowances for the days when one works harder and needs more rest and food, or for an occasional feast day, and so forth. Prudence, on the other hand, which consists in applying the means to the end, will not be a virtue if the ends are not consistent and not right; these latter qualities are brought about by the appetitive virtues.

Finally, all the virtues fall into an ordered series. For each of the virtues deals with the ordering and direction of some part of human activity toward a specific end. But ends are of their very nature in an order, from the ultimate to the most proximate. Thus, the more inclusive virtues, which are orders or dispositions (plans, arrangements) to more ultimate ends, are as form to the less inclusive.[20] And charity, which orders all our actions to the ultimate end, is (or should be) the form of all the virtues.—The life of vice is partially subject to a similar ordering, though it can never fully mimic the total order of right reason.

151. The necessity of habits

From what has been said, it will be easy to see one general need for habits. Habit is the perfection of a power which in itself is capable of many different acts so that a given action may be done

[20] An analogy may be drawn from the directing of local movement. Suppose you decide that the ultimate terminus of a trip will be New York, and that on the way you want to visit an aunt in Chicago, a cousin in Cleveland, a friend in Newark. The parts of the trip are each ordered distinctly to a distinct terminus, and each part with its term is ordered within the plan of the whole trip. This can be considered as a series of proximate and partial ends, ordered under an ultimate end, and subsumed into the order to that end.

easily, successfully, and pleasantly. Obviously, if we never progressed beyond the first laborious efforts we make to get things done, our whole life would be taken up simply with our trial-and-error struggles to keep alive—and even this result would not be assured. Habit is a means of conquering difficulties and acquiring a richer and more meaningful freedom.

In studying human instinctive activity, we saw that by nature man's instinctive reactions are generic, global. The little child, falling into an instinctive anger reaction, has his whole irascibility stimulated, and this in turn leads to violent motor reactions of his whole body more or less at the same time. A much more successful reaction would concentrate all the violence in the fist and arm and keep the feet steady. This kind of concentration is achieved by a habit-group (special apprehension of a distinct object + anger proportioned to this object + motor activity directed to retaliation). One of the major differences between a baby and a mature person is that the latter has developed habit-groups which channel his reactions so that they are appropriate to the situation. For example, the irascible reactions of a mature person are manifold: courage, determination, patience, fighting; while a grown person whose only irascible reaction is directed toward physical violence is imperfect in his being, unsuccessful in his action, and unhappy. The failure to form habitual determinations and limitations of appetite and action, or the breakdown of such distinctions later on, is a very definite kind of emotional imperfection, which even in its less evident forms causes much unhappiness, and in its extreme form leads to (or is) a kind of insanity.

These reasons may be given for the acquiring of any good habit. In addition to them, special importance and value are to be found in the moral habits. In studying the will, we have seen that our will is usually put into act by the concrete things that occur to us as ends. We have also seen that it is always possible to correct and integrate these ends. But this involves the process of regressive deliberation, which takes much time, and in addition requires some impetus. Now, the moral habits precisely regulate our apprehension of immediate moral ends. A man who has acquired these virtues will by force of them correctly apprehend as ends the things that are really good for him, and correctly apprehend as evils the things that are really bad for him. And if things should occur which are new to him, and which seem good and are not really so, the conflict between this apprehension and his good habits which will develop in the course of deliberation will be the impetus to the regressive deliberation through which he can choose rightly. Thus, a man's activity will be consistent, in harmony with himself, his own ideals, and his true good, and so will not only be productive of happiness but also morally good. Good habits make up a well-integrated personality and produce a happy life.

152. The acquiring and growth of habits

We have seen that habit is a perfection (determination, specification) of a power that by itself can produce various acts in a relatively equal way. Compared to potency in itself, habit is act or perfection; but compared to act or operation, habit is on the side of potency. Obviously, the power that is perfected by the habit cannot give itself that habit. The habit must therefore come from something which has the perfection and order that are characteristic of habit. Now, in man there is a power which moves to act (intellect-and-will), and powers which are moved to their act and directed in it. As directed by the imperium, the commanded act concretely expresses the order and perfection that the habit confers spontaneously. Therefore, the cause of acquired habits is the acts corresponding to the habits.

We have seen that the habits of first principles and of synderesis are from nature, and so, as far as the formal part of these habits is concerned, they are not acquired, but innate.[21] However, these habits are not innate as explicit judgments; they are inborn in such a way that, given the explicit apprehension of their terms, they are made easily and accurately. Hence, as complete habits, they follow upon act; as incomplete beginnings, they are innate.

[21] See above, footnote 14.

Experience also shows that some men acquire habits more readily than others. In the case of those who easily acquire habits— who sometimes even seem to be virtuous by nature—we find that they have a certain natural inclination to act in one way rather than another. Such an inclination is based on natural temperament, and so ultimately on bodily disposition. Natural inclinations do not of themselves contain the order of reason, and so are rather the material of habits than habits strictly so called. Thus, habits may be materially innate to a greater or lesser degree.

The proper cause of a naturally acquired habit is the order of reason in an act. Fully to understand this causality, we must distinguish between habits in the separated powers (intellect-and-will) and those in the organic powers (the senses and sensory appetites).

*In the habits of the intellect, if the order of reason is adequately contained in one act, that single act will cause the habit. This can be the case in demonstrative science (one act of understanding a proof in geometry may produce the habit of geometry). It is definitely not the case in prudence nor in justice. Since these habits deal with things that are to be done (operable things, *operabilia*), their whole order cannot be contained in any one act, because the matter (object) of these acts is contingent. Therefore, prudence and justice and the habits like to them (all habits of the will; art and opinion) can be gained only by some repetition of acts.

*With regard to the habits of the organic powers, some repetition is also necessary. The first reason is that, dealing as they do with operable things, the whole order of reason cannot be contained in any one act. In addition, these are material powers, and so all their action and passion takes place in time. Effects in the material world are produced by finite causes through the gradual change of material dispositions. And so there is a double reason why a repetition is necessary for the acquiring of habits in powers that are the forms of organs.

*This latter fact, however, shows that it is possible to acquire habits in material powers by mere repetition without the formal order of reason. The more such powers depend on matter, the more will this be true. Motor habits can be acquired without either understanding or desiring the act or the order of reason in it. However, if they are acquired in this way only, they are not really habits, but customs, automatisms, no longer strictly *human* perfections. This same fact also explains why some habits turn into automatisms.

From all that has been said about habit, it is clear that growth in a habit is not by the addition of part to part, but by the further, stronger impression of one and the same order (form, determination) on a power. In other words, growth in habit is always intensive, not extensive. For example, a man does not become a better mathematician by understanding more formulae of the same kind,[22] but by a deeper, more rapid, more sure grasp of the principles, the reasoning, and so forth. The excellence of a pianist is not measured by the number of pieces that he can play, but by his skill in playing any one of them.

Habits of intellect and will, since they have only one cause, can be lost or destroyed in only one way, that is, by acts which are contrary to the habit. Organic habits can be lost in this way, and also by mere non-use and time (because they are subject to the constant change which is the law of material being).

*153. Can animals have habits?

If we recall briefly the causes of habit, this question can be answered easily. (*a*) What is the proper subject (the material cause) of habit? It is a power which is not wholly determined in its act by its nature and its proper moving causes. Such a power in the first instance is will-and-reason, for freedom is to be found only in the act of choice, which is an act of will-and-reason. Secondarily, such indetermination is found in the actions of those powers in which intellect and will are operative. Since animals do not have

---

[22] This is growth by addition indeed, but not of the habit; it is an increase in the objects of the habit. Knowledge therefore grows both by addition and by intensity; but the habits of knowledge grow only in intensity.

reason, it follows that all their powers are determined to definite acts in definite circumstances. The only indetermination we can discover in animal activity is in comparison to the way in which they can be used or trained by men. So the possibility of something like habit in animals is not directly in them, but in their trainers.

(b) What is the proper efficient cause of a habit? It is a preceding act which contains formally the perfection and order of reason. This is directly and by nature to be found in the acts of intellect and will, and secondarily, in other acts, in so far as the imperium and the commanded act are one complex operation. Since the animals lack reason, they lack the proper efficient cause of habit.

In organic powers, however, customs or automatisms can be set up by mere repetition, as we have just seen. Such determinations of activity can be acquired by animals under training or by force of circumstances.

Even in the case of acquired automatisms there is a difference between men and animals. A normal man has a measure of control over his customary, automatic actions—he can usually initiate or stop them when he is clearly aware of them. An animal, on the contrary, has no control over its automatisms, but is wholly ruled by them and by the powers which actuate them (image + estimation + passion).

154. Definitions

A *habit* is a relatively permanent quality which perfects the subject in which it is and/or his operation.

An *operative habit* [23] is a permanent quality of an operative power which perfects the power in which it is by way of determination and specification, and the operation itself by making it easy, successful, and pleasant.

An *automatism* (*custom*) is the material modification of an organic power so that under initial stimulation (either voluntary or

[23] That is, a natural operative habit, which differs from a supernatural operative habit and from an entitative habit. An entitative habit is the permanent qualitative modification of a substance, which makes the substance to be in a certain way.

animal-physical) it passes into a definite act or more usually a definite series of acts, which contain an order, but not the formal order of reason.

The state of habit is an imperfect act (usually that of formal specification), which results from full act, and is between the sheer indetermination of a power in potency and the complete determination of its operative act.

Virtue is an operative habit which makes a man good and his operation good.

A virtual intention is a continuing influence of the will upon an activity, which usually begins with an act of the will or an imperium, but apart from its beginning or renewal is not fully actual, explicit, nor conscious.

Wisdom is the habit of understanding the order and value of all things and truths from the viewpoint of the highest cause(s).

A *demonstrative habit* is a habit of reasoning from principles according to one of the valid forms of inference to necessary and universal conclusions; the manner of proof and the necessity of the conclusions must be proportioned to the formal object of the habit.

Prudence is the habit of reasoning and judging correctly about things to be done, in relation to the person who acts.

Art is a habit of reasoning and judging correctly about things to be made, in relation to these things themselves.

The habit of first principles is the (partially innate) habit of the intellect by which it easily and accurately attains to the first principles of speculative reasoning.

Synderesis is the (partially innate) habit of the intellect by which it easily and accurately attains to the first principles of practical reasoning and action.

155. Proofs

A. *Habits are found only in intellect and will and in the powers subject to their imperium.*

A habit is the determinative perfection of an operative power toward easy, sure, firm or successful and pleasant operation.

But: this presupposes an indetermination in the power to be perfected and an order of reason in that perfection.

But: these are characteristics of reason and will in themselves, and of other powers only in so far as they are under the control of the imperium.

Therefore: habits can be found only in intellect and will, and in the powers whose action is one with the imperium and which are therefore subject to it.

*B. *Animals can have no habits.*

A being which has neither the proper subject of habits nor the proper efficient cause of habits cannot have them.

But: animal powers, being determined by nature and the proper moving objects, do not have the indetermination that is the characteristic of the proper subject of a habit, nor do they have an imperium by which to cause a habit.

Therefore: animals can have no habits.

156. Readings

St. Thomas Aquinas, *Summa Theologiae,* I–II, q. 49, on the nature and necessity of habits; q. 50, on the subject of habits; q. 51, the cause of habit; q. 52, the growth of habit; q. 53, the loss of habit; q. 54, the distinction of habits; q. 57, the distinction of intellectual habits.

Jaime Castiello, S.J., "The Psychology of Habit in St. Thomas," *The Modern Schoolman,* XIV (1936), 8–12; an excellent brief treatment.

W. D. Commins, *Educational Psychology* (New York, Ronald, 1937); the best treatment of the acquiring, control, and removal of habits.

Dom Odon Lottin, *Principes de Morale* (Louvain, Mont César, 1946: 2 vols.), Vol. 1, 173–175, 313–314, the only psychological treatment of the virtual intention.

G. P. Klubertanz, S.J., "The Unity of Human Operation," *The Modern Schoolman,* XXVII (1950), 75–85, on habit-groups.

Vernon J. Bourke, *Habitus as a Perfectant of Potency in the Philosophy of St. Thomas Aquinas.* Unpublished doctoral dissertation, University of Toronto, 1938. A profound textual study, stressing the metaphysics of habit.

William James, *Principles of Psychology* (New York, Holt, 1931). A classic description of habits; excellent treatment of their necessity; philosophically weak on other aspects of habit.

CHAPTER XIII

The Human Soul

157. The unity of man

In the second chapter, we considered the unity of any living thing, and we found that a living thing is substantially one. After we have analyzed the activity of man, step by step according to formal objects and powers, the unity of man should be much clearer to us. In the case of man, there are two different types of evidence that will enable us to answer the question, Is man one being? namely, internal, introspective evidence, and external evidence of observation.

If we examine our own activity, we find that the same person senses and understands. We know that man's substantial being is seen in its activity: not *what* it is, but *that* it is. We have seen how formal-object analysis discovers six levels of the experience of unity: (1) the actual indivision of our body in propriosensation; (2) the unity of external sensation in the unifying sense; (3) location in space and time in the imagination; (4) the unity as subject of action and term of passion in the estimative; (5) the self-identity of intellectual consciousness; (6) the composite unity of the imperium and the commanded act. The experience that I am one sensing, thinking, willing, and acting human being is a direct experience, not an inference, a conclusion, a supposition, or an assumption. Of course, this direct experience does not tell me how the unity is achieved, nor how it is to be reconciled with the experience of diversity and multiplicity.

There is a totally different meaning to the question, Is man one

298

being? namely, Is he the same being today that he was yesterday? This question concerns the permanence of the unity of the Ego, and its answer from internal, introspective evidence involves memory. If the question about the permanence of the Ego in time is considered before the experience of the unity of the Ego in being, and incorrectly made to be the basis of the latter, obscurity, confusion, and misunderstanding are the order of the day. Our approach is through the direct, factual experience of the unity of the Ego in being. Once that is seen and accepted for what it is worth, the problem of the duration of personal identity becomes scarcely a problem at all. The "problem of multiple personality," personality change, and so forth, are then problems of more or less partial memory-systems, as we have seen in Chapter II.[1]

To make the argument from direct experience a complete argument, it is necessary to add that vegetative life in us is clearly ordered to sense life. This is evident, because the *term* of the vegetative activities of growth, nutrition, and reproduction in man is not a vegetable, but a sentient body.

The direct experience of diversity and conflict that we have is to be explained on two grounds. The first and proximate reason is the multiplicity of operative powers that are discovered by formal-object analysis. The second and more ultimate reason is the virtual multiplicity of human nature, which we shall consider shortly when we come to define man. Because human life is vegetative and sensitive as well as rational, there is a need in man for diverse and manifold powers, and the possibility of a conflict in their activity.

The second approach to the question of the unity of man is by external observation. If the operation of a being is totally identical with its being, then that being is absolutely simple and totally self-identical (God). If the operation of a being is on a single level and itself simple, then that being is simple, undivided and indivisible in nature (an angel). If the operations of a being are of specifically different kinds, but integrated into an intrinsic unity

[1] See above, section 15.

of finality, then that being is one in nature or substance, but that nature is composite.[2]

Another preliminary observation is to be made. Material things are not perfect from the moment of their origin. Particularly is this true of man, whose perfection is to be achieved by his own activity. Now, a being which is not yet perfect is not yet as much a *being* as it can be, and so is not as much *one* as it can be. That is why the unity of human operation is partly given by nature, partly gained in the growth and perfection of personality. But the possibility of integration of activity implies the possibility of disintegration. Hence, the fully integrated activity of a man perfect in body and mind is the full actualization of the unity, actual and potential, that every man has by nature. On the other hand, the disintegration of a human being, physically, sensitively, emotionally, mentally, does not disprove the unity of a human being, but is the corollary, the obverse of his perfectibility.

The merely material activities of a human being are clearly integrated into his life, and serve as the material basis for vegetability, local motion, and the material conditions of sensation. His very composition and structure make it possible for external agents to injure him physically. This possibility merely demonstrates that man is a part of the material world.

The vegetative life of man, in turn, is subordinated to, and serves, his sensibility. The normal processes of growth, nutrition, and reproduction are directed to human sensibility, and most defects at this level are due to interference from outside causes. There are, however, some obscurely known illnesses, (e.g., cancer) which seem to indicate that perhaps some of the vegetative activities of man escape from the total finality. If such things really occur, a part of the human body would become something different, become some kind of parasitic plant (or animal). This would be a substantial change, and therefore not relevant.

The first problem begins when we find that man's sensibility can affect and harmfully interfere with his vegetative functions

---

[2] See above, Chapter II, section 11 (b).

(for example, the relation between certain emotional states and ulcers of the stomach). Our understanding of this relationship is made more difficult because we know very little about the way in which this is accomplished. However, we do know enough about this kind of thing to be able to say definitely that the basic relations of sensitive and vegetative functions are integrated, and that if they are developed in the right way, the integration becomes closer and more actual. And, as has been pointed out, the important thing is to find an essential integration and an intrinsic possibility of a complete integration.

Finally, the sensitive functions of man are ordered to the rational (of intellect and will). We have seen the basic pattern of this order in the origin of intellectual knowledge, and in the way in which intellectual and voluntary activity penetrates into the sensitive activity of man (in the unity of the imperium and the commanded act).

On this level, while the integration of functions is closer and more striking when accomplished, it is also more of an achievement than a natural gift. Consequently, at this level there is the greatest possibility for disintegration (automatisms, vice, excessively violent passion that outruns voluntary control, insanity). This sad possibility is the price of freedom and perfectibility. Is the high cost of freedom and good habits an indication of the lack of being, goodness, and unity in man? Or is the evil and disintegration of man the necessary natural [3] consequence of his power for goodness, perfection, and integration? It is only the precious things that can bring serious harm, the things that have a great power for goodness that also have a great power for evil. Looked at in this way, the actual disunity of operation in evil or unfortunately sick men is, strangely enough, an indirect argument for man's unity, in that, to the state of sheer potency in human intellect and

---

[3] The revelation of the state of original justice before the fall, and of original sin, as well as of the supernatural helps given in our present state which favor goodness, being, perfection, and unity, make it easier for us to see God's goodness in creating man. But precisely because these are matters of revelation, we do not make use of them in our present argument.

will at birth there corresponds the potential integration, unification of his sensory and even of some of his lower powers.

158. The definition of man

At the beginning of a study it is necessary to give some kind of nominal or descriptive definition, in order to designate the object of that study. In the course of this study, we have examined man and his activities. We have found that man is one substance, and that he has material, vegetative, sensitive, and rational activities. Every one of these points has been proved; the essential distinction between the various kinds of activities has also been proved.

With this background of proven conclusions, it is possible to build the *real* definition of man. Man is one of the many material things found on this earth. Together with plants and animals (as opposed to nonliving things) he has vegetative life. Together with animals (as opposed to plants and nonliving things) he has the power of sense. Finally, man is the only kind of material being that has intellect and will, or, in a single term, reason. These are the activities of man, and corresponding to them are the classes or levels of human powers. From the powers in turn we derive the names of substance. Hence, man is a substance, material, living, sensitive, rational. More briefly: man is a rational animal.

159. Does man have a soul?

In Chapter III, we saw that the word "soul" has several definitions. We decided that an investigation about the soul must begin with a nominal, descriptive definition. According to the nominal definition, the soul is the ultimate principle of life. More concretely, in the case of man, the soul is the ultimate principle by which he lives and knows.

The first meaning of the question, Does man have a soul? then is, Does man have an ultimate principle by which he lives and knows? The answer to this question is immediately evident to any man who lives and knows. For in living and knowing, he experiences immediately but very obscurely *that* there is an ultimate principle by which he lives and knows. At this level of the question, there is no difficulty and no disagreement.

The second meaning of the word "soul" is "an ultimate principle of living and knowing, distinct from the body." We are speaking, of course, not of a merely mental distinction, but of a real distinction, one which is independent of the mind, in things. Mental distinctions are distinctions between ways of looking at or knowing things. For example, we look at a man in so far as he is a part of the world and has activities in common with other living, sensing things in that world, and we call him an "animal." Then we look at man again, this time as having a proper, specific activity, and we say that he is "rational." The distinction between "rational" and "animal" is a distinction which depends on the mind, though it has a foundation in reality. A real distinction, on the other hand, is to be found in the real order, independently of any special consideration by the mind. Examples of real distinctions are those between complete beings, and also those between the real parts of one and the same being. Our question about the soul, then, comes to this, Is the soul identical with the body in reality, is it merely a different aspect of one and the same living thing? or is the soul a real part of a living thing, distinct from another real part which is the body? The answer to this question is no longer immediately evident in experience.

Man is a living thing distinct in his actions from all other material things. Yet he is not isolated from this world; he is a part of it. He lives in it, and interchanges matter [4] with other things. Man dies, and consequently no longer exists as man. Yet something

---

[4] The word "matter" is used in several senses. (*a*) Sometimes *matter* means "any nonliving material thing." (*b*) At other times, *matter* means "that generic aspect of sensible things, which is common both to living and nonliving things." (*c*) "First" or "primary" *matter* is that potential part of a material thing in virtue of which the thing is limited in its specific perfection, is individualized, and is capable of substantial change.

That which is interchanged in the vegetative processes and in death is at the present stage of discussion considered indeterminately; hence "matter" is taken in the present argument in its second sense.

of him remains, which we call his corpse, which we bury, and which reverts back to simpler compounds and elements. The change which goes on in the vegetative processes and in death is a real change, for it really happens in an existing being. Hence, man is composite, consisting of an indeterminate subject which is found both at the beginning and the end of the change, and of some principle which is the source of his special being and activities as man. This principle, really distinct from matter, is called the "soul."

To say *that* man has a soul really distinct from matter is to answer the question, Does man have a soul? But this statement tells us nothing about the nature of the soul. Yet by far the most important question about the soul is the question about its nature. Hence, this must be taken up next.

160. The nature of the human soul: I. substantiality

Man is a living thing, and we have already proved in the third chapter that every living thing has a soul, which is a distinct, simple substantial principle, the substantial form. However, there is so much more evidence available in the case of man that it will be worth our while to review the argument of Chapter III, directing our attention only upon man. This restatement of the argument will also free our philosophical account of man from any dependence upon what many persons consider less clear cases.

From the evidence and the conclusions of Chapters VIII and X (on intellect and will), we know that man has proper and distinct activities which cannot be reduced to the activities of non-human things. Activity in turn springs from the nature or essence of a thing, and the kind of activity manifests the kind of nature which is present. Hence, proper and specific activity manifests a proper nature in its specific perfection. Furthermore, in the beginning of this chapter we have seen that man is substantially one being. From these two conclusions, we draw the further conclusion that there is something in man which is proper to him alone, which makes him substantially one and different from other things, and is therefore the specifying source of his being, unity, and operations.

On the other hand, as we have seen in the preceding section, man is a part of the world. In interchanging matter with other things, man shows that there is something which is common to him and these other things. Moreover, since man is substantially one being, any interchange between him and other things is a substantial change, of a common substantial principle. This common substantial principle can be human in man, non-human in other things. Hence, the common principle in man is a potential principle in the order of substance; this potential principle is called primary matter.

Because primary matter is of itself a potential principle, in order to be a part of man it must be actualized and determined to be human. Now, there is in man a substantial part which is proper to him and is the specifying source of his being. Therefore, man is composed of a substantial potency, called the "body," [5] and a substantial act, or form, called the "soul."

In a word, the first stage of the argument concerning the nature of the soul makes us conclude that the soul of man is a substantial principle. The human soul is the substantial form of man. Therefore the human soul can be defined as "the first principle of human life in a physical body organized in a human way (as this is evident to direct experience, or is scientifically described in biology, for example)."

We are still not fully satisfied when we know that the human soul is substantial. But we cannot discover more about the soul until we examine again human operations, and see how these operations are related to the soul.

[5] "Body" here means "the potential or material part of man which is distinct from the soul." At other times, "body" may mean "the matter as informed, having the perfections of natural being, life, and/or sensation (not those of reason)." In this second meaning, "body" is distinguished from "reason" or "mind," but includes some of the perfections of the soul. In this second meaning of body, "body and mind" are not real parts of man, but rationally distinct parts, based ultimately on the really distinct parts of "body as primary matter" and "soul."

161. What kind of a cause is the soul?

All the activities of plants and animals are the operations of living, informed parts or organs. Hence, the soul is the principle of these activities only in so far as it specifies and actuates the body. In other words, the soul of plants and animals is *only* a *formal* cause—all that it "does" is to be in the body as substantial specifying principle. Consequently, expressions such as "The soul directs the growth of the cells" are not true if they are taken literally; they are to be understood as shorthand or elliptical ways of stating accurate (but frequently awkward) propositions such as "The soul as formal cause specifies certain parts of the body so that these parts direct the growth of the cells." The soul of plants and brutes is not an agent, and so it should not be called a being, but a principle of being.

The soul of man is likewise an informing principle. The activities of vegetation and sensation in man are the activities of informed parts of the body. And so when we say, "The soul is the principle of life and sensation," we mean "formal principle" and *not* agent or efficient principle. All human activities of life and sensation are therefore proximately carried on by living, informed material parts—the hormones, enzymes, and organic directive systems of which the biologists, biochemists, and physiologists speak.

But man has also "separated" or spiritual activities—those of intellection and willing. Consequently, the powers which are the proximate principles of these activities are themselves separated or spiritual accidents; they are not the forms of organs. But a spiritual accident cannot inhere in a material substance. Therefore, the operative powers (accidents) of intellect and will inhere directly in the soul.

Consequently, the whole actuality of the human soul is not taken up with informing and actuating the human body. The human soul is actually substantial also inasmuch as it is the ultimate subject of inhesion for the spiritual accidents of intellect and will. Now, intellect and will are operative powers, powers of immanent activity. Hence, through them efficient causality is exercised.[6] Consequently, the soul by itself is an ultimate principle of activity, and exercises some efficient causality.

True, the agent, and the unqualified subject, of all human activity is man as a whole. But in a limited and restricted sense (that is, inasmuch as intellect and will inhere immediately in the soul), the human soul by itself is also a subject of some human activity, that of understanding and willing.

162. The nature of the human soul: II. spirituality

A thing's nature is known from its activity. But the human soul is an ultimate intrinsic principle of spiritual action. Therefore the human soul itself is spiritual. Thus, the spirituality of the human soul is proved very simply from a consideration of man's substantial unity, and the spiritual nature of the activities of knowing and willing.

To prove the spirituality of the human soul is not necessarily to understand it; to see what it means, we need to go over the evidence from other points of view.

We have seen that the soul is really distinct from the body. Is the soul in any way independent of the body? To be independent of another is not to be intrinsically caused by another. On the contrary, to be affected by a cause is to be dependent on that thing which is the cause. How, then, is the soul related to the body? In the activities of vegetative life and sensation, the body and the soul are mutually causes (that is, as matter and form), for vegetative and sensitive activities are the acts of informed organs. As far as life and sensation are concerned, therefore, the soul is intrinsically dependent upon the body. But some of the activities of intellect and will are separated activities, as we have seen; they are not the acts of an informed organ, but of a power that has no organ. Consequently, in these activities of intellect and will, the body exercises no direct causality upon the soul; the body is not an intrinsic cause of understanding and willing.

[6] See above, Chapter V, section 51.

But, did we not find that the intellect depends for its actual knowledge upon sensation and specifically upon the phantasm? It depends in some way, yes. For the acquisition of new knowledge, the intellect depends on the phantasm as on a naturally indispensable condition and instrumental cause. However, in the actual use of at least some knowledge which deals with merely intentional being (for example, pure logic, mathematical logic), a phantasm is necessary only as the condition under which the causality of the agent intellect is exercised. (N.B. This is a question of actual knowing, not of the origin of the intelligible *species*.) Moreover, it seems that an abstract, universal, generic, and incomplete knowledge of material things can be had; for such knowledge also the phantasm would be necessary as a condition.[7] Therefore, in the actual use of some knowledge, the intellect depends on the phantasm only extrinsically (that is, as on a condition); intrinsically it is independent.

The soul is the ultimate principle of the same action of which the intellect is the proximate principle (power). Consequently, what is said of intellect is true of the soul. In some of its operations, the soul is intrinsically independent of the body, of matter. But action shows the nature of a thing. Therefore, the soul has a nature that exists by itself, without intrinsic dependence upon the body and upon matter. Therefore, the soul is spiritual.

From another point of view, the soul of man, like any other soul, is a substantial form. But it is a characteristic of all non-human forms to be principles *by which* the supposit (the existing substantial unit) exists and acts. Hence, in all non-human things the act of existing is the act of the entire supposit. But the human soul, though it is a principle by which the human being exercises physico-chemical, vegetative, and sensitive operations, is also in a limited way (as explained above) the principle *which* acts through the intellect and will. In the same way and to the same extent, therefore, the soul is a principle which has a proper and proportionate act of existing, for the mode of operation follows

[7] See above, Chapter VIII, section 96.

the mode of being. Consequently, the act of existing of a human person is primarily his soul's act of existing; the body (and so the whole being) shares in the soul's act of existing inasmuch as the soul is the form of the body and together with it constitutes human nature.

The fact that the human soul has a proper act of existing (in the limited way just explained) is expressed by calling the human soul a *subsistent* form. Now, a substantial form is non-material, in the sense that it is not matter nor composed of matter.[8] But an existing being, or an existing principle of being that is non-material, is a spiritual being, in the strict sense of that word. Therefore, the human soul is spiritual.

163. The presence of the soul in the body

The soul is the specifying form of the human body. And so the soul is *in* the body. But in what way? Our experience of sensible things shows us two ways of being present: in space and through activity. A thing that is in space is there by quantitatively occupying space. A cause is present when it acts, by its action. Now, the only things that are in space are things that are quantified.

Is the soul quantified in itself? Quantity is an accident that is due to matter. Hence, the soul, because it is a form, and because it is spiritual (negatively and positively immaterial), is not of itself in space—in other words, is not spatially present in the body.

By analysis of material things we find in them the two principles, matter and form. And so we discover another kind or kinds of presence—presence by material and formal causality. So every form is present to its matter by informing it (not by action, but by formal causality, by communicating itself).

Thus, the human soul is present in the human body by information. Where in the human body? Wherever the body is specifically human. And since the human body is entirely, part by part, human (e.g., the nose is human, the finger, the brain, the organ, the cell), the whole soul is present in the body, and in each part of the body.

[8] See above, Chapter III, section 27, and Appendix M.

Hence the whole soul is present everywhere in the body. And so, if you ask, "Where is the soul in the body?" the answer is "everywhere at once." Such a presence obviously cannot be imagined, for the imagination pictures either quantified objects or quantity itself. And a form as form is precisely not quantified. For this reason the soul cannot be directly imagined in itself and according to its own proper reality. But when we know the soul, we use the least unsuitable and most suggestive images, and *deny* the material content of these images in our intellectual judgments.

Because presence by information is presence everywhere at once in the informed body, it is a pointless, even stupid thing to look for the soul somewhere in the body. As far as essential presence is concerned, the human soul (and any form) is equally present to its whole matter and to every part of it.

By presence, we can also mean the presence of the soul through its powers. Hence, whenever a form has powers that are (accidental) forms of parts of the matter, that form will not be present to every part of the matter in the same way, and so not wholly present to the various parts. Besides this, the human soul has powers which are not the forms of any part of the body. Hence, if we are speaking of the presence through powers, the human soul is present to the body, but not wholly (for intellect and will are separate), and much less wholly present to any part. It is present to the eye according to the power of sight, and so forth.

164. The presence of intellect and will in the body

We have seen that presence can be by quantitative presence in space, by information (and reception, i.e., as matter receives form) or by efficient causality. Now, intellect and will are spiritual powers and so *not in space;* hence, your intellect and will are, strictly speaking, no *where.* And, intellect and will are not forms of any organs or parts of the body, so that they are not even *in* the body, except in so far as they are powers of the soul which is in the body by information. In that sense, the intellect and will of a particular person are in the body without being anywhere within it. Where is your intellect? As a power, nowhere in particular. But, we have seen that the agent intellect acts upons the phantasms as any principal cause acts upon its instrument. In this sense, the agent intellect is in the phantasm when it is *using* it as an instrument. And so too the possible intellect is present to the phantasm when it is receiving such influence from agent intellect and phantasm. Moreover, we have seen that in some cases reason or reason-and-will (in the imperium) uses other powers of man as instruments. In such cases, reason and will are where their causality is being exerted, and the type of presence they have is the dynamic presence of causality.

165. The origin of the soul [9]

The origin of plant and animal souls is not really a question. Only those things begin to be, which in themselves are, exist. But plant and animal souls are not in themselves; they are only the principles by which plants and animals are what they are. Hence, the only question is, How do plants and animals arise? And the answer is that in our experience plants and animals arise by generation from previously existing plants and animals. No biologist of today admits spontaneous generation—the coming-to-be of a plant or animal from previously nonliving matter—as something found in our present verifiable experience. As for the ultimate origin of plants and animals, as well as of the rest of material things, it is proved (in metaphysics or in natural theology) that all material things are *creatures*—that is, ultimately, directly or indirectly, they are by creation.[10]

[9] Though the origin and immortality of the human soul pertain to religion and are contained in revelation, they are also philosophical questions. For the soul is a real, subsisting principle of a real, natural, and even material being. Hence, we can and must raise the questions which concern its origin and its ceasing to be. The evidence we use is the soul's nature (which we have discovered after a long analysis and argument about the soul's operations). The method we use in answering these questions here is a strictly philosophical method of rational enquiry and demonstration, as can be seen from sections 165 and 166.

[10] For the place of the biological theory of evolution in relation to this statement, see below, Appendix N.

But the human soul, as we have just seen, *is* in itself, because by and in itself it acts. Hence, it is a true question to ask about the origin of the human soul. Because the human soul is spiritual, it cannot arise out of matter, it cannot be produced by working on the dispositions of matter. Consequently, since all the efficient causality of material things, man included, takes place through alteration (modification of material dispositions), the human soul cannot be produced by a material thing.

Or again from another point of view. The generative activity of man is evidently a material one. Hence, human generative activity can only have a material result or product. And the human soul, being a form as well as spiritual, cannot be divided. Hence, the new form cannot arise from the soul of the parent. And so, the human soul comes to be, without arising from a pre-existing subject or matter. Such coming-to-be is called "creation." And since it is proved in another part of philosophy (natural theology) that only God can create, it follows that the human soul comes to be by immediate creation from God.

The process is to be considered like this. The human parents each produce a cell (ovum and sperm) which are to provide the matter for the new human individual. Ovum and sperm unite, thus giving rise to a single cell with the material dispositions required for the presence of a soul. When these material dispositions have reached the appropriate degree of perfection, the human soul is created by God *in* the organized matter. (It is not possible to determine exactly when this takes place.) [11]

166. The immortality of human soul

The human soul is spiritual, arising by creation in an organized body. What happens at the moment of death? A thing can cease to be: (*a*) by being broken down into its component parts; (*b*) by the destruction of something on which it depends for its being;

---

[11] For a brief discussion of some further problems connected with the origin of the human soul, see below, Appendix M.

(*c*) by annihilation. These alternatives are exhaustive; they are based on intrinsic and extrinsic reasons for ceasing to be. Now, a thing which is composed of parts (a dog, a tree, water) obviously can be destroyed by breaking up the whole into parts. There are other realities which, though not composed of parts, depend on something which is destructible in itself; e.g., an animal soul depends for its reality on the composite (whole) which is directly destructible in itself by division into its parts. Annihilation, finally, is the reverse of creation—it is complete cessation from being, and takes place in so far as God ceases to preserve the being in existence. Now, the human soul, because it is a form, does not consist of parts which could be separated from each other. Therefore, it is not destructible in itself. Nor does the human soul depend on the body for its act of existence. Hence it cannot be destroyed in the destruction—death—of a man. Nor does God act arbitrarily in annihilating things. If He makes a being whose nature is to be indestructible, He clearly intends in the act of making it that it be in accord with its nature. Hence, in creating a soul, God shows His intention of not annihilating it. And so, the human soul, though it exists contingently with reference to the real possibility of annihilation (based on the distinction within it between essence and the act of existing), will not cease to be. Perpetual permanence in life is called immortality. And since the immortality of the human soul is according to its nature as a spiritual form, its immortality is natural.

A second (and secondary) approach to the immortality of the soul is through natural desire. Most people have a natural repugnance to the thought of completely ceasing to be, and a natural desire to continue to exist after death. Because of the universality [12] of this desire, and the way in which this object appeals to

[12] The reasons why not everybody actually experiences this desire seem to be three: (*a*) they have never actually thought of it, or have thought of it in a wholly unsatisfactory way—for example, as an eternity of harp-playing; (*b*) they have persuaded themselves that it is impossible by a fallacious argument; (*c*) they have some reason to expect eternal unhappiness.

the will, it can truly be called a natural desire, and so expresses a natural tendency of human nature.[13] But it is impossible that there be a natural tendency toward a completely non-existent object. In other words, no natural desire can be essentially unfulfillable, or, as it is frequently said, no natural desire can be in vain, can be frustrated.[14] This step in the argument presupposes that the world is created by an intelligent cause. Now it is obvious that an intelligent cause will not, and cannot in so far as it is intelligent, make a nature for an end which is not an end. But the impossible is not an end. Therefore, continuance of life after death is possible, and will be reached at least by some men, if not all.

In these two arguments we have a certain demonstration and a confirmatory sign that the human soul is naturally immortal.

A much more persuasive and concrete argument for the immortality of the human soul is that based on the implications of a rational moral order. The basis for this argument is the objective validity and the rational implications of moral values. Now the nature of the moral good is discussed in ethics or moral philosophy, and so if we want to use it here as a philosophical argument, we

[13] Objection: every being tends to the conservation of its own existence; self-preservation is the first law of life. Therefore, every being, or at least every conscious being, has a natural desire for immortality, and so should be just as immortal as the soul. But this is ridiculous, and so the argument for the immortality of the soul is not valid.

Answer. (a) as far as beings without knowledge are concerned, they naturally tend to the preservation of their *own being*. But this being is naturally corruptible. It would therefore be impossible that they naturally tend to perpetual being.

(b) As far as animals are concerned, they tend to the good which they know, for appetite follows knowledge. But sense knowledge can only attain being as particularized in the sensible objects, and cannot attain being simply (which is necessary so that "being without end" could be known). Therefore animals cannot have a natural desire for immortality. Therefore the objection is not relevant.

[14] It is frequently objected: "But so many natural desires *are* frustrated: all the seeds that never develop, the parents that cannot have children, the monsters that are born, the people that desire happiness and are unhappy." These emotional objections thoroughly miss the point. For (a) full-grown plants, children, normal offspring are real, not fictitious ends (b) which are actually reached by many beings. All that the objection proves is that created causality is not always inevitably effective. St. Thomas Aquinas says that the desire is a sign (he does not call it a proof); *Summa Theologiae*, I. 75. 6.

presuppose that ethics will establish the position from which we argue here. Furthermore, the moral order is a rational order, only on condition that the human soul is immortal. If we were to argue (*a*) that the human soul is immortal because a rational moral order demands immortality, and then later argue (*b*) that the moral order is rational, because all the rational implications of obligation are fulfilled, and among these implications is immortality— if we were to argue this way, our proof would be a "vicious circle." In point of fact, we do not argue this way, for (*a*) the first argument for the immortality of the soul which we saw above does not rest upon the moral order at all; and (*b*) obligation is not merely deduced, for there is an *experience* of obligation. Hence, the argument for immortality from the moral order is a strong, and to some extent independent, confirmation of the first argument.

In the experience of obligation, we see that there is a constraint or necessity upon us of performing certain actions, though at the same time we also know that we are free (that is, physically able) to act in accordance with this rational necessity, or to act otherwise, either by omitting the actions, or by performing contrary ones. Because we do our good or bad actions freely, we are responsible for them. In other words, our actions have consequences which justly (according to a rational equality and proportion) come upon us. Now, a good action is one which is in accord with rational nature and right reason, and which consequently is by its nature such as to bring us to an attainment of the end for which we are made and destined. A bad action is one which is not in harmony with rational nature and right reason, and consequently by its nature must interfere with the gaining of the end. Furthermore, we have seen that the appetite of man as a whole being is his rational appetite, and that the end of the rational appetite (end considered from the viewpoint of the subject which possesses it) is our happiness. Therefore, good actions are such as by their nature lead to happiness; bad actions, such as lead to the loss of happiness. This is the structure of the moral order, of obligation and moral good and evil.

When we look at the consequences which men's actions bring upon them in this present life, we see that those implications are not fulfilled. Suffering, pain, disappointment, physical evils of all sorts, are as frequently the lot of the good as of the bad man. On the other hand, morally bad actions frequently lead to success, satisfaction, gratification.—And as if this were not enough of a difficulty, the ethician shows demonstratively (and the ordinary man frequently sees without being able to prove) that complete happiness is impossible under the conditions of time, change, matter, and destructibility. Hence, in fact, the proper and proportionate consequences of our moral deeds do not come upon us in this present life.

Therefore, we are forced to a dilemma. Either there is an after life for the soul, in which the consequences of moral action are in harmony with the rational implications of good and evil, or obligation is an illusion, responsibility does not exist, and moral values ultimately mean nothing. But this second part of the dilemma involves a denial of the experience of obligation, and a denial of the ultimate intelligibility of being; it is destructive, moreover, of the entire dignity of the individual and of the bonds which make social and political life possible and hold it together. Hence, the experience of obligation and responsibility, and the objective validity of good and evil, rationally imply the immortality of the human soul.[15]

167. The final cause of the soul

So far we have discussed three of the causes of the human soul: we have seen that the soul is a subsistent *form;* that its material cause (*not from* which, but *in* which it is created) is the human body, and that its efficient cause is God. What is the final cause or end of the soul and of man? This question has already received a partial, implicit answer. For we have seen that the will is the appetite of man as a whole, as a rational being, and we have also

---

[15] Note that the argument from the sanctions of the moral law has a wider basis than the happiness of the *individual.*

seen that the end (or object) of the will is ultimately the supreme good and its possession which is happiness. The end of man and of the soul is therefore happiness. But what is happiness, and in the possession of which real good does it consist? The answers to these questions are given in ethics; [16] and at this point the philosophy of human nature demands completion by the philosophy of human action and its finality.

168. The soul's knowledge after death

What will the human soul do after death when separated from the body? [17] We have seen that though some acts of understanding and willing are in themselves intrinsically independent of any organ, they do involve an organic activity (of imagination) on the side of the object. Understanding, and consequently willing, are not naturally possible in this life without a phantasm. After death, in the state of separation from the body, there can be no phantasms, for all the powers of the soul which are the forms of various organs no longer are actual powers after death. How then can the soul know? And if it does not act, how can it be?

The extrinsic dependence of the intellect upon the body while the soul is in the body is in accord with its present mode of existence. When separated from the body, the soul has its existence in itself alone, not shared with the body. Hence, its mode of activity will be according to its mode of being. In other words, intellection and willing will then take place without phantasms. But this change in the mode of operation will entail certain changes in the object. (a) Knowledge of singular material things will be

[16] These answers are also given, more definitely and more completely, by Divine Revelation. But the fact that the answers have been revealed in no way prevents us from making a rational investigation, and from attempting to gain as complete a rational understanding as we can. On the contrary, this seeking for rational understanding is one manifestation of man's basic desire and need for truth.

[17] In asking and answering this question, we are abstracting from the moment from the Beatific Vision. In spite of that, the question is real, for it concerns the natural objects of the soul's knowledge: itself, material things, other souls and angels.

naturally impossible for the separated soul, and likewise existential judgments about material or sensible things. It will also be impossible to acquire knowledge of previously unknown material objects. Since the immanent objects of universal knowledge have only intentional being, judgments about these absolute natures can assert only intentional being. (*b*) On the other hand, in this life the soul has no actual direct knowledge of itself, because it is the form of a body. Once separated in death, it will be actually intelligible in itself, and so the soul will directly know itself as an actually existing singular spiritual substance. (*c*) Communication between separated souls and between souls and angels should be possible, at least in so far as states of mind and will are concerned. The soul's knowledge of angelic substance will apparently be by analogy with its own. (*d*) Whatever other knowledge is necessary will be given by God, in a fashion similar to the mode of angelic knowledge.

We can see that these consequences are necessary, but we cannot understand how or why. And so we cannot realize what knowing and willing will be after death, or how they take place. But that is the normal condition of analogous knowledge—and our knowledge of the state of the separated soul is analogous.

169. Definitions

"*One*" is what is not actually divided in itself.

"*Substantial unity*" or "*unity per se*" is the condition of a being that is undivided precisely as a *being*, that is, which has one act of existing.

Man is a rational animal.

Substantial form is the actual, specifying intrinsic principle of a substance that is per se one.

Primary matter (first matter) is the potential, intrinsic principle of a material substance, which is the ground of change, limitation and individuation, and of a certain community in being.

The *human soul* is: (1)   the ultimate principle by which a man lives and knows.

(II) the ultimate principle of living and knowing, distinct from the body.

(III) the substantial form of man, or: the first principle of human life in a physical body organized in a human way.

(IV) the subsistent substantial form of man, or: the spiritual first principle of being, life, and knowing, which is the act of a body organized humanly.

Real distinction is that lack of identity which is in things independently of the operation of the mind.

Rational distinction (distinction of reason) is that lack of identity (between understood aspects of a thing) which depends on the operation of the mind.

Spirituality is the condition of being or operating independently of matter.

Independence is the not being caused or conditioned by another.

Intrinsic independence is the not being caused by another.

Intrinsic dependence is the being caused by another.

Extrinsic independence is the not being conditioned by another.

Extrinsic dependence is the being limited by another as by a condition or object.

Creation is the origin of a thing which of itself was not, without a pre-existing subject out of which it is made.

Immortality is unceasing permanence in being and life.

170. Proofs

A. *Man is substantially one.*

(1) We have direct experience *that* we are one, in operation and in being. The clearest instance of this experience is this, that the same "I" which understands also senses, desires, and wills.

Therefore: as men, we are substantially one.

(2) The substantial unity of a material being is manifested by

the continuity of its parts as a condition, and by the intrinsic integration of its operations to one end.

But: a man is quantitatively continuous, and all his operations are essentially and intrinsically integrated to one end.

Therefore: man is substantially one.

B. *The soul is really distinct from the body.*

The soul is the ultimate principle of life (nominal definition).

But: human life is proper to man, specifically distinct from other kinds of life, with which man shares in matter.

But: the actual, specifying principle is really distinct from the potential, common principle which is ground of change.

Therefore: the soul is really distinct from the potential principle of man (his body).

C. *The soul is spiritual.*

Action shows the nature of a thing.

But: the human soul is the principle of operations which are spiritual, intrinsically independent of matter.

Therefore: the soul is spiritual.

D. *The human soul is created.*

A spiritual substance or substantial principle cannot come to be out of any pre-existing subject.

But: the human soul begins to be, as is evident, and is a spiritual substantial principle.

Therefore: the soul begins to be without a pre-existing subject out of which it is made. In other words, the human soul is created.

E. *The human soul is immortal.*

A being which is both intrinsically and extrinsically indestructible will not cease to be (intrinsic destructibility = possibility of ceasing to be by resolution into component parts; extrinsic destructibility = dependence in being upon an intrinsically destructible thing).

But: the human soul is both intrinsically (because it is simple, has no parts) and extrinsically indestructible (because it does not depend intrinsically upon anything destructible).

Therefore: the human soul will not cease to be.

Therefore: the human soul is immortal (immortality = permanence in life).

F. *The nature of moral activity demands that the human soul continue living after a man's death.*

Moral obligation and the intrinsic nature of justice demand that those who live according to the moral law attain their end (which is happiness), and that those who violate that law be deprived of that end toward which the law by its nature leads.

But: there is an absolute moral law, and it is evident that not all who observe it reach happiness here on earth, and that none of them can reach an unqualified happiness here; it is equally evident that some who violate the moral law have more happiness than some who observe it.

But: if there is no life after death, then the moral law is a mockery, and justice is violated on a cosmic scale.

But: both of these conclusions involve contradictions.

Therefore: there is a continuation of life after death.

171. Readings

St. Thomas Aquinas, *Summa Theologiae*, I. 75. 1–5, on the nature of the soul; a. 6, the incorruptibility of the soul; 76. 1–7, the unity of man; a. 8, the presence of the soul in the body; q. 90, the origin of the soul; q. 89 and III. 11. 2 ad 1, the knowledge the separated soul has after death.

Anton C. Pegis, *The Problem of the Soul in the Thirteenth Century* (Toronto, Institute of Mediaeval Studies, 1934), pp. 168–87.

Étienne Gilson, *The Spirit of Mediaeval Philosophy*, trans. by A. H. C. Downes (New York, Scribner, 1936), pp. 168–208.

William McDougall, *Body and Mind*, 5th ed., (London, Methuen, 1920), pp. 281–300; an excellent discussion of the unity of consciousness.

CHAPTER XIV

Human Nature: A Systematic Summary

172. The purpose of this summary

All organized demonstrated knowledge has two movements. The first begins with facts and particular conclusions, follows the lines of intelligible implication, and arrives at the conditions, causes, nature of the subject under consideration. The aim of this first movement is information and understanding. Once arrived at that point, the intellect reverses its movement, begins with the causes and nature of the subject and proceeds to the particular conclusions that can be drawn regarding properties, activity, and effects. The aim of this second movement is to see the working of the necessities that were discovered in the first movement, and thus to acquire unity, organization, and full certitude.[1]

Examples of this double movement may be taken from the sciences. Thus, in physics, it was only gradually discovered that even the lightest of gases have some weight. Then the laws of planetary motion were found. When the law of universal gravitation was found and stated, these two apparently different traits of material things were seen to be the same, and to be based on the essential mutual attraction of material bodies. Again, static electricity and lightning were known for a long time before they were understood to be manifestations of the same force, and it was a still longer time before the electron theory gave some explanation of the phenomena. Again, in chemistry, various laws of constant propor-

---

[1] Sometimes *new* information is acquired by an apriori argument (for example, we learned that the soul is immortal by a deduction from its nature), but this is not necessarily so.

tions were discovered, for example, that hydrogen and oxygen combine to form water in the proportion of two to one. When the structure of the atom was found, the reason for these constant proportions was seen.[2] Similarly, in metaphysics, after Aristotle discovered the principles of accidental and substantial change, he was able to express these principles in terms of act and potency.

In our consideration of man so far, the movement of thought has been from operation to nature. This is the only way we can come to know directly what a thing is. If we stop there, our knowledge will be incomplete, unorganized, and most likely impermanent. Throughout the second movement it will be necessary to remember that proofs and explanations have preceded;[3] it will frequently be helpful to recall them briefly.

A second purpose of this chapter will be to indicate points of contact between the matter previously discussed and other parts of philosophy, as well as to indicate points which a more adequate treatment of man would have developed at some length.

173. Intellectual substance: its place and function in the universe

It will help us to understand the nature of man, if we consider the place and function of an intellectual substance in the universe. Man has an intellect, and thus takes his place in the world of the intellectual substances; man has a body, and so he is also ranged with the world of material things. He is thus, in a kind of way, the point of juncture between these two worlds, and thus the being which binds them together.

There are two ways in which a being can possess a perfection. In the first way, a thing is perfect according to the perfection of

[2] If, as sometimes happens, the structure of the atom is taught as a principle of physics or chemistry instead of a conclusion, the student may acquire some scientific information, but he will not acquire the *habit* of science. In him, this knowledge will be human faith instead of science.

[3] If someone were to *begin* with this second movement (which is possible only by way of reading or hearing a presentation given by another), it would seem at worst to be a kind of glorified dictionary (nominalism), at best an unrealistic discussion of mere possibility.

its own being, which is proper to it according to its own nature. In the second way, a thing can possess not only its own perfection, but the perfection of other things as other. This second way of being perfect is proper to beings that have knowledge. For a thing is known when it is present to, united with, the knower. Looked at in this way, knowing is a way of being, a manner of existing, more perfect than merely possessing a perfection as subject.[4]

And so it belongs to the perfection of the universe that there be intellectual creatures. For an effect is the more perfect the more it bears the likeness of its cause in being and nature. Thus, the more closely a work of art approaches the ideal in the mind of the artist, the more perfect it is. Now, it can be proved (and is proved in natural theology) that God is an intelligent cause. And so it is most appropriate that there be intelligent creatures.

Second act is a perfection over and above first act. Now, the being and nature of a thing are its first act; its operations are its second act. In order that the universe be perfect, it is necessary that creatures be like to God, not only in being and *nature,* but also in operation. But God's operation with regard to Himself is the operation of intellect and will. Hence, there must be some creatures who have understanding and volition.

The perfection of the universe requires not only that creatures exist, but also that they act, that they themselves be causes. For, to be a cause is to communicate goodness. The causality of creatures will be a more perfect action, if their causality is like God's even in the way in which God causes. But God causes through intellect and will. Hence, the perfection of the universe requires that there be efficient causes which have intellect and will.

God's motive in creating could only be His own goodness, which He wishes to share with others by making them like to Himself. But likeness of another is found in two ways: real [5] likeness, as the fire caused in the wood is like the fire from which it was lit; and

---

[4] See St. Thomas Aquinas, *Truth,* II. 2, first half of the article.

[5] "Real" here means "physical, natural," as opposed to "intentional." This does not mean to imply that the intentional is imaginary, fictitious, or anything of that sort. See the explanation of "intentional" in Chapter IV.

the likeness of knowledge, in the way in which the knower is like the known by possessing the form of the thing known in an intentional manner. And so the perfection of the universe requires that God's goodness be shared, not only in being, but also in knowledge. But only an intellect can attain to the knowledge of the Divine goodness. Hence, there must be intellectual creatures.[6]

It is helpful to consider this question differently, and to ask, Could there be a purely material universe? Could God have created material creatures only? This question does not mean, Did or does God have the power to create only material things? It does mean, Is it consonant with God's wisdom to create only material things? Now, every being acts for an end. Moreover, in the order of ends or final causes, all secondary or intermediate ends actually cause through the causality of the ultimate end. Therefore, if there be a created universe, its end must be the ultimate end or supreme Good, which is God. Consequently, the end of all created things is God. But material things, because of their materiality and the extremely limited nature of their activity, cannot directly and immediately attain to God. Hence, if they existed alone, they would have an ultimate end which they could not reach. It surely does not seem the part of wisdom to make such beings alone. And so the very nature of created material agents calls for the existence of created spiritual beings which by their powers of intellect and will can directly attain God, and thus, mediately, bring material things to the ultimate end of the universe.[7]

From these considerations it follows that the end of an intellectual substance is God, to be possessed through the proper activities of such a substance, that is, through understanding and love. Viewed from the side of the intellectual substance, the possession of the supreme Truth and Goodness is an activity which is happiness.[8] Consequently, we can also say that the end of an in-

---

[6] See St. Thomas, *Contra Gentiles*, II, 46.
[7] *Ibid.*, II. 46; III, 17–22.
[8] *Ibid.*, III. 48. This argument does *not* prove the Beatific Vision from nat-

tellectual being as such is happiness. And in this absolute end reached by an intellectual being, the particular and limited ends of more limited natures find their ultimate meaning and fulfillment.

174. The activity proper to intellectual substance

To know is to act. There are two kinds of action, transient and immanent. Transient action is the perfection of something other than the agent. Thus, when fire is heating, that action is the perfection of something else, e.g., of the water which is being heated. But immanent action is the perfection of the agent itself, as the plant perfects itself in growth. The activity or operation of knowing has of itself no effect on any other thing; it is simply the act of the knower, and makes him more perfect than he was. Thus, knowing is an immanent activity, and so is a kind of life (where "life" is used analogously). To know is to live.[9]

"To be known" is a special way of being. When we say that a thing *is*, we are speaking of the being that a thing has in accordance with its nature. When we say that a thing is known, we speak of the being that it exercises as an object of knowledge. This special kind of being is known as "intentional being."

Within knowledge, therefore, there is always, in some sense, an opposition between subject and object: between knower and thing known, even when the thing known is the knower himself. There is in knowledge a union, a unity, even an identity of knower and known; yet this identity includes simultaneously the relational opposition of "otherness." The intentional form possessed in knowledge does not of itself perfect the knower as a natural form perfects its subject—subjectively, as his own form; it perfects him objectively.

The known form does not perfect the knower in the way in which

---

ural reason, *nor* the necessity of the Beatific Vision once we have learned about it from revelation. But it does show where the Beatific Vision as a supernatural end is "inserted" into an order of nature and end. See also, G. P. Klubertanz, S.J., "Ethics and Theology," *The Modern Schoolman*, XXVII (1949), 32–35.

9 See St. Thomas, *Contra Gentiles,* I. 100; 2. 1; *Truth,* VIII, 6; *Summa Theologiae,* I. 14. 2; 18. 3 ad 1.

a natural form perfects its matter; rather, it perfects him without reference to his or its own proper matter—that is, it perfects him immaterially. Therefore, being known implies at least so much immateriality, on the part of the thing known. And in turn, this implies an immateriality on the part of the knower. A merely material thing is in itself a thing, and it possesses only its own perfections as their subject. It is object only in the sense of being the object of transitive action or passion. When it acts, it acts to make other things like itself ("every agent produces an effect like to itself"); when it is acted upon, it becomes like its cause, and other than it was. A merely material thing can become other, for it can change; it cannot become *the other*. This is because matter is in itself exclusive—what is here, cannot be there; if one thing is here, another cannot be simultaneously here; if I completely possess a material thing, you cannot have it. Matter limits, restrains, restricts perfection. But the thing which knows cannot be thus restricted so as to be wholly wrapped up in being the subject of its own perfection, because it also has the perfection of the other. This escape from exclusiveness is to a greater or less extent an emergence from matter, a state of being higher and greater than that of mere materiality. And so, both knowing and being known imply immateriality, so that the greater the immateriality, the greater the knowledge and the knowability.[10]

Because a knower can possess the forms of other things as well as his own, acts of knowledge, and of appetency also, have a kind of infinity. The actions of understanding and of rational appetency are simply infinite as far as the scope or range of object is concerned, for the object of intellectual knowledge is all being, and the object of the rational appetency is all good. Even acts of sensory knowledge and appetency have a kind of qualified infinity, inasmuch as they can be directed to the totality of sensible objects.

Actual knowledge is an operation or activity, and like all operations it receives its specification from its object. By "object" is meant any reality inasmuch as that reality is a term of action or a

[10] See St. Thomas, *Summa Theologiae*, I. 14. 1.

principle of passion; an object, therefore, is related to the operation which it specifies either as cause or effect (term, and sometimes end).

Knowledge is an immanent operation. Therefore, it proceeds (efficiently) from the same knower whose perfection it is. In other words, the knower is the agent of that act which is knowledge. Activity which is second act presupposes that the agent is itself in act, for every being acts inasmuch as it is in act (that is, first act). But to exercise the act of existing implies having (or being by identity) an essence or form. Hence, every agent acts according to its form. And so the knower, too, performs the activity of knowing according to some form; this form is the intrinsic and immediate principle by which knowing is specified. The intrinsic and formal principle by which a knower performs a particular act of knowledge is called a *species*.

The intelligible *species* therefore is the intrinsic form by which an intellect understands. This *species* is either identical with the essence of the knower, as in God or in the self-knowledge of an angel, or it is distinct from the essence, is an accidental form, and to this extent an added perfection of the knower.

The *species* has a double function or relation: for it inheres in and specifies the knower and his operation, while at the same time it is related to the object of knowledge. As related to the subject, the *species* is the internal determination from which knowledge flows. Under this aspect, a *species* is a real being (either the essence of the knower himself or an accidental modification in the category of quality).

The *species*, however, is not merely in the knower; it is also that by which an intellect understands a definite object. In order to determine the intellect to the knowledge of a definite object, the *species* must somehow contain or be the object. The *species* as such cannot contain or be the object in a natural or physical way, else it would be a natural physical form, and its presence in the intellect would make the intellect to be some other nature (that is, be that nature whose form is contained in the *species*). What is needed is a form whose function is to make the intellect actually *knowing* some particular object. Hence, the *species* contains the object in an immaterial way, in a way which is proper to knowledge; in a single word, the *species* contains the object intentionally. In the *species*, the object of knowledge is most intimately united to the knower for the sake of the operation of knowing.[11]

Intellectual substances, therefore, or intelligent beings, will be basically of two kinds. If the intelligible *species* is an infinite form, and therefore actually representing, intentionally containing all being, the act of understanding will be single, infinite, and eternally actual. In that case, the *species* will be identical with the infinite Being, and the infinite act of understanding will be identical with the infinite, subsistent act of existing. For this reason, God knows Himself and all beings according to their proper natures and proper times in His essence, which is the infinite, eternally actual and immutable *species* by which He knows.

On the other hand, the *species* can be a finite form. In that case, even if the essence of the knower is a simple, wholly actual, immaterial substance (an angel), that essence cannot be the representative form of all being, but only of itself and of things actually like unto itself. In order that the intellect of a finite being be determined and specified to know other beings (according to its nature as intellectual substance), other *species* will be required, over and above the essence. These supplementary *species* will be inherent accidents, added to the intellect as essentially constituted.

The second kind of intellectual substance, whose nature is finite, is able to exist in many fashions, according to different proportions of potency and act in the order of being. Furthermore, the amount of act that a given intellect has will directly correspond to the actuality of the substance in the order of being. An intellect which is more in act can know many beings with but a few *species;*

[11] *Ibid.*, I. 14. 2; 54. 2; 55. 1; 56. 1, in that order.

an intellect which is more in potency needs more *species* which are more particularized and of smaller scope.[12]

Among finite intellectual substances, some are fully in act as regards their substantial perfection. These are the pure or subsistent forms, ordinarily called angels.[13] Because the angel is fully in act as regards its substantial nature, its intellect correspondingly is always in its full natural act. Hence, such accidental *species* as an angel needs for its natural knowledge are connatural, are concreated with its being, and are given by the same creative act that gives it its intellectual power. Hence, angels do not acquire natural knowledge in the course of their duration; they merely use it in one way or another.

Below the substances which are simply in substantial act (the pure forms or angels), there is another kind of intellectual substance whose nature is not wholly in act. This substance is therefore a composite of potency and act in the order of substance: that is, a composite of matter and form. This is the lowest, most imperfect kind of intellectual substance—that is, man.

175. The human intellect and the need for senses

The intellectual substance which is in potency has a proportioned intellectual power; there is therefore an intellect which is by nature simply in potency. An intellect which is by nature in potency, naturally proceeds from potency to act by a series of successive actuations. It is not to be expected that the intelligible *species* needed in this gradual process are naturally given by God, since

12 *Ibid.*, I. 14. 1–4; 55. 1–3.

13 Although the belief in the existence of created beings higher than anything in the material world is to be found among many kinds of religious beliefs, the notion of a pure form or separated substance is a purely philosophical one. St. Thomas, in the *Disputed Question on Spiritual Creatures*, art. 5, after discussing some proofs which he considers invalid, proceeds to give three arguments from reason for the existence of such beings. These proofs are subtle and difficult, and so here we will go on the assumption that such beings are at least possible.

Though we are not directly interested in the Angels in this course, the contrasts between angelic and human knowledge serve to clarify some points about the latter.

any action of God apart from creating things, conserving them in their being, and concurring (coöperating) with their activities, is a gratuitous action (miracle or grace). Hence, the *species* needed by an intellect in potency must be acquired by the action of secondary, created causes. But these *species* cannot be derived from the intellect which is in potency, because it is in potency and not in act. The human intellect must be moved by some distinct cause or causes which actually (separately or in combination) possess the required perfection in act.[14]

Moreover, because of the imperfection of an intellect which is in potency, the kind of *species* suitable for an angel are not suitable for it. Angelic *species*, as we have seen, are few in number, but enable the angelic intellect to know many beings. But an intellect in potency, if it possessed but a few *species* with which to know all beings, would be able to know only in general, vaguely. For intelligible *species*, inasmuch as they are inherent accidents, must be proportioned to the power into which they are received; the generality of such *species* would therefore have to be by way of indetermination. Hence, an intellect which is by nature in potency needs many particularized *species*, and these *species* must be acquired from distinct causes. Therefore, an intellectual substance which has an intellect naturally in potency needs passive powers or senses by which it can be moved by external efficient causes.[15]

That the passive powers needed by an intellectual substance like man are precisely *senses* will be clear from the following considerations. For the human intellect is in its origin and by nature in potency, and only successively does it pass into act. It is the kind of power which is in potency before knowing in act, and so is called a "possible intellect," that is, an intellect which can be perfected. In order to know, a possible intellect must be moved or acted upon by an intelligible being in such a way that it receives the form of that being. But the only actually intelligible beings are the pure forms (God and the angels) and separated souls. As we have seen,

14 St. Thomas, *Summa Theologiae*, I. 79. 4.
15 See *ibid.*, I. 84. 6, 7.

the human intellect is at the beginning of its existence in potency, and, according to its natural way of acting, needs to receive an inherent specifying principle in order that it may perform its activities. An intellect which is an accidental power of operation is proportioned to the operation of understanding as potency is to its proper act. Hence, it is not naturally a potency to receive actually intelligible *beings,* nor can the function of the received *species* of an accidental power be naturally performed by a separate subsistent form.[16] Nor is there any natural way in which intentional forms derived from these subsistent forms can be imprinted in the human intellect, for such supposed forms would also be more perfectly actual than the limited capacity of the human intellect would be able to receive. On the other hand, actually intelligible beings are subsistent forms; therefore they cannot naturally become or be inherent in an accidental power like the possible intellect. Consequently, we cannot directly and immediately know such actually intelligible substances.[17]

Below the level of the actually intelligible substances or forms there are potentially intelligible material things, forms-in-matter. Forms-in-matter are forms received in and limited by a substantial potency, and consequently are proportionately suited to be the directly intelligible objects for an intellectual substance that is likewise received into a substantial potency. However, though forms-in-matter are the directly proportioned object of an intellectual substance which is itself the form of a body, forms-in-matter are not actually intelligible in themselves. To be understood, forms-in-matter must become actually intelligible. The power by which potential intelligibles are made actually intelligible is called the agent intellect.[18]

---

[16] Supernaturally, in the Beatific Vision the Divine substance takes the place of an intelligible *species,* and then the intellect is raised to a higher order of perfection by the "light of glory"; cf. St. Thomas, *Summa Theologiae,* I. 12. 2 ad 3.

[17] See St. Thomas, *Summa Theologiae,* I. 54. 4.

[18] *Ibid.,* 79. 3.

The function of the agent intellect is to make actual intelligibles. Therefore it itself is not a knowing power, nor is it immediately of itself an object of knowledge. It is simply the active power of making actual intelligibles, and therefore is always in act.[19] In order to produce an actual intelligible, it is not enough that an agent intellect be present; there must also be objects which are potentially intelligible. These potentially intelligible objects are the sensed-and-imagined forms of sensible things which are called phantasms. Phantasms are of themselves only potentially intelligible, but they are actually intentional, representative forms of definite things. By the working together of these two causes (agent intellect and phantasms) intelligible *species* are produced in the possible intellect, which are actually intelligible forms of things. The causality by which intelligible *species* are produced is called "abstraction." [20] In this action, the agent intellect is as principal cause, the phantasms as instrumental cause.[21]

Because the intelligible *species* by which the intellect is put into first act are derived from sensible things through sense experience, it follows that we can have direct intellectual knowledge only of those sensible things that we actually experience or have experienced. That is why a person who lacks one sense cannot have the direct intellectual knowledge of the objects of that sense. That is also why, when the imagination is not acting (as in sleep, or injury to the brain), there is no intellectual knowledge.[22]

Because of the way in which the human intellect is first put into act—namely, by intelligible *species* derived from material things —it follows that the proper and proportionate object of the human intellect is the being or nature existing in matter.[23] All other things which the human intellect knows, it knows not immediately and

---

[19] *Ibid.*, 79. 4 ad 2; 54. 1 ad 1.
[20] See *ibid.*, I. 85. 1 ad 3.
[21] As we have seen, the notions of cause derived from sensible substances cannot be applied univocally to powers of the soul.
[22] See St. Thomas, *Summa Theologiae,* I. 84. 7.
[23] *Ibid.*

in themselves, but in terms of material things. Because material things are not only material, but also *are*, it is possible, by way of analogy, to know immaterial things, such as the soul and God.[24]

The intelligible *species* is produced by the agent intellect and the phantasm, and, more accurately, according to the *form* of the latter. Moreover, it inheres in the intellect, which is a separated, spiritual power. Hence, the intelligible *species* is directly and of itself a representative, intentional form of a material thing according to the latter's nature or essence. If the intellect knows simply according to its information by the *species*, it will have a universal apprehension of the essence or nature of a material thing. That is why direct intellectual apprehension is universal and of the essence of a thing.[25] It is correct, therefore, to use universality and necessity as certain distinguishing marks of intellectual knowledge.[26]

A material thing not only has an essence; it exists, and it exists as a singular thing. This singular material thing, through the phantasm, is the instrumental cause of the intelligible *species*, and the permanent foundation of intellectual knowledge. Hence, if the intellect "turns to the phantasm," that is, if it produces its act of knowing in contact with (or in dynamic composition with) the phantasm, then, indirectly, it can reach the being of the singular material thing.[27]

Consequently, the acts of the human intellect are of more than one kind. First of all, there is the direct (or simple) apprehension, by which the intellect, being informed by an intelligible *species*, apprehends the essence of a material thing. The most perfect and terminal act of this kind is the definition. An essence may of course be known with greater or less clarity and accuracy. Usually, we first know an essence only generically—for example, as a material substance. Upon further experience and the development of the

[24] *Ibid.*, 87. 1; and q. 88.
[25] See *ibid.*, I. 85. 1. Remember that "essence" here does not mean "essence in all its specific determinations."
[26] See *ibid.*, 84. 1.
[27] See *ibid.*, 86. 1; 84. 7.

phantasm under the guidance of intellectual knowledge already acquired, clearer and more specifically determined knowledge is acquired. Ultimately, under ideal conditions, an essence can be known in its complete specific determination.[28] When the action of the intellect is only of this kind, then it either reaches the essence or it does not, and if it does not, it simply fails. Hence, in the simple, direct apprehension of essences, there can be incompleteness; there can be no error.[29]

Because the human intellect does not immediately pass from pure potency into full act, but is actuated successively, it is necessary for it to compose and divide (separate) its apprehensions. In general, this act consists in the fact that something is not simply grasped, but is affirmed or denied. This act of the intellect is called judgment. Judgments are of two kinds, which may be called the existential and the attributive judgments. An existential judgment is one in which the existence of the subject is asserted or denied. It directly bears on the being of a thing according to its act of existing. An attributive judgment is one in which a predicate is asserted or denied of a subject. Generally speaking, the attributive judgment bears on the essence, properties, or accidents of the subject directly, and indirectly, or connotatively, bears on the act of existing (or on the relation of the subject to the act of existing). The judgment, therefore, is an act of knowledge, different from, and not reducible to, mere apprehension, for in the judgment we may attain to, know, the composition or division of apprehensions, and we always, directly or indirectly, attain to the act of existing (esse).[30]

Therefore, it is through judgment (and the apprehensions based on preceding judgments) that the human intellect goes beyond the essences of material things to metaphysics, to the knowledge

[28] See *ibid.*, I. 79. 4 ad 3; 85. 3.
[29] See *ibid.*, 85. 6.
[30] See St. Thomas, *Summa Theologiae*, I. 85. 5; 16. 1, 2. See also Gerald B. Phelan, "Verum sequitur esse rerum," *Mediaeval Studies*, I (1939), pp. 11–22; Robert J. Henle, S.J. "Existentialism and the Judgment," *Proceedings of the American Catholic Philosophical Association* XXI (1946), pp. 40–52; Francis C. Wade, S.J. "The Judgment of existence," *ibid.*, pp. 102–06.

of itself, and to the knowledge of the separated substances. Because the whole value of such knowledge is judgmental, the knowledge is analogous, derived from the directly known objects.

The third kind of intellectual act is reasoning, by which the intellect proceeds from one knowledge to another. The most important of the acts of reasoning are those in which the process from one knowledge to another in accomplished according to the way in which causality is exercised in reality.

Whenever the intellect reaches a term of understanding, it produces, forms, and expresses in itself the mental word, which is a pure sign (*medium in quo*) of the object. On the one hand, this is the knowledge itself which is signified by language, and so is the result or term of understanding. And yet it is an immanent term which the intellect forms for the sake of perfect understanding. The mental word is thus itself known. Yet it is not directly known in contradistinction to the thing-object of which it is the sign, but is constituted by the act of understanding as a wholly "transparent" medium which is formally identical with the thing, differing from the latter only according to its mode of being.[31]

176. The human soul and its body

We have seen that an intellect which is by its nature wholly in potency needs senses for the sake of its intellectual operation. Now, a sense is such that it can undergo a passion from a material singular object, and whose proper object is the material thing under some particular aspect. This means that a sense is an organic power, or an informed organ—an organ, so that it can undergo the efficient activity of another material thing; an informed organ, so that it may undergo the immaterial change which is prerequired for knowledge.

In order that a power of the soul be an accidental form of an organ, it is necessary that the soul itself be the substantial form of a body thus organized. The necessity of this conclusion derives from the relation between proper accidents and the substance

[31] See St. Thomas, *Summa Theologiae*, I. 27. 1; 34. 1 ad 2.

from which they flow and in which they inhere. For a proper accident is one which corresponds and is proportioned to the specific nature of the substance in which it inheres. The power of sense is a proper accident of the human soul, because, as we have seen, an intellect which by nature is in potency to know requires senses for acquiring and using knowledge.

Consequently, the structure and characteristics of the human body must be such that it can sense. Now, all the senses are rooted in touch. The organ of touch requires such a disposition of matter that it be intermediate between the contraries which are its formal object. This means that the body, viewed as a material structure, must contain complicated compounds, in which the various properties of matter are balanced against each other. Such a body will be easily corruptible and subject to various defects because of its very complexity. Moreover, such a body will need to have vegetative life, to be produced, sustained, and repaired. Hence, by natural necessity, man must have sensitive and vegetative life.[32]

Because the human soul is the form of the human body, the composite of soul and body is a substantial unit. Hence, all the operations of intellect and of the living body are the activities of man, so that the same person understands and senses. The substantial unity of man is expressed and manifested in the unity of imperium and commanded act, in the unity of intellectual self-consciousness, and in the unity of sense-perception through the discursive estimative, the imagination, the common sense, and propriosensation. From another point of view, the substantial unity of man is expressed in the interlocking or integration of all his various kinds of activities in an intrinsic order of finality. This means that in man the natural material activities are to serve the purposes of the vegetative life; the vegetative life in turn serves the sensitive life, in that what is generated, nourished, and sustained is the sensitive organism; and finally the sensitive activities subserve the rational, in that sensation is the instrumental cause of the intelligible *species* and a permanent foundation of intel-

[32] *Ibid.*, I. 76. 1, 5.

lectual knowledge, and in the concretization of the rational appetite. Of course, this integration is not fully accomplished by nature, for that would not be appropriate to an intellect which is by nature in potency, nor would it give any scope for the rational self-perfective activity of man. Hence, to achieve his total perfection, man needs habits and virtues, so that the order of reason may actually permeate all his actions. But the possibility of habit and self-perfection implies the counter possibility of defect, of disorder, and of vice.

177. The sensory life of man

The nature of the human intellectual soul is such that it needs senses and a body for the sake of its own proper operation of understanding and willing. This means that man, even for the sake of his specific perfection, is an animal. The animal powers which he has are not such as to derive their full actuality from their use by reason; they are also in themselves true and proper principles of activity. And therefore the sensory life of man must be considered, not only as serving reason, but in itself.

An animal needs external senses in order that it may be acted on by its environment in the order of knowledge. A sense is a passive power, and is specified by its proper moving cause, its proper object. In addition to this, a sense is directly, but secondarily, affected by the quantitative preconditions of the formal object. Man needs more than one sense, in order that the distinction between proper object and the common sensible object may be made more easily. In order that an animal be at all, it is basically necessary that it have the sense of touch, because this sense concerns the things by which the animal is nourished. We know that in fact man and the other higher animals have five external senses: (1) sight, whose formal object is actual color; (2) hearing, whose formal object is sound; (3) smell, whose formal object is odor; (4) taste, whose formal object is flavor; and (5) touch, a genus whose formal generic object is tangibility, and which is divided into at least two species: the pressure and temperature senses, whose objects are relative pressure and relative warmth.[33] Of these senses, touch and taste usually take place through contact, while smell, sight, and hearing can be affected by an object at a distance. It is clear that a perfect animal, which has the power of moving from place to place, must be endowed with at least some senses that are affected at a distance. External sensation by its very nature takes place only when the sense is affected by an object, and that is why it is strictly passive. Because of this limitation, though external sensation is necessary for a perfect animal, it is not sufficient, and in particular, it is not sufficient for human knowledge.

The perfect animal also needs internal senses. The first of these is the unifying sense, whose proper object is the act of the other senses, external and internal, and the actual sensibles known by them. Through this power, the animal knows that it is sensing, and compares, contrasts, and unites its various sensations among themselves. In addition to this, an animal which is capable of local motion needs the power of retaining the images of sensible things even when they are absent. This is the imagination, whose primary function is the retention of sensible experience. Through this power, the animal can anticipate, look for, future experience in terms of the past from which it has profited. Moreover, in the animals with a more developed imagination the retaining of images occurs in three ways: (1) simple retention of experience as it happened—the memory-image; (2) joining together or association of images according to similarity, dissimilarity, or nearness in space and time—the composite image; (3) retention of similar, salient features of experience by re-impression in which variable features disappear—the separated or abstract image (the process by which the common sensibles [extension, shape, number, motion, rest] are first known distinctly). Through the retention and combinations of past experience the experience of the present is

---

[33] *Ibid.*, I. 78. 3. It is not clear that the five senses which man has are the only possible ones, or that these five flow with absolute necessity from his nature. Hence, at this point, we can only make a statement of fact.

enriched. This function in man is particularly directed to the work of understanding. Because of the temporary and changing character of external sensation, we could never learn much about things if we had only external senses. But because the human intellect derives its intelligible *species* from the instrumental activity of the phantasm,[34] past experience is pulled into the present, and so we can come to understand what things are much more definitely and completely.

Moreover, the perfect animal must reach, not only to the objects which are directly apprehended by the external senses, the unifying sense, and the imagination, but also to the non-sensed values of things, particularly to their concrete usefulness to the individual and the species. The power of making such estimations of value is called the estimative power. In brute animals, the knowledge of the estimative power is determined by nature, since the brute has no intellect by which it could judge concrete good in terms of goodness itself. Therefore the actions of animals which flow from the estimative power are characterized by specific uniformity, relative independence of experience, and relative unadaptibility. The animal has, in addition, the power of retaining past estimations—namely, the memorative power.

Because man has an intellect, by which the judgments of his estimative power can be formed and guided, this power, as a purely sense power, needs only generic determination, leading to general reactions. Some determination by nature is needed, because there are some basic determinations which admit of no variation, and because the human intellect, which is actuated successively in time, is not able to be a guide of estimation and action from the very beginning. But once the intellect has been actuated, and has some knowledge, it can then form and guide the estimative in its judgments. As under the control of intellect, the human estimative is called the discursive estimative. Since the estimative is the highest animal power, it is appropriate that the rational discursus characteristic of the human intellect penetrate by way of the composi-

[34] Phantasm = image of the imagination in relation to intellect.

tion of the imperium and the commanded act into the center of activity of his sense nature.

Like the animal, man also has the power of retaining estimations. As mere retention and simple recall of estimations, this power is called the memorative power. When, in its work of recall, the memorative power is guided by intellect, its action is called reminiscence.[35]

178. Knowledge and appetency

Every form is accompanied by a tendency. In the things which do not have knowledge, form is found only in the way in which it determines each thing to its own proper being (substantial forms, accidental forms). Such a form is accompanied by a natural tendency which is identical with the form. This doctrine is simply the brief metaphysical statement of the dynamism of real being. Remember that being is primarily being-in-act,[36] and that being-in-potency means being in potency to some act. In this matter, we are sometimes led astray by logical or mathematical considerations, according to which it seems sufficient that a being can be known—and here we forget that the purely intelligible form is abstracted from real being, is only a being of reason or an intentional being. At other times, we are deceived by the apparent inertia of matter, forgetting that this inactivity is not complete, and that purely material being has relatively little act, a relatively imperfect form. A rapid induction should be enough to manifest the activities and tendencies which are present in things without knowledge.

In the things which have knowledge, form is present in a higher way than in those which lack it. For the things which have knowledge also have natural forms and consequently natural tendencies. But their natural form so determines their being that in addition they are able to receive the *species* of other things, as sense re-

[35] See St. Thomas, *Summa Theologiae*, I. 78. 4 and ad 1, 2, 4, 5.

[36] It is interesting to note that "act" and "action" come from the same root. So too, the Aristotelian word for act, "energeia," is connected with the verb "ergomai," which means "I work."

ceives the *species* of sensible things, and the intellect the *species* of all intelligible things. Therefore, as forms exist in things that have knowledge in a way that is higher than the way of natural forms, so it is necessary that there be in them a tendency over and above their natural tendencies. Since this higher tendency follows upon knowledge, it is necessary that it be a conscious tendency. The conscious acts of tendency we have called "appetency." [37]

Appetency follows upon knowledge. Therefore, appetency is a passive operation, whose nature is to be moved by the object as known. And since a passive operation is specified by its moving cause which is its proper object, appetency will be specified by the object as known. Therefore, if there are essentially different kinds of knowledge, there are essentially different kinds of appetency. But sensation and understanding are essentially different. Therefore, sensory appetency and rational appetency are essentially different.[38] Moreover, where the act of knowing is not identical with the act of being but flows from a distinct, accidental power, there appetency must likewise flow from a power. The power of appetency is called appetite.

179. The sensory appetite

On the level of sensory knowledge, formal objects are limited, restricted. Therefore there are many senses. Therefore, the question rises: Is there only one sensory appetite, or are there more than one?

What kind of object moves an appetite to act? Tendency is a movement to, or an adherence to, a good. Hence, the object which moves the appetite to act must be a good. Now, the senses can know what is sensibly good for the animal; in other words, they can know what is pleasant and what is unpleasant. Therefore, there is an appetite on the sensory level which moves toward what is sensibly good (pleasant), and away from what is sensibly evil (unpleasant). But the life of a perfect animal is not thus sufficiently

[37] See St. Thomas, *Summa Theologiae*, I. 80. 1.
[38] *Ibid.*, a. 2.

accounted for. Not all the goods which are necessary for the good of the individual and of the species are pleasant; some, in fact, are unpleasant. Yet it is necessary for the animal that it resist its enemies, or work with accompanying discomfort. Now, the animal has a power of knowing, by which it can grasp this kind of concrete, but not sensible, good, namely, the estimative power. Therefore, the animal has an appetite which moves toward a concrete good which is not sensibly pleasant, and may even be painful—in a single phrase, this good may be called a difficult good. The power of tending toward the difficult good is called the irascible appetite, or irascibility.[39] The distinct acts of the sensory appetites are called "passions."

180. The rational appetite; freedom

Just as there are sensory appetites, which follow form on the level of sense knowledge, so there is a rational appetite, which follows form on the level of intellectual knowledge. Now, the proper object of intellect is not limited by any kind of particularization, but is being as being, unqualified being. Therefore, on this level, there can be only one power. So, too, the rational appetite can not have a limited formal object; its formal object will be the very substance (ratio) of goodness, goodness without qualification, goodness in general. Consequently, there is only one rational appetite,[40] which is called the will.

The will is put into act by an intellectually known object which contains its formal object. (Though the intellect can apprehend abstract goodness, which is the formal object of the will considered as such, this abstract conception does not move the will to act.) The kind of causality that the known good exercises upon the will is final causality, which is the causality proper to the good as such.

Can the will be influenced by a created efficient cause? First of all, the will is the rational appetite, with a proper object which is strictly immaterial: the good without qualification, and therefore

---

[39] See ibid., I. 81. 2.
[40] See ibid., I. 82. 5.

it itself is a strictly immaterial power without an organ. In other words, the will is a spiritual power. This same conclusion follows if we consider the will as the appetite proportioned to intellect. It is clear that a material efficient cause cannot affect a spiritual being or a spiritual power. Therefore, no material efficient cause can act efficiently upon the will. Moreover, the will is the power of rational tendency or inclination to the good. A tendency or inclination simply can not be forced from the outside.[41] This is so evident that it is practically proverbial—"you can lead the horse to water but you cannot make him drink"; "you cannot make me like something." And whenever a created efficient cause acts efficiently, that is, precisely as an efficient cause, it forces the patient. Since the will as tendency cannot be forced, it cannot be influenced in the line of efficient causality by any created cause.[42]

What kind of causality is final causality, and how does it influence the will? The final cause, though it is a true cause, is not even a cause if separated from the efficient cause. Hence, the causality of the good upon the will is exercised through an efficiency upon an act of the will or upon the will as a power or nature. But no created efficient cause can cause in either way: not causing the act, as we have just seen, nor effecting the power or nature of the will, because the soul which comes into being through creation can only be produced by God. God, of course, can move the will to an act without violating its nature, because He is the author of that nature. But such a motion, though it is possible, is not the natural mode of operation of the will. Hence, the final cause exercises its causality upon the act of the will through the *nature* of the will, when it (that is, the final cause) is presented (known) by the intellect.

The nature of the will is to tend to (or adhere to) the good as such. Therefore the will is necessitated by its very nature and struc-

[41] If God should act efficiently upon a will, His action is not from the outside, but from the inside as author of its nature. Of course, God can also act upon the will in other ways, particularly by modifying the object (the final cause of the will's act), helping us to see more clearly that this object is good.
[42] See St. Thomas, *Summa Theologiae*, I. 82. 1.

ture to love the unqualified good. In other words, the will necessarily, by its very nature, tends to whatever completely and perfectly verifies and contains its formal object, and to whatever is known as absolutely necessary for obtaining such an object. Now, there are two objects which completely contain goodness as such without any defect or admixture: namely, God, Who is the perfect, complete, subsistent good; and happiness, which is the perfect and complete possession of the complete good. Consequently, when God or happiness are presented in intellect as good, the will tends to and adheres to them by the necessity of nature. However, as we have seen, in this life God cannot be known as He is in Himself, but only in terms of created, limited things. When God is known in this way, He is not possessed; hence, God must be waited for, while other goods can be possessed now. In this life, God does not necessitate the will; consequently, neither do the things that necessarily lead to Him. On the other hand, perfect happiness can be conceived, at least in general, and so a man is naturally necessitated to desire happiness when he thinks of it, and consequently also he is naturally necessitated to desire those things which clearly are seen by him as necessarily connected with happiness.

All other objects of the will can be looked at in one or more of three ways. An object which is in any sense good in itself may be considered simply in that way, under the aspect of being good, and to that extent. Or, any finite object may be looked at completely, that is, as being good, but as not completely containing the formal trait of goodness: in other words, as a finite, limited, particular good. Thirdly, there may be objects which do not contain any goodness in themselves, but which are nevertheless means of obtaining something which is good. These latter are pure means.

How does the will act in the known presence of these various objects? (1) When an end is known simply as end, the will is necessitated to it. (2) When an object is considered as a limited or particular good, that is, both as *good* and as *limited,* the will is unmoved. (3) When pure means are presented to the will by the intellect, the will's movement toward these means is necessary if the means are understood as absolutely necessary for a necessary end. Otherwise, the will's action is not necessary.[43]

By considering these three kinds of objects for the will, we have been able to discover that there are some necessary acts of the will. In order to understand what the will can do about objects which do not necessitate its action, we must recall the larger context within which the will operates. Three conclusions are particularly pertinent here. First, reality is such that though some ends necessarily involve one and only one set of means, many ends can be reached by alternative or multiple sets of means; taken separately, therefore, none of these means are necessary for the end. In other words, each set or series among multiple means is only contingently related to the end.[44] Secondly, the intellect, because of the fact that all being is included under its object, is able to work out, and thus to present to the will, the various possible courses of action by which ends can be reached.[45] Thirdly, the will is not immediately necessitated by every course of action, or every object, which occurs to the intellect.[46]

We can understand the situation of the will in the face of limited goods and contingent means by comparing that situation with the intellect and its objects. The intellect attains some truths immediately in themselves or in direct experience. But once the intellect has attained some truths, it can *move itself* to further truths. In other words, once the intellect has been put into act so that it knows the premisses in a reasoning process, it moves itself to know the conclusion. This self-motion of the intellect is not a violation of the principle that potency cannot move itself to act, because when the intellect knows the premisses of an argument, it is in act, and in an act which virtually, though not explicitly and formally, contains the following act, the conclusion.

[43] See *ibid.*, I. 82. 2.
[44] This proposition can be put more briefly: There is contingence in creaturely activity.
[45] See St. Thomas, *Summa Theologiae*, I. 83. 1.
[46] See *ibid.*, I–II. 10. 2.

The activity of the will is comparable to the activity of the intellect. Like the intellect, the will must be first moved to act in any series of actions. In this first act, as we have seen, the will is moved with natural necessity by the final causality of the known good. But once the will has been put into act with regard to an end, the will can *move itself* to further acts with regard to the means which lead to that end. Just as the intellect can move itself to a conclusion once it has been moved to the act of knowing the premisses, so too, the will can move itself to the means once it has been moved to the fact of willing and intending the end. For as the premisses are the cause of the truth of a conclusion in reasoning, so the goodness of an end is the cause of the goodness of the means to that end inasmuch as they are means.

We saw above that means can be related to an end in various ways, and that the intellect can apprehend and present to the will the various kinds of order of means to end. If the order which reason has discovered is that of a unique and necessary means to an end, then the will moves itself to adhere to those means necessarily. If, however, the order of means to end which the will has found is that of one series among alternative or multiple means to end, that is, is a contingent order of means to end, then the adherence of the will to such a means is not predetermined in any way, but is a self-determination of the will. Therefore, the will is free in choosing between alternative means, or among multiple means.[47] In the act of choice, the order of reason is as form, the impulse or movement of the will is as the essence and matter of the act.[48] Hence, the act of choice is a composite act of intellect and will.

The scope of free choice is not limited to the choice of means to the concrete ends that usually appear to us. When something comes to our mind that is known by us to be a particular limited good (by which the will therefore is not affected), we can ask ourselves whether this limited (mixed) good is or is not a means

[47] See *ibid.*, I. 82. 2.
[48] See *ibid.*, I–II. 13. 1.

to a further, unqualified good or end. Thus, the second class of objects can also become the object of choice. Finally, even those objects which first come to our minds as good without qualification (and which therefore in the first moment are willed with natural necessity) can be considered with a view to more ultimate ends. And if these intermediate ends should turn out to be only contingently related to a more ultimate, or the ultimate end, they themselves, after the first moment, can become objects of choice. Thus, through the intervention of regressive deliberation, almost all objects can become objects of choice.[49] And if we remember that non-action itself can be an alternative, and that not-to-think about something, even about happiness, may appear easier (and thus better) than thinking, then, indirectly, by shifting our consideration from the object to the thinking of the object, man can be free about any object in this life.[50]

181. The will and the other powers

The rational appetite, because it is the most universal tendency in man, is the first cause of all movement in him, in that the sensory appetites and the external members are the instruments of the will and can be moved by it, while it cannot be moved efficiently by them. The will moves through the intellect in the imperium. The imperium is an act of intellect, in that it is an order of execution, by which the means chosen are put into act so that the end willed may be attained. It presupposes the act of will, because it is the source of movement and real being. The imperium of intellect is applied directly to the imagination and the discursive estimative, and through them to the sensory appetites and action, or directly to action.[51]

The imperium and the act commanded by it together make up

[49] See *ibid.*, I–II. 15. 4.

[50] See *ibid.*, 13. 6. The phrase "in this life" is added because in the Beatific Vision there is no action which *intervenes* between our intellect and God. Consequently, the shift to the act of thought, spoken of in the text, is impossible here. Hence, the love of God in Heaven, though it is fully spontaneous, and the source of unlimited happiness, is not free.

[51] See St. Thomas, *Summa Theologiae*, I–II. 17. 7, 9.

one composite human act.[52] Through this composition, the goodness (or evil) of the will and the order of reason penetrate into the powers of man that are subject to rational control, and generate in them the habits by which man's action is progressively improved.[53] These habits will be of various kinds, proportioned to the various kinds of powers which they perfect, from the fully controllable, conscious, and deliberate habits of intellect and will to the partial automatisms of the motor powers.

182. The origin of the soul

Man is a composite material substance, and as such he is generated by secondary causes. And yet, in the generation of a man, though his parents really are the parents of the whole being, they are not the efficient causes of every part of him. As we have seen, some acts of understanding and willing can be separated from matter, in the sense that these acts are not the acts of the body nor intrinsically dependent upon the body. Now, an activity which is not material and is intrinsically independent of matter is a spiritual activity. Therefore, the power by which that activity is performed is a spiritual power. Moreover, a spiritual power is an accident inhering in a substance, and proportioned to the nature of that substance. Therefore, the substance in which a spiritual power inheres is a spiritual substance. Such a substance is the human soul.

The spirituality of the soul is so important that it will be worth while to recast the argument, both for clarity's sake, and to place the argument in terms of being rather than substance. Action follows upon being. The soul, through the power of intellect, performs an action which is intrinsically independent of the body. Therefore, the soul in its being is intrinsically independent of matter. In other words, the human soul, unlike the forms of other material things, has its own act of existing, an act of existing which is indeed shared with the body, but is primarily the act of the soul.

A subsistent, spiritual form, which is completely non-material,

[52] See *ibid.*, 17. 4.
[53] See *ibid.*, 51. 2.

cannot be produced from matter. Other substantial forms are produced in and from the potency of matter by the activity of secondary causes. But a form which is completely non-material in its nature cannot be produced from the potency of matter, and therefore cannot be produced by a material cause—for example, by the parents of the new being.

Again, material things are the efficient causes of other material effects, inasmuch as they are able to change beings from one kind to another. But if we examine case after case of the causality of material agents, we find that it takes place through change, and requires a pre-existing patient upon which the agents can act. And if we reflect upon the nature of these causes, we will see that this is necessarily so. For a material thing has its own act of existing, it is true; but this act of existing is precisely its own as an individual. Moreover, a material thing possesses an act of existing as distinct from its nature, as received in turn from a prior cause. Consequently, a material thing, or even any finite cause in general, is capable of modifying the being of some patient upon which it acts, but not of simply producing a being according to the whole reality of the effect.

This conclusion can be reinforced by a consideration of the causality of material things. For the activity of finite things is an accident, flowing immediately from accidental principles (powers), and effecting immediately accidental modifications in a patient. Even though this series of accidents is a series of instruments of the substantial nature of the agent (and thus capable of effecting ultimately a substantial change), it necessarily presupposes a subject to be accidentally modified.

From these arguments, we conclude that no material thing (living or not) can cause a being according to its whole reality, a being which does not arise from and depend upon a previous subject. Hence, if a soul is to come into being, it can only do so by way of creation by God, Who is the pure and unlimited act of existing. But souls do begin to be. Hence, individual souls are created by God.

183. The immortality of the soul

The soul is intrinsically independent of the body in the possession of its own act of existing, and this fact is made known to us
by the nature of certain actions of understanding and willing. Now,
if the soul has its own act of existing, then separation from the
body is not necessarily destruction. Other material things exist
as composites; in them, it is only the whole nature which receives
existence, and so the separation of the parts in them is the destruction of the whole and at the same time of all such parts as are not
in that very destruction made into parts of new wholes. Though
man is a composite, and exists as a composite in this material world,
still existence is primarily possessed by the soul and only in a derived way by the composite whose form that soul is. Therefore,
a human soul does not cease to be when a man dies.

Furthermore, a soul cannot be destroyed in itself. For the soul
is the form of a body, and as such it cannot consist of further real
parts by the separation of which it could be destroyed. A soul is
a spiritual substance, and so it cannot weaken or wear out. It contains no substantial potency; its only potencies are powers of
spiritual action: understanding and willing.

But someone might object that a separate soul is still a composite
being, on the ground that it is composed of a nature or essence
and an act of existing. Could not these two principles be separated,
and thus the soul cease to be? This objection has specious force
only when essence and act of existing are looked on as things, or
as substantial principles like matter and form. Really the objection
is a tautology, for "to cease to exist" means "to lose the act of
existing." This will be clearer if we try to see what a spiritual substance is. A spiritual substance is simply an act in the order of
essence, that is, it is only a form, and is not itself composed of
form and matter. Now, an essence is a potency to exist, *not* a potency to non-existence.[54] A soul is still a contingent being, inas-

[54] See the brilliant exposition of this in Étienne Gilson, *Being and Some
Philosophers* (Toronto, Pontifical Institute of Mediaeval Studies, 1949), pp.
158–66.

much as God can at any moment cease to conserve its being, that is, can cease being its creative cause. But it would be an inconsistency on the part of God to make a being which is naturally immortal, and then change His mind and withdraw His conserving influence. The human soul, therefore, will not cease to be when a man dies.

In death, the soul is separated from its body; it is no longer the form of a body. Now, we have seen that the reason why an intellect in potency begins its course of existence in body is that it may be able in this way to reach its perfection of knowing and willing. At death, an individual soul either has reached its necessary perfection, or it has not.[55] In the former case, it enters upon its new mode of life as perfected, and so as suited to receive that good for which it was made and for which it had striven rightly. In other words, the soul of a good man goes to its reward. In the latter case, when a man during his lifetime has not reached his necessary perfection, he enters upon his new mode of unchanging life as indisposed, unsuited for his end and good. In other words, the soul of a bad man goes to a state of deprivation of good.

184. Man—individual and society

Man begins his life without any inborn knowledge, and so in the state of potency to acquire his perfection as a man. Yet knowledge and virtue are his human perfections, and so it is his task to acquire them as best he can. Now, if every man began in the state of sheer potency, and could hope to gain only what he could achieve by his isolated efforts, a normal span of life would find him still struggling with the barest rudiments of civilization. In other words, the human good is scarcely to be obtained by an isolated individual.

But in coöperation with others, the human good can be reached in an incomparably higher degree. By a division of labor whose results are shared, a greater good can be accomplished. And if to

[55] It does not belong to the philosophy of human nature to inquire into the nature of human goodness, nor into the nature of the rewards and punishments for good and evil.

this is added the cumulative effect of the efforts of many generations, then indeed a high level of human excellence is within the grasp of every individual man. Thus even the essential human goods of knowledge and virtue demand the coöperation of many men.

However, precisely because coöperation involves many individuals, its successful prosecution implies order and organization. Now, where many strive in harmony and good order for a common good or end, we have a society. Hence, because the common good of man as man involves society, man is naturally a social as well as a rational animal.

In the coöperation of many men even for the essential human good many and various factors are involved. Among these are the material goods which the social animal needs for his sustenance and development as a responsible individual. Coöperation is necessary for the best production and use of material goods, and as always, the efforts of many need to be ordered and coadjusted so as best to achieve the immediate goals. This is (or should be) the function of economic society.

Other goods that can be achieved only by an organized group are the protection of individual rights, the further specification of the indeterminate principles of the natural law, and the adjustment of the relations of various individuals and groups among themselves. This is political society, whose first form is the state. Under the present conditions of world-wide communication and the exchange and interaction of economic and cultural goods, the social nature of man calls for some form of world organization whose function is not to replace existing societies, but to order and control them.

In addition to these necessary forms of organizations and institutions, other (free) associations can reasonably be formed. The goods aimed at by these organizations can be of many kinds: education, the advancement of culture or science or technology, recreation, and so on.

Moreover, man begins his life, not only with an intellect and will which need to be perfected, but, like other animals, as an infant born of parents. As an infant, man needs to be fed and clothed and cared for and educated. This is the function and purpose of the family or familial society. And the family in turn is a development from the conjugal society of husband and wife. The conjugal society, simplest and basic element of all society in one way or another, aims at a good. Primarily, of course, it aims at the procreation and education of children, and in this way the conjugal society naturally grows into a family. But secondarily and perhaps more immediately, the conjugal society aims at the good of the husband and wife. For every real society aims at perfecting its members in some way or other. Thus husband and wife in the marital society aim at perfecting each other as human beings, at achieving a greater human good than they could reach by themselves.

It has been the purpose of these last paragraphs to show that the philosophy of human nature, though it is complete in itself in one way, also points beyond itself to the philosophy of human action: to moral philosophy (ethics) or the philosophy of the goodness of human action and of human nature, both as man is an individual and as he is a member of societies.

185. Readings

The passages of St. Thomas Aquinas referred to in the footnotes.
Walter Farrell, O.P., *Companion to the Summa* (New York, Sheed and Ward, 1938–1942: 4 vols.), Vol. 1, pp. 253–344; Vol. 2, 45–63. This work follows the order of the *Summa Theologiae*, introducing, explaining, and applying the thought of St. Thomas.

APPENDICES

Part I: Philosophical Systems

Obviously, the various explanations of man cannot be presented at length. But we can indicate useful and pertinent readings; and, to help the reader, some suggestions will be made about points to be looked for in the selections. This will be followed by some suggestions for a critique, and a bibliography in which such a critique can be found completely or partly. A mere reading of these suggestions is by no means sufficient for an understanding of the system under discussion. All that can be accomplished is to alert the mind to the parts of the system that are pertinent to the philosophy of human nature.

A few general reference works will be cited first.

I. M. Bochenski, O.P., *Bibliographische Einführungen in das Studium der Philosophie* (Berne, Francke, 1948–1951).

Dictionary of Philosophy, Dagobert D. Runes, ed. (New York, Philosophical Library, 1942).

André Lelande, *Vocabulaire technique et critique de la philosophie,* 5th ed. (Paris, Presses Universitaires, 1947).

Frederick Copleston, S.J., *History of Philosophy,* Vol. 1, *Greece and Rome;* Vol. 2, *Augustine to Scotus* (Westminster, Md., Newman, 1946, 1950).

M. De Wulf, *History of Mediaeval Philosophy,* trans. by E. C. Messenger from the 6th French edition (New York, Dover, 1952: 3 vols.).

William Kelley Wright, *History of Modern Philosophy* (New York, Macmillan, 1941).

Charles Spearman, *Psychology Down the Ages* (London, Macmillan, 1937: 2 vols.).

Gardner Murphy, *An Historical Introduction to Modern Psychology,* rev. ed. (New York, Harcourt, 1949). Good; but the author thinks that there are only two theories on the nature of man: monism and dualism. He does not seem to realize that St. Thomas's "compositionism" is neither dualism nor monism.

Edna Heidbreder, *Seven Psychologies* (New York, Century, 1933). Also seems to consider dualism as the alternative to monism.

Vincent Edward Smith, *Idea-Men of Today* (Milwaukee, Bruce Pub., 1950). Semi-popular treatments of Dewey, Whitehead, Santayana, Russell, semantics, Freud.

APPENDIX A

Dualism

The Platonic Man

1. Man is composed of two substances, a soul and a body, each of which is more or less complete in itself.

2. The soul of man is purely spiritual. In many of the Platonists, the soul not only is a spirit, it belongs to the divine order. According to others, it is a created spirit. In either case, it is immortal.

3. In addition to sense knowledge, man has intellectual knowledge. His intellect sees truth immediately, with certitude. Some or all of his intellectual knowledge is intuitive (hence, Platonists usually have no doctrine of *species*). Most Platonists tend to stress the activity of the soul in knowing, and tend to minimize or to deny that the soul in knowing is affected by the thing. Frequently, this activism is applied to sensation as well as to understanding.

4. Sense knowledge is not very valuable; it may even be wholly worthless, the source of error, a merely confused knowledge, according to various proponents of dualism.

5. Hence, intellectual knowledge is independent of sense, except that, according to many Platonists, sensation is an occasion of intellectual knowledge.

6. The origin of intellectual knowledge is variously explained. According to Plato himself, our intellectual knowledge is remembering what our souls knew before union with the body, when they lived in the intelligible world. According to others, intellectual knowledge is given in the moment of the creation of the soul, and needs only to be aroused. According to still others, it is given by God or by some other spiritual substance in the course of life.

7. Freedom of the will is asserted by almost all dualists. They rarely distinguish between the will-to-end and the choice of means.

8. The reasons for holding a two-substance dualism are various. Dualism recognizes the fact that intellect and will are non-material powers. Not having a metaphysics of act and potency, dualists can account for these non-material powers by a non-material substance. Historically, Platonic dualism was reinforced by a scepticism of the senses, which Plato accepted from his predecessors, and this situation has frequently been repeated. This dualism is in some cases strengthened by the experience of moral conflict. In the case of a very few thinkers, it is the reflection of a cosmic dualism between a Supreme Good and a supreme evil.

Sources

Plato, *Phedo; Republic,* Book 6.
St. Augustine, *De Quantitate Animae.*
René Descartes, *Fourth Meditation.*
Vernon J. Bourke, *Augustine's Quest of Wisdom* (Milwaukee, Bruce Pub., 1945), pp. 237, 56–57, 103, 111–12.
S. V. Keeling, *Descartes* (London, Benn, 1934).

Critique

The scepticism of the senses can be overcome on the one hand by the distinction between substance and accident in sensible things, and on the other by the distinction between proper, common, and incidental sensibles. The truth in the experience of the non-material activity of intellect and will can be accounted for by separate powers inhering in a substantial form which is the subsistent form of the body. Dualism is then replaced by matter-form composition.

Against dualism there are three serious arguments. First, dualism destroys the unity of man, and makes the experience of unity an unintelligible illusion. Secondly, it cannot explain the origin of knowledge satisfactorily, nor the experienced dependence of intellect upon sense. Thirdly, it makes the presence of an intellectual soul in a body unintelligible, and is closely associated with a confusion between formal and efficient causality.

Sources

Aristotle, *De Anima* (*On the Soul*), Bk. I, Ch. 3, 406a407b; Bk. II, Ch. 1, 412a.

St. Thomas Aquinas, *Summa Theologiae,* I. 76. 1, 3; 79. 3; 84. 1–4, 6. These last five articles contain an appreciation of Platonic dualism, together with what is perhaps the best critique of that position.

Anton C. Pegis, *The Problem of the Soul in the Thirteenth Century* (Toronto, Institute of Mediaeval Studies, 1934), pp. 147–67.

Étienne Gilson, *The Spirit of Mediaeval Philosophy,* trans. by A. H. C. Downes (New York, Scribner, 1936), pp. 168–88. These passages of Professor Pegis and M. Gilson present the Thomistic critique of Platonism in its historical setting.

Idealistic Monism

The Spirit-man

1. Philosophical idealism, when it ventures into a discussion of human nature, either denies that there is a body at all (spiritualism, as that of Berkeley), or that the body has any intelligible part to play in man or in the universe. Hence, this doctrine has no problem of the unity of man.

2. Vegetative and sensitive life are to be expressed in purely ideal or spiritual terms. Thus, Berkeley explained sensation as the spiritual action of God upon the spiritual receptive powers of the soul, which gives rise to sensation.

3. By most of the upholders of such a system, knowledge is said to have as its object the idea or representation in the mind.

4. Many idealists proclaim the freedom of the will. Others, who deny individual personality (an individual person is a part of the Absolute), necessarily deny any real freedom. Those who maintain freedom also assert the immortality of the soul; in the others, immortality is meaningless.

5. The reasons for idealism are hardly ever to be found in the problems connected with human nature, but rather with problems in the metaphysics of being and of knowledge. Some few cannot see how such a passive thing as matter could exist (as Berkeley); others, because of their strong feeling for the presence of God in His creation, tend to a more or less complete identification of God and creature, in which case matter usually has to vanish. Most idealists are such because of the problems they have in the metaphysics of knowledge. Thus, some of them make knowledge into an instrumental sign (*medium quod,* a medium within knowl-

edge), and so conclude that they can only talk about knowledge and not about things. Most modern idealists presume that the Kantian explanation of theoretical knowledge is correct, and either work on from that point, or go on to new positions based on the Kantian analysis.

Sources

Josiah Royce, *The Spirit of Modern Philosophy* (Boston, Houghton, 1931), pp. 289, 416–18.

Brand Blanshard, *The Nature of Thought* (New York, Macmillan, 1940: 2 vols.), Vol. 1, pp. 500–20.

Bernard Bosanquet, *Value and Destiny of the Individual* (New York, Macmillan, 1913).

Critique

Pantheism is usually a failure to arrive at or at least to appreciate analogy. Without the analogy of being, pantheism or scepticism seem to be the only alternatives.

Those who base their spiritualism on the pure passivity of matter simply have an incorrect notion of material being. Idealists who hold that the object of knowledge is knowledge do not understand the nature of knowledge as a formal sign (*medium quo*, or *medium in quo*), which does not block us off from things, but brings us to them.

Kantians and post-Kantians presuppose that the material world is neither actually nor potentially intelligible; that sensation is not a source of knowledge (a Platonic position); that all knowledge is like mathematics which *constructs* its intelligible object; that pure reason necessarily falls into contradictions; that judgment is just a complex apprehension. If these presuppositions are granted *before* the Kantian critique, Kant's position is logical; if not, the Kantian critique becomes unnecessary, irrelevant to human knowledge.

Sources

St. Thomas Aquinas, *Summa Theologiae*, I. 85. 1–2; 84. 1; 86. 1.

Étienne Gilson, *Réalisme thomiste et critique de la connaissance* (Paris, Desclée de Brouwer, 1939).

André Marc, S.J., *Psychologie Réflexive* (Bruxelles, L'Édition Universelle, 1949: 2 vols.), Vol. 1, pp. 259–83, 312–35. These works by M. Gilson and Father Marc are by far the best discussions of knowledge; unfortunately, there is nothing in English that comes close to them.

Adrian Coates, *A Basis of Opinion* (London, Macmillan, 1937), pp. 120–30.

Materialistic Monism

The Mechanical Man

1. Materialism usually considers man as an aggregate of purely material parts, denying thereby his substantial unity. There have been materialisms, such as that of Averroes (1126–1198), which admitted man's substantial unity, and assigned him a material soul.

2. Vegetative life is said to be a purely physico-chemical process, and its finality is neglected or even denied.

3. Sensation is considered only in its material aspects.

4. Usually, the difference between thought and sensation is denied or minimized. Some few admit that thought is not a material activity, but assert that there is no reason why a material substance should not have a spiritual activity. Extreme materialists try to reduce thought to incipient movements of the speech organs and to other unnoticeable motor reactions (behaviorism).

5. Sensory appetite and will are explained by innate and conditioned reflexes. A reflex is a simple neuro-muscular reaction, essentially involving a receptor (organ and nerve), a connection in the spinal cord, and an effector (nerve and organ); it does not need and usually does not admit of conscious control. A conditioned reflex is one in which the response follows upon a stimulus other than the natural or original stimulus; the replacing of one stimulus by another through experience is called conditioning.

6. Modern materialism (as it is called by its proponents) insists that it can simultaneously admit irreducible levels of activity (e.g., that physico-chemical, vital, sensory, rational are distinct types of activity) while at the same time insisting that they are all equally functions of matter. Evolutionism is almost universally admitted as an "explanation" of living things and of man. Frequently, the

semantic [1] analysis of knowledge is used to bolster the position.

7. There are several paths to materialism. One of them is the failure to notice the difference between sense and intellect. This failure lay at the root of the materialism of the pre-Socratic Greek philosophers, and also of some of the present-day materialisms, especially the "reductionist" forms (so called because they admit no real qualitative differences in the universe). Sometimes materialism is chosen because any other doctrine of man involves freedom and consequently moral obligation and responsibility. Most often materialism is chosen by thinkers (*a*) because it is thought to be the only alternative to dualism and idealism; (*b*) because it is thought to be the only alternative to exaggerated "other-worldliness," the complete condemnation of nature and all natural goods that is characteristic of Puritanism and similar "Christian" supernaturalisms (when chosen for this reason, materialism is often called "naturalism"); (*c*) because some philosophers think that natural science is the only form of demonstrative knowledge (in this form materialism is now called "scientific naturalism").

Sources

Jacques B. Loeb, *The Organism as a Whole* (New York, Putnam, 1916), introduction, esp. p. viii; p. 270.

John B. Watson, *Psychology from the Standpoint of a Behaviorist* (Philadelphia, Lippincott, 1919). This is a good example of what is now called "reductionist materialism."

Manual of Civilization [anon.] (New York, William-Frederick Press, 1949). An unimportant book which presents materialism as anti-supernaturalism.

A. J. Carlson, "Science and the Supernatural," *Science*, LXXIII (1931); reprinted in the *Scientific Monthly*, August, 1944. A blunt presentation of the scientific method as the *only* form of knowledge.

Edward Lee Thorndike, *Human Nature and the Social Order* (New

---

[1] "Semantics" is a doctrine which holds (*a*) that only sensible and singular reality exists; (*b*) that knowledge alleged to be universal can be shown to be really of singulars by "language analysis"; (*c*) that propositions about nonsensible objects are meaningless. The analysis referred to sometimes employs symbolic logic, and then the doctrine is called "logical positivism." Put very simply, the analysis "eliminates" universal knowledge something like this: when we say "man," we do not understand a nature, we use a *word* as a *sign* with a universal *function;* hence, the universality is a function of the word as a sign.

York, Macmillan, 1940). A sample of the philosophy developed by a man who holds that human nature is determined by the probabilities residing in the genes; he asserts that actions are due to connections established in the nervous system.

Charles Morris, *Signs, Language and Behavior* (New York, Prentice-Hall, 1946). One of the most pretentious attempts to explain all human behavior through biology and linguistics.

Philosophy of the Future, Roy Woods Sellars, V. J. McGill, and Marvin Farber, eds. (New York, Macmillan, 1949). A collection of essays by various "modern materialists," showing the modern attempt to admit differences of activity which flow from the "same matter."

Naturalism and the Human Spirit, Yervant H. Krikorian, ed. (New York, Columbia Univ. Press, 1944). The characteristic attitudes of scientific naturalism are well represented in this series of essays.

Critique

One group of arguments for materialism is based on the notion that materialism is the *only* alternative to unacceptable positions, those of dualism, monistic idealism, or what is thought to be "supernaturalism." These arguments can be answered in two ways: (1) by rejecting the detailed criticism of the alternative positions (this is possible only where the criticism is invalid, and in any case is a long and involved argument); (2) by showing that materialism is *not the only* alternative. This latter procedure can be done much more easily by pointing out that there *is* an alternative to dualism and monistic idealism in the "compositionism" of St. Thomas Aquinas (the philosophy which this text presents), and secondly by pointing out that the "supernaturalism" which the naturalists oppose is not the supernaturalism of the Catholic faith, but either a Protestant version or a caricature. This second task is not directly the concern of a philosophical inquiry.

A second argument for materialism is based on the assumption that science is the only true and real knowledge. This assumption is shown to be an assumption by the presentation of a philosophy of human nature (as well as by the existence of metaphysics and ethics). The assumption is shown to be a false one by a reflection on the various forms of knowledge (as was done, for example, in Chapter VIII of the present work; see also below, Appendix K and the readings indicated there).

A third argument for materialism is the explanation of human activity by the conditioned reflex. This explanation is shown to be inadequate and false because it overlooks or ignores (*a*) the fact of rational control of human activity; (*b*) the fact of the difference between sense and intellect; (*c*) the proper nature of appetite, both sensory and rational; (*d*) the experimental differences between the responses to natural and conditioned stimuli.

A fourth argument for materialism is evolutionism and sensism, bolstered to some extent by a study of language. These arguments will be treated below.

Readings

St. Thomas Aquinas, *Summa Theologiae*, I. 75. 1–2.

Hans Driesch, *The Science and Philosophy of the Organism* (London, Black, 1908: 2 vols.), Vol. 1, pp. 127–30. This eminent biologist gives an excellent criticism, though his own position, a modified dualism, is not philosophically sound.

Knight Dunlap, *Habits, Their Making and Unmaking* (New York, Liveright, 1932). Clearly disproves the materialistic notion of habit. The author does not know very much about Thomism, or Christianity, or even some rather elementary moral principles; he does know materialism well, and his criticism is to the point.

Robert S. Woodworth, *Experimental Psychology* (New York, Holt, 1938), pp. 122, 788–89; *Psychology*, 4th ed. (New York, Holt, 1940), pp. 310–12; 322, 412. Excellent in its presentation of the experimental evidence that the explanation of human activity by the notion of the conditioned reflex is unsound.

Gardner Murphy, *Personality* (New York, Harper, 1947), pp. 200–01. A simple description of an experiment that supplies evidence against the theory of the conditioned reflex. The author himself, an eclectic, does not seem to draw the conclusion which stares at him.

William McDougall, *An Outline of Psychology*, 3rd ed. (London, Methuen, 1926), pp. 362, 368, 395–97, 410–11. Clearly presented evidence against materialism.

Gladys Schwesinger, *Heredity and Environment* (New York, Macmillan, 1933). This book debunks many of the materialistic theories of hereditarianism, from studies with identical twins; many sound middle-of-the-road views on these and related problems are given.

H. S. Jennings, *The Biological Basis of Human Nature* (New York, Norton, 1930), pp. 374–75. A biologist's strong insistence on the specificity of human nature and activity.

Eliseo Vivas, *The Moral Life and the Ethical Life* (Chicago, Univ. of Chicago Press, 1950), pp. 25–184. This book, a study of moral philosophy, presents in the section indicated a thorough and penetrating criticism of ethical naturalism.

Positivism:

The Unsubstantial Man

1. Either there is no substance which lies hidden under accidents, or if there is, it is unknowable and useless. Reality is activity without anything which acts.

2. All phenomena follow necessary, inescapable laws. This, however, is not held by all positivists; some have modified the necessity of nature to a statistical regularity; others tend to stress the unpredictability of the future.

3. The search for causes is useless and meaningless. It is useless, because all that makes any difference is our knowledge of the laws of activity; and even meaningless, because action is the only meaning of truth.

4. As there is no substance, and no causes, so there is no soul and no intellect—"mind is what body does." Hence, there is no importance in the distinction (or lack of it) between sensation and understanding.

5. Free choice, as an active interposition of an Ego, is clearly not admissible to positivism. But many positivists maintain a kind of freedom on ethical or sentimental grounds.

6. Positivism appears in many forms. It arose as a reaction against the deductive essentialist systems of the early modern period of philosophy, when at the same time experimental science was making great progress. As expressed by Comte, it involved a dogmatic denial of substance and cause, of metaphysics and religion.

Positivism is partly a reaction against the notion that substance is an unknown something lying hidden under the accidents which clothe it (according to the explanation of Locke, which its opponents call "the reality-peg theory"). It arose in psychology, as a special doctrine, when the question of the unity of man was viewed as being first and principally a problem of the permanence of the Ego in time.

To some extent, positivism is an acceptance of the Kantian doctrine of phenomena and the function of the categories in the unification of experience. This partial acceptance of Kant is accompanied by a rejection of the rest of his system. As influenced by Kant, it tends to become less assertive and more agnostic.

Positivism has been and is popular in this country in the form of pragmatism, instrumentalism, and related doctrines. Pragmatism holds that the speculative criteria of truth are impossible to apply, or self-contradictory, or meaningless and worthless. Hence, only that is to be considered as true which leads to successful action (the criterion of empirical verification).

Logical positivism arose as a critique of science and scientific method, and then extended its explanation of science to all forms of knowledge. In the form of general semantics, it is a revival of nominalism, attempting to reduce knowledge to sensation and the use of words.

Sources

C. S. Peirce, *Chance, Love, and Logic,* with an introduction by Morris Cohen (New York, Smith, P., 1949).

William James, *Principles of Psychology* (New York, Holt, 1907: 2 vols.), Vol. 1, pp. 338–39, 401.

A. W. Moore, *Pragmatism and Its Critics* (Chicago, Univ. of Chicago Press, 1910).

John Dewey, *Experience and Nature* (Chicago, Open Court, 1926).

William James, *The Will to Believe* (New York, Longmans, 1896), "The Dilemma of Determinism."

Critique

Positivism, like materialism, frequently defends itself as the *only* alternative. Having rejected rationalism, positivists assert that their position is secure. But between the deductive essentialism of the rationalists and the mere empiricism of the positivists there is the experiential philosophy of Aristotle and St. Thomas. Likewise, between the static and unknowable substance of Locke and the flowing, unsubstantial dynamism propounded by many modern thinkers there is the dynamic substance of Aristotle and St. Thomas. Another alternative (the favorite of Dewey and after him of many other pragmatists and instrumentalists), is that between the "spectator-theory of intellect" which, while asserting man's capacity for truth, denies his evident ability to use his intelligence in action, and the pragmatist (instrumentalist, biological) theory of intelligence which denies speculative knowledge (especially of philosophy and faith) in order to safeguard man's evident ability to modify and control nature. This extensive critique (which pretends that all its opponents maintain the absoluteness and immutability of truth in all orders) simply fails to touch an explanation like that of St. Thomas, for whom intellect is both speculative and practical, for whom some propositions are absolute and immutable, and others partial, relative, and mutable.

Sometimes positivists state that their denial of substance is based on the Kantian analysis of phenomena. This is a weak argument, since they flatly reject other parts of the Kantian system, with which the Kantian theory of the phenomenon is necessarily connected, and secondly, because the Kantian analysis is based, not on a consideration of knowledge in all its forms, but particularly on the consideration of Newtonian physics and Cartesian mathematics. The Newtonian physicist often acted as if he were a philosopher, and to put him in his proper place Kant limited him to a knowledge of phenomena. But the modern thinker who wants to get around this analysis by limiting nature in turn to phenomena should not state that he is basing his position on the great Kant when he himself so thoroughly misses Kant's main point. (There is no intention here of discussing the Kantian system; the Kantian analysis is not necessary once knowledge has been approached the way that St. Thomas approaches it.)

Finally, many of those who deny substance are basing their denial on the theories of what is now called "philosophical analysis," and used to be called logical positivism or logical empiricism. The method of philosophical analysis seems to be aimed at removing intellectual knowledge as a distinctive kind of knowledge through a special analysis of language. Philosophy, in particular, must be shown not to be a form of knowledge, and scientists kept from even looking in the direction of philosophy. The special analysis of language consists in attempting to show that all words (*a*) either refer to sensible experience of individuals (*b*) or are meaningless. Briefly, language is characteristic of man; it enables him to acquire the sciences and control nature. Language itself consists of various signs which are attached to various dispositions by means of stimuli, and so on. Now, if language is peculiar to man, it cannot be explained by biological necessities which are in fact common to all animals. But the most serious defect in semantic analysis lies in its attempt to explain the linking of the sign to the thing that is signified. For language consists of arbitrary or conventional signs, as we have seen above. What is the "convention" or "agreement" which links word or gesture to thing signified? another sign of the same nature? This would be a retreat into absurdity. Is it a natural sign? Then intellectual knowledge is admitted; with intellectual knowledge comes the possibility of metaphysics, and so the possibility of a knowledge of real substances.

Sources

Aristotle, *De Anima* (*On the Soul*), Bk. 1, Ch. 4, 407b25–408b30.

Constantine Cavarnos, *A Dialogue between Bergson, Aristotle, and Philologus* (Belmont, Mass., 115 Gilbert Rd., author, 1949).

Jacques Maritain, *La philosophie bergsonienne. Études critiques,* 3rd. ed. (Paris, Desclée, 1931).

W. O'Meara, "John Dewey and Modern Thomism," *Maritain Volume of the Thomist* (New York, Sheed and Ward, 1943).

C. E. M. Joad, *A Critique of Logical Positivism* (Chicago, Univ. of Chicago Press, 1950).

Sensism

The Animal-man

1. Sensism is implicitly a variety of materialism, and in modern times is almost always connected with evolutionism. It need not be an explicit materialism, and if it is joined with positivism, will refuse to commit itself on the question of the substantial nature of man.

2. Sensism essentially is the doctrine that all the knowing activities of man are sensation, or derivations from, and complications of, sensation. It holds that thought is imagery, or complex imagery, or imagery plus sensation and movement. It is selected as a special doctrine, because it usually takes its departure from some problem of human nature and activity, while the kindred materialism and evolutionism most frequently arise from problems in other fields. Sensisms, agreeing in this one doctrine, may differ widely in other doctrines, in their internal spirit, and in their procedures.

3. Sensationism is that form of sensism which denies the distinct reality of appetency or conscious tendency. Occasionally there have been sensationists who have experienced no difficulty in completely ignoring appetency. Usually, it is realized that some kind of explanation must be given. The favorite explanation of emotion, feeling, and sentiment is that these are the sensations of bodily reactions—feeling sad is the sensation of crying; anger, the sensation of increased pulse and breathing; fear, the sensation of shrinking and of visceral reactions; love, the sensation of slight movements of the sexual organs (so-called James-Lange theory of the emotions). Feelings and sentiments may also be the

images of such sensations. Desires are stronger emotions. Choice is said to be only a single name for a multiplicity of reactions, which range all the way from external sensation to the most complex imagery.

4. Associationism is that outmoded form of sensism which is concerned almost wholly to explain knowledge by way of the association of images or of images and sensations. By some of its founders it was called "mental chemistry"; its most important American form was called "structuralism." Its aim was to find the simple elements of all mental activity, and the laws of their combinations. These elements had to be sensations—nothing else was to be admitted. In addition to sensation, there were only images, and then the various ways of combining sensations and images.

5. Some Gestalt psychologists, though they are violent opponents of Associationism, are themselves merely sensists. Gestaltists hold that the whole is prior to the parts which are found in it. They, too, use introspective data, but concentrate on those experiences in which we meet figured or "formed" wholes. Examples of the kind of experience which they consider basic are: two lights appearing successively seem to be one light which jumps, like the lights on a theater marquee; the three-dimensional perception of two-dimensional drawings, and the perception of incompletely drawn figures as complete. Using these and similar facts as a spring-board, these thinkers try to show that thought is nothing more than a similar perception of wholes involving more complex relationships.

6. Hence, sensism implicitly or explicitly denies substantial unity, the specific distinction between sense and intellect, the specific nature of rational appetency and consequently also freedom. It also denies a substantial principle of life.

7. The reasons for accepting sensism are about the same as those for accepting materialism. Associationism received its vogue because the deductive psychology of the rationalists had wholly neglected the part of sense and phantasm in the origin and use of intellectual knowledge. It received a further impulse from the contemporary success of the natural sciences, whose methods and type of reasoning it tried to imitate. Gestalt psychology arose from the discovery of certain facts, such as those referred to above,

and from a very sound dissatisfaction with the inadequacy of associationism.

Sources

David Hume, *A Treatise of Human Nature*, L. A. Selby-Bigge, ed. (London, 1896); *Enquiry concerning Human Understanding*, Selby-Bigge, ed. (London, 1894).

Jean Jacques Rousseau, *Émile*, trans. by Barbara Foxley (New York, Dutton, 1911), Bk. 2, pp. 71, 81–82, 97–123.

Edward Bradford Titchener, *A Text-Book of Psychology* (New York, Macmillan, 1923), pp. 20, 47–48, 367, 369, 376, 17, 513, 377.

John Dewey, *Human Nature and Conduct* (New York, Holt, 1922), pp. 14–15, 22–23, 30–31, 34, 26–29, 191–92, 21, 176; *Experience and Education* (New York, Macmillan, 1938), pp. 74–75, 77–82.

Edward Lee Thorndike, *Human Learning* (New York, Century, 1931), pp. 167–68, 182.

Raymond Holder Wheeler, *The Laws of Human Nature* (New York, Appleton, 1932).

Critique

Sensism and associationism are as defective and incomplete as the materialism which they imply. In addition, they have the added weakness of refusing to recognize the distinct, proper reality of appetite.

Sources

St. Thomas Aquinas, *Summa Theologiae*, I. 84. 1, 6.

Robert S. Woodworth, *Experimental Psychology* (New York, Holt, 1938), pp. 788–89.

Wolfgang Köhler, *Gestalt Psychology* (New York, Liveright, 1929), pp. 19, 118.

William McDougall, *An Outline of Psychology*, 5th ed. (London, Methuen, 1926).

Charles Spearman, *The Nature of 'Intelligence' and the Principles of Cognition* (London, Macmillan, 1923).

David Katz, *Gestalt Psychology*, trans. by Robert Tyson (New York, Ronald, 1950). This is one of the best non-Thomistic refutations of the errors of sensism from a modern point of view.

Philosophical Freudianism

The Instinctive Man

1. The term "psychoanalysis" or "Freudianism" is actually attached to three different (though not unconnected) sorts of things. (*a*) Psychoanalysis is first of all a method of diagnosis and treatment of mental disease. Obviously, the discussion of such a method is irrelevant to the purposes of this book, and should be left to those who are competent in such matters. (*b*) Psychoanalysis is secondly a form of theoretical scientific psychology; it is sometimes called "depth psychology," or one of the types of "dynamic psychology." As such, it has the same relevance to a philosophy of human nature as what is ordinarily known as experimental psychology (see below, Appendix K). (*c*) Psychoanalysis becomes a philosophy when it explicitly denies to other philosophies the right to speak about man, or when—a more common procedure—it presents itself as giving the ultimate explanation of man and of all his activities. It is *only in this third* sense that we are considering psychoanalysis here.

2. Psychoanalytic philosophy very strongly opposes sensationism and associationism as well as all forms of radical immaterialism.

3. In the psychoanalytic concept of man, sensory appetency, impulse, or desire, is a more basic and fundamental reality than sensation (or any form of knowledge). Sensory appetency may be conceived of as sense desire, libido, or "sex" (these terms are practically synonymous in Freudian writings). By way of slight modifications, sensory appetency may be considered to be the desire for power, or achievement, or self-expression.

4. Appetency, the driving force of human nature, is modified by various factors. Among them are sensation, memory, reason, conscience (called in various forms of the theory the "censor" or the "super-ego"), and social pressure and control. These factors are frequently treated as if they were separate agents.

5. Reasoning, especially logical and philosophical reasoning, are often said to be "rationalization." By this term is meant the practice of attributing one's actions, feelings, achievements, and so forth, to allegedly reasonable motives, when in fact they flow from desire and the biological urges. Reason thus has the task of helping us to attain the satisfactions we crave, and to make us look good, first to ourselves, and then to others. Reason is not a power of knowing truth.

6. Religion is frequently assimilated to superstition. Moral codes are reduced to "taboos," or other forms of social pressure; moral values are asserted to be purely subjective. The ideal man is one who satisfies all his desires in the best way (the "best" way being the one that involves him in no conflicts, personal or social).

Sources

Sigmund Freud, *The Ego and the Id* (London, Hogarth, 1927).
Rolland Dalbiez, *Psychoanalytic Method and the Doctrine of Freud*, trans. by T. F. Lindsay (New York, Longmans, 1941: 2 vols.), Vol. 1.

Critique

We are here concerned with the critique of psychoanalysis as a philosophy. Though the system has done a service in refocusing the attention of thinkers upon the affective life of man, and has stressed the unity and dynamic interaction of all his powers, it has failed to understand some very important activities and aspects of his nature. Most basic has been the denial of intellect as a power of objective knowledge, and it is from this crucial error that most of the other errors follow. For example, the subjectivity of moral standards and values rests heavily on the misunderstanding of intellectual knowledge, as does also the misinterpretation of religion. Moreover, though psychoanalysts stress the unity of man from the viewpoint of the interaction of knowledge and appetency, they have in their own way destroyed man's unity through the apparatus of censor, id, super-ego, and the like. Psychoanalysis also presupposes evolutionism (see below).

Sources

Rudolf Allers, *The Successful Error* (New York, Sheed and Ward, 1940); *The New Psychologies* (New York, Sheed and Ward, 1938). Doctor Allers criticizes Freudianism, not only inasmuch as it is a form of sensism and evolutionism, but inasmuch as it is psychiatric method and theoretical scientific psychology. He makes this latter criticism from the viewpoint of what is called "individual psychology," itself a variety of theoretical scientific psychology. Into this disagreement we have no wish to enter.

Mortimer J. Adler, *What Man Has Made of Man* (New York, Longmans, 1937). A brilliant critique of psychoanalysis, which also attempts to accept what is good in that system.

Rolland Dalbiez, *Psychoanalytic Method and the Doctrine of Freud* (New York, Longmans, 1941), Vol. 2. This is the most detailed and most thorough critique.

Ernst Kris, "The Nature of Psychoanalytic Propositions and Their Validation," *Freedom and Experience,* Sidney Hook and Milton Konvitz, eds. (Ithaca, N.Y., Cornell Univ. Press, 1947), pp. 239–59. This criticism is quite sympathetic.

Knight Dunlap, *Personal Adjustment* (New York, McGraw, 1946), pp. 392–435. This analysis and criticism is very sharp, sometimes almost bitter; the author is a noted experimental psychologist.

Joseph Nuttin, *Psychanalyse* (Louvain, Publications Universitaires, 1950). This brilliant and profound study embodies both a presentation and critique of Freudianism and a modern development of the Thomistic theory of the dynamism of human action.

O. Hobart Mowrer, *Learning Theory and Personality Dynamics* (New York, Ronald, 1950), pp. 546–48, 550, 562–63, 567–68, summaries and criticisms of Freudianism.

APPENDIX G

Philosophical Evolutionism

The Evolving Animal

1. Evolution means development or biological change. It is used to designate a biological or scientific theory, and as such evolution will be discussed in the second group of appendices (Appendix N). Evolution (or more accurately, evolutionism) is also a philosophical theory. This philosophy states that all organisms, including the whole of man, have gradually developed through smaller or greater changes in successive generations from nonliving matter, and that this has taken place through *merely* natural and material forces.

2. Consequently, evolutionism denies the substantial unity of man, preferring a cell-group theory which allows to man only an accidental unity.

3. There is no essential difference between merely material being and life, between life and sensation, or between sensation and thought. The differences are merely complications of one and the same reality.

4. However, some recent evolutionists wish to maintain irreducible levels of activity, admitting that thought and free action cannot be explained in terms of chemistry, or physics or sensation. Nevertheless, they refuse to admit a difference in nature between things whose activities are different and irreducible.

5. Most evolutionists still hold that understanding and reasoning are simply complex processes of sense.

6. Animals have all human abilities in a rudimentary form.

7. There is no soul, and the "principle of life" is (accidental) structure.

8. Evolutionism is a form of materialism, and the reasons for it are the reasons for materialism. It has a greater appeal than brute materialism, because it pretends to be based on the same evidence that supports the scientific theory of evolution. It gives some intellectual satisfaction, in its apparent simplicity and its unification of all phenomena around a material principle.

Sources

The Outline of Science, J. Arthur Thompson, ed. (London, Putnam, 1937).

Corliss Lamont, *Humanism as a Philosophy* (New York, Philosophical Library, 1949); a confused and vituperative book; an uncritical and even naive use of "scientific data"; the author himself is almost ignorant of scientific method which he praises so highly.

See also some of the books listed in Appendix C.

Critique

At this point we are discussing only the evolutionary philosophy, not the scientific theory of evolution. As a philosophy, evolutionism overlooks all but material causality. Its argument might be paraphrased thus: "We can point out the wood from which tables develop, and indicate the various steps in the process. Therefore there is no difference between a table and lumber (overlooking formal causality), and carpenters are unnecessary figments of the imagination (overlooking efficient causality)."

Those evolutionists who deny the essential difference between physico-chemical activity, life, sensation, and thought commit their most serious error at the starting-point of their philosophy: they deny evident facts of experience on the alleged ground that they cannot be the way they are.

So-called modern evolutionists who wish to admit irreducible levels of activity and at the same time to assert that there is nothing but matter, have overlooked the basic principle of knowledge, namely, that we know what things are by what they do. These men assert that the nature of things is material, no matter what the activities of things may be. Such materialism is not only an unproved assumption; it is an assumption (in many cases a dogmatic assertion) against the facts.

See also the criticisms above, of materialism, and sensism.

Sources

Louis Vialleton, *L'Origine des Êtres Vivants*, 5th ed. (Paris, Plon, 1939).

Thomas Hunt Morgan, *A Critique of the Theory of Evolution* (Princeton, Princeton Univ. Press, 1916).

Louis T. More, *The Dogma of Evolution* (Princeton, Princeton Univ. Press, 1925).

Sir Charles Sherrington, *Man on His Nature* (New York, Macmillan, 1941), pp. 76, 316–17. These four books are written by outstanding biologists.

Erich Wasmann, S.J., *The Berlin Discussion of the Problem of Evolution* (St. Louis, Herder, 1912). Fr. Wasmann himself is a famous biologist. Though the scientific parts of this book are out of date, its criticism of materialistic evolutionism is pointed, and the historical origins of that philosophy are clearly brought out.

See also the references given below, Appendix N, "The scientific theory of evolution."

Determinism

The Pre-determined Man

1. Determinism is the doctrine that denies all real freedom to man. Of the doctrines already referred to, pantheism, materialism, positivism, evolutionism, and sensism necessarily involve the denial of freedom (for only an intellectual being can be free), whether or not they explicitly make this denial. There are, however, some dualists, some idealists, and some compositionists who also deny freedom to man.

2. Determinism may be psychological, and then it consists in saying that man necessarily chooses that which seems to him to be the greater good. Determinism may be theological, and then it asserts that human freedom is incompatible with God's foreknowledge, or with original sin, or with grace, or with the action of the First Cause in all creatures.

Sources

Gottfried Wilhelm Leibniz, *Theodicy* (New Haven, Yale Univ. Press, 1952). Freedom is in the spontaneous adherence to the greater good. This is akin to the Jansenist doctrine, expressed in theological terms, that the will follows the "victorious (greater) pleasure."

Theological determinism is especially taught by Calvin.

Critique

Psychological determinism rests on an equivocation in the term "the greater good." Obviously, there is no possibility of choosing a *lesser* good precisely under the aspect of being lesser, and for that reason. This is merely to repeat in another form the statement that the object of the will is the good. The point is that what is chosen is good as means; that the object of choice be in itself better or less good is not relevant. To say, "X is better than Y" may mean, "It is better from every point of view"; or it may mean, "It is better from one point of view and less good from another"; or it simply may mean, "It is the one I want."

Theological determinism may be a simple misunderstanding of the revealed doctrine of original sin. It has *not* been revealed that man through original sin lost his freedom of choice, and so revelation should not be used as if it said something it does not say. Theological determinism on the ground of grace, or foreknowledge, or divine causality, is anthropomorphism. If God were as limited as I am, He could not effectively foreknow the creature's action or move it to action, except by predetermining it.

Sources

St. Thomas Aquinas, *Summa Theologiae*, I. 103. 6–8; 105. 4; 115. 6; 116, on the inter-relations of causes, necessity and contingence.

William McDougall, *An Outline of Psychology*, 3rd ed. (London, Methuen, 1926), pp. 447–48, against psychological determinism.

Hubert Gruender, S.J., *Free Will* (St. Louis, Herder, 1916), a discussion of psychological determinism.

Bernard Lonergan, S.J., "St. Thomas's Theory of Operation," *Theological Studies,* III (1942), pp. 387–402; "St. Thomas's Thought on *Gratia Operans,*" *ibid.,* pp. 541–53, answers the problems of theological determinism, in an excellent, but very brief fashion; though the articles are difficult reading, they will repay careful study.

APPENDICES

Part II: Related Issues

What Is the Philosophy of Human Nature?

1. Demonstrative knowledge

The intellect is one of the powers that can be perfected by habits, as we saw in Chapter XII. Habits of knowledge modify (perfect) the way in which the intellect works. For example, by the habit of faith, a man affirms a truth (or a set or organized group of truths), not because he sees it himself, but on the authority of another who does, and he makes this affirmation easily, firmly, and with pleasure. Using a habit of opinion, a man affirms a proposition as true because there seems to be some evidence for it, while realizing that it may not really be true after all. Using the (innate) habits of first principles and of synderesis, a man affirms a truth, because he understands this truth immediately in itself when it is manifested to him in experience. Using a habit of demonstrative knowledge,[1] a man affirms a conclusion (more commonly, an organized set of conclusions), because he sees by means of a demonstration or proof that it follows from premises which are somehow necessary. Thus, a demonstrative habit is formally a habit of reasoning.

A demonstrative habit is so called because it is a habit of demonstrating or proving. A proof must be based on premises which in some way are necessary, though we must remember that there are kinds and degrees of necessity; kinds and degrees which are related to the subject matter and the way in which we come to know that matter. Because the premises are necessary, a proof or reason-

[1] "Demonstrative knowledge" and "demonstrative habit" are terms used to translate the Latin *scientia*, or the Greek *episteme*. Most Thomists merely put an English ending on the word and speak of "science" as a genus including science and philosophy. In the face of modern usage—*usus est norma loquendi*—the latter translation does not make for clarity and intelligibility.

ing on them generates some degree of certitude, which should be proportioned to the type of necessity. As a habit, the demonstrative habit implies a distinctive way of proceeding easily, firmly, and with pleasure, and derives its distinctive character from its formal object.

A demonstrative *habit* directly denotes the firm and accurate way of operating, that is, of proving; but in addition it implies a distinct formal object and principles from which and according to which the proof proceeds. Demonstrative *knowledge* is a fuller term: it denotes the demonstrative habit together with its formal object and principles as well as the main conclusions which are reached by the habit. Because the demonstrative habit uses one set of principles in a specific way upon one formal object, it follows that the conclusions in demonstrative knowledge have a unity of order; we usually say that they form an "organized and systematic body of truths (knowledge)."

2. Specification, distinction, and definition of demonstrative habits

Acts of knowledge are distinguished numerically by their subject (by being your act, or mine, and so forth), and by the times at which they are performed. This kind of distinction is not relevant to the present enquiry. Acts of knowledge are specifically distinguished by their objects. For example, I affirm "Caesar was a Roman general," or "The square of the hypotenuse equals the sum of the squares of the other two sides," or "Act, in the order in which it is act, is limited only by the potency in which it is received." These acts are distinguished from each other by their objects, and are specifically the acts that they are by these objects. Consequently, when we wish to define a demonstrative habit, we can define it completely and specifically only by reference to its formal object. The formal object, in such a definition, must be stated in specific terms (that is, not merely as "formal object").[2]

---

[2] Definitions of terms and proofs of propositions used in this Appendix are not given here; it is presumed that the reader has studied the text, or consults the text for appropriate explanations. For the basis of the type of division used here, see St. Thomas Aquinas, *Comm. in I Post. Analytic.*, lect. 41 (diversa inquantum sunt scibilia); *Comm. in Boethii de Trinitate*, V. 1 (per differentias speculabilium in quantum speculabilia).

3. The distinction of demonstrative habits by material object

In some cases, clear and obvious distinctions among demonstrative habits can be set up on the basis of material object. For example, history is easily distinguished from mathematics, for the former concerns concrete happenings in the material world, while the latter deals with abstract quantified objects (for example, numbers, shapes) or abstract relations. When a given material object cannot be shared by several sciences, we can make an absolute subject-classification of those sciences. Thus, there is no history of triangles, and no geometry of the Peloponnesian war. On this basis, there are three groups of demonstrative knowledges: (1) those which deal with real material things; (2) those which deal with abstract and/or mentally constructed objects,[3] namely, mathematics and logic; (3) metaphysics, which deals with being as being, especially natural theology, dealing with the spiritual First Cause.

4. Distinction of demonstrative habits by formal object

Sometimes, demonstrative habits can be distinguished by their material objects, as we have just seen. But on the one hand, there may be several demonstrative habits that deal with one and the same material object. For example, there are several sciences about man: anthropology, experimental psychology, biology, pathology, history. It is evident that these various sciences reach different conclusions (not contradictory, nor contrary—just different). And since conclusions and formal objects are proportioned to each other, it follows that the sciences about man have different formal objects. Consequently, there may be several sciences about the same material object, and these sciences have different formal objects.

On the other hand, a single demonstrative knowledge may deal with things which are essentially different according to their own proper natures in reality. For example, metaphysics deals with God and creature, substance and accident; chemistry deals with

[3] These objects are also from one point of view real beings, but then they are studied by philosophy and psychology. According to their proper intelligibility, they are studied as such (i.e., as triangles or syllogisms) by mathematics and logic.

living as well as with non-living things. Yet each of these is a single demonstrative knowledge, because that which they formally treat of is the same (univocally the same for chemistry; analogously, for metaphysics). Consequently, a distinct and proper formal object is necessary and sufficient to constitute a distinct demonstrative knowledge.

From the fact that a demonstrative knowledge is specified as such by its formal object, certain consequences follow. The first and most important is the starting point or principle of demonstration. For example, it should be evident that the principles of chemistry will not help a student to reach the formal object of history; that the principles of psychiatry are useless for discovering the intelligible relations of quantity.

A second consequence of a proper formal object is that a distinct demonstrative habit may have a proper method or methods by means of which it reaches that object; this point will be investigated in greater detail below. A third consequence of a proper formal object reached by proper principles through the use of a proper method is that there are conclusions proper to the various demonstrative knowledges—conclusions which cannot be reduced in any way to a single set of conclusions.

5. Knowledge and method

It has already been suggested that a demonstrative knowledge has two stages: first, the stage of discovery or enquiry; second, that of critical evaluation or judgment upon the conclusions reached; or, in other words, a stage of induction and a second stage of organization and evaluation (*via inventionis, via iudicii*).

The method of discovery or induction concerns the origin of the evidence with which one is to deal. At this point, there are two basically different methods. For some evidence is immediately presented in experience; we need but look and we can see. Logic provides us with one kind of example. By making a simple valid syllogism, we can see immediately that it is valid. In a similar way, in perceptual experience we can see *that* a being is. Again, if we see a space marked thus:

we can see, not only that the part *a* is less than the whole, but that it is *necessarily* less than the whole. These are examples of immediate insight or understanding; we can call this the method of "intelligible induction." [4]

On the other hand, many things cannot be discovered by immediate insight. For example, a stone falls; *why* a stone falls is not immediately evident. A man walks down the street every morning at 8:30; why he does so is not immediately evident. Water boils away when it is sufficiently heated; the connection between heat and evaporation is not immediately evident. Moreover, these things cannot be discovered by merely repeating the experience. At most we could perhaps conclude *that* such facts always occur under given conditions. To arrive at an understanding, we have to use roundabout methods of investigation. For example, the molecular constitution of material things is discovered; heat is then found to be the velocity of the molecules in their motions with reference to each other; finally, it is found that when this velocity reaches a certain point (different for different substances, and varying with pressure), the molecules break away from the arrangement or proximity which they had. Now we can see the connection between heat and evaporation. This roundabout and very complicated process of discovery we can call "rational induction." [5]

Secondly, we can speak of method of knowledge with reference to the stage of organization and critical evaluation or judgment. Here we have many different methods, and sometimes quite dis-

[4] This is by no means an intuitional theory of knowledge. For the truth understood is formed in the mind by the mind's own activity; an investigation into the *causes* of knowledge reveals the function of sense experience (phantasm) and agent intellect in the production of immediately understood propositions (as well as of all others); cf. above, Chapter VIII.

[5] Every form of demonstrative knowledge has therefore two moments: an experiential moment and an organized demonstrative moment. The sciences that use rational induction have an intermediate moment, which we may well call the "experimental moment." By *experience* I mean the full, non-abstractive contact with reality; by *experiment*, the selective or abstractive mediate contact (where the medium is the specialized technique or instrument). Experiential evidence is therefore *ontological* in nature, in the sense that it reveals being as it is; experimental evidence properly so called is *empiriological*, in the sense that it attains being as it manifests itself through a selective and partly artificial medium.

For the terms "intelligible" and "rational induction" I am indebted to stimulating discussions with the Reverend Robert J. Henle, S.J.

tinctive ones. For example, mathematics proceeds by definition, construction, and deduction (according to formal causality). The physical sciences organize their data by hypothesis and verification, and prove the validity of their procedures through statistical techniques and controlled observation and/or experiment.

In view of these discussions, we can reflect briefly upon the modern preoccupation with "scientific method." Many popularizers assert that scientific method is the same in all the sciences, and that it is the only method of obtaining true and certain knowledge. Such authors seem to be talking indiscriminately about the method of discovery and the method of critical evaluation. This initial confusion vitiates the entire discussion. Secondly, these writers assume that the only method of discovery is the one which we have called "rational induction," not realizing that rational induction is indeed the unique method where direct and immediate intelligibility is lacking, but is useless and frequently impossible where such immediate intelligibility is present. But even after these distinctions have been made, rational induction is not a single method. Physics and chemistry use laboratory manipulation, while history and astrophysics are not able to use it. Not even experimental methods can be reduced to a single type: the procedures of qualitative analysis in chemistry and of electronics are irreducible; an association experiment in experimental psychology is conducted in a very different way from the procedures of testing animal drives. Consequently, much of what is written about scientific method rests on confusion and on unwarranted assumptions.

6. A consequence of rational induction

We have seen that some objects manifest very little direct intelligibility, and that any detailed knowledge of such objects must arise from the use of special techniques of investigation. Two consequences flow immediately from these techniques. The first is that specialized techniques involve a selection of the characteristics of the object to be investigated. For example, suppose we want to know what fire is, and to this end we weigh a piece of wood before burning, and then weigh the products of combustion (smoke and ashes). Now, it is obvious that by this procedure we can reach only one set of characteristics of the wood and the ashes, that is, their weight. Hence, the use of a specialized technique (or a specialized instrument) always introduces selection or abstraction.

The second consequence of the use of rational induction can be seen in the same example. For our results can be stated correctly only in one way: that is, by reference to the readings on our scales. In some cases it seems to be possible to eliminate the technique or instrument from the statement of the conclusion by a further advance; [6] but in very many other instances the technique remains in the conclusion. In other words, not only is the procedure an indirect one; the very knowledge itself gained through such a technique is itself indirect, or constructural. The type of constructural intelligibility manifested in this example is often called "operational." Science also employs other types of constructs, notably (a) that of extrinsic proportionality, or metaphor (also called a "physical model," or "picture"), (b) that of schematic correlation of merely observed data, and (c) that of combining pure beings of reason (taken from mathematics, logic, and so forth) with observed or interpreted data.

Very frequently, modern science submits its data, techniques, and concepts (both direct and constructural) to the procedures of mathematics. Now, the objects of mathematics are not real beings, but, in their formal and abstract character, are beings of reason. Hence, the mathematical natural sciences (e.g., mathematical physics) are constructural from two points of view, materially (inasmuch as they contain the constructs mentioned in the preceding paragraph) and formally (inasmuch as the form of reasoning is mathematical).

7. The properties of a distinct demonstrative knowledge

It may be worth while to summarize these discussions. A demonstrative knowledge is constituted and specified as a distinct habit

[6] An example of a scientific statement that passed from the stage of indirect intelligibility to that of direct is the "law of constant proportions" in chemistry. When chemists first found the law, they knew only that chemical substances combined in constant proportions; the discovery of the molecular constitution of matter made clear the reason why chemical combination occurred as it did.

and body of knowledge by its formal object. It will use methods of discovery that are appropriate to its object, either intelligible induction or rational induction. It will also have to use appropriate methods of organization and proof. Consequently, it will use particular methods of definition, sometimes keeping the indirect methods of approach formally in its definition. And finally, it can have only that kind of certitude which corresponds to the necessities of its object, and to the extent that those necessities can be discovered and made clear.

Several examples may clarify this summary statement. We do not mean to imply that biology and physics are formally distinct habits; neither are we asserting that they differ only in material object. There are enough describable differences between the two sciences to serve the present purpose.

BIOLOGY. The formal object of biology is the observable manifestations of vegetable life. The meaning of the term "observable" is dependent upon the method or technique used. The special methods are direct ocular or sensible observation under controlled conditions if possible, the use of the microscope and other tools for discovering the characteristic structures of living things, and the discovery of characteristic functions and of functional reactions to controlled stimulations of various kinds (selection and abstraction). Its method of organization is usually through the use of conceptual constructions (cell or chromosome treated as integral parts). Its type of proof is the verification of a hypothesis, comparison with control-groups, and so forth. It defines its objects in terms of the kind of observable manifestations it has selected: for example, in terms of gross structure, as "vertebrate," or in terms of cell structure, with reference to chromosomes, genes, and so forth, or in terms of functional reactions, such as "x is that which does this under such conditions, or when stimulated in this way." It comes to its own kind of conclusions about the existence and function of hormones, vitamins, endocrine glands, the different manners in which living things use oxygen, or light, and so forth. Its conclusions admit of exceptions: there are living things which are defective in structure (monsters); there is malfunctioning of various kinds; there are diseases.

PHYSICS. The formal object of physics is the observable-measurable (non-specific) structure and activities of material things. Its methods consist almost wholly in the use of the instruments which it has devised, such as the scale, thermometer, pressure gauge, electric meter, and spectograph, which enable it to reach and usually to measure structure and activities. Its organization is almost entirely through conceptual constructs, particularly those of mathematics. Its proof lies in the verification of hypotheses by the elimination of variables. Its way of definition is in terms of its object and techniques: for example, "an electron is the sub-atomic elementary charge of negative electricity," and this means "an electron is the smallest unit of that which registers as negative according to a scale of a given kind" (abstraction and construct). Because physical definitions are by means of techniques and constructs, it is possible to have two definitions of light, as a "wave" or a "particle," because these two terms refer to different methods and instruments of observation and measurement. Physics comes to its own particular conclusions: the atomic theory of matter; the laws of forces, of gases; the mathematical formulae of electronic theory. It has its own degree of certitude, based, as far as the physicist is concerned, on the accuracy and completeness of his experimental techniques, and admitting of no exceptions within the scope of those procedures.

Philosophically speaking, the difference between biology and physics in this matter of certitude is due to the difference in necessity and contingence between living and non-living things; inanimate (non-living) things have activities that are contingent only with respect to the First Cause; living things have activities that are contingent even with respect to secondary causes (that is, their effects can be impeded by unfavorable conditions, or by defects in their own matter, as in sterility).

8. Scientific psychology and the philosophy of human nature

With these discussions, distinctions, and definitions in mind, we can compare scientific psychology and the philosophy of human nature. The ultimate subject of the two demonstrative knowledges is the same: man. From here on they differ.

SCIENTIFIC PSYCHOLOGY	PHILOSOPHY OF HUMAN NATURE

A. Starting Point

Experience and experimental or scientifically observed data.[7]	Experiential, often massive, evidences, which need not be detailed, but must be very accurately determined.[8]

B. Material Object

Behavior,[9] human and animal.	Man as revealed through his activities.

C. Method

Observation and experiment. Rational induction.	Experiential observation; reflection and/or analysis. Intelligible induction.

D. Organizing Principles

Some physical and mechanical concepts (e.g., drive); mathematical concepts (like function); constructs (e.g., conditioned reflex, complex). Hence, empiriological or perinoetic knowledge.[11]	Some metaphysical principles (e.g., act and potency); [10] some proper ontological principles (e.g., formal object). Hence, ontological or dianoetic in form.[12]

[7] See above, footnote 5. Experimental data clearly involve special techniques and/or instruments, and so are abstractive, selective. Scientific observation (other than experimentation) always involves some techniques such as questionnaires, tests, and so forth, and includes as a part of its critical evaluation the statistical theory of sampling.

[8] For the definitions and uses of these terms, see above, Chapter I, section 4.

[9] "Behavior" means all "non-automatic" or modifiable activity which can be observed, admitting both external and self-observation.

[10] This raises the problem of the relationship between the philosophy of human nature and metaphysics; see below.

[11] These terms have been invented by M. Jacques Maritain. Sciences are called "empiriological," inasmuch as the experience or experiment remains as a part of the definition or the conclusion, as we have seen. Sciences are called "perinoetic," because they deal indirectly (that is, through something else) with an object that is only indirectly intelligible, in other words, because they must use rational induction. See St. Thomas, *Summa Theologiae*, I. 13. 8 ad 2; *Truth*, IV. 1 ad 8; *In VII Metaphysicorum*, lect. 12.

[12] I call a demonstrative knowledge "ontological" in form, when it is able to use intelligible induction upon a directly intelligible object. An ontological concept or principle is one which is directly drawn from experience, and which therefore is a means of knowing an object according to the latter's own proper mode of being. M. Maritain calls this kind of knowledge "dianoetic," because it aims at the inner constitution of the being in itself. Cf. St. Thomas, *In II Analyticorum Posteriorum*, lect. 13, no. 7.

E. *Aim*

(Mathematical) laws of behavior and/or control. To reach a surrogate-sign [13] of essence.

The directly intelligible implications of activity. To reach an essence or nature through properties.

F. *Type of Definition*

Very often in terms of the experiment which is used to isolate or measure the behavior or the relationships of the latter.[14]

In terms of the principles of being; of genus and specific difference; of formal object.

G. *Formal Object*

The observable and/or measurable behavior of human and animal organisms, insofar as this behavior manifests the integrated dynamic interrelationships within the organism or between the organism and its environment.

The nature of man in relation to his being and his activities.

From these considerations, we conclude that scientific psychology and the philosophy of human nature to some extent meet in their respective starting-points, though not entirely. Both forms of

[13] Or "rationally constructed substitute for the real (ontological) essence." The term is due to M. Jacques Maritain.

In natural science, essence is quite accurately said to be "the permanent possibility of sensible verification and measurement." To express this possibility in terms of the operation and measurement is therefore a natural aim. Suppose, for example, an experimentalist defines "sight" as "the electrochemical excitation of the optic nerve." Certainly, if we were mistakenly to suppose that this were a definition of what sight *is*, it bears no direct relation to the experience of seeing, and so is meaningless, or at best highly incomplete, as being the more negligible aspect of sensation. But if we are looking for a definition that is most suitable to an experimentalist, this one makes the best kind of sense. The phrase "optic nerve" tells him where his observation and experiment is to be conducted by giving the anatomical location. The phrase "electro-chemical" tells him what instruments and techniques he can use to detect its presence, measure it, cause it. Hence, we say that natural science expresses itself in symbols or signs. These signs are surrogates or substitutes for the real essence, because it is in terms of them that the scientist defines his object. Compare the remark of Charles Sanders Peirce on the scientific definition of lithium, in *Collected Papers*, Charles Hartshorne and Paul Weiss, eds. (Cambridge, Harvard Univ. Press, 1931), Vol. 2, p. 330.

[14] For example, the "intensity" of a drive is defined by the kind of experimental situation that is used to test it: crossing an electrically charged grid so many times.

knowledge have experiential moments, and at this point evidence must be in common and commonly verifiable. But it may well be that the evidence which the philosophy of human nature uses will be only partly relevant for scientific psychology, and some of the experiential evidence used by scientific psychology, not meaningful for the philosophy of human nature. Secondly, it can happen that scientific observation may uncover some evidence which is still ontological in nature (directly intelligible), and therefore useful for the philosophy of human nature. Sometimes also ontological evidence can be discovered by the philosophy of human nature in the midst of the rational inductions made by scientific psychologists.[15] But when we consider the two knowledges at the level of organization and conclusion, there can be no direct comparison and consequently no conflict. In other words, scientific and philosophical conclusions are not directly comparable. Therefore, there can be no real direct dependence of either form of knowledge upon the other. We can speak of a partial "material dependence" of the philosophy of human nature upon scientific psychology, to the extent that there are ontological evidences among the data of scientific psychology.

In fact, however, there seem to be areas of conflict and contradiction. This apparent conflict is due either to mistakes in fact, misapplications of method, or surreptitious importations from other fields. For example, materialistic biology gets to its materialistic conclusions, not as biology, but by importing, surreptitiously, a materialistic philosophy; deterministic experimental psychology, by borrowing a philosophy of determinism; a mechanist psychology (as behaviorism), by reliance on a mechanistic philosophy. On the other hand, Cartesian dualism arrives at its conclusions, not by working as philosophy on human nature and its activities, but by using the techniques of a mathematicized essentialism; spiritualism makes use of a few pseudo-facts and some unsupported denials.

9. The unity of the philosophy of human nature

In the first chapter, note was taken of some Thomists who do not think that the philosophy of human nature is a single and unified

---

[15] For example, experiments in psycho-physics contain an ontological evidence that sensation is an operation of the composite; some experiments in hypnosis manifest the unity of the vegetative and sensitive levels in man.

branch or kind of knowledge. They consider "rational psychology," as they call it, a mere aggregate consisting of some metaphysical propositions (about the spirituality of the human soul), some propositions from the philosophy of nature (theory of powers, the matter-form constitution of human nature, and so forth), and in addition some consider that the whole treatises on vegetative life and sensibility properly belong to biology and scientific psychology.

A preliminary remark seems to be highly necessary in view of the number of times this kind of objection is raised. No single proposition can, properly speaking, be located in any demonstrative knowledge, except in some instances, materially. The center of any demonstrative knowledge is a habit of reasoning, and unless a proposition is formally engaged in an argument, it cannot of itself be assigned to any particular habit. Moreover, many syllogisms cannot of themselves be definitely assigned to a definite habit; often they can be assigned to one of several. Thus, some arguments can be assigned to one or the other of the natural sciences, or to the mathematical sciences, or to one of the philosophical disciplines. Only when the function of an argumentation is fully determinate can it be assigned to one and only one demonstrative habit.

With this in mind, it is easy to see that there is no biology or scientific psychology in the philosophical study of man, for the scientific habits in question are not brought into play. For an example, we need but compare Chapters VI and VII of this text with any standard text of experimental psychology. That the philosophical study of man is not a patchwork of metaphysics and the philosophy of nature should be evident from this, that in studying the nature of man we are at no point engaged in the study of being *as being*. Merely mentioning act and potency or the act of existing is not of itself necessarily engaging in metaphysical reasoning. To clarify this point further we must investigate the relation between metaphysics and the philosophy of nature.

10. Metaphysics, epistemology, and the philosophy of human nature

Metaphysics is that demonstrative knowledge whose material object is all beings, and whose proper object is being as being.

Like the philosophy of human nature, metaphysics uses the method of intelligible induction, reflection, and analysis. Moreover, it has been asserted above that the philosophy of human nature uses metaphysical principles for organizing its evidences. Does this enable us to conclude that the philosophy of human nature is an integral part of metaphysics, or an application of metaphysics to a part of its material object?

First of all, metaphysical principles are not used univocally [16] in the philosophy of human nature; they are used in their reference to the particular or specific nature of man. In being used thus, these principles undergo a change. There is, first of all, the obvious and easily understood change that arises from the application of universal principles to a special sort of matter. For example, the principle, "Activity (act, operation) is specified by its object," is applied in investigating the various formal objects which man's activity concerns. Such application introduces no internal change in the principle. There is a second kind of modification which is actually a different (analogous) meaning of the principle. Take the example just given. When we come to the free choice of the will, the principle, "Activity is specified by its object," has a particular, added meaning. For the principle, in all its other instances, implies a necessitating specification; in this one case, because of the specific nature of the being which acts (namely, a *rational* nature), there is no predetermining, but only a consequent necessity, and the causality is not only final, but final *and formal*. Another example is that of the metaphysical conclusion of the matter-form composition of sensible, changeable things. For, though the human soul is a principle of a material composite, it is itself subsistent. Hence, of all other substantial forms, metaphysics can say, "They do not come to be, but something else comes to be by them"; while of the human soul, the philosophy of human nature says, "It itself comes to be by creation, and by it, man comes to be."

To meet this problem squarely, it is worth while to restate the object of the philosophy of nature.[17] St. Thomas said that it was

[16] Metaphysical principles are never univocal, because being, to which they refer, is analogous.

[17] The term, *philosophy of nature*, is not being used in its traditional sense (where it would mean "the philosophy of sensible things"). The term *nature* is being used to mean "essence as principle of being and activity." Any reality

"ens mobile," which in context should be translated "thing as changeable," or, "essence as changeable." In these phrases, thing and essence mean the same, and are equivalent to quiddity—that which answers the question, "What is it?" These terms must be understood in the wide sense, as applicable to both substance and accident; primarily to substance, secondarily to accident. "Change" (in an extended usage already sanctioned by Aristotle and St. Thomas) includes all the actions and passions of creatures, even such activities as thinking and willing. "Nature" (in a similarly extended use of the term) is "the thing (essence or quiddity) inasmuch as it is the ultimate principle of change, that is, of acting and being acted on." Understood in this way, the philosophy of human nature is an integral part of the philosophy of nature, and distinguished from metaphysics as "a changeable thing" is distinguished from "being as being."

And, since their objects differ as objects, the demonstrative habits of the philosophy of human nature and of metaphysics differ. But note that they do not differ in the same way that metaphysics and mathematics differ. The philosophy of nature is in fact dependent upon metaphysics, for it uses metaphysical principles as organizing principles. Therefore, the two habits cannot be used in complete isolation from each other; metaphysics does not need the philosophy of nature formally as such, but the philosophy of nature does need metaphysics. The best name for expressing such a relationship is that the philosophy of nature is a "potential part" of metaphysics.[18]

---

that can properly be called an essence can be the object of the philosophy of nature (for example, substances, accidents). The philosophy of nature includes all finite beings which have an essence distinct from their act of existing and their activities. I consider the philosophy of nature to be a single integral whole, comprising as integral parts the philosophy of merely material nature, the philosophy of living and sentient nature, the philosophy of human nature, the philosophy of knowledge, the philosophy of angelic nature. These divisions are merely illustrations, not a complete listing; they overlap, because they are not made on any single basis of division. But they have some internal unity, and a practical validity in that they indicate areas that can be mastered in a reasonable time.

"Nature" in its narrower sense (the ultimate principle of rest and motion) is the object of the *physica* of St. Thomas, which together with the *De Anima* (and so forth) constitutes the philosophy of nature (in the wider sense).

[18] For the notion of a potential part, see St. Thomas, *Summa Theologiae,*

400 APPENDICES [K 10–11]

The relation between the philosophy of human nature and epistemology is simpler to state. Epistemology, to some writers, means the metaphysics of the true and of knowledge as a being of reason. In this meaning of the term, epistemology is an integral part of metaphysics. To other writers, the term "epistemology" means a study of the nature of knowledge. In this sense, epistemology is an integral part of the philosophy of nature. That overlapping is possible in such a division should occasion no surprise; the division into integral parts is frequently arbitrary. But for practical purposes we may say this. To arrive at the nature of man, something of the nature of knowledge must be studied. But there are some considerations of knowledge which go beyond what is needed for the discovery of the nature of man. These further considerations can constitute a field of investigation which may well be called epistemology.[19]

11. Readings

Mortimer J. Adler, *What Man Has Made of Man* (New York, Longmans, 1937), pp. 3–60, on the need, and the modern failure, to distinguish the various kinds of science. He is a non-Catholic, rather an Aristotelian than a Thomist.

Franz Alexander, "Introduction" to Adler's book just mentioned. A vigorous presentation of anti-religious and anti-philosophical scientism by a prominent psychoanalyst who really knows very little about what he is opposing.

Alexis Carrell, *Man the Unknown* (New York, Harper, 1935), pp. 30–57, on the kinds of sciences. A prominent biologist who realizes

II–II. 48. 1. An example will be the relation of the virtues of religion, veracity, and gratitude to justice. Obviously, these are four really distinct virtues. But they are not four species of a single genus. Their community is a unity of analogy. So, too, the community of metaphysics and the philosophy of nature is not that of a common genus, nor of an analogy of proportionality, but an analogy of dependence or participation. See also *ibid.*, I–II. 61. 3.

[19] The reader who is familiar with Thomistic writings will have noted that the traditional "degrees of abstraction" have not been used to solve the present problem. The reasons are (a) Degrees of abstraction do not serve to specify and distinguish knowledges, but to classify and order material objects; (b) even as classification, the degrees are not sufficient; (c) potential parts ought to be classified with their principal and perfect analogues, and so the degrees of abstraction might be used to distinguish philosophy as a whole from mathematics, but will not help to distinguish the philosophy of nature from metaphysics, or any of the sciences of nature one from another. Moreover, it seems clear that St. Thomas himself never spoke of three degrees of abstraction.

the need for something more than science, but does not see clearly how to go beyond it.

Robert S. Woodworth, "Dynamic Psychology," in *Psychologies of 1930*, Carl Murchinson, ed. (Worcester, Mass., Clark Univ. Press, 1930), pp. 327–36; p. 335, on the kinds of knowledges. Perhaps the greatest experimental psychologist of the first half of this century.

Étienne Gilson, *God and Philosophy* (New Haven, Yale Univ. Press, 1941), pp. 109–44. A brilliant analysis of some philosophies which failed to realize the distinct kinds of sciences.

Jacques Maritain, *The Degrees of Knowledge*, trans. by Bernard Wall and Margot Adamson (New York, Scribner, 1938), pp. 27–85, 165–247.

————, "Science, Philosophy, and Faith," *Science, Philosophy and Religion* (New York, Conference on Science, Philosophy and Religion, 1941), pp. 162–83. The former of these works by the eminent Thomist is the most important modern work of its kind, and its analyses are basic to any further discussion of this topic. The briefer, later article is perhaps the easier reading, and some of its expressions are better.

————, "On Human Knowledge," *Thought*, XXIV (1949), 225–43. A summary of his doctrine.

Louis-Marie Régis, O.P., "La philosophie de la nature," *Études et Recherches, Philosophie I* (Ottawa, 1936), pp. 127–56. This very important review of Maritain's theory of the philosophy of nature adds some essential qualifications. It is the basis of the last of the conclusions of this Appendix.

D. J. B. Hawkins, *Causality and Implication* (New York, Sheed and Ward, 1937), pp. 107–22.

Otis Lee, *Existence and Inquiry* (Chicago, Univ. of Chicago Press, 1949), pp. 307–09. Not a Thomist nor a Catholic. He sees clearly the difference between philosophy and science, and says some excellent things on the relation of philosophical knowledge to concrete reality.

W. Stace, *A Critical History of Greek Philosophy* (New York, Macmillan, 1934), pp. 1–13. Not a Catholic nor a Thomist, nor even wholly an Aristotelian. A keen thinker, who has come to philosophy and realism by his own reading and thinking, he is fully aware of the modern tendencies to scientism and to the cult of progress, and unhesitatingly lays their weaknesses bare.

William H. Kilpatrick, *Foundations of Method* (New York, Macmillan, 1925), pp. 6–7. A book on teaching methods, with a short discussion of the relation of method to subject matter.

Robert J. Henle, S.J., *Method in Metaphysics* (Milwaukee, Marquette Univ. Press, 1951). A brilliant study of the method employed in metaphysics, showing how philosophy has an experiential moment.

E. F. Caldin, *The Power and Limits of Science* (London, Chapman, 1949). An excellent discussion of scientific method, showing clearly how scientific knowledge is built up.

Efficient Causality in Material Things

1. The questions to be asked

Efficient causality is discussed in metaphysics, and it is likewise proper to metaphysics to discuss the analogous ways in which analogously different beings exercise that causality. Frequently the brevity of the course in metaphysics is such as not to allow this latter discussion to arise. And yet there are three important metaphysical insights which are in a way presupposed in the course on the philosophy of human nature. They can be expressed in three propositions. (The efficient causality of material things is always in space. The efficient causality of material things is always temporal. Substantial change caused by created agents always takes place through accidental change.)

2. The efficient causality of material things is always in space

Though all the accidents of a material substance are modifications of the substance itself, and inhere in the substance, yet they inhere in it according to a certain order of nature. The only strictly spiritual activities we know of in this material universe are the activities of intellect and will. Understanding and willing are immanent operations, and are principles of external, efficient activity only through other, material activities. All other activities and powers of activity are material. Now, the order found among the accidents of a material substance is such that quantity is prior, not in time, but in nature, to all other accidents. Thus, all other accidents inhere in the material substance inasmuch as the latter is affected first by quantity, therefore in a quantified subject. Consequently, all the powers of activity in the material world, outside of intellect and will, are the acts of material substance or parts of such a substance. Therefore, such powers themselves are quantified. Just as, other things being equal, a big white house has more whiteness than a small one, so, too, a big muscle, other things being equal, is more powerful than a small one, a big magnet is more powerful than a small one of the same kind under the same conditions, and so on. A rapid induction of this kind will make it perfectly clear that the efficient activity of material things is itself affected by quantity.

Now, an efficient activity that is quantified can only be received by an object (a patient) that is quantified. Material activity is directed in many directions, or all directions, or one, but at any rate, it requires that its recipient be some where, itself quantified, expanded, to receive that activity.

3. The efficient activity of material things is always temporal

The local motion of a material thing is always in time, successive.[1] Local motion in "zero time" (instantaneous, in the literal meaning of that word) was shown by Aristotle to imply an infinite power, which of course cannot be found in a material thing. Modern physics holds as the theoretical top speed of local motion the speed of light. And inasmuch as other types of material activity are preceded or accompanied by local motion, they too must be in time.

For most types of material activity this is evident to experience. Thus, chemical activity is obviously in time, though it may be very rapid. All types of radiation are temporal, though most of them proceed at speeds which seem to the senses to be instantaneous. Sensation itself is preceded and accompanied by temporal activities, though it itself is not directly in time; that is why we say that it is relatively immaterial. The only area in which

---

[1] It is said that the motion of an electron from one orbit to another within the atom takes place instantaneously. The difficulty with evaluating this statement is that what goes on in the atom is not wholly clear. Is it that this motion is the really temporal motion of a particle in space, whose electric charge, however, is transferred from one side of the electron to another? Is an electron within an atom the point of concentration of an electric charge within a relatively much larger extended part, as the mass of earth is, for the purposes of the law of gravitation, considered as concentrated in its center? And, finally, the motion of an electron within an atom is the motion of a part within a substantial unit, and so does not really belong to the present discussion.

there might seem to be a doubt is that of electromagnetic phenomena. It may be that some of these are states rather than activities, and so would be only indirectly in time. However, it is clear that the coming-to-be of these phenomena, and their increase and decrease, are in time.

What about a substantial change effected in a material thing by another material thing? Strictly speaking, and in itself, substantial change must be instantaneous. First, substance is prior to quantity, and not posterior to it, as are the active and passive powers of material things. Secondly, wherever something is directly in time, there must be succession of a continuous and gradual kind. Now, substantial forms are not capable of continuous and gradual change. Things may change, and may even change their essences; but essences themselves are what they are, immutably. A horse may die, but horseness has to be what it is. If you change it at all in any way, you have a different essence. Now, the actual principle of essence is the substantial form. Substantial form is in itself not extended and has no real parts (cf. below, Appendix M [A, B]). Therefore, it cannot be possessed partially; it is either present or absent; either informing some matter or not.

But among the activities that are experienced as temporal, is not substantial change most evidently in time? The assimilation of food into the body, for example, takes time. Here is where a distinction must be made. Substantial change, as we shall see, is essentially preceded by accidental changes (at least when caused by a created agent). The duration of these accidental changes is what gives the temporal appearance to substantial changes. The preparation for the substantial change takes time; the substantial change occurs instantaneously at the term of that preparation.[2]

---

[2] Substantial change is simultaneously the destruction of one substance and the production of another. The preparatory process of accidental change has therefore a double aspect, destructive and productive.

Moreover, it is impossible to designate a last instant in which the first substance or form would be present, followed by another instant in which the new substance and form would be present for the first time. To suppose such a possibility is calamitous for the whole theory of change. Between any two instants there is always time, no matter how brief. And so there would be a time during which prime matter existed without a form; it would thus itself be in act; and so the whole unity of being would disappear.

It is possible to designate only a last *time* during which the first substance

4. Substantial change caused by created agents always takes place through accidental change, through material dispositions

This proposition can be demonstrated briefly from the metaphysical analyses of created being and its causality. The very nature of a created cause is such that it cannot itself create. To create is to produce an entire being where there was nothing before. To produce an entire being entirely is to have power over being itself, since being is what would actually be made. That which has power over being itself has also within that power the sufficient reason for its own being. It is therefore an infinitely powerful, uncreated being. Therefore the power of creation belongs entirely to an infinite, uncreated cause. Hence, what is itself created cannot create.

It therefore follows that a created agent must have before it a pre-existing matter on which to act. And this pre-existing matter is not simply a condition; it is precisely that which receives the efficient causality. And therefore the subject of the passion or change induced by the created cause is not simply a kind of vague, universal subject, into which any form can be introduced, indiscriminately. To be able to disregard the requirements and conditions of the recipient is equivalently to be independent of the pre-existing subject in action. And that is why, when a sudden change does occur without regard to the dispositions of the patient, we rightly say that a miracle has occurred.

The activity of a created cause is an accident of that substance, and has as its proximate principle an accidental power by which that substance acts. To this accidental activity and power there correspond in the patient certain new accidental modifications. But because the accidents of the agent and the patient are instru-

---

and form are present. This time is ended by an instant at which the former substance and form are first absent, and at which the new substance and form are present. The destructive aspect of the preceding accidental change is terminated by the non-existence of the first substance and its form, and the constructive aspect of that same change by the existence of the second substance and form. Therefore, there is no time during substantial change when the substance is not either this or that kind of substance, with this or that form.

ments of the substance, therefore a new substance can be generated by means of them. Schematically:

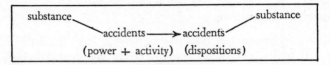

substance
accidents ———➤ accidents
(power + activity) (dispositions)
substance

This same conclusion could have been reached inductively, though not with the same universality. But a sampling of that induction will serve to show what that conclusion means.

The substantial change of food into a living body will be a clear example. The process is begun by a local motion, that of bringing the food into contact with the living thing. In the digestive system, the food is attacked by various chemicals secreted by the digestive organs. The usable parts of the food, now modified, are carried by the blood to the bodily parts that need them. There the food is absorbed into the cell, then modified, and in the course of modification built into the cell substance. Actually, in the process there is not only one, but many substantial changes.

Let us look at a chemical change according to present theory. For example, in the production of synthetic rubber, the first step is to bring the proper chemicals into contact with each other, and put them under the proper conditions of pressure, heat, and energy (all of which are changes of material dispositions). Under these conditions, it is thought, the electrical bonds of each of the distinct molecule-systems are so broken or modified that the two molecules are brought into one more inclusive system (again a gradual change of material dispositions).

Another very helpful example is that of the violent death of a living thing. A living thing has certain proper dispositions of its body: shape, temperature, pressure, and so forth. Living things can tolerate a certain amount of variation in these dispositions. But the further the disposition is varied from the one ideally suitable, the closer the organism is to death.

Suppose an animal is caught in a forest fire. At first, it will not be bothered by a slight change in temperature; a greater increase will cause discomfort, then pain. At this point, the dispositions are becoming contrary, but the matter has not yet been made wholly unsuitable to the form. But if the heating continues, the animal is killed part by part. Here, the accidental change is that of a change in temperature. In its destructive side, it will terminate in the death of the animal. On its constructive side, meanwhile, the temperature change is preparing for new molecular combinations in what used to be the matter of the animal.

Physical theory will help to illustrate this case even more. This theory says that heat is a motion of the molecules, and that the higher the temperature, the faster the motion. Chemical theory holds that many of the molecules which are found in living things are extremely complex and relatively unstable; they cannot endure under conditions of extreme heat, and so forth. Looked at philosophically in terms of virtual presence and material dispositions, this theoretical account illustrates how substantial change is effected through the change of material dispositions.[3]

[3] For a correlation of this doctrine with the theory of equivocal generation, and for a full set of references to St. Thomas for it, see G. P. Klubertanz, S.J., "Causality in the Philosophy of Nature," *The Modern Schoolman*, XIX (1942), 29–32.

Some Corollaries about the Soul as Form

A. *Every soul is simple, inextended.*

Those formal perfections which presuppose quantity are quantified either in themselves or in their subject—for example, shape and color. A colored surface is big or small, and this refers to the color as well as to the extension. The same is true of similar qualities. But some qualities have no reference to quantity. Substantial forms are the intrinsic substantial principles of specific perfection. Now, is iron more or less iron? (not: is a piece of metal more or less pure iron?). A ton of iron is just as much of the nature of iron as an ounce. It is nonsense to speak of an increase in a given specific perfection.

From another point of view, we can ask: Can an essence change as essence? If "horseness," for example, changes at all, it ceases to be itself. This is evident. But substantial form is the actual principle of essence. Therefore it is even less susceptible of change. Therefore it does not admit of more or less. And so, substantial form is not quantified.

We can take still another point of view. In metaphysics it is proved that quantity is an accident which in the order of nature is posterior to substance, and inheres in a being by reason of the matter. Hence, substantial form is what it is prior to, and without intrinsic relation to, quantity. Hence, substantial form is not quantified.

B. *No soul can be directly divided, though new living organisms can arise by division.*

Division can be into any type of parts. If the parts are real, there can be real division. If the parts are not real, there can be only logical division, for example, division into genus and difference: plant = living/material substance. No soul has quantitative parts, as was just explained. No soul has essential parts, because it is the ultimate actual principle of specific perfection. Therefore, no soul can be divided.

But most plants and some animals (and all animals at some stage of their growth) can be divided into two or more new beings by cutting or some similar kind of division (for example, a branch of a willow tree, if cut off and planted, will grow into a new tree). How is this? We have seen above that, where structure is relatively homogeneous, a (sufficiently large) part of the organism contains the whole virtually.[1] Therefore, a mere cutting off is a sufficient cause for the production of a new living thing.

We may wonder: What about the soul? Is the soul divided in these cases? We have seen above that a substantial form is by its nature not quantified, not extended. Therefore, no substantial form can be divided. And, even if a substantial form could be divided, the problem would become more difficult, for part of the specification would be in one of the new beings, part in the other, so that each would be specifically different from the other, and from the original being which was divided. So, then, the soul of the original being to be divided is not itself divided. What happens to it? Strictly speaking, nothing happens to it, for it is not a being, but only a principle of being. Where a part is cut off from the whole, the original being remains, and continues to be informed by the same soul, but part of the matter is withdrawn from that information. Where the whole being is divided into two or more parts, the original being ceases to be, and consequently ceases to be informed by the first soul.

What about the soul of the new being or new beings? In general, form is in the potency of matter, and is actuated in the matter. When a form is virtually present in a part of a living thing, it is in potency that is very close to act. By mere separation that virtuality is reduced to act. And so, to the extent that we can speak of a form being produced, it is produced by the material causality of the dispositions [2] of the separated part or parts.

How can this be? how did these parts acquire such power? They

[1] See above, Chapter II, section 14.
[2] See above, Appendix L, section 4.

acquired this power by the immanent, efficient activity of the living being itself whose parts they were. Like a jack-in-the-box— open the lid and up it comes. Nobody pushes it up, but somebody or something pushed it down. Similarly, what produces this new perfection? Here and now, no efficient cause is needed beyond the cause of division; an efficient cause was needed to bring the material cause to that state of perfection, and that efficient cause was the previously existing living being.

C. *Identical Human Twins.*

We have seen above that the human soul is spiritual, that it can arise only by creation, and that it is immortal.[3] We are not sure just at what moment in the generative process the creation of the soul occurs.[4] It is quite probable that the human soul is created at the moment when the new individual is formed by the union of ovum and sperm. If this is what happens, then, in the division of the embryo by which identical twins are formed, the individual soul remains in one of the parts (it is impossible to tell in which one). Meanwhile, as soon as the other part is fully separated, and so removed from the information of the already created soul, a new soul is created for the second twin.

Thus, the formation of identical human twins differs in two ways from similar happenings in animals. In animals, the original being ceases to be in the division, and so its soul no longer is a principle

[3] Above, Chapter XIII, section 162, 165, 166.

[4] It is possible (though most Catholic writers say it is not probable) that the human spiritual soul is created at some moment during the transition from the embryonic to the fetal stage (at about the third month of growth); at least, some biologists so consider it. If this is the correct account, then the origin of human identical twins is by simple division of the embryo.

Under this supposition, the embryo, though it is human, is not formally a man. It would possess a sensitive (mortal) soul, whose nature it would be to prepare a human body for the reception of the formally human spiritual soul. At the moment of the creation of this spiritual soul, the preceding preparatory soul would be reduced to the potency of matter, that is, would no longer inform the body. (NB: even if this were proved to be the case, directly willed abortion would not thereby cease to be a serious sin.)

For the whole matter of this note (4) see for example Edouard Hugon, O.P., *Cursus Philosophiae Thomisticae* (Paris, Lethielleux, 1927), Vol. II, *Philosophia Naturalis*, pp. 199–204; E. C. Messenger, *Theology and Evolution* (Westminster, Md., Newman, 1950), pp. 259–83, 327–32; Meth. M. Hudeczek, O.P., "De tempore animationis foetus humani sec. embryologiam hodiernam," *Angelicum*, XXIX (1952), 162–81.

of being; and the two (or more) new beings are produced by separation, from the virtuality of the parts of the original being, and they are informed by their proper souls in the same process. In human beings, on the contrary, the original human individual does not cease to be, but loses half of its matter; and in the new being thus formed by division a new soul is created.

D. *The Plant Soul Is "Material."*

Vegetative activities, though they are specifically different from those of non-living things, are still wholly material and quantified. They are entirely concerned with matter (ingesting and assimilating it, adding to the quantitative increase, bringing forth a new individual in matter). They make use of the ordinary physical and chemical properties of matter. Hence, vegetative life is material. As the source and principle of such life, the plant soul is said to be material, wholly limited by matter. When the plant soul is called "material," this does not mean that it contains matter, or is of itself quantified, but simply that the activities to which it gives rise are completely concerned with matter.

Philosophy and the Scientific Theory of Evolution

1. The scope and purpose of this discussion

As a scientific theory, evolution is to be critically evaluated by the scientists who proposed it as an explanatory hypothesis; it is not directly pertinent to philosophy. Indirectly, through the evidence accumulated by various scientists, and through further conclusions drawn from it, evolution has an interest for a philosopher. And this interest becomes an important factor because very many people who are neither biologists nor philosophers take the scientists' statements for literal and exact expressions of absolute truth on which they can build their lives. Hence, it is important and valuable to relate the empiriological propositions of the scientists to reality as directly known and to the ontological statements of common knowledge and of the philosophy of human nature.[1]

2. The question and the problem

We know that this universe has not always existed in its present form, and all modern theories are agreed that at some time in the past our world was not inhabitable for any living thing. Secondly, we know that most animals cannot live directly on the ordinary products of the chemical activity of inanimate nature; they need to have their food prepared for them by plants. For these and other reasons, it seems that at one time the only living things on the earth were plants, and that animals came later on. The ques-

---

[1] The relation between the sciences and the philosophy of human nature is discussed above, Appendix K.

tion then is: How did life begin on this earth? and have animals somehow come from plants? Have the many kinds of plants and animals descended from just a few kinds?

But on the other side of the picture, there seem to be difficulties. Modern biologists maintain that life comes only from life—at least at the present time. And philosophers say, "There can be nothing in an effect which was not in some way in the cause"; and "Every agent produces an effect like to itself." If the cause was non-living, how can the effect be alive? If the cause was a plant without sensation, can its effect have that perfection? If the parent was one kind of plant or animal, can its offspring be of a different kind? Or should we say that every new event in this universe requires the special creative intervention of God? Perhaps it does; and yet, we know that God usually works, in the natural order, *through* the secondary causes which He has made.

3. Untenable solutions

Some writers assert that nothing really new has come into being —a man is really nothing more than so many chemicals—and so there is nothing to explain. Some say that there are no things; there are only happenings, changes which follow one another without any particular reason. Some say that causality is a law of thought, not a law of reality, and that there is no objective (that is, real) reason why anything cannot come from anything at all, or something from nothing. Some say that since the alternatives are either to admit creation or a purely "natural" (that is, materialistic, physico-chemical) origin of life and of man, we must choose the latter.[2]

We are not going to discuss these theories here, for they are

[2] "Creation" in its strictest sense means "the production of an entire being according to its whole reality, nothing whatever being presupposed (that is, without a pre-existing material cause)." As far as I know, no Christian thinker held that the distinct species of living things were separately created, in this *strict* sense of creation. In a wide sense, "creation" means "the production of a being from pre-existing matter, which matter (including all the created causes) did not contain the perfections of the effect either formally or virtually." When Catholic philosophers and theologians say that God specially created the distinct species of living things, they are using the word "creation" in its *wide* sense.

philosophical, not scientific. Some of them have been discussed in the first part of tho Appendices; others involve errors in metaphysics or in the theory of knowledge. These erroneous theories are listed here, in order that we may make it clear what we are *not* discussing.

4. The meanings of the term "evolution"

(*a*) In its most general sense, "evolution" means change. Now, one can scarcely avoid admitting that changes do occur, and so in this sense practically everyone admits evolution. But in admitting this, we have not admitted anything significant. Yet the point needs to be belabored, because many writers argue, If you admit that changes occur, you by that very admission admit the truth of the scientific theory of evolution. Put this briefly, the argument seems unbelievably childish; yet some biologists, who are extremely cautious and exact in their scientific work, are capable of loose thinking when they philosophize.

(*b*) Evolution, as a scientific theory, says: The very large number of kinds of living things has been derived by means of a tremendously long series of usually very small (perhaps occasionally large) cumulative changes, from a very few (perhaps only one) living ancestors.

(*c*) Evolution (evolutionism), as a philosophical system, holds that the complexity of kinds of things is due to accumulated changes brought about by the activity of merely material things, all causality on the part of a Creator being excluded. This philosophical theory has been considered and evaluated above in Appendix G.

5. The evidence for evolution

How did life begin? Were birds, for example, actually descended from flying reptiles? We have no witness that such was the actual fact,[3] for there was no human observer around to tell us what happened. If we are to answer these questions, we can answer them only on the basis of reasoning. And, this is what biologists do: they adduce certain facts and evidences from which they conclude

---

[3] See also below, section 8 and footnote 16.

that evolution occurred, and that it probably occurred in this or that way, or to this or that extent.

The evidence for evolution falls into four classes, drawn from the four fields of paleontology, comparative anatomy, physiology and biochemistry, embryology, and genetics. Because this evidence is so well known, or at least is so easily available in both scientific and semi-popular presentations, we will only indicate the general directions that the argument takes.

A. *Paleontological Evidence.* In general, paleontological remains preserved in caves and buried strata give a kind of pictorial history of life on this earth. Earliest in time was a very lush vegetative growth. When animal life appears, it seems to have been of a low form of sensibility, and frequently great size—the dinosaurs, with their great bodies and their tiny brains, are considered characteristic. As time went on, animal species became more numerous, more differentiated, with a more perfect sensibility. Man is a relative late-comer on this scene.

In particular, the history of certain animal forms can be discovered. Thus, there is a series of animal skeletons, all of which have some relation to the skeleton of a modern horse. If these remains are arranged in their chronological order, they turn out to be arranged in a series in which the most similar remains are close together, and in which a general direction of change is apparent. A number of other cases turn out to be fairly similar.

With regard to man, there is also some evidence. The earliest certainly human remains are somewhat different from the present-day human skeleton. These early remains seem to have a smaller cranial capacity, chinless face, and a more or less sloping forehead. These characteristics would have made the human body at that time much more like the bodies of some of the anthropoid apes.

B. *The Evidence from Comparative Anatomy, Physiology, and Biochemistry.* The evidence from comparative anatomy and physiology is detailed and quite numerous. Its trend, in brief, lies in this direction: similar functions are performed by similar structures even among kinds of living things that at present seem to have no connection. The evidence would seem to point to a common ancestor for these various lines of descent, which originally had those traits, most likely in a less developed fashion. Sometimes, the remains of such an ancestor have been found.

The evidence from biochemistry is perhaps not so plentiful as that from other fields. Among other things, biochemistry has established this point, that the osmotic pressure of the substances dissolved in the human system is very close to that of other animals, and is approximately equal to that of a salt solution of the same concentration as that of ocean water. Biochemists have established similarities of digestive and assimilative processes among various animals; have found that the same hormones are secreted by the glands of very different animals. In general, biochemists are finding that there is a kind of basic pattern of animal functioning common to many if not most animals.

C. *Embryological Evidence.* Here again there is a great mass of evidence, which can be put into two large groups. In one group, there are various evidences that the young (embryos, fetuses, or immature specimens) of various animals are much more alike than the fully developed adults. For example, the Bay-breasted and the Black-poll warblers, when first hatched, are scarcely distinguishable. Yet the adult males of these two kinds differ strikingly in color and markings. Again, some whales have teeth; the adult whalebone whales do not. Yet in the fetus of the latter, there are a large number of tiny teeth, which, as the fetus develops, are resorbed.

The second group of evidence is called by the question-begging name of "atavisms." These consist in this, that in the course of embryonic development, certain organs or structures appear, and again disappear before birth. Moreover, it is hard to see what place they have in the development of this being as it is now found. For example, the baby tadpole is a water-breathing animal that looks like a fish, and grows into a four-legged air-breathing frog.

Similar evidences are found in the human body. For example, a baby's legs have about the same proportion to its trunk as those of a chimpanzee at birth, but the adult man's legs are proportionately much longer than those of any anthropoid. In the early fetal stages, the hands and feet of the human fetus are quite similar to

Unfortunately, due to an historical accident,[4] the philosopher seems to be talking about the same thing as the biologist, for both of them talk about genera and species. (Incidentally, the logician uses these same terms.) When a philosopher looks at a material being, he sees that it is composed of a substance and a number of accidents or added inhering perfections, both necessary and contingent. As far as the substance is concerned, he sees that it can be considered (a) from the viewpoint of its constitutive perfections (these taken together he calls the "essence"); it can also be considered (b) in the particularized and limited mode in which these constitutive perfections are found (and this mode he calls *individuation*). The essence, considered in its full determinateness, is called a *species*,[5] because the philosopher finds that some indi-

---

[4] The terms "genus" and "species" first became technical terms in the philosophy of nature and logic. Much later, when biologists who had been trained philosophically began to look for terms for their classifications, they naturally made use of terms they knew. To some extent, they may have thought they were using them in the same sense as they had been used in philosophy. From this arose confusion and disagreement.

[5] How does the philosophical species correlate with the biological species? As was indicated in footnote 3, they seem to have been intended to be the same. In modern times, opinions vary. Many Thomists take the two to be the same. Others, among them Mortimer Adler, say that the only species are the four degrees of the hierarchy of being (inanimate, plants, animals, men). If we take species as defined above, then philosophical species must differ essentially. Does a cow, for example, essentially differ from a horse? or a cat from a lion?

This matter may become clearer if we see how a philosopher and a biologist go about identifying a species. In biology, most animals are classified by combinations of merely material or vegetative characteristics (for example, *large, tawny, quadruped* are identifications based on merely material characteristics, size, color, shape; *vertebrate, cud-chewing*, and so forth, are vegetative characteristics). In philosophy, species are identified by differences which are to the genus as act to potency (Cf. St. Thomas Aquinas, *Summa Theologiae*, I. 50. 4 ad 1; 76. 3.). Now, is *vertebrate* a philosophical difference which further determines sensitivity? Evidently not. Suppose we define an animal generically; it will be defined thus: a substance, material, living, sensitive. If there is an essential difference among animals, it ought to be a further determination in sensitivity. We might suggest this point of view. Animals, which generically have sensitivity, will be specifically different kinds of animals according as they sense in different ways: for example, with one or several or five external senses; and again, from there on, by differences in internal sensation, especially in the innately determined estimative power (compare the interesting suggestion of St. Thomas that some animals are preponderant in irascibility, *Summa Theologiae*, I–II. 46. 51. 1, and *In Psalmos,* ps. 17,

those of many apes; by the time of birth there are import
ences in structure.

The so-called atavisms are also found in human deve
As summary examples, we may recall that the human em
a true external tail, with seven to nine rudimentary ve
this tail disappears before birth, and the vertebrae are 1
in number to four or five; the human fetus is for a time c
with a fine hairy growth, which usually disappears before b

D. *Evidence from Genetics.* Much of the work in geneti
dealt with hybridization and pure strains, and these problen
not relevant here. Two things have been discovered which
of some significance. The first is that changes in inheritance
cur by way of sudden, usually small variations. The offsp
which has acquired a characteristic not possessed by its pare
or lost one that its parents had, is called a "mutant" or "spo
Most mutants are defective; occasionally, there is a change whi
is not a defect and which is from then on inherited (this is whe
"natural selection" comes in). An example is that of the odorle
marigold which was found among the descendants of the commo
ill-scented plant. The second fact which may be of some impor
tance is that if the developing ova are subjected to radiation, the
number of mutants is greatly increased.

6. A preliminary question: What is meant by "kinds" of living things?

This, then, is the evidence on which the scientific theory of evolution has been erected. Does this evidence prove that the kinds of
living things have changed in the course of centuries-long descent?
Before we can answer this question, it is necessary to know what is
meant by "kinds" of living things.

Biologists classify the kinds of living things, beginning with the
most inclusive category, into phyla, classes, orders, families, genera,
(subgenera), species (subspecies), and varieties. These are scientific terms in biology, and so it is the biologist's task to decide
what they mean, to set up and evaluate the criteria by which living
things are so classified, and so forth. The philosophy of nature has
neither direct interest in nor concern with these classifications.

viduals possess the same essence. The essence, considered indeterminately (that is, by abstracting from one or more of the constitutive perfections), is called a *genus*, because he finds that several species, when considered indeterminately, have the same indeterminate essence.

Moreover, the philosopher adds two further considerations. When he compares the different species and genera among themselves (species and genera being taken in their philosophical sense), he finds that they can be arranged in an order of perfection, of which the highest, man, possesses all the essential constitutive perfections of the lower genera, and the perfection of rationality in addition. Below man are the animals, which possess the essential generic perfection of plants, and in addition, the perfection of sensitivity. This order of perfection is sometimes called the degrees of being, the scale of being, or the hierarchy of being.

Secondly, when the philosopher looks at living things, he finds that over and above the species, there are stable groups with more or less permanently inherited characteristics, like the races of men. All men have the same essential perfections, and so all of them belong to one and the same (philosophical) species. But there are groups of men with particular inherited characteristics of color, size, and even, to a limited and relative degree, shape. These racial differences are not essential, not formal. Hence, they must be material dispositions.[6] Once "races" have been found within the group of men who are certainly known to possess the same essential perfections, the concept of race can be extended over the whole field

---

1). I do not know of anyone who has attempted to work out such a classification in detail.

[6] The possibility of inherited characteristics which are not formal, but on the side of material dispositions, is peculiar to living things. At first sight, it seems to conflict with the principle of activity: "Every agent acts according to its form." But it must be remembered that the generation of living things is not wholly comparable to ordinary transient activity. In transient activity, with which the principle quoted is concerned, no part of the agent becomes the effect. In generation, a part of the parent, prepared by the immanent activity of that same being, is separated, and becomes the new being. In other words, not only the formal perfection, but a part of the matter of the parent, is transmitted to the offspring. Therefore, there can be traits and dispositions, which from the viewpoint of species and definition, are material (and individual), but which likewise, from the viewpoint of inheritance, constitute a distinct and stable "race" within the species.

of living things. The term "race" shall then, for the rest of this Appendix, be understood to mean "a group of living things with relatively stable and particular inherited characteristics, not differing essentially from other groups with different inherited characteristics."

When inherited non-essential traits are changed in the series of generations, we shall call this change "inter-racial evolution." If essential perfections are gained or lost in the series of generations, we shall call this "essential evolution."

If these terms are understood, it should be clear that a proved occurrence of inter-racial evolution does not prove even the possibility of essential evolution.

7. Philosophical evaluation of the evidence for evolution

The question about evolution can be subdivided into four questions: (a) did evolution happen? (b) if not, could it happen? (c) did it not happen? (d) is it impossible? And, since we have distinguished two radically different kinds of evolution, these questions can be asked about each kind. For the purpose of our present discussion, we are not interested in inter-racial evolution. Consequently, if an evidence goes to prove only inter-racial evolution, we shall leave the consideration of the four questions to someone else.

(a) The ascending series of modified skeletons in the *paleontological* museum can be paralleled neatly by the ascending series of improved models of automobiles in an automotive museum. Such an arrangement may be perfectly sound, and may give us much valuable information. But of itself it does not prove either that essential evolution happened, nor that it could happen.[7] The detailed evidence about horses and other animals, and about changes in the human skeleton, concerns modifications of clearly non-essential characteristics. If we grant to the scientists that this is a proof, *what* it proves is inter-racial evolution, not essential evolution.

---

[7] It is true that similarity proves a common cause; but that common cause may be either external to the series (the Creator—as the human mind is external to the series of automobiles), or internal to it as the common ancestor. The paleontological evidence is not sufficient of itself to decide which of these possibilities actually is the true one.

(b) The evidence from comparative anatomy, physiology, and biochemistry directly proves similarity—that the organisms are made according to "a common plan." Similarity may be a good confirmatory proof for common descent; or, *proved* common descent may be a good explanation for similarity. The evidences gathered under this heading therefore prove neither that essential evolution happened nor that it could happen.

(c) The stages of embryonic development are frequently considered to be a kind of stream-lined and slightly modified recapitulation of the evolution of the species. Suppose we grant that some evidence gained from embryology is a real proof of evolution (for example, that a whale at one stage has teeth which as an adult it does not possess). The kind of evolution thus proved is inter-racial, not essential evolution. To evaluate the other evidence adduced, we must ask two questions: (1) Is it one and the same embryo which develops to become the adult animal? (2) Is there ever a point at which we can say of a dog embryo, for example, "This is a fish"? Now, (1) if it is clear that it is one and the same being which develops through a series of structural and quantitative modifications, and (2) if a dog is always recognizably dog from fertilized ovum to barking watchdog,[8] then embryology does not prove essential evolution. In this area, also, it is true that essential evolution would be a simple and even a very illuminating explanation of the series, if it were proved.[9]

(d) The evidence from genetics is up to the present time wholly within the area of racial characteristics. If we grant this to be a proof of evolution,[10] the kind of evolution that is proved is inter-racial evolution. Incidentally, genetics shows us much about the

[8] Cf. Sir Charles Sherrington, *Man on His Nature* (New York, Macmillan, 1941), p. 76, who states that the human being even in its very first starting-point is recognizably specifically human.

[9] To talk about "vestigial organs," or "atavisms," is to beg the question. Frequently, biologists argue: this structure is useless now; therefore it is an atavism. This argument is worthless; no matter how you look at it, the conclusion does not follow from this premise. Of course, if you insert a second premise (for example: But useless organs are remains of evolutionary descent), then the logic is corrected, but evolution is assumed instead of being proved. Frequently, people speak of atavisms to conceal the fact that they do not know what the functions of certain organs are.

[10] Not all biologists grant this; they say that the "new" characteristic was there all the time, but was regressive.

mechanism of inter-racial evolution, and suggests a possibility of the mechanism of essential evolution, as we shall see later.

Even when we take all these evidences together, they do *not* *prove* that essential evolution historically occurred; they do not even prove that it is possible. Note that we are not discussing the scientific evaluation of the scientific theory; for many, if not for most, scientists, a theory is considered proved when it affords valuable understanding, and leads to further hypotheses, understandings, and information. For a most brilliantly successful theory in a science may be from the philosophical, as well as the common sense point of view, an empiriological construction.

Nevertheless, these evidences strongly suggest that the present complexity of living things (including even the human body) may have been derived by means of a tremendously long series of cumulative changes from a very few living ancestors, perhaps even from a single one. The simplicity and the sweeping character of this suggestion make evolution a very appealing theory.

But before we can go any further, there are two more questions left unanswered. They are: do we know that evolution did not happen? is evolution impossible? The former question is a question about an historical fact, and at the present time almost everyone is ready to agree that we do not know certainly that evolution did not happen. Do we then know that evolution is impossible? Some philosophers think that they can prove the impossibility of evolution, and they do this by an appeal to two principles: that an effect cannot be more perfect than its cause; that an effect is of the same kind as its non-cognoscitive cause.

8. Equivocal Generation

Is it possible that offspring be essentially different from (in the sense of possessing more constitutive perfections than) its immediate parent? [11] Before we answer this question, let us recall a remark

[11] "Regressive evolution," in which the offspring would be essentially less perfect than its parent, would be simply an instance of a lesser perfection virtually contained in a greater.

On the scientific level, an instance of regressive evolution is the parasites; there is sound evidence that parasites are descended from organisms that were capable of an independent life.

which Aristotle made apropos of chance and contingency in the world of nature.

The action of individual natural causes is necessary, predetermined. When we are talking about causes that do not act through free will, and we have a case where A causes B, then the nature of B is completely and necessarily predetermined by the nature of A, except to the extent that A or the pre-existing matter of B is defective. But, Aristotle continues, though the individual lines of causality in the world of nature are necessary, there is no necessity about their crossing or interference. At the level of the created causes concerned, this interference is uncaused, and so contingent.

Now, it is to be expected that the chance interference of two lines of causality will usually result in spoiling the effect produced. But it is theoretically conceivable that one line of causality, as interfered with by another line, should be completely *equivalent* to the causality proper and proportionate to a nature higher than either of the interfering causes themselves.[12] Since in such causality, there would no longer be a community of nature between cause and effect, it is very appropriately called "equivocal causality" or "equivocal generation."

Note that at the level of secondary, created causes any chance event is uncaused; the meeting or interference of two independent lines of causality is inexplicable, unintelligible. But a chance event just happens only with regard to the created causes involved. If we take into consideration all the causes involved, there is no chance. What is chance with regard to creatures is planned by God. And because the two independent lines of causality are unified in the Divine intellect, there is a unified cause to account for the single effect. Thus chance + Providence can explain the origin of effects that are higher than their created causes.

9. The possibility of Essential Evolution

If we apply the theory of equivocal causality to the generation of living things, we can see that essential evolution is possible. It

---

[12] How this is to be understood is explained in Appendix L. Cf. the important text, *Summa Theologiae*, III. 75. 6 ad 1 (esp.: "nihil prohibet arte fieri aliquid cuius forma . . . [est] forma substantialis").

has been found that during the processes of mitosis (for single-celled living things) and meiosis (in bisexual reproduction), living things are particularly susceptible to outside interference. If, during the formation of the new living thing, or the formation of the germ cell, we suppose an interference [13] (perhaps by radiation) which so modifies the living process that a different cell structure is obtained, we have the basis for the possibility of evolution. We would have to suppose that the developmental process would begin with a rather simple, relatively undifferentiated form of life, and proceed by way of extremely small but sudden changes.[14]

The same explanation can perhaps be used for the origin of life itself. It is again possible that the right chance occurrence of a whole group of particular lines of causality, unified in the Divine plan, should result in the formation of a single living cell.

The effort of scientists to produce a living cell in the laboratory would work along the same lines. For these scientists use the natural, necessary, predetermined activities of various natural compounds, and, acting as intelligently unifying causes, try to find the right combination of interfering causalities which would produce the material dispositions requisite for life.[15] If they succeed, the living result of their efforts will be produced by equivocal causality

[13] This interference is a chance occurrence with regard to each and every proximate cause. But, as has just been explained, whenever we take the viewpoint of chance, we are professedly taking an incomplete point of view. The other side of the theory of chance is Divine Providence and the direct action of God on creatures. Hence, in the supposition with which we are dealing, the origin of specifically different kinds of living things is by equivocal generation and the direct intervention of God.

This explanation differs from the so-called "origin of life by direct creation," in that the latter supposes a *miraculous* intervention of God (that is, an immediate production without regard to the pre-existing dispositions of matter), while the present hypothesis supposes an intervention according to the ordinary laws of generation from previously disposed matter. In such intervention, the secondary causes would be instruments of God.

[14] Most of the scientists who use this language seem to think that, when they have enumerated all the secondary causes involved, they have given a complete explanation. It is possible that in a particular case the scientists would be able to discover all the created causes of an equivocal generation. Philosophers and theologians would then accept these findings, as far as they go, but not the implicit or explicit denial of God's part in the change.

[15] Here the material elements and compounds would be the instruments of the human cause, which would be, relative to them, the principal cause.

under formal unification of the secondary, dependent providence of the scientist's mind.

Moreover, it seems possible that the human body itself could take its rise in this way. The complexity of the interference required staggers the imagination, but it does not seem to be impossible. What is required is that, either during the formation of the germ cells or at the moment of their union, the material parts undergo such a modification that they become like the human ovum and sperm, or the fertilized human ovum. Then, at the instant when the proper material dispositions are present in this being, God would create in the matter thus essentially disposed a human soul, in the same way in which He creates the soul in the course of normal human generation. Remember that from this analysis of possibility it is impossible to say what did occur,[16] for it is certainly not the only way in which man could have come to be.

To sum up. Essential evolution of living things up to and including the human body (the whole man with his spiritual soul excluded, for the reasons we have seen in Chapter XIII), as explained through equivocal causality, chance, and Providence, is a possible explanation of the origin of those living things. The possibility of this mode of origin can be admitted by both philosopher and theologian.[17] On the other hand, the factual occurrence of such evolution in the case of particular organisms, which actually existed in a given time in world history, is a question of fact whose establishment by any direct means is extremely difficult if not impossible. Scarcely any of the sciences of living organisms are concerned with the question of fact in just this way. For, as we have seen, a scientific theory is often considered "proved" and is accepted by the scientists in the field, when it effects a systematic organization and unification of data, and leads to further investigations, insights, and theories. The scientific theory of evolution per-

---

[16] Above, in section 6, we referred to a "witness." There is of course a witness, God; and He can reveal the order in which living things came to be if He chooses. At the present, it is not clear that he has revealed the order, sequence, and interconnections of the origins of living things.

[17] There are some theological problems involved in such an admission; these problems do not concern us here. Suffice it to say that at least some competent theologians think these problems can be solved; at any rate, a difficulty does not of itself constitute a refutation.

forms these functions. This is why scientists almost universally accept it, and from the viewpoint of present evidence and biological theory, apparently with sufficient scientific justification for a scientific theory.

10. Bibliography

A. *Presentation of Evidence*

Edward O. Dodson, *A Textbook of Evolution* (Philadelphia, Saunders, 1952). A straight-forward and quite complete presentation of evidence; does not presuppose technical acquaintance with specialized scientific terms and theories.

G. G. Simpson, *The Meaning of Evolution* (New Haven, Yale Univ. Press, 1949). The first two parts contain an easily read presentation of the course of evolution. The third part (which is non-scientific in character) is rambling and inaccurate.

J. F. Ewing, "Précis on Evolution," *Thought*, XXV (1950), 53–78. A short general summary.

Edouard Boné, S.J., "L'Homme: Genèse et Cheminement," *Nouvelle Revue Théologique*, LXIX (1947), 360–89. An excellent account of the facts of human paleontology.

Raymond W. Murray, C.S.C., *Man's Unknown Ancestors*, 2nd ed. (Milwaukee, Bruce Pub., 1948). Very good and readable account.

R. Goldschmidt, *The Material Basis of Evolution* (New Haven, Yale Univ. Press, 1940). This book concentrates on physiology and genetics.

T. Dobzhansky, *Genetics and the Origin of Species*, rev. ed. (New York, Columbia Univ. Press, 1941).

Evolution, G. R. de Beer, ed. (Oxford, Clarendon Press, 1938). Two of the essays are excellent and to the point of the present consideration, "Embryology and Evolution," pp. 57–78, and "The Values of Interspecific Differences," pp. 79–94.

W. L. Strauss, "The Riddle of Man's Ancestry," *Quarterly Review of Biology*, XXIV (1949), 200–33. A discussion of the lines of evolution proposed for the human body.

William C. Boyd, *Genetics and the Races of Man* (Boston, Little, 1950).

Glenn L. Jepsen, E. Mayr, and G. G. Simpson, *Genetics, Paleontology, and Evolution* (Princeton, Princeton Univ. Press, 1949). Some excellent essays on the title subjects.

Frederick Zeuner, *Dating the Past*, 2nd ed. (New York, Longmans, 1951). Though the general topic is somewhat specialized, the author gives a critical chronology of human fossils which is more directly pertinent to this consideration.

B. *The Relation of Evolution to Philosophy and Theology*

E. Amann, "Transformisme," *Dictionnaire de Théologie Catholique.*
Gives, among other things, the latest views of Catholic scholars on the
subject.

Louis Eugene Otis, *Le Doctrine de l'évolution* (Montréal, Fides,
1950: 2 vols.). The first volume summarizes the evidence, the second
considers it from the point of view of philosophy and theology. The
philosophical considerations are good but not complete.

Cyril Vollert, S.J., "Evolution of the Human Body," *The Catholic
Mind,* L, no. 1071 (March, 1952), 135–54. A brief, but very clear,
accurate, and readable account.

Achille Cardinal Liénart, "Le Chrétien devant le progrès de la science," *Études* (December, 1947), 289–300.

Humphrey J. T. Johnson, "Catholics and Evolution," *Downside Re-
view* (Autumn, 1949), 375–94; "Unity of the Human Race," *ibid.*
(Summer, 1950), 324–40; *The Bible and Early Man* (New York, Mc-
Mullen, 1948).

E. C. Messenger, *Evolution and Theology* (New York, Macmillan,
1932); *Theology and Evolution* (Westminster, Md., Newman Press,
1950). The first is a classic work on the subject; the second is a sequel,
answering criticisms. On the whole, the philosophical treatments are
not very satisfactory.

G. H. Duggan, S.M., *Evolution and Philosophy* (Wellington, Reed,
1949). The general treatments are valuable and very well put. But
there is no detailed explanation of the causality at work in evolution.

C. *Special Considerations*

St. Thomas Aquinas, on the interpretation of the first book of Gene-
sis, *In II. Sent.,* d. 12, q. 1, a. 2; *Summa Theologiae,* I. 71. 1; 72; 74. 1.
2; *In Hebraeos,* c. 4, lect. 1; *De Potentia* 4. 2 ad 22, 23, 33, 34 and ad 5
in contrarium.

Edward T. Foote, S.J., "Prologue to Evolution," *The Modern Schoolman,* XIX (1941), pp. 7–11.

G. P. Klubertanz, S.J., "Causality and Evolution," *ibid.,* pp. 11–14.

Truth and Error in the Senses

Truth and error are to be found wherever a mind judges (affirms or denies) that a thing is or is so, when it is, or that it is not, when it really is not (truth), or on the contrary, judges that a thing is so when it is not, or that it is not when it is (error). Thus, it is clear that truth and error in the strict, formal sense are to be found only in a judgment (this is discussed both in logic and in metaphysics). The judgment is an intellectual act; no sense power judges, affirms. Hence, in the strict and primary meaning of the words, only the intellect can attain truth or be in error.

But truth and error are used in another, closely related way. Thus, we speak of "false teeth"—where we use the adjective "false" to mean "looking like," or "serving the purpose of, but not really being." In this meaning, a true thing is what it seems to be; in other words, it is the kind of thing that by its appearance leads an intellect to truth about itself; a false thing is one which appears to be what it is not, and so would easily and upon surface acquaintance lead an intellect into error about itself. It is only in this meaning of truth and error that the question of the truth or error of sense knowledge can be asked.

Properly to answer this question, it is necessary to recall to mind the three kinds of sensible objects: proper, common, and incidental sensibles.

Do the senses lead to error concerning their proper sensible objects? External sense is a passive power, and must be put into act by a cause. Precisely as acted upon by the external cause, the external sense receives its determination; it adds nothing of its own. When I judge that "I see red," there is no possibility that I should be both seeing and not-seeing at the same time, nor that some other act of my eye should mislead me into judging that I am seeing. Since, moreover, the act of seeing is specified by its proper object, so that the act of seeing red is what it is in virtue of the red which is seen, it follows with the same kind of necessity that I cannot know myself to be seeing red and not seeing red, and that the red which I see cannot be simultaneously not-red. It follows also that the object (that is, the thing precisely in the way in which it is causing this sensation) is and must be red. Every word in these propositions must be taken literally and strictly and is not to be applied any further than it goes.

The word "object" means that a thing is being considered, not precisely as it is in itself, but as it is, or can be, in some relation of causality. Now, material things exist. In so far as they are able to affect some sense, and be known by it, they are called "sensible things." When they are actually known, they are called "sensed" things, or "sensible-in-act." The different proper sensibles, however, are related to the things considered in themselves in different ways. That which is tangible (the proper object of touch) is such merely by being material. The audible, the odoriferous, and the flavored, must be acting in a suitable medium (air or water) before they are sensible. The visible must, in addition, be actuated by light before it can be acting in its medium. Schematically:

THING (SUBJECT)	SENSIBLE OBJECT	OBJECT-IN-ACT SENSATION
Material thing	= the tangible ⟶	the touched–touching
Material thing vibrating + medium of air (etc.?)	= the audible ⟶	the heard–hearing
Material thing diffusing + medium of air (etc.?)	= the odoriferous ⟶	the smelled–smelling
Material thing diffusing + medium of water (etc.)	= flavored ⟶	the tasted–tasting
Material thing + light + medium of the translucent	= the visible ⟶	the seen–seeing

For example, the red object I see may be potentially white (that is, having a surface capable of reflecting all the colors of the spectrum equally), but actually red (when the white surface is illuminated by a pure red light). My eyes tell me only that it is actually red. Or, the red object may be striped dark red and white when it is at rest, but as a whirling surface it is actually red. Similar care must be used in making judgments about the proper objects of the other senses.

It is well known that some kind of sensory excitation can be "non-proper"—the seeing of "stars" produced by a blow to the eye or head; "lights" or "noises" produced by electrical stimulation. On the basis of these and similar experiences, some psychologists have worked up a theory of "specific nerve response": every sensory nerve, no matter by what means it has been stimulated, has as its specific response a particular sense quality. Now, this is not yet entirely certain; the stimulus may arouse a memory image, as was suggested above.[1] Even if the theory is correct, a conclusion about the unreliability of sensation is not justified because (a) no one confuses the experiences here referred to with ordinary sensations, for they are experientially different; (b) we know from other sources (facts referred to above) that sensory stimuli do differ qualitatively.

Do the external senses lead to error with regard to common sensible objects? Here even greater care must be used. We have seen that common sensible objects are known in two ways: concretely and directly by the external senses; separately and distinctly by the imagination. To the extent that the external senses report the common sensibles, they report accurately. For example, that the red I see is in itself an extended (quantified) red, is still necessary. But its size is a matter of interpretation, dependent upon its proper location as regards distance from the eye; this location, as we have seen, involves the use of the abstract image of space, and past experience. Its shape, in a two-dimensional sense (in the plane offered to vision), seems to be known as directly as its quantity. But that its surface actually lies in this plane is not given directly—a round plate, held at an angle, may well seem to be an ellipse. But its action upon me, when held at this angle, is the action of an ellipse, not a circle. Again, the partly submerged stick appears broken, and because of the double medium of air and water, it is acting brokenly. If I judge that the plate is elliptical in itself, or the stick broken in itself, I am going beyond the direct data of external sense. The judgment about number is about the same as for extension and shape. Rest and motion, relative to other objects in the same plane of vision, are given directly, in the sense that either the background or the object or both are at rest or in motion relative to each other. Rest and mo-

[1] Above, Chapter VI, footnotes 2, 3, and 7.

tion relative to the subject are not data of the external senses; much less absolute rest and motion.—When the common sensibles are taken out of their concretion and known directly in their abstract images, and then applied in perception to sensed objects, the possibilities for error are wide open.

Experimental psychologists and popular "scientific" writers make much of certain illusions of visual space perception. Situations are designed such that the ordinary signs of depth are missing. To point out the "unreliability of sense perception" in such instances is to confuse judgment with perception and perception with sensation, and to take advantages of the lack of information of ordinary non-scientific readers.

Incidental sensibles are in no wise guaranteed by the necessary dependence of effect upon cause, except in so far as the direct formal object of another power of knowing might be concerned (as when, seeing a sensible object, we know by intellect that it is a being). Of course, there is no necessary bias in favor of error here; incidental sensibles may just as well be true as false.

Imagination and memory are open to both truth and error. In them, there is complex knowledge, with all the possibilities that arise from the complexity itself.

Nevertheless, one thing emerges: the basic act of a power on its formal object cannot lead to error. Because there are such acts, truth and certitude are possible, simply by depending in the proper way upon sense and intellect.

APPENDIX P

The Measurement of Intelligence

1. The Question

In the chapters dealing with intellect, will, and the soul, quantity (especially extension) is used as a necessary and universal criterion of materiality. Where there is quantity, there is matter; where matter is, quantity must be, too. Conversely, spirituality and lack of quantity go together. Can what is not quantified be measured? [1] The argument we used concluded that the intellect is spiritual. Yet experimental psychologists and teachers can measure intelligence. Does not this fact prove that intelligence is quantified and therefore material?

2. The Answer

First, we must decide what an intelligence test measures. As all the experimentalists admit, such a test partly tests achievement, and necessarily so. Philosophically, this is quite reasonable, since a power can be known only in its act. What kind of an achievement, therefore, does this test measure? It partly measures memory, that is, the sensitive retention of images of things, words, mathematical symbols; partly, it measures the use of imagination as under the guidance of reason; partly, it does measure understanding, intellectual appreciation, judgment, and so forth.

Secondly, we must decide how an intelligence test measures memory-retention, use of imagination, and understanding. Here, the test scale itself gives the clue. For the result of the test is not directly a pointer reading or anything like that; it is a statistical

[1] Anthony Standen, in *Science Is a Sacred Cow* (New York, Dutton, 1950), pp. 85–86, points out that some "things" which did not exist have been very accurately measured. Cf. above, Appendix L.

432

rating on qualitative grounds. The tests have been given to thousands of people, and the results classified according to age, and so forth. A typical score on such a test now gives a picture of achievement-and-ability as compared with those of other persons of the same age (or other condition).

This expression of qualitative results in quantitative terms is quite natural to man, who after all does not know spiritual things in their own terms, but only in terms of sensible reality, as we saw in Chapter VIII. St. Augustine's dictum is pertinent here: "In spiritual things, to be greater (larger) is to be better."

Briefly, an intelligence test measures memory-retention, the rationally guided use of the imagination, and understanding, according to an analogously applied statistical scale of relative qualitative perfection. To be subject to measurement in this way does not imply quantity in what is measured.

APPENDIX Q

Freedom, Hypnosis, and Post-hypnotic Suggestion

1. The Facts

A hypnotized person will spontaneously and indeliberately carry out the suggestions and commands of the hypnotizer, at least in so far as these do not go counter to his own personal moral convictions and/or virtues. Under hypnosis, a person will answer questions, carry out bodily motions, become insensitive to pain if that is suggested, and so forth. An adult, told to stab a third person in the back with a rubber knife, did so; given a real knife, he woke up. It seems that a command or suggestion that goes against a strong personal moral conviction and/or virtue shocks the person out of hypnosis. It seems also that where a personal conviction is lacking, and behavior has been directed out of human respect or refinement of taste or similar factors, there is very little limit to the suggestibility of the patient.

In post-hypnotic suggestion, a person will carry out a command which was given to him under hypnosis, and this even when he was told to forget what he had been commanded. This seems to be subject to the same restriction as obedience under hypnosis itself. Moreover, post-hypnotic suggestion can be used to determine attitudes and feelings; for example, a smoker can be told that he dislikes cigarettes; given a smoke upon awakening, he will not enjoy it.

2. Interpretation

Can a person be hypnotized against his will? As far as all evidence goes, no. A person who is unable to concentrate for a long time, or in the face of an insistent distraction, will find that his actual present knowledge can fall under another's control. In such a case, his power of deliberation is removed; this affects, not the will directly, but the *object* of the will. This sort of thing is similar to the disturbance of the imagination by passion or by physical agents, which was discussed in Chapter X. This is an interference with freedom by way of an interference with one of the conditions of freedom, and does not affect the argument of that chapter.

Secondly, a person may be tricked into an acceptance, in that he agrees, consents to let his attention follow the lead of the hypnotizer, in ignorance of the result. We have also seen how knowledge is a condition of freedom, on the side of the object.

Hypnosis, therefore, may be either voluntary or involuntary, but in neither case is it a control of another person's will, nor a direct interference with the activity of that will. It does result in a control of the sensitive and motor powers and activities. However, even this control is not complete and absolute, as we have seen. Nevertheless, in the hands of an unskilled or an unscrupulous person, it is dangerous, not only because of the actions that may be suggested, but also because it leads to an unhealthy heightening of suggestibility, and tends to lead to a disintegration of human activity. In the hands of a skilled and reputable physician, it can, under carefully controlled conditions, be an instrument of healing.

Very much the same is to be said about post-hypnotic suggestion. In this case, there are, in addition, introspective reports which make the situation even clearer. A subject had been ordered to open a window at an assigned time, and told to forget that he had received this order. At the appointed time, he arose and opened the window. When questioned, he said that the room had become warm and stuffy. Reports like this make it clear that the force of the suggestion or command does not bear directly on the will, but rather on the object of the will. It affects directly the sensory apprehension and appetite, and so modifies the way in which the intellect receives its object to present to the will. Hence, post-hypnotic suggestion can interfere with freedom in the way in which passion and error limit it; but when it is used to remove erroneous apprehensions or irrational sense desires and aversions, it can help to restore freedom in the way in which truth is a condition of freedom.[1] What was said above about the use of hypnosis applies also to the use of post-hypnotic suggestion.

[1] Somewhat the same sort of thing is to be said about certain drugs and forms of torture which are popularly thought to destroy or weaken will power. The direct effect of these drugs and procedures is upon the central nervous system, thoroughly and sometimes permanently weakening it. Their direct effects are thus upon the internal senses, either greatly increasing suggestibility to external stimuli so that rational control becomes impossible, or so weakening them that they cannot maintain a single object in continuous sensory awareness. In either case the conditions of freedom are absent.

Index

Absolute nature, 174, 181, 333-34
Abstract idea, 161-62
Abstract image. *See* Image
Abstraction, 81, 112, 181, 391; degrees of, 400
Acceptance, 233, 240-41
Accident, 14, 35, 71
Act, 35, 47; and potency, 6-7, 398
Act of existing, 175-76, 179-80; knowledge of, 187
Action follows being, 15
Activity, 15-17, 65, 71, 89-91, 100; and act of existing, 94; immanent, 47-49, 55, 90, 326; power, substance, 98-99; specified by object, 89-90, 101; transient, 48, 55, 89-91, 100, 116; *see also* Operation
Actus perfecti, 77
Adaptation, 42, 45
Adler, 377, 400
Affirmation. *See* Judgment
After-image, 129
Agent intellect, 170-72, 190, 191, 199, 201-02, 322-33
Alexander, 400
Alford, 156
Allers, 377
Alteration and generation, 404-05
Amann, 427
Analogy, 6, 50, 70, 165
Analysis, 9; philosophical, 370
Angel, 329, 330
Anger, 267
Animals. *See* Brute, Plants
Appetency, 62-63, 83, 196, 205-08, 224, 225, 341-42
Appetite, 134-35, 224, 225; rational (*see also* Will), 222-23; sensory, 222-23, 225, 252-53, 260-77, 342-43
Apprehension, 173-75, 199, 334; complex, 178-79

Aristotle, 9, 23, 286, 322, 341, 360, 369, 371, 399, 423
Art, 296
Assent, 177
Assimilation in knowledge, 64
Associationism, 373
Association of images, 130-31
Atavism, 416
Attention, 145-46, 252
Augustine, 359
Automatism, 274-75, 294, 295, 301
Aveling, 259
Averroes, 3, 6
Aversion, 206-07, 215, 267
Avicenna, 23
Awareness, 62, 124-26

Bachhuber, 165
Beatific Vision, 326, 332, 348
Beauty, 166
Behavior, 395
Behaviorism, 364
Being, 165-66; knowledge of, 179-80, 186-88
Benevolence, 220
Benignus, 38
Berkeley, 361
Bernard, 155, 285
Biology, 392
Blanshard, 362
Bochenski, 357
Body, 56, 305; and mind, 56
Bodily resonance, 206, 208-10, 216, 224, 261
Boldness, 267
Boné, 426
Bonnet, 38
Boring, 122
Bosanquet, 362
Bourke, 297, 359
Boyd, 426
Brute, 123-34, 151-55, 160, 196

437